REGNUM STUDIES IN MISSION

Diakonia in a Gender Perspective

Series Preface

Regnum Studies in Mission are born from the lived experience of Christians and Christian communities in mission, especially but not solely in the fast growing churches among the poor of the world. These churches have more to tell than stories of growth. They are making significant impacts on their cultures in the cause of Christ. They are producing 'cultural products' which express the reality of Christian faith, hope and love in their societies.

Regnum Studies in Mission are the fruit often of rigorous research to the highest international standards and always of authentic Christian engagement in the transformation of people and societies. And these are for the world. The formation of Christian theology, missiology and practice in the twenty-first century will depend to a great extent on the active participation of growing churches contributing biblical and culturally appropriate expressions of Christian practice to inform World Christianity.

Series Editors

A full listing of titles in this series
appears at the end of this book

REGNUM STUDIES IN MISSION

Diakonia in a Gender Perspective

Edited by
Stephanie Dietrich
Knud Jørgensen
Kari Karsrud Korslien
Kjell Nordstokke

First edition published 2016 by Regnum Books International

Regnum is an imprint of the Oxford Centre for Mission Studies
St. Philip and St. James Church, Woodstock Road
Oxford, OX2 6HR, UK
www.ocms.ac.uk/regnum

09 08 07 06 05 04 03 8 7 6 5 4 3 2 1

British Library Cataloguing in Publication Data
A catalogue record for this book is available from the British Library

ISBN: 978-1-506475-56-1

Typeset by Words by Design
Cover design by Words by Design

regnum

The publication of this volume was made possible by the generous financial assistance of Digni and VID

Distributed by 1517 Media in the US and Canada

Contents

Foreword

The life of the church always suffers from the areas neglected in preaching from the pulpit. In the mission movement in Norway we have had a strong focus on 'saving souls' through preaching. Our calling as Christians to love our neighbour and take care of, help and support our fellow humans has received less attention – even though most of us, in the northern part of the world, have a greater possibility of standing up for our neighbour and the stranger than ever before.

It seems that every Christian group, at a given time in history, reads the Bible differently – in the sense that different aspects of the book are given more priority and a stronger focus, while other aspects are downplayed.

The Christian tradition of prayer houses in Norway held a strong focus on the preaching of the gospel, whilst giving money for mission work was all about 'saving souls' – full stop. The idea of *diakonia* was not much focused on in teaching from the pulpit. Mission work was also very much related to this overarching aim. Being a disciple was related to evangelizing and praying for your neighbour.

It so happened that I had the opportunity to work in the Ethiopian Evangelical Church Mekane Yesus. Here 'holistic ministry' was at the centre of the work. God, in his word, is very clear that we should care about body, soul and spirit. The message from the pulpit was not about saving souls only; it was equally about taking care of each other, our relatives, our neighbours, the stranger and even the enemy. The story where Jesus divides the sheep and the goats (Matthew 25), and the story of the good Samaritan (Luke 10), and the words of Jesus when he talks about the Great Commandment – loving God and loving our neighbour (Matthew 22) – were equally important to the message to 'go into the world and make disciples'.

Diakonia is not a minor issue in the Bible – it is a major one. God really wants us to care for each other – not only in our prayers and thoughts and good intentions. He challenges us to take each other by the hand and make life better for everyone. His calling is to give bread, water and clothing, and to provide practical support in the everyday life of the people who come our way. *Diakonia* is something God wants because he loves all of his creation equally, and he wants all of us to live dignified lives. He calls us to serve him through serving our fellow humans, unconditionally.

Gender was another issue, which was not valued in the Christian culture where I lived as a young person. There were fixed roles for men and for women, with men holding all the honourable and leading positions – and this was not questioned. Instead, it was presented as God's plan for us human beings.

In church and in society – be it Norway where I grew up or Ethiopia where I lived for some years – people are not treated equally. Far from it! Some criteria are highly valued in different cultures, but the bottom line is that people are valued according to these criteria. People who are rich and powerful are treated differently from those who are poor and powerless. Colour, education, physical strength and other cultural criteria are decisive when the value of a person is assessed.

One group stood out – women: half the world's population. Women have been, and are, in most societies treated as second-rate, they do not experience the same opportunities as men, and they do not have the same rights. Their role and standing do not reflect the fact that God has given all humans the same value. In most cultures, the male is placed above the female in the social hierarchy. So if a person is a poor woman, this person is suffering twice over – as a poor person, and as a woman. Even in societies where we would expect equal rights to prevail, there is clear discrimination. If we look at business, political or religious leadership, there is an overwhelming majority of men. It seems that, without reflecting on the actual practice, most people just follow the cultural pattern where they live – and thereby uphold this injustice.

Even in church, where the Bible clearly speaks the message of God-given values to all, such injustice prevails. Women often make up the majority of members – but it is the men showing off on the platform.

It is time to change this situation. It is time to take God's calling and challenge seriously and treat each other as God's creation – all with the same value. Women and men have a God-given obligation to raise the human dignity and value of every person. Women and men are called to lift our voices when injustice is done, even when it incurs cost to ourselves. It is not acceptable that one of the sexes is placed above the other; it is not acceptable that women are beaten and raped; it is not acceptable that girls are circumcised; it is not acceptable that they are given away in marriage against their will; it is not acceptable that girls are deprived of education; it is not acceptable that men are paid more than women for the same job; it is not acceptable that there are jobs that women cannot hold; it is not acceptable that women cannot own land; it is not acceptable that women do not inherit as men do. The list is endless. It is a shame on all of us, women and men, that we accept the unjust cultural or religious patterns between men and women. We are facing major challenges in our world today, and we are losing out on half of the world's potential when we do not give women the same rights and opportunities, the same honour and respect, as we give men.

So it is time to change! It is time to lift our eyes and see the bigger picture. It is time to bring *diakonia* and gender justice to the fore. Women are as strong as anybody! They can challenge society. It is together that we, women and men, can do our outmost to bring dignity, respect and equal opportunities to all. We can do it! It is all about joining hands, standing together, working together, challenging together, and not giving in until change has come.

The two issues covered in this book – *diakonia* and gender – have been playing 'second fiddle' for quite some time. Now is the time to make a difference, now is the time to fulfil the dreams of every person on earth to live a dignified, purposeful life. We need to put on our *diakonia* lenses, and see the world as God sees it – and fulfil his purpose in taking care of each other and taking care of the planet.

I congratulate the editors of this book on its focus: *Diakonia in a Gender Perspective*. In our efforts to build a better world, this is a major issue, and it needs continued attention for years to come. I especially like the way the book is organized. This is not only a research book, it is a book where we see the research, the abstract thinking and the theological reflection go hand-in-hand with case studies where daily life shines through the text and makes the book more interesting and more relevant. We therefore give thanks for this valuable contribution to the struggle for holistic ministry and for a holistic view of creation

We are all God's creation. He has given us all equal value and the challenge of serving each other. There are no second-rate citizens. All persons, women and men, are entitled to a fulfilled life – and we can make it happen!

Jørn Lemvik
General Secretary of Digni – the umbrella organisation for the long-term development work of twenty Norwegian mission organizations and churches

Introduction
Diakonia in a Gender Perspective

Stephanie Dietrich, Kari Karsrud Korslien,
Kjell Nordstokke and Knud Jørgensen

This book is written within a context of academic reflection on the theory and the praxis of *diakonia*. It is the second book on *diakonia* published by Regnum Books International, and follows up *Diakonia as Christian Social Practice: An Introduction* (2014). By academic context is meant postgraduate studies, and this is expressed by the fact that many of the authors belong to VID Specialized University in Norway (Oslo and Stavanger campuses), which offers Master's Degrees in Diakonia and Christian Social Practice, Theology, and Intercultural Studies, as well as PhD programmes in Diakonia, Values and Professional Practice, and Theology. The editors of the book are all linked with Campus Diakonhjemmet, Oslo. At the same time, the authors of the various contributions of this publication come from many different parts of the world, and thus a broad variety of different contexts and diaconal working fields are presented and discussed.

The authors are not mere specialists in gender studies, but they are all especially concerned about the role which gender plays within the theory and practice of *diakonia*, and want to elaborate on that through their contributions. Most of the authors also have experience as diaconal practitioners. The academic context of this publication is thus not gender studies *per se*, but an interdisciplinary approach where diaconal theory is deepened through the lenses of a gender perspective, and where a number of examples and case studies are provided in order to exemplify the non-negotiable impact of a gender perspective on diaconal theory and practice.

The *Church of Norway Plan for Diakonia*, defines diakonia as:

> The caring ministry of the Church. It is the Gospel in action and is expressed through loving your neighbour, creating inclusive communities, caring for creation and struggling for justice.

The study of *diakonia* at an academic level is marked by an interdisciplinary approach as it aims at bringing together knowledge from different disciplines, primarily theology and social sciences. The goal is to perform both empirical research related to what is (or what could be) designated as diaconal praxis, as well as to develop theoretical and normative frameworks when analyzing and evaluating diaconal work in a gender perspective. The publication is carried out and sponsored jointly by VID Specialized University, Institute for Diakonia and Leadership (Oslo) and Digni, an umbrella organisation for the long-term development work of twenty Norwegian mission organizations and churches.

Diakonia may be presented as the social ministry of the church, and as an academic discipline it is often located within the area of practical theology. It is carried out individually and collectively, in a congregational or communal context, through institutions and internationally, through development work and advocacy. *Diakonia* is social ministry carried out in the framework of or motivated by faith-based practitioners or organizations. The field of *diakonia* is not primarily related to normative theological assignments, but is a study object for social and political research which supports the claim that *diakonia* as an academic discipline must be done in an interdisciplinary manner, bringing together knowledge both from the theological and social sciences, especially gender studies.

The authors of this book largely subscribe to an understanding of *diakonia* which may be found in contemporary documents like *Diakonia in Context: Transformation, Reconciliation, Empowerment*, published by the Lutheran World Federation in 2010. Without giving a strict definition of *diakonia*, this document maintains some fundamental assumptions when elaborating on the understanding of *diakonia*:

> One is that diakonia is a theological concept that points to the very identity and mission of the church. Another is its practical implication in the sense that diakonia is a call to action, as a response to challenges of human suffering, injustice and care for creation. This rather open-ended understanding of diakonia is also due to the fact that the concept itself does not allow for a precise definition, not even when used in the Greek New Testament. The present use of the word has largely been shaped by how Christians have tried to be faithful to the biblical call to be a neighbour throughout the history of the Church.[1]

Diaconal studies are thus concerned about describing and analyzing life conditions of people in different contexts, with the aim of finding methods to improve diaconal practice. Obviously, gender perspectives play a core role when it comes to both the theory and practice of *diakonia*.

The *gender perspective* looks at the impact of gender on people's opportunities, social roles and interactions. Gender is an integral component of every aspect of the economic, social, religious, daily and private lives of individuals and societies, and of the different roles ascribed by society to men and women, thus also within the field of diaconal theory and practice.

[1] Lutheran World Federation, *Diakonia in Context: Transformation, Reconciliation, Empowerment* (Geneva: Lutheran World Federation, 2010), 8.

Social scientists and development experts often use two separate terms to designate biologically determined differences between men and women, which are called 'sex differences', and those constructed socially, which are called 'gender differences'. Both define the differences between men and women, but they have different connotations. Sex refers to biological characteristics common to individuals in all societies and cultures, while gender defines traits forged throughout the history of social relations. Gender goes far beyond the physiological and biological specifics of the sexes in terms of the roles each is expected to play. Gender differences are social constructs, inculcated on the basis of a specific society's or religious community's particular perceptions of the physical differences and the assumed tastes, tendencies and capabilities of men and women. Gender differences are transformed over time and from one culture to the next, as societies change and evolve.

Gender relations are accordingly defined as the specific mechanisms whereby different cultures and communities determine the functions and responsibilities of each sex. They also determine access to material resources, such as land, credit and training, and more ephemeral resources, such as power. The implications for everyday life are many, and include the division of labour, the responsibilities of family members inside and outside the home, education, leadership roles and a voice in policy- and decision-making.

Gender analysis is part of this process: It is a tool to understand the disparities between women and men's realities in any context. The same issue affects women and men differently and disproportionately, and challenges the idea that everybody is affected by a given issue in the same way, regardless of their contexts. Therefore, gender analysis may bring to light previously hidden or obscure anomalies – like differing social realities, socialization processes, role expectations, economic circumstances, or access to and power over resources.

The chapters of this book will deal with a number of these issues.

Part 1 Provides Biblical and Theological Perspectives

Stephanie Dietrich explores and discusses systematic theological arguments which are relevant for developing a gender perspective on *diakonia*. Her contribution includes a critical discernment of the theological concept of a 'creation order' and its impact on the church's *diakonia*. She emphasises the need for a gender perspective within diaconal studies in order to find 'ways of transforming human life, leading towards empowerment and reconciliation of all human beings, in accordance with God's intention for the whole human creation'.

The aim of *Elaine Neuenfeld's* article is to find correlations between some Old Testament narratives about women's experiences and the active role of care and service in the community, with studies that highlight women's diaconal practices. A critical approach of a gender justice perspective is found in the analysis in the article.

Kjell Nordstokke investigates the role of women in the New Testament, starting with the question: Did Jesus envisage a discipleship of equals, in the sense that women and men would share tasks and responsibilities? This issue is explored from a diaconal perspective and is related to the use of the so-called *diak*- words (διακονια, διακονειν, διακονος) and how they reflect gender roles. It starts with the assumption that women played a more active role in the life of the early church than is depicted in the New Testament writings, and that they also held leadership positions. The development of patriarchal structures resulted in women being expected to perform caring services, but under the guidance and control of male leaders. This development is described as the feminization of *diakonia*, suggesting that diaconal work is an activity that in the first place engages and involves women, with the consequence that *diakonia* is considered less important compared with other church matters – such as proclamation, sacraments and leadership – areas often dominated and decided upon by men. In other words, the feminization of *diakonia* leads to the marginalization of *diakonia* in the life of the church. A new and critical reading of the New Testament may provide incentives to reinterpret *diakonia* as an integral dimension of the being and the mission of church, and Christian discipleship as a ministry where women and men equally are called to share and serve.

Elieshi Mungure writes about women's empowerment and gender equality. These two need to be given priority in ongoing discussions globally as we strive to close the existing gap of gender relations. In order to bring transformation, churches and communities in Africa are called to advocate and pay attention to socio-cultural, theological and pastoral factors that particularly affect women's empowerment and gender relations in their various contexts whilst trying to achieve gender equality.

Part 2 Explores Learning from the Praxis of Engendered Diakonia

Kristian Larsen describes diaconal work from the Mekane Yesu Church in Ethiopia that used Diapraxis as a method to stop female genital mutilation (FGM). Through Diapraxis, the religious dimension of life was taken into account, in part releasing the potential for changing traditions and beliefs that were falsely justified by religion. Hence, in addition to FGM largely being abolished, transformation, reconciliation and empowerment took place at a community level because of this project.

In the interview with *Father Alexi Chehadeh*, the Director of the Department of Ecumenical Relations and Development (DERD) of the Greek Orthodox Patriarchate of Antiochia and All the East (GOPA), Father Alexi gives a picture of his organization's work for the people in Syria in time of war and persecution. The unstable situation causes huge difficulties for all vulnerable groups, and Father Alexi provides examples of specific gender-based programmes offered by his organization. He also discusses the understanding of a gender-based approach in the light of his own Orthodox theological tradition, emphasizing the understanding of *diakonia* as 'the liturgy after the liturgy' and the specific role of women in peace-building and community development in a war-torn country.

Atola Longkumer describes how indigenous and predominantly Baptist Naga Christians have a complex practice of the concept of *diakonia*. Patriarchal and androcentric ecclesiastical policies relegate women to a complex location within the church organisation. While not excluded from acquiring theological education, women are limited to gendered space and roles. The article affirms the renewed development of the concept and practice of *diakonia* in the ecumenical movement and pleads for employing this towards a prophetic *diakonia* that advocates gender-inclusive communities in such contexts as the Naga Baptists in Northeast India.

Starting with the question as to whether secularism is bad for women, *Annette Leis-Peters'* chapter analyses how deaconesses negotiate their professional and gender roles in the expanding Swedish welfare state. The development of the comprehensive Swedish welfare state can be interpreted as a process of secularisation. The empirical material of the study includes ten in-depth interviews with deaconesses who started their service in the 1940s and 1950s. They decided on a religious and gender-hierarchical lifestyle at a time when the influence of the church was fading and gender equality was high on the political agenda. The interviews show that the deaconesses did not end up in conflict with society even though they experienced situations of conflict. Instead, they focused almost entirely on the negotiation of gender and professional roles within the church. Secularisation seems to have affected them much less than outside observers might expect. This points to a need for more research about women's religiosity, both with regard to their professional and their gender roles, and not least in the context of secularisation.

Kari Karsrud Korslien's chapter is called 'Conviviality, Diakonia and Gender'. It gives an example of diaconal work among and together with women living in a multicultural contexts. The deacon co-operates with people in the local community where they have a gym called 'Mountain in Movement'. The author reflects on the question why a gym is an important expression of *diakonia*. She also asks in what way the practice of conviviality and diapraxis can influence opportunities, and open up and help realise women's capabilities.

Heidi Holt Zachariassen's chapter is about awareness-raising, competence-building, and learning as the key factors shaping the gender mainstreaming programme, Women's Empowerment and Gender Equality (WEGE). It was initiated and run by DIGNI, a Norwegian umbrella organization for twenty mission and faith-based organizations (FBOs) which work co-operatively with churches and faith-based organisations in the global South. This chapter provides a short introduction to the concept of gender mainstreaming. It further shares the strategies and conditions that the partners and projects in the WEGE programme experienced to be important in order to do gender mainstreaming in practice and obtain a better life situation for men and women. Some of the strategies used are described by using examples from one project that took part in the WEGE programme.

Christa von Zychlin has been listening to women leaders among Lutheran-linked churches and organizations of the Mekong Mission Forum. Her article documents the use of a modified Contextual Bible Study method, whereby marginalized female voices of the Bible empower diaconal reflection and ideas for action in Mekong communities.

Hector Fernandez shares experiences and insights from the diaconal action that is performed in El Salvador through the work of the Esteban Ecumenical Diaconal Institute. In particular, he focuses the work with young people who live in situations of social and economic risk, youngsters that – in order to survive – are attracted to join gangs, or to seek a better future abroad, most of them wanting to emigrate to the USA. Through programmes of diaconal accompaniment, these youngsters are empowered to overcome sentiments of hopelessness and to see possibilities with their own reality. The diaconal accompaniment envisages a process of walking and reflecting together, and of helping each other to live with hope and to see a future of dignity and justice for all.

Drea Fröchtling's article is based on Focus Group Discussions with migrants carried out in South Africa, the Philippines and the Netherlands. It explores gender and gender-based violence as a push factor in the decision-making process before migration, and highlights areas of gender-violence and injustice in the actual course of migration. A final section looks at the intersection of *diakonia* and migration and suggests locating diaconal engagement amidst dislocation and diaspora.

In *Zo Ramiandra Rakotoarison's* paper, the empowerment of women in Madagascar is considered through a church project called 'Use Your Talents'. The paper concludes that this project as a diaconal endeavour has transformed women's lives. Even so, certain aspects of community life remain unchallenged.

Terese Bue Kessel explores in her article the movement Femmes Pour Christ (FPC), or 'Women for Christ', in Eglise Evangélique Luthérienne au Cameroun (EELC) and its care for the individual through their diaconal community. While they mutually share care and compassion to relieve suffering in local neighbourhoods, they demonstrate that their care practices did not originate from western theology. Nevertheless, inspired by Christian faith, they have Africanised pastoral care and diaconal practices.

Marit Breen's case study describes how development interventions engage with a whole range of power relations and affect the contexts in which they are implemented. The article emphasises how crucial gender relations are. By applying the gender analytical framework of Naila Kabeer to the Western Ethiopia Women's Empowerment Programme, the article demonstrates how a gender analysis is useful in order to improve the way development work is conducted – and particularly that which engages with women's empowerment.

The Third Part Provides Reflection and Deals with Key Issues in Diakonia and Gender

Isabel Phiri and Chammah J. Kaunda's chapter engages the concept of power in *diakonia* from a gendered perspective through the lens of African feminist post-colonial theory. It argues that *diakonia* is entrenched with power that if used in life-giving ways has the potential to allow people on the margins to gain greater control over their lives. Yet the diaconal capacity that can produce this liberation is too often entangled within a web of power struggle which unintentionally marginalises the very groups it aspires to emancipate. The chapter argues that engaging power in *diakonia* within the framework of pilgrimage of justice and peace and post-colonial feminist spirituality brings transformation of social relations to empower women and sexual minorities.

Knud Jørgensen writes about 'Mainstreaming Gender Leadership in Diakonia' as the process of addressing gender from the beginning to the end of any planned action. It is a strategy for making women's as well as men's concerns and experiences an integral dimension of the design and implementation, monitoring and evaluation of policies and programmes in all political, economic and societal spheres so that women can benefit equally and so that inequality is not perpetuated. Such a gender approach is needed in diaconal work. This includes both practical and strategic dimensions. The church arena is still lagging behind when it comes to gender and leadership. The author believes that *diakonia*, by seriously mainstreaming gender leadership, will set an example that will challenge the church at the local and the national level. The leadership models chosen by *diakonia* will mirror values inherent in a broad understanding of *diakonia* (go-between, mediator, advocacy) and will bring to light the assets of *diakonia* (including ethos, relationships, trust, moral authority), and in that way contribute new thinking towards both secular and Christian leadership.

Marianne Skjortnes describes how the Malagasy Lutheran Church is an active religious entity with strong roots in local Malagasy society in large parts of the country. The church is therefore an effective diaconal force with a high level of legitimacy and credibility. At the same time, religion shapes gender-order in ways that both stand out as a hindrance to change and as an agent of change. A greater gender equality is not an automatic result of commitment to the Christian faith.

Hans Morten Haugen reviews five gender-relevant theory traditions, identifying whether or not they promote personal and societal transformation. He then clarifies central concepts and approaches within a human rights-based approach to development, asking why this approach has been preferred by those diaconal practitioners working in the realm of international development, but less so among other diaconal practitioners. The article also asks if there are risks in applying a human rights-based approach, using Lutheran churches as examples.

Anne Austad's article addresses how gender positions may be explored in pastoral care and counselling. By using Dialogical Self Theory as a conceptual framework, gender positions are unfolded as intersected with various positions in the dialogical self. The discussion refers to both a personal and a socio-cultural perspective. Further, a dialogical approach to pastoral care and counselling is discussed as a way of creating openings for liberating change.

Tormod Kleiven's article explores the understanding of sexual misconduct (abuse) from a gender perspective in the context of the church. The author claims that a discussion of this topic from a gender perspective has to include a power-analytical approach in which power is not only understood as a position (personal or structural), but also mainly as a relational and mutual exercise. The author emphasizes the need of developing a culture in which relationships and organizations increase transparency, especially in the risk zones connected with vulnerability in order to prevent sexual misconduct. It also emphasises the appropriateness of focusing on the interplay between power and powerlessness, and creating opportunities for 'competing masculinities' and perhaps also 'competing femininities' in the context of the church.

It is our hope that the following chapters may contribute to a broader understanding of the concept of *diakonia* in a gender perspective.

Part 1

Biblical and Theological Perspectives

'Poverty Has a Woman's Face': Theological Arguments for a Gender-based Approach to Diakonia

Stephanie Dietrich

Introduction

In this chapter, I want to explore and discuss systematic-theological arguments, which are relevant for developing a gender perspective on *diakonia*.

First, I will give an introduction on some main themes within gender approaches in theology, focusing especially on feminist theologies and their critical discernment. Secondly, I will discuss main aspects of theological anthropology – namely, the theology of creation order and of biblical anthropology supporting the idea of the dignity and equality of *all* human people, men and women. Thirdly, I want to show how a gender perspective on *diakonia* is relevant for diaconal theory and practice.

What does it mean to apply a gender perspective on diaconal studies and diaconal practice? In addition: why do we need such a perspective? When one asks for a gender perspective within theology and *diakonia*, one subsequently experiences either a total refusal or an understanding that such a perspective is non-negotiable. Maybe there is something in between these two approaches? My main argument is that a gender perspective on *diakonia* is necessary and should be developed on the background of an understanding of *diakonia*, which focuses on community and the dignity of *all* human people as created in the image and likeness of God – both men and women.

Critical Approaches to a Gender Perspective

One of those who generally speak very critically on the application of a gender perspective is the Pope. Pope Francis addressed the question several times during 2015.[1]

---

[1] http://w2.vatican.va/content/francesco/en/audiences/2015/documents/papa-francesco_20150415_udienza-generale.html (accessed 9th February 2016). Pope Francis, St Peter's Square, 15th April 2015.

> Modern contemporary culture has opened new spaces, new forms of freedom and new depths in order to enrich the understanding of this difference. But it has also introduced many doubts and much scepticism. For example, I ask myself if the so-called gender theory is not, at the same time, an expression of frustration and resignation, which seeks to cancel out sexual difference because it no longer knows how to confront it. Yes, we risk taking a step backwards. The removal of difference in fact creates a problem, not a solution. In order to resolve the problems in their relationships, men and women need to speak to one another more, listen to each other more, get to know one another better, love one another more. They must treat each other with respect and co-operate in friendship.

Obviously, the Pope has an understanding that gender approaches are necessarily equivalent to a specific strain of feminist theories emphasizing that there is no difference between women and men. Surely, this is typical of a rather simplified understanding of feminist theories by a traditional church leader. Nevertheless, being aware that his critique is rather common in much of traditional Christianity, there is indeed a need to investigate feminist theologies more thoroughly in order to discuss their legitimate or non-legitimate relevance for the Christian church. Are gender theories equivalent with eliminating the difference between men and women? A thorough reading of theologies which place themselves within the feminist-liberation strain show that the picture is much more multifaceted than the Pope's and other critical remarks on gender theories can reveal.

The Pope emphasised that eradicating male and female identities does nothing to solve the problem of unfair and disrespectful treatment based on people's gender. He criticizes gender theories for eliminating the differences between man and woman, which, according to him, are rooted in the structure of creation and 'the Creator's plan'.

> Let's think of the nuclear arms, of the possibility of annihilating in a few instants a very large number of human beings; let's think also of genetic manipulation, of the manipulation of life, or of the gender theory, that does not recognize the order of creation.[2]

It is obvious that the Pope refers to gender theories that emphasize the similarity of both sexes, and the understanding that, to a major degree, gender is a cultural construct, more than a biological given-ness. This critical approach to whatever is called a 'gender perspective' seems to be widespread in many Christian traditions, like parts of the Roman-Catholic and the Orthodox world, but also what might be called 'conservative streams' of the Protestant world.

Thus, there is a need to look critically and constructively at what it means to have a 'gender approach' to *diakonia*.

---

[2] http://ncronline.org/news/vatican/francis-strongly-criticizes-gender-theory-comparing-nuclear-arms (accessed 9th February 2016).

Quite often, criticism is based on some basic assumptions concerning gender approaches:

- Gender approaches within a Christian tradition represent a threat to traditional theological understandings of family life and the relationship between men and women.
- Gender approaches are mainly critical towards an 'order of creation'.
- Gender approaches are threatening the church's traditional teaching on power and the relationship between men and women.
- Gender approaches are related closely to feminist theology, which is strongly influenced by western secularized contexts.

These assumptions need to be discussed, in order to be in dialogue with the different traditions, and to develop and establish a good theological basis for our further elaborations on '*diakonia* in a gender perspective'.

Gender Theories, Gender Approaches and Feminist Theology

Gender theories have become an integral part of the curriculum of many different studies, and also of the study of *diakonia* as Christian social practice. Gender studies is a field for interdisciplinary study, focusing on gender identity and gendered representation. Gender studies is a wide field, and there are different strains and theories within this field which cannot be explored fully here.

A number of gender theorists focus on the understanding of masculinities and femininities as social and cultural constructions. One of the best-known basic assumptions in this connection was expressed by Simone de Beauvoir: 'One is not born a woman, one becomes one.'[3] Other gender theorists would carry opposing views and emphasize that gender should be studied as a *practice* rather than as a condition.

Feminist theories have had a strong impact on gender study disciplines, especially within theology. Some researchers have tried to break down gender into the categories of gender identity, gender expression and biological sex, i.e. into cultural, social and biological constructs. Gender theorists often emphasise that femininity and masculinity are fluid entities and that their meaning fluctuates depending on various social and cultural conditions.

This emphasis on the fluctuation and constructed-ness of gender identity might be one of the reasons why different historic faith traditions express their critical approach to gender theorists, as the latter seem to threaten a traditional understanding of the given-ness and immutability of gender identities.

Feminist theology is part of the field, having both a critical and a constructive side. On the one hand, it includes a power-critical perspective, especially towards patriarchal structures in churches and societies while, on the other hand, theological models are sought – models that may further equality,

[3] Simone de Beauvoir, 'The Second Sex' (Paris: Gallimard, 1949, 1989).

dialogue and reform. There is a wide range of different approaches of Christian feminist theologies. One might say that the search for either a feminine *or* a gender-transcendent divine is common to all those who define themselves as feminist theologians. While some feminist theologians have tried to reform the church with their new approach to theology, others emphasise the impossibility of reforming the church in a gender-just way, and have therefore left the classic church structures.

Philosophers like Judith Butler have argued that feminism as a term is illegitimate, because it reinforces the stereotype of femininity. The gender divide between male and female itself is, according to Butler, an artificial social construct and therefore needs to be challenged. In *Gender Trouble: Feminism and the Subversion of Identity* and *Bodies that Matter: On the Discursive Limits of Sex* (1990/1999), Butler emphasises that those who maintain 'traditional' gender distinctions and roles are immoral because, by implication, this condemns those who want to choose their own gender. Butler develops a concept of gender performativity which becomes essential in feminist and gay scholarship. In particular, the assumption that heterosexuality is 'normal' and homosexuality/lesbianism is 'deviant' is offensively discriminatory against homosexuals/lesbians. While Butler is not a theologian, such thinking is increasingly influential in feminist theological circles.

It is easy to see that Butler's approach, widely respected by many modern feminist theologians and gender theorists, stands in clear opposition to traditional theological approaches emphasizing that God created men and women in a specific pattern and order, which is God-given and therefore unchangeable.

Many post-Christian feminists replace 'God' with 'Goddess/es', or with an abstract verb 'Be/ing', or with a universal principle which can be identified with creation/humanity. Such a post-Christian feminist spirituality is also present in different fields of culture and arts, as in the poems of Ntozake Shange:[4] 'I saw God within me and I loved her fiercely' is one of her famous quotes. Post-Christian feminists usually maintain that 'God' is not 'other' – s/he is within us.

Nevertheless, in our context, I want to address feminist theology – which still perceives itself as a part of the Christian tradition and wants to reform it – rather than leave it aside. One reason for choosing this reformist part of feminist theories, rather than the radical, post-Christian part, is that the goal of discussing a gender perspective on *diakonia* is situated within the tradition of

---

[4] www.encyclopedia.com/topic/Ntozake_Shange.aspx (accessed 21st February 2016). In *For Colored Girls Who Have Considered Suicide,* poems dramatized by female dancers recall encounters with classmates, lovers, rapists, abortionists and latent killers. The women survive the abuses and disappointments put upon them by the men in their lives, and come to recognize in each other the promise of a better future. In unison, at the end, they declare, 'i found god in myself / and i loved her / … fiercely.'

Christian faith. There is a need to rethink the impact of a gender perspective on the theory and practice of *diakonia*, understood as social practice situated in the framework of the Christian tradition.

Even though there are a huge number of different approaches within feminist theology, all feminist theologians agree on the issue that the patriarchal model for doing theology, developed and maintained over almost two thousand years, must be addressed critically. Another issue, on which most feminist theologians agree, be they revolutionary or reformist, is the central role of *experience* in their theologising.[5] Diaconal studies put a strong emphasis on human experience as decisive for the development of its theories, in order to improve diaconal practice. Since *diakonia* has a specific focus on unjust power relations, oppressive practices and marginalization, and gender theories contribute to unmask such practices, a gender-based approach is decisive for the development of diaconal theory and practice.

According to Rosemary Radford Ruether, who belongs to the 'reformist camp', the tendency to treat the use of experience as unique to feminist theology, and to see it as distant from the 'objective' sources of truth of classic theologies, is based on a misunderstanding. All theology has an experiential base. Ruether maintains that what have been called the objective sources of theology, scripture and tradition, are themselves codified human experience. Human experience is the starting-point and the end-point of the hermeneutical circle. For Ruether, her involvement in feminist theology led to a radical critique of oppressive structures in church and society. In her book *Liberation Theology: Human Hope Confronts Christian History and American Power* (1972), Ruether attacked the Christian tradition wherever it discriminated against Jews, blacks, women and Latin Americans. Ruether's most influential book to date is *Sexism and God Talk: Towards a Feminist Theology* (London, 1983/2002). It presents her basic thesis: 'The critical principle of feminist theology is the promotion of the full humanity of women. Whatever denies, diminishes or distorts the full humanity of women is, therefore, appraised as not redemptive.'[6]

Another feminist theologian who is relevant for the development of a gender approach to *diakonia* is Elisabeth Schüssler Fiorenza. Her best-known work is *In Memory of Her: A Feminist Theological Reconstruction of Christian Origins* (London, 1983). For Fiorenza, the critical issue for interpretation is that of securing justice and freedom for all. Biblical interpretation is above all a tool for becoming aware of structures of domination, which must then be abolished. Feminist theologians are not mere academics: they should be part of a social movement for emancipation. Theological arguments are to be judged as to whether they are empowering wo/men in their struggles for survival and

---

5 For an overview, see Denise Ackermann, 'Feminist Liberation Theology: A Contextual Option', in *Journal of Theology for Southern Africa*, 1988, No. 62, 14-28.

6 R.R. Ruether, *Sexism and God-talk* (Boston, MA: Beacon Press, 1983), 18.

transformation, or whether they are supporting structures of domination and oppression.

Both Rosemary Radford Ruether and Elisabeth Schüssler Fiorenza are important stakeholders when it comes to developing a gender perspective on *diakonia*. Their radical demand for re-reading the biblical texts with a perspective from below, asking for the liberating power of the gospel and criticizing unjust structures based on gender discrimination and patriarchal structures, are indeed important when it comes to understanding *diakonia* as the social practice of the church.[7]

The *diakonia* of the church encompasses the call to serve the poor and oppressed, to address injustice and to fight for the value and dignity of all human people, regardless of their sex. Thus, feminist theologians and the stakeholders of the church's *diakonia* share a common concern to advocate for people in need, creating just and solitary societal structures and engaging proactively to create structures for women and men's access to sustain their own livelihood.[8]

Theologians like Elizabeth A. Johnson emphasized in her book *She Who Is* (1992) – a book which is widely seen as a classic text of feminist theological discourse – that we need a new way of speaking about God which reflects the human dignity and equality of all people. Johnson describes God as 'the creative, relational power of being who enlivens, suffers with, sustains, and enfolds the universe'.[9] Johnson's project was to translate the classic theological doctrines, like the doctrine of the Trinity, into a new and inclusive way of God-talk.

> In the end, the Trinity provides a symbolic picture of totally shared life at the heart of the universe. It subverts duality into multiplicity. Mutual relationships of different equals appear as the ultimate paradigm of personal and social life. The Trinity is pure relationality, and moreover, epitomizes the connectedness of all that exists in the universe.[10]

For Johnson, the triune image of God as community becomes a profound critique of patriarchal structures in church and society. Since God in God's very nature is relational, God is a community shaped by equality and mutuality. This image of God should, according to Johnson, be the basis for all human community.

---

[7] R.R. Ruether, *Sexism and God-talk.*

[8] For an Introduction into the theories of *diakonia*, see S. Dietrich, 'Reflections on Core Aspects of Diaconal Theory', in Stephanie Dietrich, Knud Jørgensen, Kari Karsrud Korslien and Kjell Nordstokke (eds), *Diakonia as Christian Social Practice: An Introduction* (Oxford: Regnum, 2014), 13-27.

[9] Elizabeth Johnson, *She Who Is: The Mystery of God in Feminist Theological Discourse* (New York: Herder & Herder 2007).

[10] Johnson. *She Who Is*, 222-23.

The Order of Creation – A Critical Perspective

The theological basis

Within a Lutheran tradition, the theology of 'Order of Creation' refers to a doctrine of theology asserting God's hand in establishing social domains, and basic structures and patterns of life such as the family, the church, the state and the economy. The doctrine became highly discussed and rejected by theologians like Karl Barth and Dietrich Bonhoeffer after its misuse during the 1930s and 1940s, when it served in legitimizing the Nazi regime. The Nazis had used the doctrine to emphasise their racist ideologies and primacy of the so-called 'Arian race'.

Also, the Roman Catholic Church emphasises in its catechism that men and women are, from creation, characterised by equality, complementarity and difference. Within the Roman Catholic tradition, the emphasis on a God-given structure and order between the sexes is based mainly on their understanding of the Thomist-Aristotelian tradition of natural law. There are nevertheless similarities to the Lutheran understanding of an order of creation, a doctrine that still seems to be alive or even sometimes revitalised in parts of the conservative Lutheran tradition.[11] The emphasis that there is an eternal order of created relationship between women and men, founded by God according to his eternal will from the time of creation, stands in stark contrast to most feminist models of understanding.

The Roman Catholic catechism emphasises that men and women have the same dignity, but are from creation onwards, and through the hands of the creator, designated to be different.

> Man and woman have been created, which is to say, willed by God: on the one hand, in perfect equality as human persons; on the other, in their respective beings as man and woman. 'Being man' or 'being woman' is a reality which is good and willed by God: man and woman possess an inalienable dignity which comes to them immediately from God their Creator. Man and woman are both with one and

---

[11] Carl E. Braaten wrote an article on 'God in Public Life: Rehabilitating the 'Orders of Creation'' (www.firstthings.com/article/1990/12/god-in-public-life-rehabilitating-the-orders-of-creation): 'We have lost our way in a labyrinthine antinomianism that leaves it up to each individual to intuit his or her way out of moral dilemmas. In any ethical situation, Christians are told to rely on what the Spirit nudges them to do on the spur of the existential moment, which in practice often amounts to people doing pretty much what everybody else is doing. This approach to moral questions has now been adopted by the churches, so that eliciting sample opinions from a cross-section of the population becomes an avenue to the discovery of God's will on any issue. The pluralism and relativism built into this sociological approach are the latest substitutes for the theology of law and the orders of creation that framed the ethical discussions of the church in the past.'

> the same dignity 'in the image of God'. In their 'being-man' and 'being-woman', they reflect the Creator's wisdom and goodness. [12]

Critical discernment

In the context of this article, I cannot go into depth concerning the broad discussion on creation order or natural law versus feminist theology. Surely, there are several obstacles concerning their relationship: first, the emphasis on human experience as opposed to the emphasis on the church's tradition; secondly, the patriarchal systems of power, which are often a part of the structures of authority within the churches, are opposed to the emphasis on the need to overcome patriarchal systems.

One of the challenging aspects of theologies emphasizing the 'order of creation', is the way this theological approach is used to argue for the subordination of women. Based on the second story of creation, women are depicted as sinful, of secondary importance and created out of Adam's rib. Thus, their value is not equal, but based only on their relationship with a man, and on their being derived from a man, even physically. Women, according to this view, are the source of temptation, carry the main responsibility for humankind's fall, and are leading men away from God and from mankind's true destiny.

Historically, and especially within the church's tradition, such theology has served to oppress women, to deprive them of their God-given dignity, equality and value and to create structures of subordination, in both church and society. It has been used as an argument to exclude women from positions of power, designating them as the weaker sex and reliant on their male counterparts. Also, within the history of *diakonia*, women have been widely excluded from positions of power, even though women have always played a strong part when it comes to the church's service to the world.

From a diaconal point of view, there are many good reasons to question the theology of an order of creation when it serves to create and sustain oppressive structures. Designating the role of women and men so strictly, and in addition emphasising that this subordination is God's will – and thus non-negotiable – and that women have an inferior role from creation until the end of the world, has had and still has a devastating effect when it comes to women's life conditions. In addition, such theology contributes to systemic injustice, since it gives the power to define solely to men. Since the church's *diakonia* is concerned about creating and sustaining communities, where both women and men equally can contribute and partake, the theology of the order of creation has to be discussed fundamentally.

---

[12] www.vatican.va/archive/ccc_css/archive/catechism/p1s2c1p6.htm (accessed 21st February 2016).

The Need for a Gender Perspective in Diakonia

Diakonia leading towards transformation and empowerment

In an adequate, biblically grounded, theological anthropology, men and women reflects God's image. This anthropology is basic and decisive for all diaconal theory and practice. Every human being, irrespective of sex, has equal value and is created in the image and likeness of God. Taken as a starting-point in this very basic diaconal value, this leads towards a non-negotiable defence of the dignity of both women and men.

Diakonia thus contributes to empowerment, reconciliation and transformation. This includes the recognition of the potential and abilities of every human. Such an anthropology does not result in a neutralised, colourless equality of humanity in which it becomes difficult to speak of male and female. The transformative model refers to Paul's vision in Galatians 3:27-28: 'There is no such thing as Jew and Greek, slave and freeman, male and female; for you all are one in Christ Jesus.' Women and men are addressed together, not merely to partake in some future vision, but to become involved in the practical and present application of such an anthropology. That includes breaking down patterns of domination in society. The model of transformation does not imply the neutralising of the sexes. The experience of being a woman or a man contributes through its own particular and different appearance. Recovering our createdness in the image and likeness of God, our *imago Dei* leads towards the transformation of structures in church and society. Diaconal transformation leads towards both a newly integrated self and a newly integrated social and societal order.

Thus, there are clear aspects of similarity between diaconal theory and the transformational approaches of feminist theorists. When diaconal theorists emphasize that *diakonia* relates both to the individual in need, but also to structures of justice, to care for creation and the creation of inclusive communities, this is very much in accordance with transformative models as developed by Catharina Halkes and other feminist researchers.[13]

Halkes' transformative model seeks the attainment of full personhood for both men and women, whilst realising the simultaneous need for societal change. The transformative model seeks a theological base in the concept of *imago Dei* based on Genesis 1:26-28. Halkes, sometimes described as 'the

---

[13] Catharina J.M. Halkes, *New Creation: Christian Feminism and the Renewal of the Earth* (Louisville, KY: Westminster John Knox, 1992). Also her 'Humanity Re-imaged: New Directions in Feminist Theological Anthropology', in *Liberating Women; New Theological Directions, 2nd-6th September 1991* (University of Bristol, Dept. of Theological and Religious Studies, 1993).

founding mother of feminist theology in Europe',[14] remained within the reformist feminist tradition, trying to reform rather than leave the church and its tradition.

When putting our emphasis on everybody's created-ness in the image and likeness of God and thus intrinsic and God-given value, both conservative theologians and theologians emphasizing the need to start with women's experience of oppression and fighting it, should be able to unite in a common concern to affirm the liberating role of faith for the community of women and men. The Lutheran World Federation emphasizes this in its document, 'It will not be so among you!':

> To be human means to be male and female because that is how God had created us to be – different but equal. Together we are the image of God and together we are expected to reflect this image.[15]

In addition to this basic aspect of Christian anthropology, emphasizing the equal value and dignity of all human beings, there can be a common reference to Jesus' teaching as empowering gender-just attitudes.[16] Jesus' dialogue and encounter with many women, even in the morning of his resurrection from the dead, make very clear that Jesus himself went beyond the gender stereotypes and expectations of his time and thus became a model of inclusive church leadership. 'Above all, Christ's empowering of women serves as the model that could be embodied by men in leadership and partnership that would help break the chains of oppressive cultures and norms.'[17]

Diaconal theology between experience and tradition

The emphasis on human, and especially women's, experience is an important aspect of feminist theology and gender perspectives on theology, which has often caused tensions between those claiming to defend the *tradition* of the church against what is perceived to be individualistic and subjective claims of godly experience. Acknowledging that there is a tension between theologies emphasizing divine revelation through tradition, and theologies putting their main emphasis on the encounter with human experience, there is a need for a discussion on the relationship between revelation and experience, and not least

[14] Mary Grey, Catherina Halkes – In Memory and Appreciation: http://feminismandreligion.com/2011/07/26/catharina-halkes-in-memory-and-appreciation-by-mary-grey (accessed 21st February 2016).

[15] 'It will not be so among you!' (Mark 10:43): A Faith Reflection on Gender and Power (Geneva: LWF Department for Mission and Development, 2010): https://www.lutheranworld.org/sites/default/files/A%20Faith%20Reflection%20on%20Gender%20and%20Power.pdf (accessed 21st February 2016).

[16] Compare Nordstokke's and Jørgensen's contributions in this publication.

[17] 'It will not be so among you!', 33.

between the location of revelation in women's experience and its location in the tradition of the Christian church.

This question is also discussed within feminist theology. Mary Catherine Hilkert asks:

> On the one hand, in what sense can the Catholic Church (or even the larger Christian Church) claim to be faithful to the life and mission of Jesus when it is so fundamentally distorted by patriarchal structures and sexist attitudes and practices? On the other hand, at what point are Christian feminists no longer identifiably Christian in belief, ritual, or practice?[18]

In any situation in which women suffer the injustice of oppression in patriarchal structures, both in family life and society, feminist theology remains primarily a critical theology of liberation.

Gender theories do not imply an elimination of the difference between male and female; rather they emphasise that human beings, as male and female, created in the image and likeness of God, in difference and diversity *together* form the human community. This implies a raised awareness of gender justice, as described by Christian Aid: 'Christian Aid believes that gender justice means, in part, 'just power relations between women and men in which both are valued equally in society and empowered to pursue their human rights and fundamental freedoms'.'[19]

Gender justice has therefore become an integral part of the commitment of many churches and confessional bodies, like the Lutheran World Federation (LWF): 'Gender as a methodological tool can explicitly bring out the disparity in power relationships based on the biological differences of sex. This could facilitate public policies that advocate citizenship rights, and transform unjust structures, thus promoting fundamental inclusiveness for all human beings.'[20]

Christian communities have the goal of being 'inclusive communities'. Creating and sustaining inclusive communities is a part of the diaconal call of the church. As long as there are women and men who are excluded from the community, there is a need to sustain and uphold a gender perspective to counteract this exclusion. The LWF emphasises that gender has to be internalized and deliberately used as a tool for analysis and action, in both a practical, conceptual, strategic and systemic way.[21]

The LWF emphasises that such a gender perspective on *diakonia* has to lead towards:

---

[18] Mary Catherine Hilkert, 'Experience and Tradition – Can the Center Hold?', in Catherine Mowry Lacugna (ed), *Freeing Theology: The Essentials of Theology in Feminist Perspective* (Harper Collins: New York, 1993), 59-82 (76).

[19] *Gender Justice for All:* Christian Aid's strategy for achieving just and equitable power relations for men and women, 2014.

[20] 'It will not be so among you!', 7.

[21] 'It will not be so among you!', 47-48.

- Offering and receiving such services as are intended for both men and women, but service should be distinguished from the servitude that is often required of women. Service is a free offer women extend willingly, while servitude is a subjugating imposition on them by others.
- If *diakonia* is promoted over the existing development paradigms, one needs to look into whether gender as an analytical tool would be integral in *diakonia* as it has been for development.
- • Most importantly, it should ensure that in diaconal deliberations, women are not once again relegated to being the traditional, humble service providers with less option to be practitioners and leaders, with less or no remuneration, and fewer opportunities for leadership, and to be relegated once again to the traditional feminized areas of service.[22]

Conclusion

Christians affirm the equality of men and women in God's sight. This means that every community shaped by Christian theology should be one in which women and men live alongside one another in peaceful and just relationships.

It is a well-known fact that the reality is far from this ideal. Religious leaders often do not address or challenge gender-based injustice, but rather, in many places and cultures, the faith communities support oppressive and unjust practices.

Women from the global South have emphasised that 'Poverty has a woman's face'. In many places, women face the multiple burden of pregnancy, child-bearing, child-rearing and domestic unpaid work; they have been denied opportunities for education and are without access to adequate health care, education or income. Women comprise half of the world's population, yet they are the majority of those living in absolute poverty today.

Faith-based development agencies report on gender-based violence, legal and cultural exclusion and lack of educational and economic opportunities. We also know that, especially in situations of war and disaster, women and children tend to become the most vulnerable parts of the conflicts. Thus, there is a need for increased awareness on gender-based violence especially in places of armed conflict and natural disasters.

Discussing why and how a gender perspective becomes relevant within the field of diaconal studies thus becomes not just a question of the understanding of gender, whether it is better to place emphasis on what men and women share in common or the distinctiveness of men and women, and whether their difference is natural or socially constructed. Applying a gender perspective on *diakonia* is rather about analyzing the different contexts and their hidden and revealed patterns of gender injustice, applying a profound Christian anthropology that emphasizes the dignity and value of all human beings to

[22] 'It will not be so among you!', 49.

address the situation, and trying to find new and better ways of living together in our world. Applying a gender perspective on *diakonia* includes finding ways of transforming human life, leading to the empowerment and reconciliation of all human beings, in accordance with God's intention for the whole creation.

Women's Religious Experiences and Gender Justice Perspectives on Biblical Narratives: Building Bridges to Diaconal Practices

Elaine Neuenfeldt

Building Bridges – Gender Justice Perspectives in Diakonia

The aim of this article is to find correlations between some Old Testament narratives where women have an active role of care and service in the community, with studies that highlight women's diaconal practices. It is not the intention here to seek diaconal practices in Old Testament texts. This would be a fallacy of reading ancient texts with concepts that have been introduced later in history. The intention is to read of some practices that come under women's responsibilities and roles, with a perspective that can build a wider understanding to what is called *diakonia* in the New Testament.

This follows a perspective in feminist biblical hermeneutics that affirms women's autonomy and leadership as a continuous process in the biblical world. It overcomes also a perspective that sees only in the New Testament, and especially with Jesus' practices and attitudes, that women have received value. If in the New Testament women have been active, and stories show that women followed Jesus as disciples, it is because there was a tradition of women being leaders in the ancient Israelite society and culture.

Among many definitions of *diakonia*, in this essay the classical Greek notion of a 'bridge-builder' or 'go-between' role will be used. The importance of this particular way of defining *diakonia* is that it will interact with a gender justice perspective, where the work done by women is an important and crucial part of the church ministerial work. In that sense, central to *diakonia* is the criterion of relationship. 'Diaconal activities are relational, in the sense that all diaconal activity, including those addressing immediate needs, are embedded in a comprehensive mandate of building relationships.'[1]

The Lutheran World Federation document *Diakonia in Context* is using the same concept of go-between and bridge-builder:

---

[1] Kari Jordheim, 'Bridge-Builder and Go-between: the role of the deacon in church and society', in Stephanie Dietrich, Knud Jørgensen, Kari Karsrud Korslien and Kjell Nordstokke, *Diakonia as Christian Social Practice* (Oxford: Regnum, 2014), 198-99.

> The task of being a bridge-builder is integral to the very nature of diakonia. In the Ancient Church, the deacon was called 'the ear and the mouth of the bishop'. It was the deacon who had the responsibility for bringing the stories from the margins, from the lives of the poor and the sick into the church. The mission of go-between is successful if distances can be bridged. When this happens, diaconal involvement can contribute to transformation of the church – both in the centre and on the periphery.[2]

This notion of building bridges and being a go-between highlight the hermeneutical approach to Old Testament texts, taking women's active roles in the community as a call and a ministry to build relationships and keep the community in peace and order. It is a ministry that cares for wholeness of life, for restoring relationships and mediating forces to keep peace in the community.

Analyzing these practices with a gender justice perspective implies a critical look at the power relations embedded in diaconal practices. Are activities developed by women considered on the same level as those developed by men? What are the opportunities and possibilities for women in the diaconal work of the churches? How are we to read the diaconal work, as ministerial service, developed with dignity and not as servanthood, based on oppression and obligations?

A gender justice perspective 'implies the protection and promotion of the dignity of women and men who, being created in the image of God, are co-responsible stewards of creation. Gender justice is expressed through equality and balanced power relations between women and men, and the elimination of the institutional and interpersonal systems of privilege and oppression that sustain discrimination.'[3]

Women are carrying in their bodies the reality of life and death. In biblical times, but also in a considerable part of today's context, women are responsible for maintaining life in borderline moments like pregnancy, delivering a child, caring for sick or dead bodies. This social and cultural task has a religious implication. Women perform religious activities and rituals at these moments. These moments are not always connected or even recognized by institutional religion. Mostly, in today's context, these practices come under the responsibility of women and are performed in domestic spheres, where this service is not yet specialized and outsourced to specific agencies, like hospitals and care centres. But, even if those practices are performed by specialized agencies, women are still mostly the workers in these centres; women are the majority of care-givers and nurses.

---

[2] Lutheran World Federation, *Diakonia in Context: Transformation, Reconciliation, Empowerment. An LWF Contribution to the Understanding and Practice of Diakonia* (Geneva: LWF, 2009), 46-47.

[3] The Lutheran World Federation Gender Justice Policy (Geneva, LWF, 2013), 7.

To analyze some biblical texts, the concept of 'go-between' is also helpful in avoiding a reading of these religious practices in opposition to an official religious doctrine, performed in the temple or later in synagogues. The diaconal key of being a bridge-builder helps to see these activities not in contradiction to but as different aspects of religious life in a community. Women are responsible for a ministry of care and dignity for the integral nature of the human body, and therefore, for the community as a whole.

A Methodological Approach to Analyse Women's Religious Experiences and Practices in Old Testament Texts

Reading Old Testament texts, using gender as an analytical tool, raises some methodological questions that expand interpretative possibilities. The intention is to amplify the scenario of probabilities, going beyond gender stereotypical roles attributed to and expected of women. These analytical tools are also helpful in order not to isolate women as a segregated group, but to see their experiences and practices as interconnected in the social, cultural, political and economic fabric of society. This approach will move beyond the idea of making women visible in the biblical narratives; it will ask for the power relations interwoven in the tapestry where these practices happen.

To analyse women's religious experiences and practices, daily life needs to be taken into account, as a place where the relationship with the sacred and divine come together. This relationship with the divine will includes objects, elements and things that correspond to this quotidian space, like food, clothes, pans, fire, salt, oil, flour, bowls, river, water, trees, earth, animals, etc.

My starting-point is to highlight experiences of ordinary women and their ordinary life, and see how these experiences may have a religious significance. It is this interconnectedness of daily life and religious significance that will be explored in the following paragraphs.

To do the exercise of rebuilding what could encompass women's participation in the religious life of ancient biblical times, some questions may guide the research.[4] There are several communitarian and public religious activities, like pilgrimages, feasts, victory celebrations or national convocations narrated in the Bible. What was the role of women related to these activities? How were the activities divided according to gender roles, and what were specifically the roles of women? From which kind of activities were women specifically excluded and why? From which activities were men excluded and why? What are the implications of religious obligations for social life? Are these implications different for men and for women? The intention is to discover a variety of roles, differentiated by gender expectations, and to

[4] These questions are based on a broader study developed by Phyllis Bird, *Women's Religion in Ancient Israel*, in Barbara S. Lesko (ed), *Women's earliest records: from Ancient Egypt and Western Asia* (Atlanta, GA: Scholars Press, 1987), 292.

rediscover how some activities provide the possibility of empowering or disempowering women.

On Attributed Gender Roles and Women's Religious Practices

The roles of women in the cultic life of ancient biblical times were closely related to the gender-based division of work.[5] Women were relegated to reproductive functions and responsible primarily for work in the domestic sphere. The social roles of each sex were determined by expected gender roles instituted according to the patriarchal and androcentric values of society.

This spatial delimitation has consequences for a differentiated participation and performance in the social and cultural institutions, and more specifically in the religious life. Thus, leadership in institutional worship is rarely, if ever, a function occupied by a woman. The activities performed by women are normally restricted to the needs of the domestic sphere. Public religious activities normally reflect male perspectives and expectations, and do not reveal women's realities and daily life, and normally did not even allow women's participation

Such a categorization of functions and spheres for women and men provokes an asymmetric access to power. Women are denied access to public spaces, and also have limited decision-making power in private spheres. Also, in the private sphere, women are under the authority of the patriarch, father and lord. This domestic sphere, at home, must be seen as a *locus* where women develop their religious life – sometimes parallel or in opposition to the public and male-dominated religious practices.[6]

What this article wants to explore is the relationship between domestic activities performed by women and the assigning of religious value to a given activity. Specifically, the analysis will focus on what women do around death. Crying/weeping or caring for dead bodies are social or cultural activities developed only by women, or do they have embedded religious values? To what extent will a cultural or social activity have a religious connotation? The division between the social, cultural and religious is a modern concept, and normally a western/occidental assumption, used mostly in academic settings, which differ from ancient and non-occidental societies where social and religious values interact closely.

Caring for Life and Death

Jeremiah 9:17-22 is one text in focus. Verse 17 reads: *Consider, and call for the mourning women to come; send for the skilled women to come.* One

[5] Phyllis Bird, *Missing Persons and Mistaken Identities* (women and gender in ancient Israel) (Minneapolis, MN: Fortress Press, 1997), 86.

[6] Phyllis Bird, *Women's Religion in Ancient Israel*, 297.

immediate observation concerns a different translation for a concept when applied to women or to men – clearly a translation guided by gender stereotypes – why weeping women cannot be considered wise, while men are. A considerable number of versions translate this as *skilled* women; but the root of the Hebrew word is clearly connected with a word that means *wisdom.* The same root is translated as 'wise' or 'wisdom' in verse 23, where the word refers to men: *the wise boast in their wisdom.*

Verse 20: *Hear, O women, the word of the Lord, and let your ears receive the word of his mouth; teach to your daughters a dirge and each to her neighbour a lament.*

The ritual weeping performed by the mourners was a wisdom/knowledge passed from mother to daughter (Jer. 9:20). Here is the unique situation where God is calling women directly – and the use of these specific verbs reinforces the prophetic calling and sending: *Hear, O women... Let your ears receive the word of his mouth... teach to your daughters.* Similar verbs are used in Deuteronomy 4:1, when God is talking to the people and giving the law; or in Esdras 7:10, when Esdras, is teaching the commandments to the people.

Certainly, belonging to a group of professionals confers a position of influence and status. Belonging to such a group that is responsible for public laments will confer on women a distinct position which is crossing the borders of the domestic and limited spaces, and their role as wives, mothers or daughters.

Their function is catalytic; their weeping should animate the congregation, the group. They weep loudly and represent the collective. 'We are devastated.' The formation of the lamenting women finds room in the family, so that the house and the public are firmly connected. The mother teaches the lament to the daughter: the right gesture, the right clothes, and the right behaviour in dealing with the other mourners at the funeral, and she teaches a possible matching song or text of the song for the funeral. 'So we have the commitment with the oral tradition to pass this practice from one generation to the other.'[7]

Weeping for the dead is a public action, learned in private and domestic life, and it is also a social action with religious meaning, which confers a characteristic of moving beyond the border, or between frontiers. This trespassing of borders and being between social and religious, domestic and public frontiers can be seen in the following texts.

Rizpah lamenting the death of her sons, in 2 Samuel 21:10-14 is one very emblematic text. A mother will take care of dead bodies for more than six months, according to the text. She will be sitting in a ritual, wearing sackcloth, as instructed in other texts (Gen. 37:34; 2 Sam. 3:31; Job 16:15, etc.). Her action – sitting and caring for the bodies of the deceased– is a prophetic resistance. Her action reminds us of today's realities of so many women who

[7] Silvia Schroer, *Häusliche und außerhäusliche religiöse Kompetenzen israelitischer Frauen,* 7.

are seeking the bodies of their beloved sons and daughters, assassinated by military dictatorships, drug traffickers, or as a result of other kinds of violence.

Other texts where weeping is a political action are the narrative of destruction in Zechariah 12:10-14 and Jeremiah lamenting the death of the king, in 2 Chronicles 35:25.

Most of the references to rituals and practices surrounding death are inserted in the realm of women's responsibility and power; these practices have to do with the care of life and death. Women are responsible for all issues that deal with preserving life, like health, fertility, menstruation, reproduction, pregnancy, labour and childbirth or death, funerals and burials. Pregnancy and childbirth are women's domains; midwives perform the rites of passage for the newborn from delivery, to washing, anointing and scrubbing the newborn. These are some of the specific roles of women, and it is expected that women will be in these areas of danger and power. In these areas the performance of rituals that are embedded in spirituality, led by women, will take place. Official religious performers, who are mostly men, do not enter these spaces. It might be because women experience in their own body the borderline realities of life and death, with menstruation, or carrying a life inside their own body for nine months, or giving birth, that confers on women the power to deal with these moments of danger with our being unclean, or dying.

In Ezekiel 16: 4-6 some elements of these rituals can be found: cutting the umbilical cord, washing, rubbing with salt and wrapping with clothes. Other texts concern the presence of midwives (Ex. 1:15-21; Gen. 35:17; 1 Sam. 4:20) and give some indication of the presence of women serving in a health care – and possibly also a religious – capacity.

All these practices aim at preserving family religion which has a two-fold meaning:

> The one afforded the family a sense of continuity and tradition; the other provided a way of asserting and maintaining a local identity. Both aspects of family religion also had a legitimizing function. Through the cult of the ancestors, the paterfamilias was confirmed in his position as successor to his forefathers. The devotion to the family god, on the other hand, had the attendant effect of legitimizing the social station of the family, since health, wealth and a good reputation were celebrated as his gifts.[8]

The family, as a social centre, furnishes communitarian and collective identity to individuals. The family deity establishes the connection with the city patron deity and so will build a connection among families and with the temple and public worship in the city. Public worship in the temple will sustain ideologically the palace, the king and his kingship. This is the role of family religion: it is to be dialogue, to build bridges between social groups and

---

[8] Karel van der Toorn, *Family Religion in Babylonia, Syria and Israel: Continuity and Change in the Forms of Religious Life* (Leiden/New York/London: Brill, 1996), 11.

ancestral deities, locally and nationally. This reading of family religion avoids the notion of opposition and condemnation of family religious practices, but highlights the role of family spiritual practices that cultivate and nurture communitarian relations.[9]

Caring and ritualizing the realities around death require an immense field of knowledge and wisdom – about taboos, impurity and danger, restrictions and so on. Biblical narratives as well as surrounding cultural practices testify to these realities.

In connection with reading women's tasks and responsibilities in caring for the dead, which is attested in Old Testament narratives, an emblematic passage in the New Testament is the text in all the gospels, about how the women are going to take care of Jesus' body, on that third morning, the day of Resurrection. They are going to take care of Jesus' body because it was expected they should do so. They had the knowledge about the use of the spices, the hour to go, the clothes and ritual to be carried out. Their *diakonia* – the service of caring for the dead body – was nothing unexpected or extraordinary. What became extraordinary is that through this service they became disciples. Through their ordinary caring role, a domestic service that women were used to performing, a new significance was established as they testified to the resurrection.

Touching and Restoring Life and Relationships as a Prophetic and Diaconal Action

In 1 Kings 17, the story of one of the widows of famine, or the widow of drought, this interaction between prophecy and restoring relationships between a woman and a prophet can be seen. At the beginning of the chapter (17:1), it says that there was no rain in the land; widows and sick or dead children are so common when there is no rain. The widow is the mother of an only son. And he dies. And she cries out questioning the prophet – in her understanding, the death of her son is because of her sin. She feels guilty – which is a very common feeling for women, especially mothers, and even more after the death of a child. Crying out to request some action from the prophet is what this woman is doing.

The prophet, going against the purity law that prohibits touching corpses, at the risk of becoming impure, took the dead body in his arms, and laid it down; then he stretched himself upon the child three times and cried out to the Lord. The Lord listened to the voice of the prophet and the life of the child came into him again, and he was revived. Bringing this son back to life is crucial so that this family group is restored in this social context. For a widow to be alone would be a pathway to more suffering and loneliness, hunger and increased poverty.

---

[9] Karel van der Toorn, *Family Religion in Babylonia, Syria and Israel,* 20-33.

The prophetic task here is to restore life, restore family relationships, bring back a widow's son. It is a religious experience that enters into the home, deals with the concrete issues of daily life: drought, empty pots of food, sick people. It is a religious practice that goes beyond the temple, the sanctuary and its traditional rituals and ceremonies formatted in the officially instituted spaces. The prophet also seems desperate: he demands God's intervention: *Have you brought calamity even upon the widow with whom I am staying, by killing her son?* Death and suffering question faith: going through moments of doubt, disbelief, scepticism – especially when facing difficulties like death and loss – is what the prophet experiences.

It is in touching death, in the encounter with the suffering, that life is restored. The prophecy here takes place through embracing, touching body with body, through a kind of ritual that restores life, restores hope and reconnects relationships. The text says that the breath came back to the child; he started breathing again and his life was restored.

Prophecy is the courage to act to restore life to a dead body. It is the brave gesture of touching death in order to re-establish relationships – because life comes first; life in its wholeness and fullness. Faith experiences at the margins of life, and when life is at its limits, it can restore breathing. And then life returns and relationships are restored.

The prophetic announcement cries out that God's love and compassion will enter homes, fill pots and tables and touch bodies, breaking down any notion of impurity, untouchability – and life will be restored, breath will come back, and bodies are going to feel the warm breath of life again.

In the New Testament a related story is found in Luke 7, the widow of Nain. Here again, a widow is weeping over the death or her son, her only son; will her dignity be restored by Jesus' miracle of bringing life back to the son's body? After this miracle, Jesus is glorified as a prophet, and they recognize through this restoration of life and dignity that God has visited his people. A prophetic diaconal action of God is affirmed in this text – visiting a widow in her mourning. A domestic situation of mourning a dead son is the space and place for God revealing his presence, being present, visiting the one who is in a fragile, marginalized situation, because of being a widow and now losing her only son.

Would it be possible to read these touching stories in the Bible about carrying the suffering in the arms or God visiting a widow, as a prophetic gesture, as a way in which *diakonia* should be exercised? That's the aim of bringing these biblical stories and experiences of women in dialogue with the notion of *diakonia* as go-between and bridge-builder. It is to see these biblical testimonies as a way of inspiring diaconal practices today.

In times when it is so difficult to look someone in the eye, to see the suffering, stay in solidarity, take diaconal responsibility for whoever is next – the stranger, the one who is alone, who is in trouble – suffering is a strong message in these stories. The widow, in the story in the book of Kings, understood prophecy as a life-restoring responsibility, and demanded it from the prophet. It is in listening to the cry for justice and dignity that life was restored. The people around Jesus understood the miracle of bringing back the son of a widow as God's presence, healing and visit of solidarity. The cry of women, as prophetic action, calling for resistance and resilience, is an inspiring reversal of the understanding of crying. Culturally, there is no value attributed to women's crying; it is instead a symbol of weakness. Reversing this understanding, questioning it, using gender-critical lenses, is the new insight that this reading of the biblical text can produce. Interweaving a critical gender perspective with prophetic *diakonia* will open a new path of discovering the meaning of these biblical texts for today's world.

Go-between, Building Bridges and Prophetic Diakonia – Transforming Gender and Power Relations

The prophetic dimension of *diakonia* transforms the notion of 'service' in a liberating action. Serving in a context of hierarchy and injustice is based on one person negating her/himself; while service in a context of transformative relationships, based on justice, dignity and love, is empowerment that impels to critical consciousness to take autonomous decisions and transform the existing reality of exclusion and injustice. This is especially important for women, as traditionally, based on gender stereotypes that are neglecting women's autonomy and agency, the notion of service was used to subjugate women's work and practices. These stereotypical divisions of tasks received a religious and sacral atmosphere in the church – a theology of service that relegated women to a limited position of being responsible for caring for the community, serving food and caring for aged people and children, disconnected from decision-making and the exercise of power.[10]

In the prophetic text of Jeremiah 9, God called the women to weep, as a prophetic mandate. Caring for the dead is a prophetic action in a society where death becomes trivialized. Mothers in Central America, in Colombia, in South American military dictatorship regimes, are vivid examples of this prophetic cry for the dead. Crying is a political action. Weeping is an action of resistance and resilience. Searching for dead bodies in the middle of danger, caring for the integrity and dignity of the corpses, is a prophetic *diakonia* done by women. It is a courageous act of resistance, an affirmation of justice in life and relationships.

[10] Rogerio Oliveira Aguiar, 'A Diaconia Cristã como Contestação ao Discurso Sexista', in André Musskopf, Marcia Blasi, *Ainda feminismo e gênero* (Histórias, gênero e sexualidade, sexismo, violência e políticas públicas, religião e teologia) (Sao Leopoldo: CEBI, EST, 2014), 160.

A critical gender analysis on women's practices regarding care and bodily experiences interwoven with a notion of *diakonia* as go-between and bridge-building contributes to re-defining women's diaconal ministry in the churches.

An understanding of *diakonia* connected with women's bodily experiences, in daily life, and with balanced power relations, questions the hierarchical division of domestic service and ministry. This is an embodied *diakonia*. Therefore, it is an approach that looks to the experiences of those, who resist oppressive power relations, and it also criticizes the power architecture that relegates women to a position of servanthood. This critical approach to *diakonia*, with gender justice lenses, brings in the notion of responsibility – caring is not a burden, a service that has a minus value – but is part and parcel of a responsibility for building justice and dignity for all people.[11]

Bibliography

Jordheim, Kari, 'Bridge-Builder and Go-between: the role of the deacon in church and society', in Stephanie Dietrich, Knud Jørgensen, Kari Karsrud Korslien and Kjell Nordstokke, *Diakonia as Christian Social Practice*. Oxford: Regnum, 2014.

Lutheran World Federation, *Diakonia in Context: Transformation, Reconciliation, Empowerment. An LWF Contribution to the Understanding and Practice of Diakonia*. Geneva: LWF, 2009.

Bird, Phyllis A., *Missing Persons and Mistaken Identities: Women and Gender in Ancient Israel*. Minneapolis, MN: Fortress Press, 1997.

Bird, Phyllis A., 'Women's Religion in Ancient Israel', in Barbara S. Lesko (ed), *Women's earliest records: from Ancient Egypt and Western Asia*. Atlanta, GA: Scholars Press, 1987.

Schroer, Silvia, 'Häusliche und außerhäusliche religiöse Kompetenzen israelitischer Frauen – am Beispiel von Totenklage und Totenbefragung', in *Lectio Difficilior*, Bern. n. 1, 2002: www.lectio.unibe.ch/02_1/schroer.htm

Toorn, Karel van der, *Family Religion in Babylonia, Syria and Israel: Continuity and Change in the Forms of Religious Life*. Leiden/New York/London: Brill, 1996.

Aguiar, Rogerio Oliveira, 'A Diaconia Cristã como Contestação ao Discurso Sexista', in André Musskopf and Marcia Blasi, *Ainda feminismo e gênero: Histórias, gênero e sexualidade, sexismo, violência e políticas públicas, religião e teologia*. Sao Leopoldo: CEBI, EST, 2014.

Pletsch, Rosane, 'Diaconia e corpo. Categorias relevantes para repensar o conhecimento na perspectiva de gênero e cidadania', in Marga Stroeher, Wanda Deifelt, André Musskopf (eds), *À flor da pele. Ensaios sobre gênero e corporeidade*. São Leopoldo: Sinodal, CEBI, EST, 2004.

---

[11] Rosane Pletsch, 'Diaconia e corpo. Categorias relevantes para repensar o conhecimento na perspectiva de gênero e cidadania', in Marga Stoher, Wanda Deifelt, André Musskopf (eds), *À flor da pele*. (Ensaios sobre gênero e corporeidade. São Leopoldo: Sinodal, CEBI, EST, 2004), 222-23.

The Feminization or Engendering of Diakonia: New Testament Perspectives

Kjell Nordstokke

Introduction

Did Jesus envisage a discipleship of equals, in the sense that women and men would share tasks and responsibilities? Elisabeth Schüssler Fiorenza who published the book *In Memory of Her* in 1983,[1] has proposed a reconstruction of the early church from a woman's perspective, based on the view that the authors of the New Testament have downgraded the role of women when telling the story about Jesus and his followers.

This chapter seeks to explore this question from a diaconal perspective. What is the role of women in *diakonia*, understood as discipleship and as sharing in the caring ministry of church? In what follows, we shall first present some of the findings of Schüssler Fiorenza and a few other scholars who have studied the role of women in the New Testament. Then we shall turn to the so-called *diak-* words (διακονια, διακονειν, διακονος) in order to find out whether their use reveals gender roles. In doing so, we shall be aware of the claim of feminist theologians that patriarchal structures soon became dominant in the early Christian communities, and that this development largely influenced the authors of the New Testament – all of them males – and the manner in which they refer to women.

This point of departure supports the assumption that women played a more active role in the life of the early church than is depicted in the New Testament writings, and that they also held leadership positions. The development of patriarchal structures resulted in women being expected to perform caring services, but under the guidance and control of male leaders. In many ways, the modern diaconal movement, starting in Germany in the 1830s, imitated this structure: in the majority of diaconal institutions, women, trained and commissioned as deaconesses, did the diaconal work, while men, usually ordained ministers, had the position of leaders.

---

1 Elisabeth Schüssler Fiorenza, *In Memory of Her: A Feminist Theological Reconstruction of Christian Origins* (London: SCM, 1983, 2nd edition, 1994).

We may describe this development as a feminization of *diakonia*.[2] It suggests that diaconal work is an activity that in the first place engages and involves women. The consequence will often be a view that considers *diakonia* as less important compared with other church matters, such as proclamation, administering the sacraments and giving leadership – arenas often dominated and decided upon by men. In other words, the feminization of *diakonia* leads to the marginalization of *diakonia* in the life of the church.

Without doubt, several social and cultural factors have contributed to this development. However, theological factors also count, not least the normative role that the New Testament maintains in setting standards for the understanding of the mission and the ministry of the church. It is therefore appropriate to ask if the biblical texts contain a broader picture of gender roles than male-dominated interpretation has been able to discover. This may be an impulse to reinterpret *diakonia* as an integral dimension of the being and the mission of the church, and Christian discipleship as a ministry where women and men equally are called to share and serve.

Jesus and Women

Luke lets us know that among those who accompanied Jesus when he travelled through cities and villages were 'some women who had been cured of evil spirits and infirmities'. Three of them are named; Luke makes it clear that there were 'many others, who provided (διηκονουν) for them out of their resources' (Luke 8:1-3 NRVS).

Three comments regarding this text: where NRVS translates the Greek verb διηκονουν 'provided for', NIV reads 'were helping to support'. The classical King James Version (KJV) has 'ministered unto him of their substance'. Comparing these translations, KJV comes closest to the Greek terminology, understanding διηκονουν as 'performing a ministry', thus more than providing food or taking care of some practical matters. What these women are doing is an expression of their vocation as disciples: they follow Jesus and serve.

This takes us to the second comment: whom did they serve? In the early Greek versions of this text, two variants are handed on, one saying that they 'ministered unto him', as KJV translates, while the other says 'them'. This latter version has the strongest support in the oldest manuscripts; therefore most translators opt for it. The meaning could then be that the women have an equal share in the communal life of the group of disciples, but also that they participated in the mission of Jesus, bringing the good news to cities and villages.

[2] Feminization is here interpreted as a negative process that constructs divisions between women and men, and tends to devalue the role of women. The alternative, and positive, term is 'engendering' – this affirms equal opportunities for women and men, and values the practice of sharing gifts and roles.

Thirdly, Luke explains why these women had become disciples and chosen to follow Jesus: they had been cured of evil spirits and infirmities, which means a radical experience of liberation and transformation. Antiquity did not distinguish between possession and sickness; rather, it regarded them as expressions of impurity, which meant shame and stigmatization for the victims. When Jesus healed such persons, he did not only cure their physical and mental illnesses; he also restored their social and religious life, so that they could again be part of the community from which they had been excluded. Even more, he empowered them to be his disciples and to follow him. People would probably look with suspicion on them; antiquity was not familiar with women who played such roles in a religious movement. It seems, however, that these women freely opted for this ministry, as an expression of gratitude and generosity.

We see similar traits in the Gospel of Mark. It presents stories with women that, according to contemporary moral and religious standards, are excluded. When meeting with Jesus, they experience healing, inclusion and affirmation of their dignity. One example is the haemorrhaging woman (Mark 5:25-34). Her suffering has many dimensions: she has been sick for a long time; she has spent a lot of money on physicians who could not heal her; her situation makes her unclean and a risk to people who might get close to her. When hearing about Jesus, she takes the initiative of getting close to him. To her surprise, Jesus does not see her uncleanness, but her faith. He empowers her to be a whole person; she is healed and free to go in peace.

Another example is the story about the Syrophœnician woman (Mark 7:24-30). She also had heard rumours about Jesus. Knowing that he is passing by her neighbourhood, she imagines that he can heal her daughter possessed by a demon. She acknowledges that everything counts against a meeting with Jesus: being a women, a Gentile, and in addition coming from a household made unclean by her daughter. Against all the odds, she manages to bring Jesus into a dialogue with her, appealing to him to grant her space close to the table of sharing, even under the table where the dogs eat the children's crumbs. Her words move Jesus to see her misery and struggle; he announces the healing of her daughter. Doing so, he defies the rules of impurity that would exclude her from the communion of the table; instead he affirms her faith and dignity.

The story about the woman who anointed Jesus (Mark 14:3-9) is another remarkable example. On her own initiative, she enters a space reserved for men, she interrupts what is going on and, when anointing Jesus, she takes upon her the prophetic role of announcing his messianic ministry. Those present react with anger and scold her; Jesus, however, defends her and declares her act as a good service for him, stating that 'wherever the good news is proclaimed in the whole world, what she has done will be told in remembrance of her'.

There is a surprising contrast in the Gospel of Mark between men and women in their relationship with Jesus. The author presents the group of twelve – all men, of course – as unable to grasp the liberating significance of the good news; they fight among themselves about positions, and at the most critical moment of discipleship, they all flee. With the women followers, this is different. In their own life, they have experienced the newness of life that Jesus brings; therefore they serve him and they remain faithful, even at the foot of the cross.

We sense a message behind Mark's indirect polemic against the male disciples and his recognition of female discipleship. Mark seems to have become concerned when observing the development of the young Christian communities and the establishment of patriarchal structures, introducing patterns of dominance and submission.[3] Therefore, he reminds them of the clear statement of Jesus: 'It is so not among you!' (Mark 10:43a), said on the occasion when two of the disciples expressed an ambition for high-rank positions, which occasioned Jesus to announce the nature of his ministry: 'For the Son of Man came not to be served (διακονηθηναι), but to serve (διακονησαι), and to give his life as a ransom for many' (10:45).

The admonition 'It is so not among you!' seems to have gained new relevance at a time when the church was beginning to adapt to its social and religious environment, and to limit opportunities for female discipleship. To be a follower of Jesus implies following his example, and serving as he did: 'Whoever wants to be first must be the last of all and servant (διακονος) of all' (Mark 9:35). It is interesting to note that Mark never uses the verb διακονειν related to male disciples, but to Jesus who applied it when making clear the distinct nature of his ministry, and on two occasions related to women. The first appears when Jesus heals Simon's mother-in-law; once the fever had left her, 'she began to serve (διηκονει) them' (1:31). The second is a parallel to Luke 8:1-3, about the women that had served (διηκονουν) him when he was in Galilee and 'had come up to Jerusalem with him' (15:41).

It may well be that among the factors that motivated Mark to write down 'the beginning of the good news' (Mark 1:1) was the increasing need to keep alive the memory of the nature of true discipleship, by which the marginalized and excluded were lifted up and empowered to follow Jesus. That may be why he depicts women as positive models of discipleship, as persons that by their actions affirm their faith in Jesus. They challenge churches that seek patriarchal honour and hierarchical authority; while 'rule by power' is exclusive, their way of 'serving' (διακονειν) is inclusive and life-giving.[4]

Evidently, the gospels present a double message in this matter, as Turid Karlsen Seim has shown in her study of gender patterns in Luke and Acts.[5] On the one hand, Luke gives women considerable prominence; they participate in

---

[3] Schüssler Fiorenza, *In Memory of Her*, 323.

[4] Hisako Kinukawa, *Women and Jesus in Mark: A Japanese Feminist Perspective* (Maryknoll, NY: Orbis Books, 1994), 105-06.

[5] Turid Karlsen Seim, *The Double Message: Patterns of Gender in Luke & Acts* (Nashville, TN.: Abingdon Press, 1994).

the ministry of Jesus and exhibit ideal virtues of leadership. On the other hand, they are not allowed to exercise leadership, which was clearly demonstrated at the crucial moment when some of them bore witness to the resurrection: their word turned out to have no credibility among men. Moving from the Gospel to Acts, women become less visible and more silenced, concludes Karlsen Seim. While Jesus had dared to cross social and religious barriers, the church accommodated its mission to the public sphere of the world of men.

Women in the Early Church

The fact that the New Testament refers to two distinct historical periods – one focusing on the Jesus event and the movement of followers it caused, the other reflecting the life of the young Christian communities some 25-50 years later – is challenging. It is tempting to idealize the first and be critical about the second, especially because of the increasing move towards patriarchalization and the ascendency of a hierarchical leadership. One of the effects of this process was that women were marginalized and silenced; their discipleship was largely restricted to service within what was understood as women's spheres.

On the other hand, every historical process must be analyzed according to its specific context, taking into account the socio-economic and cultural-religious conditions in which it is embedded. This helps us discern better the strengths and weaknesses whenever the church takes historical form, and it helps us acknowledge that no such form is absolute. This is also the case for the early Christian communities. The New Testament does not present a standard model of Christian discipleship or of how to organize the church. Its aim is to give witness to how the apostles interpreted faithfulness to the gospel and the newness of life in Christ. The letters of Paul indicate that this was a demanding venture, at times more marked by weakness, conflicts and failures than by success.

The memory of the words and deeds of Jesus must have remained a crucial point of reference in such critical times. It motivated Mark and others to create the literary genre we call 'gospel', with the purpose, as Luke states, 'that you may know the truth concerning the things about which you have been instructed' (1:4). As we have seen, the authors of the gospels tell this story influenced by their own background and concerns. We need, therefore, to read them, as all biblical writings, critically, as Schüssler Fioranza claims:

> As androcentric texts, our early Christian sources are theological interpretations, argumentations, projections, and selections rooted in a patriarchal culture.

> Therefore they need to be read critically for their theoretical-theological androcentric tendencies and their polemical theological patriarchal functions.[6]

This approach helps us discover a double message also in the letters of Paul. Paul got his theological education within the Jewish Pharisee tradition which categorized women together with children, and even slaves, for legal religious purposes. Growing up in a Hellenistic environment, he knew however that the actual socio-religious status of women to a large degree was determined by their economic autonomy and social roles.[7]

Lydia, who came to play an important role when the church in Philippi was established, illustrates this. Luke tells that she was a 'dealer in purple cloth' (Acts 16:12-15, 40); she appears to be well off, both economically and socially, and when converted, she opens her house to Paul and provides a meeting place for the Christians. We do not know whether Lydia was a Jew or a Gentile; Luke informs us that she was 'a worshipper of God' (σεβομενη τον θεον). The term indicates that she belonged to a group of 'devout persons' (σεβομενοι), similar to those Paul later met in Athens (Acts 17:17), Gentiles who sympathized with the Jewish faith. For different reasons they were not fully integrated into the Jewish community; as a woman Lydia would have encountered more hindrances than men. When listening to the preaching of Paul, 'the Lord opened her heart', which made her see the radical significance of the gospel. Through baptism she is fully included in the community of believers; this act empowers her to active discipleship, offering hospitality to Paul and to the newly established church. Luke emphasizes that Lydia is the one who takes the initiative – 'she prevailed upon us', he remarks. Thus, she comes forward as an example of the transformative power of faith: from being a marginal member of a Jewish circle in which she could never receive the covenant sign, she becomes a central figure in the local Christian church and the first baptized convert in Europe.[8] In line with the women that followed Jesus and 'served' (Luke 8:3), Luke portrays Lydia as an example of true discipleship: a person that freely opts for serving the others and leaves her resources and talents at the disposal of the mission of the church.

Persons like Lydia must have inspired Paul to state: 'There is no longer Jew or Greek, there is no longer slave or free, there is no longer male and female; for all of you are one in Christ Jesus' (Gal. 3:28). This is not in the first places a dogmatic statement referring to the unity of all human beings in their relationship with God; it is a prophetic witness to the healing and reconciling power of belonging to the body of Christ even now. Thus it reflects what Paul experienced in many house churches, often lead by women and men together,

---

[6] Elisabeth Schüssler Fiorenza, *Bread Not Stone: The Challenge of Feminist Biblical Interpretation* (Boston, MA: Beacon Press, 1984), 108.
[7] Schüssler Fiorenza, *In Memory of Her*, 109.
[8] Ben Witherington III, *Women in the Earliest Churches* (Cambridge: CUP, 1988), 149.

as must have been the case of Prisca and Aquila (Rom. 16:3-4a), and most likely of Andronicus and Junia whom Paul considered to be 'prominent among the apostles' (Rom. 16:7).

On the other hand, Paul also claims that 'women should be silent in the churches' (1 Cor. 14:34). When presenting the list of persons who had met Jesus after the resurrection, he excludes the women who went to the grave (1 Cor. 15:5-8). We do not know why Paul thus contributes to the downgrading of the role of women in the church. Was it because of reports from Corinth that seem to have presented female behaviour as indecent and disorderly? Or do we discern social and cultural challenges linked with the process of transition from house churches to a more public way of being church? When Paul tells women to be silent, he argues that this is what the Law says (1 Cor. 14:34). It gives the impression that Paul here exchanges freedom in Christ for the order established by the Law. We do not know if this is an impulsive reaction due to unfortunate episodes that in his view could harm the reputation of women, and consequently also of the church. It could also be interpreted as a demonstration of a more restrictive position championing behaviour according to what was considered established order.

This attitude gained strength as the church grew and spread even beyond the borders of the Roman Empire. The first generation of Christians was convinced that the end-time was imminent, which empowered them to adopt an alternative lifestyle and to relate to each other as sisters and brothers in Christ. Now the Christians recognized, however, that that would have to wait; it obliged them to establish teachings and structures that would keep the church faithful to its nature and mission, and to protect it against false teaching and accusations of immorality. It became more dependent on fixed structures of leadership, which soon were reserved exclusively for men. As we shall see in what follows, it had not always been like this.

Female Leadership in the New Testament

In the last chapter of the letter to the Romans, Paul introduces Phoebe, 'a deacon (διακονος) of the church at Cenchreae'. She is evidently about to travel to Rome, and the apostle urges the congregation there to welcome her 'in the Lord' and 'help her in whatever she may require from you' (Rom. 16:1).

The fact that Paul describes her as a deacon, in the masculine form of this title, and not deaconess, is worth noting.[9] It indicates that Phoebe had a leadership role in her congregation, similar to that of Apollos and Paul in Corinth, both referred to as deacons in 1 Corinthians 3:5. Cenchreae is the seaport of Corinth, and it is therefore likely that the title 'deacon' has the same

[9] The Revised Standard Version (RSV) translates 'deaconess', a term that came into use only in the fourth century. The New Revised Standard Version (NRSV) has corrected this reading to 'deacon'.

meaning in both places, thus indicating a ministry that both men and women could exercise. Paul adds that Phoebe 'has been a benefactor (προστατις) of many and of myself as well'. It is not immediately clear what 'benefactor' means; scholars claim that it corresponds to the Latin term *patronus*, a person that would use his authority to protect others. Paul has personally experienced Phoebe in that role, as *patrona*, most likely in the role of offering generous hospitality or protection when he was in some kind of difficulty, perhaps even in prison.[10]

Opinions may differ whether the Pauline congregations at this early stage had already established offices in the sense that would be the rule a few decades later. What seems to be unquestionable is that the *diak-* words were gaining a prominent role when conceptualizing leadership responsibility in the church. Paul describes himself as διακονος (Col. 1:23.25) and presents his ministry as διακονια (2 Cor. 4:1; Acts 20:24). In my view, the early church opted for the *diak-* terminology because it reminded them of the ministry of Jesus. Paul always emphasizes that his διακονια relates him to Christ who has authorized him to serve in his name. This corresponds to the saying in John 12:26: 'Whoever serves (διακονη) me must follow me, and where I am, there will my servant (διακονος) be also. Whoever serves (διακονη) me, the Father will honour.' Again, we see the close connection between discipleship as following the example of Jesus and serving as he served.

While the memory of Jesus inspired the leaders of the early church to use διακονια as a preferred term for leadership or ministry (or *ministerium* as the Latin Vulgate translates this term), other titles would soon be introduced that established a more hierarchical understanding of leadership that eventually would lead to the threefold order of bishops, priests and deacons. The New Testament gives two examples of the pairing of bishops and deacons, one in Philippians 1:1 where the author mentions them in his opening greeting; the other in 1 Timothy that lists qualifications for those who aspire for the office of bishops (3:1-7) and deacons (3:8-13). Here it is evident that only men can aspire for the office of bishop. It is less clear whether women could still be deacons; a key question here is the interpretation of γυναικας in verse 11. While translators in the past (for instance KJV) here read 'wives', modern (for instance, NRSV and NIV) prefer 'women', which clearly points in direction of female deacons, and not wives of deacons. The fact that the ministry of the deacon continues to be the theme also in the following two verses, seems to support the understanding that the author of 1 Timothy reflects a practice where men and women still could be deacons.[11]

---

[10] Schüssler Fiorenza, *In Memory of Her*, 47-48; Ben Witherington III, *Women in the Earliest Churches* (Cambridge: CUP, 1988), 113-14.

[11] John N. Collins, *Deacons and the Church: Making Connections between Old and New* (Leominster, UK: Gracewing, 2002), 99-100. Against James Monroe Barnett, *The*

On the other hand, the letter indicates that the author was not quite conformable with this practice. He clearly supports those who want to limit the freedom of women in the life of church. In 2:11 he tells women to 'learn in silence with full submission', and in the instruction regarding the female deacons, he admonishes them not to be 'slanderers (διαβολους)'. Marianne Bjelland Kartzow claims that it had become a conscious strategy to present women as addicted to gossip, with the purpose of downgrading their position in the church.[12] In her view, the Pastoral Epistles link gossip with false teaching, as an expression of deviance. Thus slandering is more than unethical behaviour and unreliable speech; it is submission to the 'devils of gossip', as some commentators translate διαβολους in 3:11.[13] διαβολος is included in the list of awful things that will happen in the last days (2 Tim. 3:3-9); to limit the freedom of women would therefore be a logical measure at a time when the faithful are admonished to turn away from 'profane chatter' and talk that 'will spread like gangrene' (2:16-17).

We thus observe a process that aimed at excluding women from leadership positions in the church, including the office of deacon. The hierarchical order of bishop-priest-deacon that was eventually established, with the deacon as the first and lowest step, had no space for women. Women certainly continued to play an important role in the life of the church; they were now organized in groups of widows and virgins. The group of widows especially attracted many women, according to 1 Timothy 5:3-16, so much so that the author proposes restrictions and warns against giving them too any opportunities in the life of the church. In order to be registered as a widow, 'she must be well attested for her good works, as one who has brought up children, shown hospitality, washed the saints' feet, helped the afflicted, and devoted herself to doing good in every way' (5:10). In today's language, we would describe the diaconal practice presented here as an arena where women have their natural outlet for service. This observation affirms the assumption that the marginalization of women leads to the marginalization of *diakonia*.

The Modern Diaconal Movement and its Feminization of Diakonia

Here is no room to present the development of female discipleship throughout the centuries that followed.[14] Women were among the devoted Christians who

---

Diaconate – A Full and Equal Order (Valley Forge, PA: Trinity Press International, 1995), 40: he concludes that they are 'probably wives of the deacons'.

[12] Marianne Bjelland Kartzow, *Gossip and Gender: Othering of Speech in the Pastoral Epistles* (Berlin: Walter de Gruyter, 2009).

[13] Jerome D. Quinn and William C. Wacker, *The First and Second Letters to Timothy: A New Translation with Notes and Commentary* (Grand Rapids, MI: Eerdmans, 2000), 276.

[14] Jeannine E. Olson, *One Ministry, Many Roles: Deacons and Deaconesses through the Centuries* (St Louis, MO: Concordia, 1992).

left the organized churches and moved to the desert for prayer and meditation – for instance, St Mary of Egypt who died c. 420, having lived as a hermit for forty-seven years. Others formed communities of celibate women; by the second part of the fourth century, some of these founded the first monasteries. The monasteries provided new openings for female spirituality, and also for female leadership and for diaconal services.

The emergence of the modern diaconal movement should be partly understood against this background. Theodor Fliedner, the Protestant pastor in Kaiserswerth, Germany, who in 1836 established what would soon develop into the first Deaconess Motherhouse, had the vision of renewing what he understood to be the diaconal ministry of the New Testament. He both referred to the example of Phoebe and the group of seven appointed to be responsible for the '*diakonia* of the table' (Acts 6:1-6), based on the view that they all had been involved in charity work, caring for the sick and poor. However, he was equally inspired by the work of the *Ladies of Charity* (French: *Dames de la Charité*), a religious order for women founded by Vincent de Paul in 1617.[15]

The Motherhouse in many ways replicates a Catholic religious order for women. The deaconesses formed a community of sisters, led by a Sister Superior. When admitted, they committed themselves to chastity, poverty and obedience, virtues well known from monastic life. In spite of being a community of women, the Motherhouse would have a male head leader, normally a pastor. In addition to the role of administrative director, he would also be the spiritual leader of the house, conduct worship services, supervise the spiritual training of the probationers, and sometimes serve as business manager and public relations director

The deaconesses received training as nurses and social workers; within a few decades hundreds of diaconal institutions were established, which allowed the deaconesses to pioneer the development of modern health in a remarkable way. There were also institutions that educated male deacons; their number remained relatively small compared with the Motherhouses, which contributed to the perception that *diakonia* was, in the first place, a service for women, with a focus on health and social care.

Without doubt, this movement opened a new space for women as professional workers, led to a tremendous upgrading of health work, and represented as such a valuable response to burning needs in contemporary society. It contributed, however, to the feminization of *diakonia* and also to its marginalization, due to the fact that most of this work was performed within the framework of diaconal institutions, at some distance from local congregations and ordinary church structures.

---

[15] Ruthild Brakemeier, *Die Mutterhausdiakonie und ihr Weg in die Zukunft* (Kassel, Germany: Kaiserswerther Verband, 2002).

Conclusion

The gospels affirm that Jesus called both women and men to follow him and to serve. As we have seen, for some of the women, meeting with Jesus became a radical experience of healing, inclusion and empowerment. In a special way, their discipleship gives testimony to the newness of life that Jesus announced as 'good news' (Luke 4:18). Their service (διακονια) should therefore be considered not only a consequence of being a follower, but as an act of obedience. Much more, their service expresses the very nature of the gospel, of belonging to the new community of disciples who in Jesus Christ was liberated and empowered to participate in God's mission for the healing of the world.

From this perspective, *diakonia* is rightly considered an integral dimension of the gospel, as stated by the Church of Norway Plan for *diakonia*:

> Diakonia is the caring ministry of the Church. It is the Gospel in action and is expressed through loving your neighbour, creating inclusive communities, caring for creation and struggling for justice.[16]

This way of understanding *diakonia* as a dimension of the Gospel lays the ground for the view that both women and men are equally called to discipleship. As we have seen, the early church already had difficulty in living up to this standard; it introduced interpretations that downgraded the role of women in the narratives from the time of Jesus, and created structures that excluded women from full participation in the life and the mission of the church. In our view, this had as its consequence, not only an unfortunate marginalization of women, but also a marginalization of *diakonia*.

To overcome this situation, we are challenged to re-read the biblical texts in a gender perspective. In addition, the task of engendering diaconal practice is imminent, allowing both men and women to find equal roles of participation in the diaconal ministry of the church. Such a development requires a change in the way of conceptualizing *diakonia*. In the past, *diakonia* has often been underpinned by a servant-language, as 'self-denial, self-abnegation and self-sacrifice', as Elizabeth Schüssler Fiorenza rightly describes 'service-ecclesiology' generated by patriarchal-hierarchical church structures.[17] It will be different when *diakonia* is understood as discipleship of equals, in the spirit of freedom and mutual sharing.

Bibliography

Barnett, James Monroe, *The Diaconate – A Full and Equal Order*. Valley Forge, PA: Trinity Press International, 1995.

---

[16] https://kirken.no/globalassets/kirken.no/om-kirken/slik-styres-kirken/planer-visjonsdokument-og-strategier/plan_diakoni_2010_english.pdf

[17] Elizabeth Schüssler Fiorenza, 'Waiting at table': A Critical Feminist Theological Reflection on Diakonia (*Concilium* 198, 4:1988), 84-94.

Bjelland Kartzow, Marianne, *Gossip and Gender. Othering of Speech in the Pastoral Epistles*. Berlin: Walter de Gruyter, 2009.

Brakemeier, Ruthild, *Die Mutterhausdiakonie und ihr Weg in die Zukunft*. Kassel, Germany: Kaiserswerther Verband, 2002.

Collins, John N., *Deacons and the Church. Making Connections between Old and New*. Leominster, UK: Gracewing, 2002.

Karlsen Seim, Turid, *The Double Message: Patterns of Gender in Luke & Acts*. Nashville, TN: Abingdon Press, 1994.

Kinukawa, Hisako, *Women and Jesus in Mark: A Japanese Feminist Perspective*. Maryknoll, NY: Orbis Books, 1994.

Olson, Jeannine E., *One Ministry, Many Roles: Deacons and Deaconesses through the Centuries*. St Louis MO: Concordia, 1992.

Schüssler Fiorenza, Elisabeth, *In Memory of Her: A Feminist Theological Reconstruction of Christian Origins*. London: SCM Press, 1983, 2nd edition 1994.

Schüssler Fiorenza, Elisabeth, *Bread Not Stone: The Challenge of Feminist Biblical Interpretation*. Boston, MA: Beacon Press, 1984.

Schüssler Fiorenza, Elisabeth, 'Waiting at table': A Critical Feminist Theological Reflection on Diakonia. *Concilium* 198, 4:1988, 84-94.

Quinn Jerome D. and William C. Wacker, *The First and Second Letters to Timothy: A New Translation with Notes and Commentary*. Grand Rapids, MI: Eerdmans, 2000.

Witherington III, Ben, *Women in the Earliest Churches*. Cambridge: CUP, 1988.

Women's Empowerment and Gender Equality: Pastoral-Theological Reflections from Africa

Elieshi Mungure

Introduction

The changes globally from Women in Development (WID) to Gender and Development (GAD) are a clear indication that God's human creation needs each other for a sustainable world where peace, justice and equality will reign. Although women in a development perspective enhanced an understanding of women's development needs,[1] some feminist and development theorists have remained unconvinced by the WID approach, arguing that it does not address the fundamental factors that structure and maintain gender inequalities.[2]

Theologians in Africa, through 'The Circle of Concerned African Women Theologians', have since its inception realized that it is the patriarchal culture in Africa which bends women not to participate fully in the mission of the church. The 'Circle' therefore wants to destroy the instruments of their oppression embedded in the many-layered forms of patriarchy, which requires taking a radical and critical attitude towards culture and traditions.[3]

The adoption of the Beijing Declaration and Platform for Action at the Fourth World Conference on Women in 1995 laid the foundation for action towards gender equality in all aspects of economic, social, cultural and political life globally. As women's empowerment and gender equality emerge as a goal of sustainable development agenda,[4] the world needs to work on the implementation and actualization of these goals through many and diverse ways. This is referred to by the UN Secretary General Ban-Kimoon in a speech

---

[1] C. Overholt et al, *Gender Roles in Development* (West Hartford, CT: Kumarian Press, 1984), 67.

[2] J.L. Parpart et al, *Theoretical Perspectives on Gender and Development* (Ottawa: International Development Research Center, 2000), 53.

[3] Mercy Oduyoye, 'The Story of a Circle', in Konrad Kaiser, Thomas E Best (eds), *On Being Church: Women's Voices and Visions*, in *The Ecumenical Review*, Vol. 53 (1st January 2001), 97-100.

[4] ILO COOP Publications on 'Women's Empowerment and Gender Equality in Co-operatives', 2015.

at the launching of a high-level panel on Women's Economic Empowerment' affirming that '… empowerment of the world's women is a global imperative'.[5]

This article is a contribution to an ongoing discussion on women's empowerment and gender relationships. I will focus on socio-cultural, theological and pastoral factors that impact women's empowerment and gender equality in African church and societies. The paper will also highlight challenges and initiatives taken by both governments and the church in Africa in empowering women and on gender relationships in the continent. Furthermore, the paper argues that, unless women's empowerment and gender equality are given priority in the church and society, it will be difficult to close the gap of relationships that exist in many societies in Africa. While some general examples might be taken from various countries in Africa, specific examples in regard to this topic are taken from Tanzania, my native country.

Key Terms in this Paper: *Empowerment* and *Gender Equality*

Empowerment

According to the Concise English Dictionary, 'Empowerment means give strength and confidence to'.[6] A further explanation adds that '… empowerment stands for processes that endow the individual with resources, material as well as symbolic, and strengthen internal sources of power on various levels'.[7] Empowerment as a process allows individuals to have control over resources, both intellectual, physical and financial, which help one to transform one's life from one stage to the next. It is through empowerment processes that better gender relationships are achieved, individuals are affirmed and have equal rights to life, while development and independence leads to life transformation. Therefore, women's empowerment is key in the holistic mission of any church. It is through empowerment that policies, strategies and processes for achieving an inclusive society are built and implemented.

According to McKim, gender (from Lat. *genus 'kind', 'sort'*) refers to attributes and behaviours shaped by culture to describe either males or females.[8] Togaresai and Chitando added that gender refers to culturally constructed differentiation between men and women in terms of expected social roles.[9] Being socially constructed by society, gender can then be

---

[5] www.unwomen.org/en/news/stories/2016/1 (accessed 21st January 2016).

[6] Soanes and others (eds), *Concise Oxford English Dictionary*. 11th edition (Oxford: OUP, 2004), 468.

[7] Josefina Hurtado Neira (ed), 'Women's Empowerment' in *Mission 21*, in Protestant Mission Basel, Women's letter (November 2014), 9-10.

[8] K. Donald MacKim, *Westminster Dictionary of Theological Terms* (Louisville, KY and London: Westminster, John Knox Press, 1996), 112.

[9] Togarasei, Lovemore and Ezra Chitando, 'Teaching religion and gender in contexts of HIV/AIDS in Africa', in Ezra Chitando (ed), *Mainstreaming HIV and AIDS in*

deconstructed for better relationships since it is neither divinely nor naturally acquired.

Women in the Eyes of God and in African Culture

Human beings are created in the image of God and reflect this image by being co-creators with God (Gen. 1:28). The fact that they were all blessed, asked to multiply and take the role of stewardship is clear evidence that God values both females and males, and intends to let them share power with peace, justice, love and joy as they journey towards full salvation in Jesus Christ. In explaining the intention of a just society to both genders, the Lutheran World Federation (LWF) *Gender Justice Policy* says:

> Gender justice implies the protection and promotion of the dignity of women and men who, being created in the image of God, are co-responsible stewards of creation. Gender justice is expressed through equality and balanced power relationships between women and men, and the elimination of the institutional, cultural and interpersonal systems of privileges and oppression that sustain discrimination.[10]

Culture has created a gap by the humanly constructed patriarchy tradition in Africa. In some African societies, there are several factors that contribute to gender inequality due to patriarchal traditions which call for empowerment and transformation. Some research indicates that patriarchy is the leading factor contributing to this disparity: patriarchy enforced education and economic rights in favouring men. In African communities, among the Bahaya of north-western Tanzania, or the Chagga and Meru of Northern Tanzania, for example, land culturally belongs to men. Even when a woman inherits land from her parents, she is not allowed to sell or give it to another person; instead she is required to return it to the clan or brothers when she gets married or wants to give it away. For women not having the power of inheritance or owning land – which is the main asset that people own – this leaves them with low economic power, forcing them to become dependent on men who do own land and other major assets in the family.

Women and Leadership Roles in the Church

The same patriarchal tradition prevents the church from having full *koinonia* among its members. Although women account for large numbers in church pews, their role in decision-making bodies is still small.

Theological Education: Experiences and Explorations (Geneva: WCC Publications, 2008), 211-23.

[10] LWF Gender Justice Policy, 2013.

Sr Bernadette Mbuy-Beya from the Democratic Republic of Congo observed that, generally speaking, the church does not perceive women differently than the way society does at large.[11] Comparing what is happening in society and in the church regarding the status of women, Mbuy-Beya finds that, in society, women are victims of physical, psychological and moral violence, while in the church there are different possibilities for women's participation in different roles and therefore some hope of full participation in God's mission.

However, she warned that discrimination, which is still evident in the church – for instance, in men refusing to accept women's leadership roles or denying the ordination of women – should be denounced as sin and therefore something to be repented of, and that women should use all opportunities available to them in collaboration with men today.[12]

Philip Jenkins[13] and Philomena Mwaura[14] who researched the response to gender equality in African Independent and neo-Pentecostal/Charismatic churches, are of a different view. Jenkins is convinced that the newer churches have arisen in the societies with conservative notions of gender roles and naturally gravitate to Bible passages that support these ideas. For him, even the efforts made by women theologians to give women a voice and to share roles in the church is not successful since the methodology and approach used are far beyond grassroot levels. He suggested using a simple explanatory methodology like that of the Samaritan woman which suggests Jesus' willingness to violate traditional rules about gender, and, like Ruth, to generate discussion about solidarity across tribal lines and ethnicity.[15]

However, Mwaura sees that both men and women are pioneering the spread of the gospel in the continent. In the African Initiated Churches (AIC) and neo-Pentecostalist churches, women receive social, spiritual, psychological and material benefits, and feel affirmed and their dignity upheld. She continues that, in AIC, women are given a chance to recover their status and the position that had been undermined by the teachings of the mission churches. They hold leadership positions in ministry and decision-making bodies because church hierarchies are rarely determined by formal education but rather by spiritual gifts and seniority.[16]

---

[11] Bernadette Mbuy-Beya, 'Women in the Churches in Africa: Possibilities for Presence and Promises', in *The African Synod: Documents, Reflections and Perspectives* (Maryknoll, NY: Orbis Books, 1996), 177.

[12] Mbuy-Beya, 'Women in the Churches in Africa, 186.

[13] Philip Jenkins, *The New Faces of Christianity: Believing the Bible in the Global South* (Oxford: OUP, 1996), 159-60.

[14] Philomena Mwaura, 'Gender and Power in African Christianity: African Instituted Churches and Pentecostals', in Ogbu Kalu (ed), *African Christianity, an African Story* (Trenton, NJ: Africa World Press, 2007), 366.

[15] Philip Jenkins, *The New Faces of Christianity*, 177.

[16] Philomena Mwaura, 'Gender and Power in African Christianity', 366.

Observations by the above scholars are still more or less the same in churches in Africa.[17] It is also important to say that, due to empowerment programmes that are carried out, changes are taking place in the church today. A significant improvement in having women as equals in the ministry and leadership of the Evangelical Lutheran Church in Tanzania (ELCT) can be seen in the way women have been enrolled in theological institutions for training in leadership. From 1968 to 1979, ELCT had less than ten women theologians. In 1990, ELCT decided to ordain women to the pastoral ministry and became among the first Lutheran churches in the continent to do so.

Almost 90% of these ordained women have different leadership positions in the church, mostly at parish level. In the leadership of the higher learning institutions, there are three women theologians who are instructors, a dean, and one at the level of a vice-chancellor of the university.

According to recent statistics, ELCT has a membership of about 6.5 million and more than 50% are women. However, this percentage is not reflected in the high-level decision-making bodies and other levels of governance in the church. For example, in the Executive Council of ELCT, the highest decision-making body after the general assembly, there are only five women among its 52 members. In similar leadership bodies at national level or in the dioceses, the percentage is only 20% of the members.[18] Some initiatives are being taken to change the situation, but results are still minimal. This has been a persistent challenge since these bodies are largely made up of clergy who are mostly men. And due to the patriarchal mindset, even where a position does not necessarily require a man, people will still nominate a man instead of a woman who is often more capable than the man.

In the course of a ten-year period after the establishment of Tumaini University (now known as Tumaini Makumira University), 1997-2007, out of 333 students that graduated from the faculty of theology with diploma, bachelor of divinity or a Master of Theology, only 34 were women.[19]

ELCT passed a resolution to ordain women for the ministry of word and sacrament in 1990, and by 2012 there were 153 ordained women in the 18 (currently 24) dioceses of ELCT while the whole of ELCT has about 3,000 pastors. When the 2015 women theologians and pastors' conference of ELCT met in Bukoba in the North Western Diocese in May 2015, it was realized that many of the ordained women were still given 'nurturing' and ceremonial

[17] Faith Lugazia and Juvenal Rwamunyana did research on 'The Effects of Culture on Gender Roles in the Protestant Church: A Case Study of Churches in the Huye District of the Southern Province in Rwanda' in 2013. They found that gender equality in the church in Rwanda remains a challenge. For many, the culture is holy and unquestioned. The positive development identified by the study came basically from the government of Rwanda and some of the churches that had initiated profound policies on gender equality.

[18] www.elct.org/social.html (accessed November 2015).

[19] Tumaini Makumira University records (accessed 2015).

leadership positions like leading women's and children's departments, hostels, girls' vocational school, retreat and recreation centres of the church, while some, although in the parish, were working under the supervision of male pastors. For a church like ELCT, with a long history in the LWF, one should expect 50-50 participation at all levels, and that the issue of gender roles should no longer be under discussion but a core value for a church, shedding light on the rest of the community, including secular society. More education in cultural transformation and change in society and empowerment programmes are still urgently needed for the full participation of men and women in God's *oikos*.

Education as a Tool for Women's Empowerment and Equality in Africa

Education is one of the most crucial tools for empowerment, liberation and self-determination of individuals and communities. A good, quality education aims at transforming people's lives, both formally and informally. In most countries in Africa, including Tanzania, formal education came with Christianity and colonialism. One of the diaconal arms of Christianity was education while others were health care and the proclamation of the gospel. It began with simple arithmetic, reading and writing, and later grew to include more formal schooling with grade systems.

However, the type of formal education which was first introduced to Africa was mostly of a low quality, mainly to enable Africans do simple jobs for their colonial masters. According to Tripp, the colonial system that ruled Tanzania until 1960 'was class-biased as well as mean and racialist'.[20] The colonial educational system also reinforced gender-related discrimination due to reliance on male-only institutions of education that had developed throughout Europe. In university education of earlier days, a western ethos, standards, values, research and thinking were ingrained in both students and staff.[21]

Low formal education of women is another effect of patriarchal culture because women were thought of as reproduction agents and giving them education was wasteful. Even when formal education was introduced for women, it was restricted to domestic management so that women could be good mothers and wives. And of course men's education was preparing them for assumed leadership responsibilities, regardless of their capabilities or talents. However, there was some progress in regard to gender equality in Tanzania due to multiple initiatives by both NGOs and the government.

Since independence, the education system in Tanzania has grown from only one institution of higher education (a university college) in 1961 to more than

[20] A.M. Tripp, *Changing the Rules: The Politics of Liberalization and the Urban Informal Economy in Tanzania* (Berkeley, CA: University of California Press, 1997), 87.

[21] I.M. Omari, *Psychology and Education in Changing Societies: New perspectives from Tanzania* (Dar es Salaam: Dar es Salaam University Press, 1982), 185.

200 tertiary training institutions by 2006.[22] The policy of universal education for all, regardless of gender (for example, in 1976 and subsequent educational policies) has also contributed to more girls attending school and institutions of higher learning.

More positively still, in recent years, the possibility of the government offering grants or loans for students at higher learning institutions or university, has enabled more students even from low-income families to further their education and career paths. Recently there have been more girls remaining in education and attending institutions of higher learning.

When social policies are patriarchally-dominated and coupled with religious hindrances and a lack of education, some teenage girls may get pregnant at a very early age – a result of not continuing with school, while others, due to harmful traditions and culture, become victims of early forced marriages. UNICEF research indicates that 49% of rural women and 23% of urban women are married before the age of 18. The 1971 Marriage Act which is used in Tanzania allows a girl to be married at the age of 14 but her male counterpart at 18. Lugazia sees the above situation as an act of oppression for women since someone at that age cannot be a full participant in the marriage union but rather obeying what her counterpart says.[23] Thus communities still need to have their voices heard through different strategic ways of advocacy in order to empower girls to acquire education equally with boys without interruption, and to use education as a tool for transformation.

Economic Empowerment for Women in Africa

About 75% of Africa's population live in rural areas and are dependent on agriculture for their survival. Women play an active role in farming and food processing, and often have the primary responsibility for household nutrition.

Education in entrepreneurship through small-scale loans and credit (commonly known as SACCOS) has changed the mindset of women in Tanzania. Apparently, today in Tanzania women are increasingly becoming income-earners in their household and having a say in decision-making on matters that they previously would not have had. However, there are still some challenges.

Although women peasants bear more than half the responsibility for agricultural labour, their agricultural productivity and their access to markets are generally very low. Social prohibitions on women's movement, low formal education, exclusion from land ownership and social biases – among other forms of discrimination – add challenges to women's economic

---

[22] http://siteresources.worldbank.org/INTWBISFP/Resources/0_Prof_Msolla.pdf (accessed 8th February 2016).

[23] Faith K. Lugazia, *'Naweza' Masomo ya Biblia kwa wanawake Wakristo Tanzania* (Bukoba, Tanzania: North-Western Publishing Company, 2015), 62.

empowerment.[24] When it comes to the cash economy, they end up as smallholders and small entrepreneurs. Therefore, gender concerns must be considered when validating the work done, their contribution to the national GNP, and in policy decisions.

Furthermore, while economic power at the household level gives women room to participate in decision-making, this has not been the case at community or national levels. This might be caused by the fact that there are more fundamental reasons why women are found at the periphery on larger schemes of economic resources. These may include women not owning permanent property such as land or houses in most communities, but also, as mentioned above, low education and patriarchy which set them 'behind the curtain', and affect their determination to attempt substantial business for fear of failure or because they simply do not trust themselves to succeed. The impact of patriarchy is felt in most aspects of people's lives, even in liberating initiatives like business.

Church Initiatives in Meeting Gender Disparity

For its part, the LWF has played a significant role in promoting women's empowerment and gender equality, particularly in member churches in Africa. These include the historical resolution of the LWF Seventh Assembly in Budapest, Hungary, in 1984 to ensure 40% men, 40% women and 20% youth participation in all LWF leadership and events. This was followed by the reaffirmation of the Budapest resolution at the Eleventh Assembly in 2010 with the 'LWF principles of inclusivity' regarding gender balance for all LWF leadership and participation and Executive Staff at the Communion office; and finally, by the endorsement and affirmation of the LWF 'Gender Justice Policy' in 2013. Member churches are taking it up for implementation.

These initiatives have served as strategies to commit the churches to gender equality, challenge patriarchy and ensure that the gifts of both men and women are acknowledged and valued.

Women's Empowerment and Gender Roles in Africa: Pastoral Perspectives

As seen above, women's roles in church and society in Africa have been much influenced by their historical or traditionally prescribed gender roles. In most cases these roles have been related to either domestic care and service or production and reproduction. Strategic advocacy and policies need to be put in place in order to influence change, beginning from the grassroots.

---

[24] Ruth Besha, 'Communion and Economic Power', in Musimbi Kanyoro (ed), *In Search of a Round Table: Gender, Theology and Church Leadership* (Geneva: WCC Publications, 1997), 96-98.

From a pastoral perspective, it means discerning and critically reviewing the leadership of women in the church, whether it is gender-inclusive and what its specific roles are. Leadership in the church needs to listen to the discernment of the Spirit of God who is the helper, guide and giver of wisdom. Some forms of language and ideology – such as what one leader told me: 'Women in African churches should be content as they are studying theology and being ordained' – needs a liberation of its own so that gender justice will prevail in the church.

The Way Forward

In order to bring change, the church and especially theological institutions need to establish a process to mainstream gender in the curricula. This will empower theologians and pastors to emerge from their training well equipped with the needed skills and expertise on gender and women's issues. Chammah Kaunda (referring to Phiri) has identified four crucial challenges for theological education in Africa which are 'to re-define the identity of African women theologians, empower women to study theology and teach in theological institutions, engender the theological education curriculum in Africa, and to collaborate with Africa male theologians'.[25]

Furthermore, transformative changes in practical theology must positively reflect the following areas:

The contextualization of theological and hermeneutical reflection

It is important to consider the numerous ways in which human beings encounter God and are able to share God's story through their own interpretation and life experience as they read and exegete the scriptures. The incorporation of life experience into biblical criticism methods, for example, and adding social scientific interpretations to unmask patriarchal and exploitative paradigms will allow for a true contextual understanding. In the process, then, it is important to invite, listen to and experience how people in different groups read, interpret and reinterpret scriptures. Churches and theological institutions particularly should use human resources as a resource available and reliable to create a new ways of interpreting scripture. In Africa so far, we have liberation interpretation, African interpretation, feminist and other such interpretation which, well used, will help even marginalized groups to be heard and enrich both God's story in the community of believers and our own theological practices.

---

[25] Chammah Kaunda, 'Towards an African Theological Education for Gender Justice and Peace: An African Theological Reflection on the Concept of Justice Peace', in Isabel Phiri (ed), *Journal of Gender and Religion in Africa* (KwaZulu-Natal: South Africa, Vol. 18, No.1, 2012).

Working on the ecclesiological question

As churches struggle to be transformed towards gender equality and pastoral ministry, the question about their own self-understanding as *koinonia* must be raised: what does it mean to be a church and who belongs to this community which is the body of Christ? The church is not only an institution with sacred scriptures, a hierarchy, sacramental structures, canon law, liturgical norms, orthodoxy and moral imperatives, though all this is important, but is also an expression of the love of God that is open to the vulnerabilities of inclusiveness. Such a church should bear in mind that her mission is to share responsibility with all her members as equal participants in *missio Dei*. It carries a pastoral dimension of being church. As Everist and Nessan affirm, 'We need distinct offices and roles within the church, but together as the priesthood of all believers we are transformed into being the church in the world…'[26] Here the church is called to action through its prophetic voice, advocating for the marginalized while empowering through diaconal actions to take up the various roles for themselves.

Transforming oppressive cultures through justice

Culture explains a people's way of life, it tells about the identity and things that people keep sacred, hence is mostly passed on from generation to generation. In Africa, like other societies in the world, there are beliefs and taboos that are held as part of people's identity and help in guarding the social norms. Most African culture embraces the patriarchal system where gender disparity is very clear. In such societies, the discussion of women's empowerment for equality is very limited. Unfortunately, churches may feel very comfortable under patriarchy and not challenge or transform it. The process towards transformation should be governed by justice either in the church or in society. This will check imbalances in gender and power relations. The prophet Micah says, 'He has told you, O mortal, what is good; and what does the Lord require of you but to do justice, and love kindness, and to walk humbly with your God (6:8)?' God wants people to remember the saving acts through which God has shown fidelity to the covenant. Hence people should offer themselves through a life of justice so that no-one is victimized but rather all relate in justice.

Transforming the Christian family

By its nature, a Christian family is a place where the people of God are cared for, nurtured and meet for worship. These are the basic characteristics of being church at home. It is important for the family to take its core responsibility of empowering its members through teaching from the word of God about equal relations. Themes like transformative masculinity and gender justice could be introduced, accompanied by the right raising of children of both sexes as

---

[26] Norma C. Everist and Nessan Craig , *Transforming Leadership: New Vision for a Church Mission* (Minneapolis, MN: Fortress Press, 2008), 200.

equals. Also, dialogue on harmful practices and the effect of patriarchy could be addressed here. This is where transformation through educational empowerment begins, and however informal that might be, it sets the agenda for future direction.

Conclusion

This paper has discussed the need for empowering women in church and society in order to end gender parity for the equality and health of African societies. Patriarchy is seen as a hindrance to gender parity even though Christ is beyond culture; the power of culture still dominates in many churches and in African society. Efforts made by both governments and churches are still blocked by a patriarchal culture. The paper has, however, indicated some developments achieved in education and economy for liberation and transformation by giving a few examples from both ELCT and the government of Tanzania. It ended by encouraging communities to be creative in strategizing and mainstreaming policies with clear processes which thirst after gender equality.

A pastoral approach to gender equality should focus on sharing opportunities, rights and responsibilities in all structures of the church and community.

As there is a will and desire for transformation, let policymakers in collaboration with government and church leadership take up their responsibilities. And the motto should be: 'Together we can make a difference!'

Bibliography

Everist, N.C. and Nessan L. Craig, Transforming Leadership: New Vision for a Church in Mission. Minneapolis, MN: Fortress Press, 2008.

Jenkins, Philip, The New Faces of Christianity. Believing the Bible in the Global South. Oxford: OUP, 1996.

Kaunda, Chammah, 'Towards an African Theological Education for Gender Justice and Peace: An African Theological Reflection on the Concept of Justice Peace', in Isabel Phiri (ed), *Journal of Gender and Religion in Africa.* KwaZulu-Natal: South Africa, Vol. 18, No.1, 2012.

Kanyoro, Musimbi (ed), *In Search of a Round Table: Gender, Theology and Church Leadership.* Geneva: WCC Publications, 1997.

Lugazia, Faith K., *'Naweza' Masomo ya Biblia kwa Wanawake Wakristo Tanzania.* Bukoba, Tanzania: North-Western Publishing Company, 2015.

Lugazia, Faith, and Juvenal Rwamunyana, 'The Effects of Culture on Gender Roles in the Protestant Church: A Case Study of Churches in the Huye District of the Southern Province in Rwanda', in *Family, Gender and Community Development.* Huye: PIASS Publication, Series No. 5 (2013), 53-81.

Lutheran World Federation, *Gender Justice Policy,* Geneva: LWF, 2013.

McKim, K. Donald, *Westminster Dictionary of Theological Terms.* Louisville, KY and

London: Westminster, John Knox Press, 1996.

Maluleke, Tinyiko Sam and Sarojini Nadar (eds), 'Breaking the Covenant of Violence Against Women', in *Journal of Theology for Southern Africa.*(2002), 5-15.

Mbey-Beya, Bernadette, 'Women in the Churches in Africa Possibilities for Presence and Promises', in African Faith and Network (eds), *The African Synod: Documents, Reflections, Perspectives.* Maryknoll, NY: Orbis Books, 1996.

Mwaura, P. Njeri, 'Gender and Power in African Christianity: African Instituted Churches and Pentecostal Churches', in U. Ogbu Kalu (ed), *African Christianity, an African Story.* Trenton, NJ: African World Press, 2007.

Nasimiyu`-Wasike, Anne, 'Christology and an African Women's Experience', in Robert Schreiter (ed), *Faces of Jesus in Africa.* Maryknoll, NY: Orbis Books, 2005.

Oduyoye, Mercy-Amba and Musimbi Kanyoro (eds), *The Will to Arise: Women, Tradition and the Church in Africa.* Maryknoll, NY: Orbis Books, 1992.

Omari, I.M., *Psychology and Education in Changing Societies: New Perspectives from Tanzania*. Dar es Salaam: Dar es Salaam University Press, 1982.

Overholt, C. et al, *Gender Roles in Development.* West Hartford, CT: Kumarian Press, 1984.

Parpart, J.L. et al, *Theoretical Perspectives on Gender and Development.* Ottawa: International Development Research Centre, 2000.

Phiri, Isabel (ed), *Journal of Gender and Religion in Africa* (KwaZulu-Natal: South Africa), Vol. 18, No. 1, July 2012.

Raiser, Konrad (ed), 'On Being Church: Women Voices and Visions', in *The Ecumenical Review*, Vol. 53, No. 1, January 2001.

Togarasei, Lovemore, and Ezra Chitando, 'Teaching religion and gender in contexts of HIV/AIDS in Africa', in Ezra Chitando (ed), Main Streaming HIV/AIDS in Theological Education: Experiences and Explorations. Geneva: WCC Publications, 2008, 211-23.

Tripp, A.M., *Changing the Rules: The Politics of Liberalization and the Urban Informal Economy in Tanzania*. Berkeley, CA: University of California Press, 1997.

Websites

http://siteresources.worldbank.org/INTWBISFP/Resources/0_Prof_Msolla.pdf
www.tanzania.go.tz.gender.html
www.unwomen.org/en/news/stories/2016/1
www.elct.org/social.html

Part 2

Learning from the Praxis of Engendered Diakonia

Diapraxis in Response to Female Genital Mutilation

Kristian Larsen

> I was circumcised when I was ten years old, and it was so painful and horrible! I was just so scared. I became sick afterwards and had to lie in bed for over a month. I got a fever and infection, but the worst thing was the pain. It felt like my entire insides were on fire. And when I needed to urinate – it was like being stabbed with knives! I couldn't even sit up for a long time afterwards. When I turned 14, I was forced to marry a man who was 21. I had seen him in our village a few times but I had never actually met him or talked with him. I got pregnant when I was 16, but when it was time to give birth – well, I just couldn't make it happen. I don't remember much of what happened, but I know I lay there for three days and that they ended up having to take me to hospital. By then the baby was dead and I was completely torn to pieces down there. They said it was because I had been circumcised. Things didn't get better after that. I had no control over my bladder and I couldn't be near others. I smelled so bad… I was so ashamed, it was all so embarrassing. I was so scared about what others would think and what they would say about me. My husband beat me because of it. Even when he lay with me, my urine would just run out of me, I was so scared. I wasn't well and I became afraid of everything and everyone. But then I heard about this anti-FGM project that had come here, that they wanted to talk with girls who had the same problems as me. After a while I mustered up the strength to come here to find out more.[1]

Introduction

Amina shared her story with me while I was in Ethiopia studying how the Mekane Yesus Church (EECMY) worked to stop female genital mutilation (FGM), a harmful traditional practice used by both Muslims and Christians. In this article I will focus on one specific project[2] and on the diaconal method that had been developed through its work, which was formed as a means of eradicating the practice of FGM. I will then describe the method as diapraxis

---

[1] Kjell Kristian Larsen, *Diapraksis som diakonal metode i endring av skadelig tradisjonell praksis. Masteroppgave i diakoni* (Oslo: Diakonhjemmet Høgskole, 2012).
[2] Project 10568. EECMY/NLM-Sinana Dinsho FGM Elimination Project. The projected was supported by the Norwegian Lutheran Mission (NLM) through Digni/NORAD.

and then evaluate the strengths and weaknesses of this diapraxis from a gender perspective.

Presentation of the FGM Project

The results of the project's work with FGM were very good. Yearly reports, evaluations and interviews all confirmed that the practice of FGM was almost completely eradicated in the project area, and that a pervasive change had truly occurred. The method that was used to cause such results also proved to have a ripple effect on other areas of society. I was a personal observer to these events over a longer period of time in connection with visiting the project and later with data gathering. I was able to observe at a few larger outdoor gatherings related to the project how women and men, Muslims and Christians and religious leaders from both the Orthodox Church and Muslim mosques interacted as a group. Women spoke in public at these gatherings, openly sharing their personal experiences and viewpoints on the subject. Before the project started, it would have been unthinkable for women to share in an assembly where men – even religious leaders – were present. Yet the religious leaders expressed their satisfaction with what had occurred. They appreciated how they had been given a 'new language' to speak about a subject considered taboo – something they themselves openly admitted would have been completely impossible to do just a short time before. Many of those who spoke pointed to the importance of receiving assistance on how to correctly interpret their traditions in the light of their holy scriptures, and how they could work in fellowship to address the greater issues of FGM practice and other traditions as well.

The project's overarching goal was to assist in the abolition of FGM within the project's target area. The project is based on the values inherent in the International Declaration of Human Rights and those built into Ethiopian legislation, both of which forbid the practice of FGM. Equally important to the project is the value of human life as expressed in the Christian faith and the biblical view of creation.

The project's primary method used in reaching its goals was described as a 'Community Conversation' (CC).[3] In its original form, the method was based on six stages that prepared a community to engage in dialogue on a particular issue:

1. Relationship building: The religious leaders were considered key persons for bringing change and were thus invited to be involved in the planning of the project even as early as the first project cycle. The practice and method of the project developed over time without necessarily following a prescribed format

[3] Community Conversation was initiated in Ethiopia in 2002 by the National HIV/AIDS Prevention and Control Office (NHAPCO).The original set-up encompassed eighteen discussion sessions of 50-70 people.

or plan, but adjustments were made in the light of new insights and experiences that arose through interaction with the target group. It should be stressed here that religious leaders were seen as respected and important figures of the community; their spiritual and general advice was very important to members of the community. It was desired that an exchange of experiences as well as invitations to visits and further debate would arise from the discussions between the various religious leaders.

2. Identifying the problem: Within the project target area, FGM was not tied to religion as such but was more closely tied to ethnic affiliation. However, FGM is still perceived as a consequence of religious requirements and regulations. The project document points to the fact that religious leaders play a key role in convincing the population that FGM has no real connection to either the Bible or the Qur'an; this should make possible both the condemnation and the eradication of the practice of FGM.[4]

3. Dialogue on identified problems and/or concerns: The men in the target area were greatly touched when the women began to share their personal stories about the problems they encountered as a consequence of having been circumcised. In addition, the women's stories, information and instruction based on health and psychological perspectives, were discussed within the framework of theological interpretations. The result of this approach was a mutual agreement among the religious leaders that female circumcision could not be endorsed by their religions. Muslims and Christians alike were able to affirm that FGM was a violation of God's creation and of how God had created women.

4. Decision-making processes and building a commitment to action: An interesting aspect of the project was the care given to those who previously had practised the surgical execution of FGM. These individuals were incorporated into the project as resource persons and, as a reward for their decision to discontinue the practice, they were offered a new means of earning income. The project was careful not to refer to these persons as 'problems'; instead, work was done to ensure that they felt included and given a sense of value within certain frameworks and conditions. The target group was given responsibility for choosing the individuals who would form the project committee, persons who became important players in the planning, implementation and evaluation of the project's plans and goals.

5. *Implementation:* When one reads the initial annual reports,[5] there is a clear expression of surprise that the community's response was so positive, and

---

[4] EECMY 1. Project Document 2006-2008. EECMY Wabe Batu Synod, FGM elimination project (Archive Digni, 2006).

[5] EECMY 3. Annual Plan 2006. EECMY Wabe Batu Synod, Sinana Dinsho FGM elimination project 10568 (Archive Digni, 2006). EECMY 4. Annual Plan 2007. EECMY Wabe Batu Synod, Sinana Dinsho FGM elimination project 10568 (Archive Digni, 2007).

that the goals set for each year were reached without great challenges. According to project reports and evaluations, the practice of FGM had been abolished within the target area, and many of the project's measures went further and reached more people than what had been anticipated. Already during the first year of the project a large portion of the community had expressed interest in participating in the project as a means of abolishing the practice of FGM. The legal system was also influenced by the project during its early years, with the community backing measures to create laws punishing those who performed FGM. Close co-operation developed between the police, the legal system and the region's public office for women's affairs.

6. *Reflection and evaluation:* The project's evaluation reports indicate that the involvement of religious leaders, locally-based organizations, women's groups, FGM practitioners and others directly or indirectly involved with the issue of FGM, together with sufficient implementation and follow-up, were important success factors for the project. The project succeeded in gathering these diverse groups into a concerted effort to combat FGM in their region. 'Unity in diversity' appears to be the 'best practice' in the fight against FGM and should be incorporated into future measures.

Change Process and Awareness

The Mekane Yesus Church has developed a holistic vision for its work, in which the social aspects of the work were just as important as the evangelistic ministry to the community. This understanding of *diakonia* requires that diaconal work is actively incorporated into the preaching of the gospel. In other words, *diakonia* must be viewed as foundational (constitutive) and not merely a consequence (consecutive) of the preaching of the gospel. One of the more distinctive aspects of this project is the care and concern in promoting the quality of life of individuals in the community that belong to a religion other than their own. This kind of understanding and reasoning can also be developed with the help of the creation account in the Old Testament. In many ways, the practice described in the project can be seen as supporting the understanding of *diakonia* described in 'Diakonia in Context'.[6] Transformation, reconciliation and empowerment describe the process of what happened in the project area as a consequence of the project. Old harmful practices stopped, and people with different backgrounds started to interact in positive ways to improve the conditions of life for their community. Women were empowered to take part in life in a new way and were given a voice in contexts that used to belong only to men.

---

[6] LWF, *Diakonia in Context. Transformation, Reconciliation, Empowerment. A Lutheran contribution to the ongoing ecumenical discussion regarding the understanding of diakonia and diaconal structures and practices in churches and congregations* (Geneva: Lutheran World Federation, 2009).

The established space as a diaconal method

As described in the presentation of the project, the project's method had generally developed in six stages based on the concept of Community Conversation. One way to describe the method and to place it within a theoretical model is by combining praxis and specific theories on FGM with *diakonia*. According to Nordstokke,[7] diaconal science is characterized by experience and theology combining with other academic fields as influences on diaconal praxis and theory. Diaconal practice is most often characterized as a praxis developed over time through the experience of coming into contact with human need.

The model can be interpreted from an *instrumental perspective* which employs stages that are to be followed in order to move up to the next level. Another approach to the model is to view these stages as creating new and various 'spaces' for action, where each 'space' provides a new potential for transformation. The process itself becomes essential in such an arena, in which a person in fellowship with others expands both the space for action and his or her potential for action within that space. One of the strongest impressions from my field visit came from observing the co-operation of people from different religious backgrounds. This particular project had truly succeeded in creating safe spaces for dialogue, expressed feelings, shared traditions and faith, all combining to create a space for action.

With this type of approach, the model can be divided into various spaces in which each of the six stages can be nurtured and formed. These are more than merely physical spaces; they are intentionally formed opportunities, safe places in which diverse individuals can meet and together create platforms for interpretation and understanding on shared interests and issues that become the basis for decisive action.

Space to see in the light of theological reflection

In the first stage of the process, a space is created in which the religious leaders of a community can gather. Spaces are created for leaders from a specific religion to gather together, as well as spaces for leaders from various religious backgrounds to come together. From interviews with these leaders it became clear that they had felt both resistance and uncertainty in having been invited or requested to enter into this space. However, the project was able to create a safe place for these leaders to meet, a space where faith and doubt could be expressed during the discussions and dialogues with other leaders from their own religion. Two arenas were created for dialogue, one to meet with those who were members of the same religion, and another to meet in fellowship with 'the others'. Sharing with each other was an important dimension in these

[7] Kjell Nordstokke, *Liberating Diakonia* (Trondheim: Tapir akademisk forlag, 2011), 34.

meetings. 'Diakonia in Context' [8] also points to the importance of this – not only the sharing of words, stories and experiences but also the sharing of food and drink. Within this context a dining table is more than a piece of furniture; it becomes a metaphor for that space and place where people meet to share a meal together and to give gifts to each other in order to express and build a common identity. In this space a common understanding was created on how to interpret what the Qur'an and the Bible teach on FGM. When this space was established, it expanded into something greater than itself.

Space to evaluate through awareness and knowledge

I have chosen to call the second space a space for awareness and knowledge. When the religious leaders had arrived at a consensus as to what their respective religions said (or did not say) in regard to FGM, a step was taken into this next space. Within this space, the religious leaders met together with all the local leaders, elders and informal leaders, both men and women. A report on circumcision[9] states that it has been important to involve recognized and respected religious leaders in order to convince others that the practice of circumcision has nothing to do with religion. Leaders of the religion are thus involved in building an atmosphere of security, in part by affirming the identity of each person in the room as either Christian or Muslim. In addition to religious instruction, representatives of the project give instruction on the other aspects of the FGM issue. All assumptions and arguments for the practice of FGM are brought up and discussed in the light of scientific knowledge on the subject. The laws and legal implications of the issue are also treated as an integral part of this meeting. This process may require several meetings before it is complete. At the end of the process the group appoints persons to the Anti-FGM Committee. As one Orthodox priest explained afterwards, 'This project has created laughter among us!' Laughter can be seen as a liberating power within a secure space, a power that contributes to create secure social bonds – even between those who are members of a religion other than their own.

Space for action

The project's own documentation and evaluations show how people were made accountable and empowered to take action. The method that the project used to achieve this was empowering the community to choose representatives whom they wanted as leaders in the work; even the youth were allowed to choose their own representatives. The respective groups then chose from their members those who would be trained as instructors for the greater community. However, responsibility for further planning and guidance of the project rested in the hands of the project committee based on pre-approved plans and

---

[8] LWF, *Diakonia in Context,* 33.

[9] Marit Berggrav (ed), *Kjønnslemlesting. Hva skjer, og hva gjør Norge?* (Oslo: Norad Rapport 13/2011, 2011), 9.

guidelines for the project. The organizing of the work testifies to its local ownership and sustainability. A good example of this is reflected in the comments of Sheik Ibrahim, who stated that his community would continue the work even if the project ended tomorrow.[10]

What is Diapraxis?

Diapraxis is defined in terms of inter-religious co-operation. Diapraxis describes the interaction that occurs when people from different faiths work together in order to improve the quality of life of their people. The Danish theologian Lissi Rasmussen introduced the term as *dialogue as action*, so that 'doing' comes before 'knowing'. While *dialogue* is described as the centrality of talking together within a relationship, *action and common praxis* are the essential elements in diapraxis, from which true dialogue may spring.[11] Rasmussen further states that there is a need to see society as an integrated whole.[12] Diapraxis is holistically oriented and includes shared experiences and activities as well as common social and political goals and interests.[13] The Lutheran World Federation also offers key criteria in evaluating diapraxis which is defined as *the meeting of people from various faith traditions in order to take action, in a solidarity that promotes human rights, improves quality of life and meets the felt-needs of their community.*[14] Within this understanding, transformation, empowerment and reconciliation are seen as consequences of diapraxis. It is this understanding of diapraxis that is used in this paper. The various spaces presented above have as their purpose to promote action, where each space contains the potential for transformation. Within the context of this particular project, a transformation took place in that women were listened to, with the result that their self-confidence increased as they spoke in public. Another transformation occurred when religious leaders and their followers were able to come together in order to work towards common goals. This particular transformation arose when old dividing lines were overcome, allowing people to help each other and share aspects of their daily lives in ways never seen, an unexpected yet positive result that went far beyond the original vision of the project.

Very little academic literature can be found dealing with the diapraxis approach. However, diapraxis is becoming an accepted term to describe any

---

[10] Larsen, *Diapraksis som diakonal metode i endring av skadelig tradisjonell praksis,* 48.

[11] Lissi Rasmussen, *Diapraksis og dialog mellem kristne og muslimer i lyset af den afrikanske erfaring* (Aarhus, Denmark: Aarhus universitetsforlag, 1997), 35.

[12] Rasmussen, *Diapraksis og dialog mellem kristne og muslimer i lyset af den afrikanske erfaring,* 70.

[13] Rasmussen, *Diapraksis og dialog mellem kristne og muslimer i lyset af den afrikanske erfaring,* 35-36.

[14] LWF, *Diakonia in Context,*89.

type of inter-religious co-operation. For Christians, diapraxis is founded on Christian values that all people share in the call of the Creator to love their neighbour by caring for those who are in need. This is illustrated in the parable of the Good Samaritan (Luke 10). The Samaritan helped a man in need even though the man practised a different faith than his own. The parable aids us in seeing diaconal work as something more than the giving of care to only those within one's own religious context. Against this background, diapraxis can be related to EECMY's co-operation with Muslims in giving women a better quality of life through the abolition of the practice of FGM. However, diapraxis does not promote religious neutrality or the relativizing of all religions. What is important in this understanding of diapraxis is the foundational respect of the values of others, in combination with an understanding that God has equipped all people with the ability to do good work. Such an understanding makes it possible for Christians and Muslims to work side-by-side in fighting the practice of FGM. Diapraxis is also the recognition of other people's faith as a positive resource to promote good living conditions and compassion. Diapraxis is thus based on a process in which change must be seen in each group involved – not just in 'the others'. While neither the project nor the church had heard of the term 'diapraxis' before beginning the work against FGM, the practice of the project lies within the above definition and understanding of the term.

Strengths and Weaknesses of the Project's Method

As described earlier, the results of the project's efforts are strongly positive in terms of the nearly complete abolition of the practice of FGM within the project area. However, it is still important to evaluate the method, in particular from a gender perspective, since the project's main target group were women while those who played a central role in the project were male religious leaders (who had had very little training in listening to women). This may indicate that a number of dangers may be inherent in the method, beginning with setting up religious leaders as spokespersons and standard-bearers for an entire society. History reveals that religion can be either liberating or oppressive. One element in the method described for this type of project can be the danger of legitimizing the power held by religious leaders, especially when there is the potential for that power to be wielded in a negative manner. On the other hand, the project had the positive result that women participated in the project and that they were willing to speak in front of public assemblies to stand against FGM and to share how the practice had negatively affected their lives. Many women also shared how the project had given them greater self-confidence, using words and descriptions that fell within the term 'empowerment'.

In order to gain oversight of these concerns and compare them with the project's clear advantages and possibilities, I have created a SWOT analysis[15] based on the project's work in relation to certain external factors.

Strengths	Weaknesses	Opportunities	Threats
Gives women the right to speak Religion is promoted in the public space Religious leaders are made accountable Anchored in the community Community-based ownership Democratically oriented Builds relationships Enables sustainable change Is anchored in religion Is anchored in national laws and rights Is supported by the governing authorities	Exposed to negative influences from leading voices / religious leaders Small, isolated areas that are influenced from the outside	Religion can positively energize towards motivation, inclusion, participation and sustainability Strengthens civil society Works against religiously based conflict Builds experience in organizing Builds knowledge Creates a better society to live in Improves human relationships	Religious leaders may misuse their authority and use religion for negative purposes Radicalization of Muslim leaders with contacts abroad Strengthens religion's general power to oppress The FGM practice may go 'underground' Resorting to the old practices when outside focus subsides

The SWOT analysis shows the strength of the project in that it endorses the role of the religions represented by the participants, and that religious leaders work openly in interacting with other leaders and with women. Women's personal experiences with FGM are respected and women are given authority

[15] A SWOT analysis is a structured planning method used to evaluate the Strengths, Weaknesses, Opportunities and Threats involved in a project or in a business venture.

to interpret and define the practice. This in turn leads to increased responsibility and the democratization of the religious leaders, or alternatively leads to the removal of non-compliant leaders by their community. I believe this is due to the participation of religious leaders in high positions and reputation who stand for positive attitudes and values in relation to the goals and vision of the project. The project's method and praxis are built on the participation of the community and not on the efforts of a few individuals who happen to be highly motivated towards action. The project is anchored in the local community, offering training and experience in democratic leadership and thought. The project promotes the building of relationships across entrenched dividing lines, as well as creating an arena where women can take action and participate equally with men. Another strength of the project is that it is established within the national legal system and is supported by the governing authorities.

Weaknesses of the project can be many, but I have chosen to focus on the possibility of negative influence by strong religious leaders who may have their own agendas. Though the project may work to encourage this, I see this as a remote possibility in relation to the strengths of the project mentioned above. Another weakness is the real possibility of very small, isolated communities being inadvertently influenced by what happens from outside the area. One possible solution for this is to ensure that the target area is large enough to be able to cope with such a threat from the outside.

One opportunity available through the project lies in the capacity of religion to offer its authority and energy towards motivation, inclusion, participation and sustainability. This includes the opportunity to strengthen civil society through the experience of democratic organizational experience, the dissemination of knowledge and the prevention of conflict. However, there could be the danger of religious leaders being given too much legitimate – or unquestioning – authority.

My conclusion of this analysis is that the positive elements of the project are so overwhelmingly significant that the potential of them working towards the prevention of the project's weaknesses is greater than the potential of them working towards strengthening these weaknesses. Excluding religious leaders from the project is not an option, since they are part of the external framework that the project must work within and recognize in order to get the job done; exclusion would overlook the religious dimension of the people's understanding of the practice of FGM.

Conclusion

The core of diapraxis is the arena in which action and shared praxis are the essential elements for which genuine dialogue can flourish between various groups. In order for this to function, no group can claim a monopoly of the truth or of correct interpretation; instead, the focus must be placed on the *process*. A question related to the project is whether the focus should be exclusively placed on eradicating negative actions and attitudes, or whether the method's actions and attitudes may indeed hold an inherent and positive force. Experience gained from the project points to the fact that the method releases something positive for everyone involved, something that has a ripple effect that reaches far beyond the purposes of the project; that, for example, women are viewed by their communities more as positive resources and less as problems.

Diapraxis as defined in this paper works to highlight a problem and experience that can be relevant in other situations, situations in which people from different faiths can work together towards a common goal. Even though this specific project functions within a context and framework that are indicative of Ethiopia, I believe that the model can be transferred, adapted and used within other contexts. The project can give increased understanding for development work and for the interface between development work and religion, and create an arena where women are given position and influence.

The leadership of the project had given no conscious thought to the diaconal dimension of the project's method and work. The project was clothed in the language of development work and was completely disassociated from the language of the church. Though the leaders were Christians, what was most important to them was that the project would serve to end a practice that was immensely damaging to all women, no matter from what religious background they came.

Much of the diaconal work of the churches in the South may well be characterized in this way: a practice that develops within the church's thinking and view of humanity, but that most often is not described. Such experiences therefore do not often stand out as examples of best practice and valuable inspiration and learning. This applies both within their own context and beyond their own borders.

Bibliography

EECMY 1. *Project Document 2006-2008.* EECMY Wabe Batu Synod, FGM elimination project (Archive Digni, 2006).

EECMY 3. *Annual Plan 2006.* EECMY Wabe Batu Synod, Sinana Dinsho FGM elimination project 10568 (Archive Digni, 2006).

EECMY 4. *Annual Plan 2007.* EECMY Wabe Batu Synod, Sinana Dinsho FGM elimination project 10568 (Archive Digni, 2007).

Kjell Kristian Larsen, *Diapraksis som diakonal metode i endring av skadelig tradisjonell praksis. Masteroppgave i diakoni.* Oslo: Diakonhjemmet Høgskole, 2012.

Lutheran World Federation, *Diakonia in Context. Transformation, Reconciliation, Empowerment. A Lutheran contribution to the ongoing ecumenical discussion regarding the understanding of diakonia and diaconal structures and practices in churches and congregations.* Geneva: Lutheran World Federation, 2009.

Marit Berggrav (ed), *Kjønnslemlesting. Hva skjer, og hva gjør Norge?* Oslo: Norad

Rapport 13/2011, 2011.
Kjell Nordstokke, *Liberating Diakonia.* Trondheim: Tapir akademisk forlag, 2011.
Lissi Rasmussen, *Diapraksis og dialog mellem kristne og muslimer i lyset af den afrikanske erfaring.* Aarhus: Aarhus universitetsforlag, 1997.

Diakonia in a Practical Perspective: Orthodox Reflections on the Background of the Syrian Crisis

Interview with Abouna Alexi Chehadeh, Damascus, Syria

Father (Abouna) Dr Alexi Chehadeh serves as the Director of the Department of Ecumenical Relations and Development (DERD) of the Greek Orthodox Patriarchate of Antiochia and All the East (GOPA), co-ordinating the development and relief work of DERD in Syria. Father Alexi is an Orthodox priest and holds a PhD from the University of Münster, Germany, on 'Islam, Staat und Gewalt. Hassan al-Turabis islamistisch-politisches Denken' (Islam, State and Violence. The Islamist-Political Thoughts of Hassan al-Turabi). He has a Master of Arts degree in Islamic Studies from the University of Hamburg. He has lectured on a variety of topics at the University of Balamand (Lebanon), at the Institute of Mission, Ecumenism and Religious Studies, and at the Asia-Africa Institute, University of Hamburg. In addition, he has participated in many international consultations on peace, the ethics of peace, the war in Syria, and Christian-Islamic conversations. From 1993 to 2013, he served as priest of the Antioch-Orthodox Archdiocese of Europe, between 2000 and 2007 he was Vicar of the Metropolitan, and since 2007 'Exarchos of Antioch-Orthodox Archdiocese of Germany'. At the end of 2013 His Beatitude Patriarch John X asked Father Alexi to move to the Middle East to assist him in the main residency in Syria and Lebanon. He is also a member of the Lutheran-Orthodox Joint Commission and Chief Editor of the patriarchal magazine 'AL-NASHRA'.

The interview was conducted in March 2016. The interviewer was Stephanie Dietrich, one of the editors of this publication.

Father Alexi, you are the Director of the Department for Ecumenical Relations and Development in the Greek Orthodox Patriarchate of Antioch and All the East. Could you please describe your work in a country struggling with internal war, millions of internally displaced people and terrorism?

Our beloved Syria has been suffering for more than five years and the general situation remains unstable, lacking the vision for peace.

Since 2011, the complexity of the situation and the absence of safety have led to an increase in the number of vulnerable persons all over the country, due to warfare and fighting in most areas. Consequently, many are either displaced or affected, while some have fled from Syria, seeking peace. As for the majority which remains in Syria (about 13½ million), according to the latest OCHA[1] needs assessment reports, they are in huge need of basic living services in order to overcome the difficult conditions they are facing on a daily basis.

As for our role as a humanitarian organization, we immediately rushed to take responsibility in co-operation with other international humanitarian practitioners to help our affected Syrian citizens.

Our field experience, based on our aid work towards the Iraqi refugees, has enabled us to respond rapidly and professionally through extending a hand of support, to Internally Displaced Populations (IDPs) and affected Syrians. We have taken immediate steps to train teams required for rapid response. In addition, we have improved our logistic services to meet the increasing and changing needs.

We therefore established a number of liaison offices in most of the Syrian governorates, which have received a large number of internally displaced persons and have started responding to the urgent needs of our vulnerable people.

The GOPA-DERD has launched many programmes to meet the needs of the Syrians. One of them is the Food and Non-Food Items (hygiene kits, kitchen sets and bedding sets, in addition to summer and winter clothing and stoves) within the Distribution Programme to reduce the economic burden of the affected population.

In addition, we are well known for our ability to respond quickly during emergencies, thanks to the team that demonstrates faith in action and professional training, enabling them to provide services in accordance with international standards. This can be seen through the diversity and multiplicity of our programmes – in Education, Livelihood, Psycho-social Support, Capacity Building, Health and Nutrition Awareness Campaigns, Delivery and Life-Saving Surgeries, Shelter Rehabilitation, WASH (water, sanitation and hygiene), and Community Service Programmes.

Our team assesses the status of displaced and affected persons while responding to their needs, either directly through our offices located in the majority of Syrian governorates, or through our network with other humanitarian practitioners on the ground, to make referrals of some cases when necessary, as our main concern is giving those disadvantaged people a helping hand, regardless of the source of help.

We know that the war affects all people in Syria, but especially the most vulnerable. In a situation of war, there needs to be an increased focus on gender-based violence, human trafficking and sexual slavery. How would you describe the situation for women and children in your country after more than five years of war? How does the war affect family life?

---

[1] OCHA: United Nations Office for the Coordination of Humanitarian Affairs.

The conflict and displacement have affected all layers of the Syrian community, especially women and children. Loss of documents, unstable security situations and other protection concerns have hindered the access of Internally Displaced Population to services specific to their needs, while specialized services have become scarce and limited to some areas only.

Violence, family separation, and lack of adequate services have further increased the vulnerability of the population, and many families have resorted to negative coping mechanisms in order to meet the needs of their families.

Psychological problems such as high levels of fear, anxiety, depression and a sense of isolation have steadily increased. At the same time, social support networks have been weakened and the resources of the communities have been depleted.

The current crisis is aggravating and creating new vulnerabilities. We have observed through our Community Service Programmes an increase of inter-family violence and domestic violence, as well as a development of harmful coping mechanisms related to gender survival (child marriage) since the ongoing crisis is affecting children and adolescents physically, psychologically and socially, leaving them subject to violations of their human rights and making them face specific protection risks, including dropping out of school, kidnapping, sexual exploitation, trafficking, child labour, abuse, neglect, separation from their families and recruitment into armed groups. Psychological symptoms, including withdrawal, anxiety, fear, denial, anger, sadness, restlessness and regression are particularly prevalent among children and adolescents.

More than five million children are reported to be in need of humanitarian assistance; two million children are not attending school and 2.4 million children below five years of age are at risk of malnutrition. A child's sense of well-being is jeopardized and the impact of the crisis on children and their development can have tremendous consequences for their adult lives if they are not provided with appropriate support and healing mechanisms. Parents and relatives may not be in a position to support and care for their children as a result of the crisis and its implications for economic hardship.

As for women, their vulnerability has increased dramatically, as they have been subject to displacement, disrupted livelihoods and access to public services, carrying additional workloads within and outside the home in the absence or loss of male family members. Keeping up with new realities on the ground and taking the role of a breadwinner, they have been scattered within the informal economy or home-based small business with very low pay or irregular wages due to their limited education and vocational skills, or due to the reproductive roles that occupy their time and mobility. Besides, in the long run, undermining interventions for women and girls can reinforce inequalities in a post-conflict context and result in the downgrading of the role of women in peace talks and reconstruction processes.

The unstable security situation and the lack of safety have led to the appearance of different types of violence among the IDP communities. Women and girls are in particular risk of sexual violence due to forced displacement as well as early/forced marriage, while incidents of Sexual and Gender-based Violence (SGBV) are on the rise.

Does your organization offer specific gender-based programmes?

One of the main focuses through our community service programmes is raising the awareness of sexual gender-based violence cases, through conducting special campaigns to spread information within communities, especially the most vulnerable ones, on how to tackle this very sensitive issue in a social friendly manner.

Awareness materials are developed based on discussions with the community and in consultation with our partners, in order to meet the specific concerns of different groups. International standards combined with cultural sensitivity and a respect for traditions are considered when developing the materials.

Through our specific SGBV campaigns, we address topics like women's rights, domestic violence, sexual abuse and women's empowerment by targeting females, males, adolescent boys and girls.

Such sessions are provided in locations most appropriate for the participants and as close as possible to the community; a minimum level of privacy is ensured during the sessions, which are provided by male or female staff who have received the training on the basics of SGBV and Training of Trainers in awareness. Our staff engaged in awareness sessions are working in accordance with the SGBV guiding principles which ensure that the 'Do No Harm' principle is respected and some sessions are complemented with the distribution of dignity kits to women and girls.

Afterwards, a follow-up management is done on special cases, whether they have been referred to livelihood activities, a gynæcologist, a psychiatrist or a lawyer in order to give the SGBV survivor suitable advice for her case.

Also, establishing community-based women's committees is one of the means of building the capacity of the community members, to prevent and respond to protection issues affecting women and girls and to play a key role in community awareness on SGBV and empowerment of women's leadership and decision-making in the community. The committees are established in shelters and/or within the community.

This year GOPA-DERD will carry out advocacy campaigns through the media to spread information all over the country via road advertising billboards, TV shows, brochures and pamphlets containing messages that should stick in the minds of people in an indirect way to educate them about women's rights and the proper manner of solving problems or family conflicts, and encouraging peaceful communication, to help in building solid family relationships which will be the starting-point for reconstructing our Syrian society.

Millions of people are internally displaced or are living as refugees in the neighbouring countries of Syria. Many people try to escape to Europe as well. What is your recommendation to the people in your church – do you ask them to stay? Is the situation for women the same as for men when being internally displaced or being refugees?

Syrian women and girls are living through the most damaging conflict in the region's recent history, especially when being refugees, as they are sometimes subject to sexual violence and more frequently suffering from harassment and abuse. For the women of Syria, the process of reintegration and recovery at the individual and community level will be long and complex.

But one of my main duties towards the people of my church, regardless of their age, gender, social, economic or personal situation, is to encourage them to stay by trying my best to plant seeds of hope in their hearts, as our country is in need of its entire population being built again, and one of our fears as religious leaders is to have an old Syrian generation as a result of massive emigration of youth to Europe and other foreign countries. Consequently, our beloved Syria will suffer even more by importing external expertise and human resources for the rehabilitation process to be accomplished properly and as required.

That's why as GOPA-DERD, we are very aware of this fact, working together to combine our efforts, plans and ideas, in order to create new opportunities for our youth generation by increasing the proportion of livelihood programmes, through developing vocational training courses based on market needs, providing small business loans with technical support, as well as creating better opportunities for those who get the skills to teach other people a certain profession. All of this is being done to give our youth the means of becoming independent and supporting their families financially, as well as raising awareness of the importance of creating solutions instead of waiting for others to do so. The whole purpose is to help our young population to stay and have a better hope for the future.

Within Orthodox theology, one might say that there has not been a wide focus on 'gender-based approaches'. As a church leader from the Orthodox Church, do you think Orthodox theology can make a specific contribution when addressing social practice from a gender perspective?

In the Epistle of St Paul to the Galatians, he emphasises that there are no differences between genders. He clearly says that there is no male or female, since all people are one in Christ (Gal. 3:28). Accordingly, Christ made women and men equal and both share in the image of God. Given this understanding of the equality of men and women, none of them is more honoured by God than the other. This is stressed in the Orthodox tradition in connection with the mystery of salvation. The Orthodox Church does not include the priesthood of women in her tradition; women assume their own roles for the rehabilitation of the broken image of God. The Divine Revelation is in this case the foundation of the understanding of the Orthodox Church, when she considers both God and the humans. According to Psalm 118:27, it is clear that God has acted to provide us with insight into who he is and likewise who we are.

In addition, we understand that God is the creator of both men and women. Each has his or her origin with God. This firm belief is further underpinned by our perception that Christ has come to save both men and women equally and to restore both men and women to communion with the Creator (Col. 1:20).

In other words, the biological differences between men and women do not indicate any kind of inferiority or superiority of any of them before God. Both genders are called to the sanctification of their souls, bodies and life, to be part the faithful, who are saved and selected on the basis of their belief, and to strive in order to participate in the Holiness of the Lord (1 Peter 1:15). According to this understanding, the Orthodox Church venerates her Saints, who are men and women, and the list of the female Saints from the beginning of Christianity is long.

The Orthodox tradition focuses on community between all human people as being united in the body of Christ. Maybe one could say that your focus is on community rather than diversity. Could you explore this approach a little further for us?

According to John 17:21, Jesus prayed for the unity of the faithful: 'I pray that they might be one.' In my Church, we consider women and men, laity and clergy, as united in faith and by baptism in the body of Christ, so that all of them form the community. According to St Maxim the Confessor: 'Men, women, children (...) all receive from the Church one nature which is beyond corruption – the nature that is not affected by the numerous and profound differences by which people differ from each other (...) in the Church, no-one is at all separated from the common, as everyone is as if dissolved in one another by the simple and invisible power of faith.' The guarantee of this unity is the Holy Spirit, whom the faithful receive by baptism, and who is given to the church in general 'so that she can unite those who are divided by different races and conditions. For the aged and the young, the poverty-stricken and the wealthy, the infant and the adolescent, the woman and the man, every soul becomes one thing' (St John Chrysostom, Homily on Ephesians 9:3) in the body of the church whose Head is Christ himself.

We emphasize in the Orthodox Church that we are one body. This is very clear according to the teaching of St Paul (1 Cor. 12:12-27) and in the parable of the 'True Vine' (John 15:15). In this way, the Orthodox Church respects the role of each individual, but insists on the importance of the community as a whole. We should take into consideration the teaching about the Trinity, who is one in three persons, God Father, God Son and God Holy Spirit. Each of them has his own attitudes; yet all of them are united in one. The differences in their attitudes do not nullify their unity. The same applies to humans; we should not consider our diversity as a reason for differentiation, but rather as a richness for the community, so that the strong should help the weak among us (Rom. 15:1).

The orthodox tradition has developed a specific understanding of diakonia *and the church's social practice as 'the liturgy after the liturgy'. What does that mean, especially in your context in Syria, where the majority of the population is Muslim?*

First, I would like to define the expression 'liturgy'. It is derived from the Greek word *leitourgia*, which is derived from the words *leitos* (public, from *laos,* people) and *ergon* (work). The Eastern Churches, especially the Orthodox Church, use this *terminus technicus* to allude to the celebration of the Eucharist, which means the offering of the gifts of bread and wine and their consecration through the Holy Spirit to become the body and blood of the Lord. Through participation in the Holy Communion in the body and blood of Jesus Christ, the faithful, included the celebrants, become united with Christ and with one another.

This unity with Christ does not mean only sharing with each other his body and blood, but also following in his footsteps in his mission and service towards the world, regardless of any ethnic or religious consideration. This service is clearly illustrated in the Parable of the Good Samaritan. Furthermore, the Holy Gospel according to St Matthew (25:31-41) emphasises the duty of the faithful to comfort the suffering, to feed the hungry, to help the homeless, and to visit the sick people and prisoners, as we would do this for Christ himself. This is another way in which we are united with Christ through the service towards the world and the humans.

Accordingly, we realize that the church cannot be content with preaching the gospel to fulfil its mission of salvation. She invites the faithful to charity work and *diakonia*, what she calls 'the liturgy after the liturgy'. She aims through this to improve the spiritual-moral and material condition of the world. We, as DERD, understand our diaconal work towards the world and the humans in this sense, namely, not only to distribute kits, but to express our love to the world and to each other as a contribution to the salvation plan of the Lord. Therefore, my church and her charity arm, DERD, enter into co-operation with various international organizations and civil associations to get help, which in turn helps us to witness in the mission of love and charity in the world.

In other words, the dynamic movement of the Divine Liturgy cannot be limited within the walls of the church or to the Eucharistic assembly. This movement goes beyond the gathered faithful in the church to serve the community as well as all humans outside the church. The dynamics of the Divine Liturgy send the faithful, equipped by the Holy Spirit and unified with Christ, to celebrate the 'sacrament of the brother and the sister' outside the church, in any place and house where we encounter persons who are in need, the wounded, sick, marginalized, hungry, thirsty and suffering. In the gospel we read: 'If you are offering your gift at the altar and there remember that your brother or sister has something against you, leave your gift there in front of the altar. First go and be reconciled to them; then come and offer your gift' (Matt. 5:23-24). Reconciliation with our brothers and sisters means also to care for them, to share our time and goods and chattels with them, and to share with them our daily bread. To offer a sacrifice on the stony altar in front of God can't be completed and meaningful without offering a sacrifice for the 'temple of the Holy Spirit', namely the human for whom Christ died. My church calls the extension of the liturgy from the Eucharistic assembly into the daily service of the people outside the temple 'the liturgy after the liturgy', which points to the connection between the liturgy and *diakonia*.

Do you think that women play a different role from men in peace-building?

Definitely, since the participation of women is critical to the success of any peace-building process; excluding half the human population would make it impossible to achieve peace. Women peace-builders bring different perspectives and priorities than men, and their role in re-establishing the social fabric in the aftermath of conflict is vital. The role of women in peace-building is recognized in many international agreements and resolutions, and the Nobel Peace Prize has been awarded to several women round the world, as a public recognition of the impact of women peace-builders. But whilst women peace-builders have made vital contributions to peace processes in diverse places, the reality remains that women are denied meaningful participation in many peace processes.

As regards the role of Syrian women – even though many of their own dreams may have been ruined – resilient women have not lost hope and have never stopped believing that life could one day be better for their children. If we are to see that these hopes do not die, it is important that we ensure that women and girls are provided with adequate access to services and safe supportive spaces where they can heal and rebuild their lives. It is becoming apparent that, in the aftermath of this conflict, Syrian women will be empowered – women who will be active agents in bringing about peace and reconstruction in their war-torn country.

That's why as GOPA-DERD, we are engaging women in most of our programmes to strengthen their role in the peace-building process, empowering them to become active participants in their communities, within the early recovery stage that we are passing through, as their role is vital and every single endeavour is needed for comprehensive efforts to build our society.

Culture, Baptists and Diakonia: Naga Christianity from a Gender Perspective

Atola Longkumer

> The hungry need bread, and the homeless need a roof; the oppressed need justice and the lonely need fellowship; the undisciplined need order and the slaves need freedom. To allow the hungry to remain hungry would be blasphemy against God and one's neighbour, for what is nearest to God is precisely the need of one's neighbour.
>
> Dietrich Bonhoeffer[1]

Introduction

Since the beginning of the Suffragette movement in the late nineteenth century, women have gradually gained much freedom and the right to participate in society. While women did not enjoy absolute equality within Christianity, there have nevertheless been active and gifted women in almost all centuries, 'excavated' in recent years by excellent scholarship.[2] Gendered historiography and the development of feminist theology[3] have contributed enormously to the debate and achievements of women's movements, beginning in the last quarter of the twentieth century.[4] That women are excluded is not the argument, but that women and their perspectives and equal participation continue to be marginalised is the point. The marginalisation of women is shared across a

---

[1] Dietrich Bonhoeffer, *Ethics* (New York: Macmillan, 1955), 163.

[2] For some examples, see Averil Cameron and Amélie Kuhrt (eds), *Images of Women in Antiquity* (Oxford: Routledge, 1993); Mary L. Bitel, *Women in Early Medieval Europe, 400-1100* (Cambridge: CUP, 2002); Dana L. Robert (ed), *Gospel Bearer, Gender Barriers: Missionary Women in the Twentieth Century* (Maryknoll, NY: Orbis Books, 2002).

[3] This term is used as a rubric for the liberation movements of women that includes the different strands of race, ethnicity, class, geo-political regions, etc.

[4] Carol P. Christ and Judith Plaskow (eds), *Womenspirit Rising: A Feminist Reader in Religion* (New York: HarperCollins, 1979); Rosemary Radford Ruether, *Sexism and God-talk: Towards a Feminist Theology* (Boston: Beacon Press Book, 1983); Elizabeth Schüssler Fiorenza, *In Memory of Her: A Feminist Theological Reconstruction of Christian Origins* (New York: Crossroad Publishing, 1994).

broad range of socio-cultural, economic, regional and denominational categories.[5] In a generalised assertion, the marginalisation of women persists because of an entrenched kyriarchal-patriarchal cultural orientation and practices derived from this fundamental social hierarchy.[6]

To be sure, the word 'gender' is more than the dual binary of female-male categories; gender encompasses more than the traditional binary categories and recognises the fluidity around gender. For instance, a seminar in Princeton Theological Seminary is proposed to discuss gender fluidity from a theological perspective. Jacqueline Lapsley, professor and director of the Centre for Theology, Women and Gender, at Princeton Theological Seminary, has introduced the complexity of gender identity in contemporary time: 'Gender is a topic of great interest today, especially for young people; they are questioning the gender binaries – male and female – and some are forging new gender identities in accordance with their self-understanding. There is also a keen awareness that an appreciation of gender diversity can move our society towards real justice for women and other persons who are marginalized because of gender and/or sexuality.'[7] The category of gender encompasses identities more than the social construct of male-female identities that dominated the discourse on equality of women.

While the topic is on gender and its critical engagement with an aspect of Christian mission, *diakonia*, the present chapter will work with data and the social realities of women among Naga Christianity. Non-availability of data and resources pertaining to the larger concept of gender that incorporates sexual orientation and sexuality is the only reason for limiting the treatment to the conventional category of women.[8]

The chapter will argue that the church in Naga society in general has been inadequate in its diaconal responsibility towards its excluded members, such as women and the culturally defined 'others' in Naga society. To develop this argument, a description of Christianization of the Naga people in the nineteenth century from a patriarchal/oral tradition society will be juxtaposed with the restructuring of Naga society in tandem with the modernisation process as a by-product of Christianization. A critical analysis of existing cultural practices and

---

[5] See: www.un.org/womenwatch/directory/statistics_and indicators_60.htm

[6] Elisabeth Schüssler Fiorenza coined the term 'kyriarchal' as an analytical term to articulate in a more comprehensive way the systemic oppression of women seen across socio-political structures of a complex web of domination more than the conventional term 'patriarchy'. 'Kyriarchy' locates sexism and misogyny in a wider spectrum of oppression and interstructures of domination; see Schüssler Fiorenza, *Rhetoric and Ethic: The Politics of Biblical Studies* (Minneapolis, MN: Fortress Press, 1999), 5; Gerda Lerner, *The Creation of Patriarchy* (Oxford: OUP, 1989).

[7] See: www.ptsem.edu/indexmobile.aspx?id=25769809906 (accessed 26th February 2016).

[8] The fact that there is still no viable and sincere conversation on the issue of sexuality among Naga Christians is itself quite telling of rigid cultural boundaries.

the Baptist mission will be included. The critical reading of Christian mission and the cultural practices that survive makes it imperative for the church to embrace *diakonia* as a missional spirituality and a radical advocacy for gender equality in contemporary Naga society. Probing this micro context, a theoretical question on the impact of local culture on the goals of transformation of communities into inclusive communities is highlighted.[9] The concluding section will identify three areas wherein a deliberate policy of *diakonia* in the churches as a fundamental need of a prophetic community may be developed.

A Survey of Naga Christianity

The Naga are an indigenous people of the Indo-Myanmar region, a majority of them living in the north-east Indian states of Nagaland, Manipur, Arunachal and Assam. The Naga people are a confederation of many sub-tribes/clans having different dialects but sharing many religio-cultural practices. Orality in transmitting community knowledge, proximity to nature, an age- and gender-derived social hierarchy, a warrior tradition, and a land-centred, patriarchal, shamanic religion are some shared traditions. Colonialization by the British beginning in the early nineteenth century and being Christianised by Baptist missionaries from America in the late nineteenth century are also shared experiences of the Naga people.[10] While most of the Naga tribes are Christians today, there are still a few that practise and live in the traditional way.[11] For obvious reasons, the issue addressed in the chapter pertains to the Christians among the Nagas.

The espousal of Christianity by the Naga people took place relatively *en masse* and within a short space of time. Significantly, the participation and role of early native converts in the evangelisation of the people has been identified as crucial in the establishment of Christian communities.[12] Inadvertently, the transition to Christianity stipulated immense adaptation to a new way of life, not just in allegiance to a new God, but also an enforced rejection of socio-cultural practices. The enormity of transition to a new way of life, demanded

---

[9] John L. and Jean Comaroff, *Of Revelation and Revolution: The Dialectics of Modernity on a South African Frontier,* Volume 2 (Chicago: University of Chicago Press, 1997); Andrew F. Walls, 'The Gospel as Prisoner and Liberator of Culture', 'Culture and Coherence in Christian History', 'The Translation Principles in Christian History', in Andrew F. Walls, *The Missionary Movement in Christian History: Studies in the Transmission of Faith* (Edinburgh: T. & T. Clark, 1996).

[10] While there is a growing production of micro history, for a macro narrative and ethnographic portrayal of the Naga people, see Julian Jacobs, *The Nagas: Hill Peoples of Northeast India* (London: Thames & Hudson, 1999).

[11] See Robert Eric Frykenberg, *Christianity in India: From Beginnings to the Present* (Oxford: OUP), 2008.

[12] See Robert Eric Frykenberg, *Christianity in India*, 433.

by the change in religion, is best exemplified by phrases used to describe the encounter, 'from darkness to light', 'from head-hunters to soul hunters', among Naga Christians.[13] Today, Christianity among the Naga people is a defining marker of their modern identity, in that the cultural practices and beliefs of Christianity is a way of life for many, and the church is an influential institution. The church serves as a common platform for the Naga and wields authority in many facets of society. The authority of the church among the Naga is, however, more complex; it is not akin to a centralised state-church relationship as found in some European nations. The church and its influence in Naga society are more tacit and subtle, sustained more by a traditional understanding of the church as the institution representing God. Hence those who serve the church in whatever ecclesiastic roles are to be respected and honoured. This notion of the institutionalised church is not without its adverse impact on the larger Naga society.

Among the many changes that Christianity wrought in Naga society was the invariable introduction of modern education. The reception of modern education by the native was enthusiastic, according to mission records and oral stories of early converts. The enthusiastic embrace of modern education is evident in the formation of a people's forum such as the Naga Club in 1928, to enable for elite Nagas to voice their socio-political identity. Today, the literacy rate is high among the Naga people; in fact, some tribes account for a higher literacy rate than the national rate in India, according to the latest census (80.11% vs. 64.8% on the national level).[14] While the literacy percentage need not translate into favourable societal transformation, it makes the fundamental point of the embrace of modern education among the Naga people, an erstwhile oral-based community, and its subsequent impact on modern Naga identity. The archival records tell of a Naga chief imploring missionaries to come to his village and teach his children to read the written word. It is important to note also that women were initiated early into the modern education system. In fact, there are records of classes conducted for the young mothers who stayed at home taking care of the young ones when the other elders were away for the day's work in the rice fields.[15] Both men and women began receiving modern education at the same time. When education was introduced, there was neither discrimination nor resistance against women attending school; hence both men and women began to participate in modern society with their respective skills and professions. It remains the same today for many Naga women – that there is no overt discrimination in access to acquiring education and pursuing

---

[13]For instance, the theme song for the quasquicentennial celebration of Nagaland Baptist Church is entitled, 'Out of Darkness into Light'. See NBCC, *Nagaland Celebrates Quasqui Centennial* (Kohima: NBCC, 1997), 24.

[14] www.census2011.co.in/literacy.php

[15] Narola Imchen, *Women in Church and Society: The Story of Ao Women* (Jorhat, Assam: Eastern Theological College, 2001); Aphuno Chase Roy, *Women in Transition: Angami Naga Women from 1878 to the Present.*

modern professions. While the initial period of transition from a shamanic oral culture witnessed equal opportunity for Naga women, the role and participation became curtailed in conventional positions as secondary roles at best or excluded at worst, once the church became an established institution with its own structures and functions.

Gender Location in Naga Christianity

Beneath the embrace of Christianity was the traditional Naga socio-cultural web of hierarchy, grounded on characteristic clan- and male-centred gender relationships. The gender hierarchy and its practice were, however, more complicated than a simple bifurcation of society along the binary category of male and female. Naga women enjoyed relative freedom and rights before conversion to Christianity despite the fundamental patriarchal culture. Naga women participated in community life such as performance of rituals, possessed shamanic gifts, could steward ancestral land, albeit without 'owning it', and contributed equally to community well-being. In other words, women were not restricted in many aspects of the community by reason of their gender identity. In many instances, a woman could be identified as a shaman who performed the shamanic rituals on behalf of individuals or the community. Unlike some cultures, where women were segregated and isolated from the larger society, Naga women enjoyed relative freedom of mobility and rights as individuals, albeit within the purview of the clan stipulations. The clan structure and its practices served as normative for any social interaction for any individual. The normative derived from the clan ways of life ensured democratic values and the protection of every member in the community. Despite the relative freedom and clan rights available to women, the decision-making council was out of reach of Naga women. Pre-Christian Naga socio-cultural structure did not allow women to participate in the decision-making council. The council of the community was strictly composed of male representatives of the clans.

Into such a socio-cultural backdrop, Christianity was introduced and embraced among the Naga people initiating enormous changes in many aspects of society. That transformation of the Naga people from an oral, warrior culture to a modern, professional society cannot be denied. The encounter between Christian missionaries and Naga people has been dynamic and mutually transforming.[16]

Women were not denied education and were incorporated into the institutions and structures of modern society, as necessitated by the colonial power and the establishment of the church. Right from the beginning, Naga women studied alongside male members in Bible schools, theological colleges and universities. They also served as leaders of women's societies, women's

---

[16] See John L. and Jean Comaroff, *Of Revelation and Revolution*, 28.

departments in the church, Bible women, and other professions such as nurses and teachers, and in clerical positions such as administrative support aides. Women were also part of the local economy limited to agricultural produce and handcrafts.

While a general freedom to pursue modern ways of life was not curtailed for women, ironically, the church and its function excluded women from its decision-making bodies and the Eucharistic ministry. Naga women had access to modern education, served in every profession under the state, even pursued theological education and became professors of future pastors, but they were excluded from the pastoral ministry and decision-making bodies such as the deacon boards. The challenge for Naga women pursuing theological studies is after completion of their studies, because the church, being a culturally influenced community, has very little opportunity for a woman.[17] What the missionaries transplanted of the gender hierarchy as existing in the mission period has more or less remained rigidly implanted among Naga Christians.

The position and participation of Naga women in both the church and the larger society posit critical questions to the understanding of the liberative dimension of the Gospel and its inherent values among Naga Christianity. The concept and practice of *diakonia* in the church provides a potential resource to make some proposals for policy and practice in the Naga church, drawn from a theological foundation of God's kingdom as an inclusive community.

In the remaining part of the chapter, the concept of *diakonia* and its understanding and practical implication for gender justice will be discussed, particularly among the Naga Baptists who represent a complex gender hierarchy.

Diakonia as Prophetic Service

In conventional Christian perception, the term *diakonia* is understood as serving and service to the world. Such an understanding of the concept of *diakonia* has been sustained by the interpretation of the Greek word *diakonia, diakonos* and the verb *diakonein* in the New Testament. These terms appear both in the gospels and the Pauline epistles (for example, Matt. 8:15; 22:13; Mark 1:13; 10:45; Luke 22:27; John 12:2; Eph. 1:23; Rom. 11:13; 1 Tim. 3:8-13) where they relate to serving, service, and ministry. In the *Encyclopedia of Christianity Online*, Richard Boeckler describes *diakonia* as derived from the Greek word *diakoneo*, meaning 'serve', in response to the needs of the people either by deeds or by words as taught by the gospel.[18] The interpretation of the

---

[17] I have discussed this in detail in another essay: see Atola Longkumer, 'Tetsur Tesayula: Christian Mission and Gender in the Ao Naga of Northeast India', in Christine Lienemann-Perrin et al (eds), *Putting Names with Faces: Women's Impact in Mission History* (Nashville, TN: Abingdon Press, 2012), 187-206.

[18] Richard Boeckler, 'Diakonia' in Encyclopedia of Christianity Online. Brill Online,

term as service and ministry has influenced ecclesiastical organisations and practice immensely. In particular, such an understanding of the New Testament term and its usage as 'the social ministry of the church' has been instrumental for the northern European and Scandinavian churches, particularly of those belonging to the Lutheran reformation.[19] Derived from (or based on) such an understanding of service of the church to the social needs of the times, the formation and movement of deaconesses and deacons began in Germany in the nineteenth century. *Diakonia* as compassionate service was also undergirded by the basic Christian principle of 'love your neighbour as yourself' which found expressed implementation in the social context of nineteenth-century Germany. Beate Hofmann writes: 'Some German Christians became so desperate about the horrible living conditions of the working poor that they started to organize diaconic work in a more professional and institutional way.'[20] Hofmann illustrates this movement with the service of a social nature provided by Theodor Fliedner who founded the first deaconess motherhouse in Kaiserwerth, Dusseldorf, in 1836 to take care of sick people and children. Another example of such social service provided by the church was the Rauhe Haus in Hamburg, started in 1833 by the Lutheran pastor Johann Hinrich Wichern.[21] These social services organised by church people were efforts in alleviating the socially deprived poor of the time.[22]

With its history of concrete practice in the church as compassionate service provided to the downtrodden and the vulnerable rooted in the social conditions of nineteenth-century Europe, particularly Germany, the concept and practice of *diakonia* has expanded beyond its specific locale. *Diakonia* as social service certainly was actively implemented in conditions of marginality in many parts of the world, not least in the global South. Boeckler states that the social conditions of poverty and deprivation 'have enabled the church in modern times to reach an unprecedented degree of consensus regarding *diakonia*' and 'declared their solidarity with the poor'.[23] From its basic meaning of serving the poor in society, the term *diakonia* has evolved into a practice with concrete form and substance, established to enable the community of faith to incorporate deliberate actions for justice. For instance, the Church of Norway has

---

2016. Reference. Princeton Theological Seminary, 11th March 2016: http://ezproxy.ptsem.edu:2087/entries/encyclopedia-of-christianity/diakonia-D229

[19] 'Introduction: Diakonia as Christian Social Practice', in Stephanie Dietrich, Kari Karsrud Korslien, Kjell Nordstokke and Knud Jørgensen (eds), *Diakonia as Christian Social Practice: An Introduction* (Oxford: Regnum, 2014), 1.

[20] Beate Hofmann, 'Diakonia between Church and Society: Learning from German Experiences and Challenges', in *Currents in Theology and Missions,* 42:3 (July 2015).

[21] Beate Hofmann, 'Diakonia between Church and Society.'

[22] The historical background is only to anchor the argument of the paper; for a detailed and elaborate treatment of the historical development and interpretation of the concept, see the chapters by Stephanie Dietrich and Kjell Nordstokke in the present volume.

[23] Richard Boeckler, 'Diakonia' in Encyclopedia of Christianity Online.

developed a *Plan for Diakonia* which elucidates the understanding of the concept in the following way: 'Diakonia is the caring ministry of the Church. It is the Gospel in action and is expressed through loving your neighbour, creating inclusive communities, caring for creation and struggling for justice.'[24] Another important document has been published by the Lutheran World Federation in 2009, entitled *Diakonia in Context: Transformation, Reconciliation, Empowerment.* This document emphasises the theological assumption in the usage of the New Testament term *diakonia*, as fundamentally a missional aspect of the church. The theological understanding of *diakonia* as mission is further elaborated in the practical imperative to action. Hence, *diakonia* is the church's response 'to challenges of human suffering, injustice and care for creation'.[25]

From its basic meaning of service driven by the subjective emotion of compassion amidst suffering, the concept of *diakonia* has been enlarged to incorporate issues of justice and advocacy. This movement of *diakonia* as service for social justice is observably led by Protestant churches, notably churches in northern Europe, with a history and experience of having established organisations and the allotment of resources. *Diakonia* as a movement for social justice has been integrated into the ecumenical movement in such a way that the crystallisation of the concept as intrinsically connected with the church is highlighted. Within the ecumenical movement, *diakonia* is emphasised as a mission of the church. The vision and action emphasised in *diakonia* as service to the needs and demands of social conditions is a task of the church. Such an understanding of *diakonia* then 'enhances bold, some would say prophetic, expressions of diaconal action, in solidarity with marginalised and suffering people, moving away from traditions of conceptualising *diakonia* as humble service'.[26]

The development of *diakonia* as an ecumenical concept that incorporates inclusive justice provides the global Christian community with a conscious platform for anchoring its missional task for the marginalised and the excluded in communities round the world. Stephanie Dietrich describes 'prophetic *diakonia*' as the understanding and practice of corporate service for justice in the context of unjust social structures. Prophetic *diakonia* is undergirded by a rights-based approach to serving the needs of the socially deprived. Compassion is not limited to the provision of material and physical needs, but prophetic *diakonia* seeks security, human dignity and inclusivity.[27]

---

[24] Stephanie Dietrich, ''Mercy and Truth are Met Together: Righteousness and Peace Have Kissed Each Other'(Psalm 85:10): Biblical and Systematic Theological Perspectives on Diakonia as Advocacy and Fight for Justice', in Dietrich, Korslien, Nordstokke and Jørgensen, *Diakonia as Christian Social Practice*, 4.

[25] Quoted in Stephanie Dietrich, 'Mercy and Truth are Met Together', 2.

[26] Stephanie Dietrich, 'Mercy and Truth are Met Together'.

[27] Kjell Nordstokke, 'The Study of Diakonia as an Academic Discipline', in Dietrich, Korslien, Nordstokke and Jørgensen, *Diakonia as Christian Social Practice*, 43.

The concept and practice of *diakonia* as a prophetic mission of the church can be applied to contexts of exclusion and discrimination of women in church and society across a wide spectrum of traditions. The conditions and practice of Naga Christians in relation to women members represent a context wherein *diakonia* as prophetic mission of the church can be a resourceful platform for seeking inclusive justice.

Diakonia for Gender Empowerment

Gender justice and empowerment continue to pose a challenge to the mission of global Christianity.[28] The persistent exclusion and discrimination of women across the broad spectrum of social structures and economic contexts make it imperative for churches to deliberate on the issue with prophetic zeal. The concept and practice of *diakonia* as a movement for serving communities towards inclusive justice bring global Christianity into conversation and co-operation across diverse contexts. It is this context, the complex socio-religious location of Naga women in the church and the larger society, which provides a case in point for prophetic *diakonia* as a common project.

The Naga people are an indigenous group of people who espoused Christianity in the late nineteenth century, and today Christianity serves as a defining marker of their modern identity. The church has a central role, function and authority among Naga Christians. Within this pre-eminent position of the church, the women among Naga Christians are discriminated and excluded from positions of authority and participation in decision-making. There are no explicitly stated normative rules laid down against women, in that Naga women enjoy equal access to modern education including theological education. Naga women serve in the church and the larger society in gendered spaces such as the women's department in the church, educational institutions and other professional platforms. Ironically, it is within the church structure that Naga women are most excluded.

The Christianity that was transmitted to the indigenous culture of the Naga people was surely a child of its time with its own gender views and practices, influenced both by a reading of the scripture influenced by pre-feminist hermeneutics and Victorian gender norms prevailing in the cultures of the missionaries. While Christian mission has been a vehicle of social progress and economic empowerment for women across many contexts, women both as agents and recipients of Christian mission were second-class members.[29] In the

---

[28] I have discussed this elsewhere: see Atola Longkumer, 'Not without women: Mission in the Third Millennium', in *International Review of Mission,* Vol. 10, 2, November 2011.

[29] Among the many resources, see Dana L. Robert, *American Women in Mission: A Social History of their Thought and Practice* (Macon, GA: Mercer University Press, 1997).

organisation of the nascent Christian community, gender roles and practices still favoured a patriarchal structure. The Naga Christian community was no different. All church organisational leadership was assigned to males: pastors, deacons, even the *chowkidar* (equivalent to sexton).[30] Women could teach and preach within the gendered space of the women's department and the Sunday school. Some Naga Baptist churches have ordained women in the late twentieth century, but these are mere tokens, since women are still not welcomed as fully-fledged pastors. Ironically, there are many theologically trained Naga women who teach future pastors in theological colleges.

Naga churches also have an idiosyncratic understanding and practice of deacons in the church. Deacons consist mostly of men that are educated and placed in important social and bureaucratic positions in the state. In a way, deacons of the church are an elite male club. The deacons form the deacon board which is the decision-making body, in most cases with authority over the pastor. Contrary to the biblical concept and understanding, deacons are not those who serve but those who decide among the Naga Baptist Christians. In most Naga churches, seating arrangements have also assigned space for deacons. The deacons' space is allotted facing the pulpit either on the left or the right of the altar. The position and role of deacons among the Naga Baptists therefore is almost the exact opposite of the primary meaning of the biblical concept of deacon. Whereas in New Testament times, deacons carried out service, including social care of the downtrodden, Naga Baptist deacons are power-wielders and arbiters.

Such a lopsided practice of deacons adds another dimension to the understanding or misunderstanding of the term *diakonia* – that it is not about service but about privilege. Therefore, the ecumenical movement of *diakonia* as a missional task of the church that includes advocacy for inclusive justice is an imperative task required of the church. The mission document of the World Council of Churches entitled *Together Towards Life* (TTL) has also reiterated the prophetic mission that embraces the margins produced by any systemic structures of exclusion and discrimination. The call for a prophetic *diakonia* that advocates justice is spelt out in the mission document:

> Jesus Christ relates to and embraces those who are most marginalized in society, in order to confront and transform all that denies life. This includes cultures and systems which generate and sustain massive poverty, discrimination and dehumanization, and which exploit or destroy people and the earth. Mission from the margins calls for an understanding of the complexities of power dynamics, global systems and structures, and local contextual realities. Christian mission has at times been understood and practised in ways which failed to recognise God's alignment with those consistently pushed to the margins. Therefore, mission from

[30] Renthy Keitzar, *Good News for North East India: A Theological Reader* (Jorhat, Assam: Eastern Theological College, 1995).

> the margins invites the church to re-imagine mission as a vocation from God's Spirit who works for a world where fullness of life is available for all.[31]

The interpretation of *diakonia* as advocacy and action for inclusive justice in contexts of discrimination is also emphasised by the WCC in the following words: 'Diakonia may also imply social action, aimed at dismantling oppressive cultures such as patriarchy, racism, casteism, xenophobia and other discriminatory and exclusionary practices.'[32] Ideological stances, cultural practices and institutional policies that are oppressive and exclusive are not limited to the larger society, but they have existed in churches, which have made the churches complicit with oppressive cultures. And therefore, 'the churches too need to repent of the presence and practice of these [oppressive] cultures right within, and for their derisive attitudes and theological constructions that stigmatize certain sections of society'.[33] As the preceding narrative of the gender location of the Naga women vividly depicts a complicated locus of exclusion almost to a practice of an 'institutionalised injustice', the understanding and practice of *diakonia* provides a platform for re-imagining gender-equal participation in the Naga churches. *Diakonia* as prophetic service for gender justice in the context of Naga Baptists and women in the church and the larger society calls for advocating changes in policy and practice in the church's organisation and functions. Three areas are highlighted that can be developed in this light: theological education, ecclesiastical policy, cultural critique. This also includes the existing diaconal services that are lived-practices of the Naga Christians. Existing diaconal services are an illustration of 'walking the (diaconal) walk without talking the (diaconal) talk'.[34] While compassionate service and practices for the common good do prevail among the Naga as part of their indigenous cultural worldviews, it needs to be underscored that these are performed within the patriarchal context and via gendered roles.

Diakonia and Gender in Theological Education

Theological education is the backbone of the Christian community. The integrity and quality of theological education provide the Christian community with its direction and continuity of its understanding of faith. Apart from the teaching of traditions of the faith, theological education also plays a crucial role in clarifying and contextualising faith tenets. Theological education that is

---

[31] Jooseop Keum (ed), *Together Towards Life: Mission and Evangelism in a Changing Landscape* (Geneva: WCC Publications, 2013), 37.

[32] 'Theological Perspectives on Diakonia in the 21st Century': www.oikoumene.org/en/resources/documents/wcc-programmes (accessed 4th April 2016).

[33] 'Theological Perspectives on Diakonia in the 21st Century'.

[34] For this perspective, I am grateful to Kjell Nordstokke for comments received in an earlier draft.

contextual engages the socio-cultural challenges and seeks to bring edification and awareness. Theological education therefore provides a viable platform for the concept and understanding of *diakonia* as prophetic service for inclusive justice. The University of Heidelberg has established an Institute of Diaconal Science to initiate critical inquiry and develop a discourse on practice implementation of the *diakonia* as social service. In the same manner, theological institutions should make deliberate efforts to introduce into their curriculum and pedagogy the concept and practice of *diakonia* as a social service. Theological institutions welcome women students and theological education; however, more efforts are needed towards gender inclusion.[35] In contexts like Naga Christianity, wherein women are not excluded from theological education but not given equal opportunities post-graduation, the concept of *diakonia* as a right-based movement provides a platform to advocate for their equal participation in the church's organisational structure.

The fact that Naga women were neither excluded from education nor from theological education provides significant foundation for larger gender empowerment in contemporary times. Furthermore, when Christianity was initially introduced, Naga women served as Bible women taking the good news of the new religion to the neighbouring villages. Gender identity did not limit them in participating in the evangelisation of the people. This participation, albeit limited, illustrates a germinal concept of gendered *diakonia*, which can be further extended towards equal participation in every aspect of the church and its ministry.

Diakonia and Ecclesiastical Policy towards Gender Inclusion

Re-imagining the understanding of *diakonia* beyond diverse social service helps position churches to review policies and practices that are parochial and gender-oppressive. *Diakonia* as a movement for just and inclusive communities calls for gender equality in ecclesiastical organisations.[36] The organisation of the Naga Baptist church bespeaks of explicit male-centric ecclesiastical policy and practice. While such policy and organisational structure may be traced to the mission period, it requires interrogation from a theological perspective of inclusive ethics. Ecclesiastical policy and practice that discriminate based on gender identity need to be laid bare of its theological limitations over against the foundational principle of the sovereignty of the Triune God. The practice of *diakonia* as prophetic service becomes a catalyst in such an ecclesiastical structure. The interpretation of *diakonia* as the mission of the church for social

---

[35] See Atola Longkumer, 'Gendered Theological Education: A Reading from India', in Steve Bevans, Teresa Chai, Nelson Jennings, Knud Jørgensen and Dietrich Werner (eds), *Reflecting on and Equipping for Christian Mission* (Oxford: Regnum, 2015).

[36] Theological Perspectives on Diakonia in the 21st Century': www.oikoumene.org/en/resources/documents/wcc-programmes (accessed 4th April 2016).

justice should express itself in candid critique of the traditions and practices within the church that are exclusive and discriminatory. Hence, the ethos and language of *diakonia* provide for churches to move towards a transformation of ecclesiastical practices that are parochial and fossilised remnants from the mission period.

Within the androcentric ecclesiastical organisation among the Naga Baptists, there are roles and space for women, which are diaconal in nature. The paradox lies therein. Women are active agents of diaconal services in the church – in fact, most of the crucial diaconal services of compassionate, missional and evangelism activities are performed by women members and the women's department of the Naga Baptist church. During different life seasons such as childbirth, death, illness and marriage, it is the women members who visit the homes for prayer and support. Women form the backbone of the community through their participation in prayers and personal support. An example of women's participation in diaconal service can be vividly observed in the Naga church movement for an alcohol-free society. In order to implement this principle of an alcohol-free community, vehicles and visitors to villages are inspected at the village gate. This inspection to ensure that alcohol and other substance are not brought into the village is carried out by the women members. To be sure, this practice presents a multi-layered analysis and the question of success at curbing alcohol consumption requires a major analysis. The point is the participation of women in diaconal services for the good of the community, without being labelled as such. These unnamed albeit existing in practice of women performing diaconal activities on behalf of the church do serve as signs and opportunitiesthat can be transformed into the more pronounced and equal participation of women in ecclesiastical organisations.

Diakonia from a Gender Perspective and a Cultural Critique

Culture remains a potent category from many aspects of discourse, not least theological and missional. Criticisms as well as the embrace of culture are traditions of human encounters in its diverse forms. Gender discrimination in many instances is rooted in cultural notions and practices: for instance, the Naga women and the complex role allotted to them in the church are derived from the larger Naga culture. The pre-Christian Naga gender relationship was one of stratified hierarchy, wherein women were excluded from the male-only decision-making forums. While women enjoyed relative freedom and rights within the clan structures, they were still excluded from the clan council, which served as the authority. The conversion to Christianity did not alter this gender hierarchy; rather, it was transplanted into the church organisation structure, solidified by gender roles prevailing in the missions. The Naga Baptist church and its gendered participation demonstrate the need of cultural critique. The concept of *diakonia* as prophetic service and as advocacy makes it impartial and objective; hence, *diakonia* becomes a vehicle for cultural critique. *Diakonia* boldly denounces injustice derived from cultures that are parochial.

Conclusion

The above discussion of *diakonia* as a concept and practice that is repositioned as a crucial action towards inclusive and just communities is fundamentally undergirded by the theological conviction of God's sovereignty over creation. The church participates in God's mission of reconciliation and embrace of all, and *diakonia* with its diverse actions of compassionate service, advocacy and solidarity provides a channel for translating the vision of healed and inclusive communities into lived realities. Contexts such as Naga Christians and their gender hierarchy, conditioned in a complex manner by both indigenous cultures and Christianity, bring a dual dimension to the crucial discourse of *diakonia* as an advocacy service for inclusive justice. Particularly from a gender perspective, the renewed development of *diakonia* enables communities to critique and construct inclusive communities. The platform and discourse of *diakonia* as a movement towards inclusive justice serve as a significant prophetic mission of the church towards the transformation of parochial and exclusive structures into communities that are foretaste of God's kingdom.

Women's Religious Agency: How Swedish Deaconesses Negotiate Secularism and Changes in Welfare Society in Everyday Life

Annette Leis-Peters

Introduction

'Is secularism bad for women?' asks the British scholar in religious studies, Kristin Aune, in a contribution to the internet discussion forum opendemocracy.net.[1] Her question is a conscious reversion of a question asked by women's rights activists and political scientists in the 1980s and 1990s, namely: Is religion and multiculturalism bad for women? The latter question emerged from the experience that the positive vision of multiculturalism as a peaceful co-existence of different cultures within a society resulted in the deprivation of the rights of some groups, among them women who belonged to certain ethnic, cultural or religious minority communities. Prominent examples that were used in the debate to illustrate how women were forced to live under disadvantaged social conditions due to gender-hierarchical values and practices in their minority community are polygamist family models or (full-face) veils.[2] But does secularism disadvantage religious women?

In international studies about values and beliefs, the Nordic countries often score as among the most secular.[3] Even though the majority of the population is still in membership of the former Lutheran state churches, these value studies show that Nordic citizens believe only to a low degree in the key teachings of Christianity and rarely practise their religion.[4] However, as in the whole of Europe, globalization and immigration have put the issue of religion in the public sphere on the agenda of the Nordic countries again. In a Nordic setting,

---

[1] Kristin Aune, 'Is secularism bad for women?', in *Opendemocracy.net*: https://www.opendemocracy.net/transformation/kristin-aune/is-secularism-bad-for-women (accessed 30th March 2016).

[2] Susan Moller Okin, 'Mångkulturalism – kvinnor i kläm?', in Susan Moller Okin (ed), *Mångkulturalism – kvinnor i kläm?* (Göteborg, Sweden: Daidalos, 2002), 13-30.

[3] Pippa Norris and Ronald Inglehart, *Sacred and Secular: Religion and Politics Worldwide,* 2nd edition (New York: Cambridge University Press, 2011).

[4] Thorleif Pettersson and Yilmaz Esmer, *Vilka är annorlunda? Om invandrares möte med svensk kultur* (Norrköping, Sweden: Integrationsverket, 2005).

where religion has been moved to the private sphere during the period of industrial society, religion is discussed as a 'unique' source of difference that has the potential to come in conflict with the general values of society. The Swedish ethicist Hans Ingvar Roth claims that religion is more exclusive than other collective identities, because a person normally has only one religion, but can embrace several languages or ethnicities.[5] Therefore, the Swedish authorities tend to avoid debates about religion.[6] What does such a secularized setting mean for newcomers who take religion in the public sphere for granted? What does it mean for women who have chosen a religious lifestyle?

Inspired by the current debate about the new visibility of religion, the chapter looks into recent contemporary history in order to find examples of negations of religion in the secularized Nordic context. It focuses on deaconesses in Sweden, a group of women who choose an entirely religious lifestyle, and asks what ongoing secularization has meant for their identity as women and as professional workers.

The chapter starts with explaining the example of deaconesses in Sweden in the decades between 1950 and 1970, then sets a theoretical framework for studying women's religiosity in secularized frameworks, presents the empirical material of in-depth interviews with retired deaconesses before it analyses the interviews by asking how secularization influenced the gender and professional identity of these women.

The Case of Deaconesses in Sweden

Deaconess motherhouses are part of the international and ecumenical diaconal movement of the nineteenth century. The industrialization and urbanization of the European countries of this time weakened the social structures of the societies that had previously been rural and caused poverty and social misery. The bad social situation brought many Christian social initiatives into being that attracted not least (unmarried) women. The initiatives were often formed as independent associations and only loosely connected with the established churches. The Kaiserswerth model of deaconess motherhouses was one of the most successful initiatives for women's diaconal work. The German pastor Theodor Fliedner and his wife Caroline were both inspired by the texts about deaconesses in the New Testament and by Catholic religious orders for women that cared for injured soldiers in the wars all round the world. They developed a model of a Protestant women's community with obligations and rights similar

5 Hans Ingvar Roth, *Mångkulturalismens utmaningar* (Lund, Sweden: Studentlitteratur, 2005), 21-22.

6 See, for example, Karin Borevi, Annette Leis-Peters and Anna-Sara Lind, 'Layers of inconsistency: A Multidisciplinary Analysis of the Swedish National Agency on Education's Guidelines on the Muslim headscarf', in Anna-Sara Lind, Mia Lövheim and Ulf Zackariasson (eds), *Religion, Law and Democracy: New Challenges for Society and Research* (Lund, Sweden: Nordic Academic Press, 2016), 179-98.

to those of Catholic orders. Women who joined the community and became deaconesses were not allowed to marry, could not choose the location of work (they were sent by the institution), and did not get any income of their own. Their identity as deaconesses was visible for everyone due to the deaconess dresses that they had to wear. In return, they were supplied and cared for within the institution throughout their whole life. Since women at that time were generally dependent on having husbands who provided for them, religious communities like deaconess motherhouses became an attractive alternative, not least in times of hardship.[7]

Deaconess motherhouses on the lines of the Kaiserswerth model were also the most successful type in Sweden. Even though some of the institutions were founded with other ideas and paradigms, most of them adapted to the Kaiserswerth example during their first few decades (including the Samariterhemmet in Uppsala that is the focus of this chapter). Many of the institutions focused on health care and nursing when they were founded. They ran their own hospitals in order to train nurses and they sent trained deaconesses into various parishes all over the country where it was intended they would provide primary health care.[8]

The diaconal institution Samariterhemmet followed the same example and expanded in the field of local primary health care. In addition, it was involved in a number of institutions for children and young people which it had taken over on the request of the municipalities. However, when Sweden entered an economic upswing directly after World War II and prioritized the upgrading of the welfare state, the standing of diaconal institutions changed rapidly. The Swedish welfare state became stronger and stronger and no longer needed independent welfare providers like the diaconal institutions. In particular, primary health care and care for children and young people were two areas where the state aimed at a nationwide network of public services for all citizens that was supposed to be provided by the municipalities. By the mid-1940s, the public primary health care system had been developed so well all over the country that deaconesses were not needed any more.[9]

Due to the changed situation, deaconesses who were sent to the parishes no longer worked in nursing (even though they had been trained as nurses) but were involved in all kinds of parish activities such as children's and youth work, scouting or the care of elderly people. While the deaconesses' new role in the parishes often went ahead smoothly, the changes in children and youth welfare services were more dramatic. When the municipalities took back these

---

[7] Jutta Schmidt, *Beruf Schwester: Mutterhausdiakonie im 19. Jahrhundert* (Frankfurt am Main, Germany, and New York: Campus, 1998).

[8] Bengt Ingmar Kilström, *Kyrka och diakoni I +II* (Åbo, Finland: Åbo akademi, 1986).

[9] Annette Leis-Peters, *Den kyrkliga diakonins roll inom ramen för två välfärdssystem. En jämförande fallstudie av två diakoniinstitutioner in Sverige och Tyskland* (Uppsala, Sweden: Diakonivetenskapliga institutet, 2004).

services, this practically meant that they closed down the institutions (and, with them, the diaconal institutions) that had run these services before, often for several decades. At the time of the closure of diaconal children and youth institutions emerged struggles in which the (male) representatives of the diaconal institutions often acted and spoke out in very apologetic ways. They expressed their disappointment about their rejection by the state and society both in the internal communication within the institution and through external channels. Their perspective was that the important contribution of church and *diakonia* was neglected and that this was a loss for society.[10]

In addition to the smooth transition and contested take-overs, co-operation between diaconal institutions on the one hand and state and municipalities on the other was a third scenario in the expansion of the Swedish welfare state. This scenario was most likely in fields where the technical development and rising expectations of the users resulted in considerable cost increases. Typical examples were hospitals. In the 1950s and 1960s, both the buildings and the facilities of the diaconal hospitals were often old and outdated. To stay in the hospital business, diaconal institutions had to upgrade. Since they did not have the resources for these upgrades, they had to join forces with the municipalities. Common funding implied common management of the hospitals. The common hospital boards became arenas where the representatives of municipality and diaconal institution fought for a diaconal versus a secular profile of the hospital.[11] All three scenarios could be described as secularization of the field of welfare.

The development of the Swedish welfare system is closely connected with the project of gender equality. Sweden was among the first countries that replaced the model of the male family provider with the model of two family providers. From the 1960s, new laws were introduced that gave women an independent position within the welfare system, including retirement benefits and taxes.[12] According to the new paradigm, women were supposed to have full-time employment and leadership positions just like men. The task of the welfare services was to support women in this endeavour – for example, by establishing a comprehensive network of full-time day care institutions for children all over the country that also served hot lunches.[13] The Swedish

---

[10] Elisabeth Christiansson, *Kyrklig och social reform. Motiveringar till diakoni 1845-1965* (Skellefteå, Sweden: Artos & Norma, 2006); Annette Leis-Peters, 'Hidden by civil society and religion? Diaconal institutions as welfare providers in the growing Swedish welfare state', in Pirjo Markkola and Ingela Nauman (eds), *Religion and the Welfare State,* Special Issue of the *Journal of Church and State*, 56:1 (2014), 105-27.

[11] Annette Leis-Peters, *Den kyrkliga diakonins roll inom ramen för två välfärdssystem: En jämförande fallstudie av två diakoniinstitutioner in Sverige och Tyskland* (Uppsala, Sweden: Diakonivetenskapliga institutet, 2004).

[12] Anders Bäckström, Ninna Edgardh Beckman and Per Pettersson, *Religious Change in Northern Europe: The Case of Sweden* (Stockholm: Verbum, 2004).

[13] Yvonne Hirdman, *Att lägga livet till rätta – studier i svensk folkhemspolitik*

welfare state, together with the liberation movements of the 1960s and 1970s, redefined traditional gender roles.

Against the background of these changes, the monastery-like lifestyle that the deaconesses had chosen seemed exotic at its best. They lived not only in economic dependency, but were also governed by a religious institution when it came to workplace, sexuality and outfit. Bearing in mind that churches were among the advocates of a traditional family model and represented lifestyles like the deaconess mother houses, the establishment of new frameworks and patterns for women in society could also be interpreted as a kind of secularization of gender roles. It is not surprising that the Swedish deaconess motherhouses were among the first in the world to abandon the strict rules of the Kaiserswerth model. However, it takes much longer to change a lifestyle that an individual has chosen and maybe does not even want to change. The deaconesses who started their service in a still traditional model around the 1940s were not only challenged by changing gender roles, but also by changes in their professional setting. From being a part of welcomed diaconal work in society, they became either superfluous (for example, in the case of primary health services) or contested (in the case of welfare services for young people and children), or they had to co-operate with municipalities in much more secular settings (in the case of hospitals). What did this mean for them? How did they negotiate the changes in their professional and gender identities?

Women, Religion and Secularization

Before we go to the narratives of the deaconesses and the interpretations of their lives, we should take a look at theoretical approaches to help us analyze what they report. Comparisons of women's and men's religiosity often argue that women are more religious than men.[14] This includes both what they believe and how they practise religion in their everyday lives.[15] Does an extension of this hypothesis mean that women are more affected than men, when the frameworks of society become more and more secular?

At the same time that secularization is used as a buzzword in public debates, it is important to remember that there is no such thing as *the* secularization theory; there are many different approaches that, from different levels, look at the relationship between religion and society. Secularization is, for example, often related to functional differentiation, which can be explained as an effect of the transition from rural to industrial society. The logic of industrial society is rationalization and specialization. This has an impact on all institutions of

(Stockholm: Carlssons, 2010).

[14] Kate Miriam Loewenthal, Andrew K. MacLeod and Marco Cinnirella, 'Are women more religious than men? Gender differences in religious activity among religious groups in the UK', in *Personality and Individual Differences,* 32:1 (2002), 133-39.

[15] Grace Davie, *The Sociology of Religion: A Critical Agenda* (London: Sage, 2013).

society including religion. In a more and more differentiated society, the social relationships of religious institutions change at least at three levels: between religious institutions and society as a whole, between religious institutions and other institutions in society, and between religious institutions, groups and individuals. If religion is no longer a 'canopy' that holds together the whole society,[16] religious institutions also have a different and weaker role in relation to other social institutions that they have traditionally been involved in, such as school or social and health care. If religious institutions are less present in other social institutions, they also have fewer opportunities to influence and control the lives of individuals.[17] These processes can be interpreted in various ways. Pettersson and Leis-Peters[18] refer to the Japanese scholar of religious studies, Keiichi Yanagawa, who interprets the religious changes that have been caused by functional differentiation in three ways. The first interpretation is that the phenomena of religion become smaller and smaller in society until they disappear totally. The second understanding is that religion gets separate, clearly limited, space in society, and the third understanding is that traditional forms of religion diminish while new forms emerge.[19]

Since both the gender and the professional identity of deaconesses are based on religion, all three ways of religious change that Yanagawa describes are likely to be perceived by deaconesses, but in particular the latter two. With regard to their welfare work, they are supposed to experience how their room for manoeuvre becomes more and more limited at the same time as traditional forms of religion (that they represent through the gender roles that are part of the lifestyle they have chosen) diminish in society. There are no studies that focus on this development from the perspective of deaconesses.

However, there are studies that show how challenging it is to handle a public religious identity in secular Sweden. The Swedish anthropologist Maria Zackariasson has, for example, interviewed 21 young people between 15 and 21 years of age who were active in Christian youth organizations.[20] The interviews illustrate that these young people are aware of (or anticipate) that religious commitment is connected with a particular collective identity. This collective identity is supposed to be different from the mainstream Swedish youth culture that is formed by hedonism. In relation to the mainstream culture, religiously active young people are a minority that stands out. The collective

[16] Peter Berger, *The Sacred Canopy: Elements of a Sociological Theory of Religion* (Garden City, NY: Doubleday, 1969).

[17] Per Pettersson and Annette Leis-Peters, 'Religion i Sverige: Kontinuitet och förändring', in Mia Lövheim and Magdalena Nordin (eds), *Sociologiska perspektiv på religion i Sverige* (Malmö, Sweden: Gleerups, 2015), 37-52.

[18] Pettersson and Leis-Peters, 'Religion i Sverige: Kontinuitet och förändring'.

[19] Keiichi Yanagawa, 'Introductory thesis: Beyond the secularization thesis', in *Journal of Oriental Studies,* 26:1 (1987), 1-4.

[20] Maria Zackariasson, 'Being Yourself: Identity and Self-presentation among Youths in Christian Youth Organizations', in *Young,* 22:2 (2014), 153-70.

identity that they are labelled with could be described as negative stereotypes 'of being strange or boring'[21] or too well-behaved. The interviews show that young people develop different strategies to handle this labelling, which Zackariasson groups in three stances. One strategy is to avoid the issue of religious involvement with friends and schoolmates outside the church. The opposite approach is to take a stand and be open about one's church involvement. This implies being prepared to be categorized in a certain way and to defend oneself. The third stance is what Zackariasson calls 'handling categorizations'. Young people who are using this strategy filter and form the public information that they give about their church engagement according to the negative stereotypes that they anticipate. All information is meant to contradict the stereotypes.

There are obvious parallels between the situation of the deaconesses in the expanding Swedish welfare state and the position of active young church members in hedonist Swedish youth culture. Both groups are placed in a separate limited room, and both relate to traditions that are becoming more marginal. Do deaconesses use similar strategies like the young Christians to deal with increasing secularization?

Secularization theories place in a bigger picture the challenges that deaconesses are likely to meet in the secularized, gender-equal Swedish welfare state. Other studies on negotiations about religion and gender help to create awareness of strategies and agency in the narratives of the deaconesses.

The Material

The empirical material of the chapter consists of ten in-depth interviews with retired Swedish deaconesses. The interviews were conducted in 2009. All interviews were taped and transcribed.[22] They followed a tentative interview guide with the following six thematic areas: socialization, vocation as a deacon, professional role, gender, social challenges, and spirituality and theology. A list of sub-questions was developed to help the interviewer to cover the different areas of the guide and to make the narrative flow. The interviews lasted between one and 2½ hours. The interview guide was not developed to answer a specific research question, but to collect the experiences and narratives of deaconesses, who were well advanced in years.[23]

---

[21] Zackariasson, 'Being Yourself: Identity and Self-presentation', 165.

[22] The interviews were conducted and transcribed by Deacon Rosita Borum-Halvars (master in diaconal studies).

[23] For parallel projects, see Silke Köser, *Denn eine Diakonisse darf kein Alltagsmensch sein: Kollektive Identitäten Kaiserswerther Diakonissen 1836-1914* (Leipzig: Evangelische Verlagsanstalt, 2006); Ute Gause and Cordula Lissner, 'Einleitung: Auf der Suche nach dem Alltagsgedächtnis einer Institution', in Ute Gause and Cordula Lissner (eds), *Kosmos Diakonissenmutterhaus: Geschichte und Gedächtnis einer*

During almost all their history from the 1830s until today, deaconess motherhouses have been characterized by a gender dichotomy and gender hierarchy placing the women in the role of daughters and service providers while the institutions were governed by male directors. This explains why the historical documentation of deaconess motherhouses is dominated by the men in charge, neglecting the perspectives of the much more numerous female workers. Consequently, there is a need for complementing the male-dominated documentation of the institutions' history with material and sources that make visible how women contributed to and experienced the development. All the interviews have been with deaconesses at the diaconal foundation 'Samariterhemmet', the second-oldest deaconess institution in Sweden (founded in 1882), based in Uppsala, sixty kilometres north-west of Stockholm.

The interviewed deaconesses were born between 1920 and 1935. Nine of them had been installed as deaconesses between 1946 and 1959. One them had been working within the institution for a long time, but was not installed until the mid-1980s. This means that all of them – as representatives of a deaconess motherhouse and a lifestyle that was experienced as quite extreme both socially and religiously by Swedish mainstream society – have experienced the expansion of the Swedish welfare state and the development of the Swedish model of gender equality.

Experiences from Being a Deaconess

In the thematic content, analysis of the interview's two perspectives are highlighted: encounter with the welfare state and gender negotiations.

Encounter with the expanding welfare state

In general, the interviews are evidence of the deaconesses being very positive about the welfare state and gender equality. They refer to the professional work that was done in the realm of public welfare services. Likewise, they mention that many female leaders were installed in the public welfare services during their professional career and that they believe that these women did a very good job as leaders.

They are positive, even though all the three above possible scenarios of encounter between diaconal institutions and expanding welfare state were experienced by at least some of the interviewees. Some have worked all their professional life in parishes. These deaconesses tell about their education in nursing, but also about their tasks which were mostly of a pedagogical nature (Sunday school, groups for children and young people, afternoons for elderly people). None of the interviewees questions that they, as educated nurses, should work as a kind of 'curate' as several of them formulate it. They seem

---

protestantischen Frauengemeinschaft (Leipzig: Evangelische Verlagsanstalt 2005, 9-32).

content with what they have done and often express that they had a very good relationship with the local pastor. At the same time, they are aware of the boundaries to primary health care, and experience it as a delicate task to avoid crossing the line. However, one of the deaconesses tries to overcome the lines that have been drawn between parish and local primary health care. She makes contact with both the responsible local physician and with the public primary health nurse. Her offer to help in primary health care is first rejected by both physician and nurse. However, when she repeats her willingness to participate, the nurse involves her finally in a case of terminal care. The co-operation at the deathbed leads to a continuation of the co-operation. The deaconess has become a resource for primary health care.

Another group among the interviewees spends all its working life in hospital. The interviewees witness that the funding body changes from a diaconal institution to a municipality. Nevertheless, the deaconesses often choose to continue to work at the same hospital. One of the deaconesses remembers that she was not alone having a Christian background. Many of her colleagues in the secular hospital also had a Christian training. Sometimes it is even possible to give the work a diaconal profile within a secular setting. One interviewee mentions that they organized prayers at her ward in a secular hospital and that all the colleagues were positive about that.

One of the deaconesses worked at an institution for young girls that got into conflict with the public authorities and some representatives of the media. Society asked if the diaconal institution really did meaningful work among the young girls while the deaconess herself experienced how all the staff were working hard for the girls. This made a deep impression on the deaconess. When asked for challenges with regard to changes in the welfare system, she refers directly to this situation as the only challenge that she remembers.

Overall, the deaconesses give a positive picture of their co-operation with the expanding welfare state. Instead of perceiving the public welfare services as competitors, they find ways to collaborate and even to bring a religious dimension into the work. The only negative experience comes from an institution for youth welfare services which is in direct conflict with the public authorities. As long as conflicts and competition can be avoided, collaboration goes smoothly for the deaconesses both in secular and church settings. However, this presupposes either that the deaconesses continue to work for the same institution even if it has become secular, or that the parishes find new tasks for deaconesses after their participation in primary health care becomes unnecessary.

Gender negotiations

The interviews contain only very limited material about gender negotiations with the majority society. The deaconesses seem to have taken a conscious decision regarding their lifestyle which they do not have problems in motivating afterwards. This is true both for those interviewees who maintained a traditional deaconess lifestyle all their life, and for those who married later in life but kept contact with the deaconess motherhouse. Some of the deaconesses told how their parents and families did not like their decision to become deaconesses because of the monastic lifestyle. This indicates that they considered the gender roles of society before becoming deaconesses. None of the interviewees reflects explicitly on gender equality or sexual liberation either. The only aspects that are taken up in the interviews are that women become (good) leaders in public welfare services and that the retirement pensions change during their time as deaconesses.

The gender negotiations that the deaconesses talk about most take place in the church and the parishes. Several of the interviewees mention that the parishes were expecting deaconesses to be poorly educated women who were prepared to help with whatever was needed, but not educated professionals with a competence of their own. These expectations reflect the existing church hierarchy. One of the interviewees recalls: 'We were considered as a kind of maidservant, in particular by the wife of the vicar. So we were expected to help in the vicarage when they had invitations.' Another deaconess remembers that a male parish member said clearly in a professional discussion that he did not expect the deaconesses to be intellectual. The examples show that there was need of gender negotiations in the parishes. Some of the deaconesses had difficulties in being accepted as professionals. While the vocation made the male pastors into professionals and authorities, it seemed to have the opposite effect for some of deaconesses. By being an ordained deaconess they had to be available for whatever work that was needed. The fact that almost all the interviewees touch upon this challenge indicates that this is not only about single cases. While the rest of society undertakes huge steps towards more gender equality, the deaconesses are still in a gender-hierarchical universe.

While the deaconesses are critical about how they were perceived by some of the parish representatives, and while they demand respect and equality, at the same time they reproduce the traditional gender roles in the case of the ordination of women into the pastor's office (a reform that the Swedish state imposed on the Church of Sweden as a state church in the year 1958). Some of the interviewees remember this reform as one of the major challenges that they experienced during their working life. Even though it is highly politically incorrect in today's Sweden to refuse the ordination of women, several of the interviewees indicate that this is what they did. While the deaconesses demanded more rights for themselves, they did not hold the same view when it came to the rights of other women within the church hierarchy. In the case of the ordination of women into the pastor's office, they argue with traditional theological arguments for gender dichotomy.

Interestingly, the arena for gender negotiations for deaconesses is the church and the parishes, and not the majority society. While they see and criticize when their agency is limited due to religious traditions, some of them use the religious traditions themselves to limit the agency of other women in the church. In this respect, their gender negotiations could be characterized as ambiguous.

Conclusions

At the beginning of this chapter, we asked if secularization was bad for women. The empirical material is far too limited to give a comprehensive answer. Nevertheless, the case of the deaconesses can contribute with some interesting aspects that might enrich the debate. From an outside perspective, it seemed natural to assume that the deaconesses negotiate mainly with society about the general. The interviews illustrate that they actually are negotiating more within the church. Thus, the ongoing process of introducing gender equality in Swedish society affects them. Because of this, they pay attention to and remember situations in which their professionalism and their equality were questioned within the realm of the church. This shows that society still has a strong impact on the structures of the church while the influence of the church in society is decreasing. On the other hand, the deaconesses reject the influence of society – which they nevertheless make use of for themselves, when it comes to the demands of other women in the church. Their ambiguity in this question can be interpreted as an illustration of how the power balance between church and state shifts in favour of the state (one of the developments that are described as secularization). The deaconesses refuse the interference of the state in the church (in the case of the ordination of women into the pastor's office), but at the same time they acknowledge that some of the gender reforms of the state have improved their own position (gender equality in professional life, retirement pensions).

With regard to the negotiations with the secularizing, expanding welfare state, the rootedness of the deaconesses in the church gives them a collective identity that helps them to interact with the welfare state in a collaborative and constructive way. Almost all narratives about the encounter with the welfare state are positive, but at the same time the deaconesses also experience situations that require strategies that have some parallels with the strategies that Zackariasson has developed in her study about how religiously active young people who negotiate with the majority youth culture. Like them, some of the deaconesses have to filter information and activities in the collaboration with the public welfare state (for example, in hospitals and primary health care). Like them, they are also avoiding the religious dimension when needed (again in hospitals and primary health care). Only if they are challenged – for example, in the fights related to diaconal youth institutions – do they take a stand.

However, another important finding from the interviews is that the deaconesses in general would rather talk about the church than about welfare services. This indicates that they have made a decision for a lifestyle that is publically recognisable as religious. Changes in society do not make them want to reverse this decision.

To answer the question from the beginning: the deaconesses seem to be not very affected by secularism. Why not, one could ask, bearing in mind all the changes in society that would give them reason to be affected? Compared with the young people in Zackariasson's study who struggle so hard with their identity in relation to the majority youth culture, the deaconesses seem to be satisfied with their position as representatives of religion and the church in society. One explanation could be that they have made a conscious decision when they were younger and there is no reason for them to reverse this decision just because things around them are changing. Another explanation would be that they got what they wanted. That religion gets a separate, more limited space in society is one way of describing secularisation. To become a deaconess according to the Kaiserswerth model means opting for a separate, more limited space. However, the case of the deaconesses shows that such a limited space is not necessarily identical with isolation, but can imply both collaboration with society and agency. It would deepen the understanding of women's religiosity if the case of the Swedish deaconesses could be compared with cases of other religious women in other contexts.

Bibliography

Aune, Kristin, 'Is secularism bad for women?' in *Opendemocracy.net*: https://www.opendemocracy.net/transformation/kristin-aune/is-secularism-bad-for-women

Bäckström, Anders, Ninna Edgardh Beckman and Per Pettersson, *Religious Change in Northern Europe: The Case of Sweden* (Stockholm: Verbum, 2004),

Berger, Peter, *The Sacred Canopy: Elements of a Sociological Theory of Religion* (Garden City, NY: Doubleday, 1969).

Borevi, Karin, Annette Leis-Peters, and Anna-Sara Lind, 'Layers of inconsistency: A Multidisciplinary Analysis of the Swedish National Agency on Education's Guidelines on the Muslim Headscarf', in Anna-Sara Lind, Mia Lövheim and Ulf Zackariasson (eds), *Religion, Law and Democracy: New Challenges for Society and Research* (Lund, Sweden: Nordic Academic Press, 2016).

Christiansson, Elisabeth, *Kyrklig och social reform. Motiveringar till diakoni 1845-1965 [Church and Social Reform. Motivations for diakonia 1845-1965]* (Skellefteå, Sweden: Artos & Norma, 2006).

Davie, Grace, *The Sociology of Religion: A Critical Agenda* (London: Sage, 2013).

Gause, Ute and Cordula Lissner, 'Einleitung. Auf der Suche nach dem Alltagsgedächtnis einer Institution' [Introduction: In Search of the Everyday Memory of an Institution], in Ute Gause and Cordula Lissner (eds), *Kosmos Diakonissenmutterhaus: Geschichte und Gedächtnis einer protestantischen Frauengemeinschaft* [Cosmos Deaconess Motherhouse: History and Memory of a Protestant Women's Community] (Leipzig, Germany: Evangelische Verlagsanstalt 2005).

Hirdman, Yvonne, *Att lägga livet till rätta – studier i svensk folkhemspolitik [To Arrange Live – Studies in Swedish People's Home Policy]* (Stockholm: Carlssons, 2010).

Kilström, Bengt Ingmar, *Kyrka och diakoni I + II [Church and Diakonia]* (Åbo, Finland: Åbo akademi, 1986).

Köser, Silke, *Denn eine Diakonisse darf kein Alltagsmensch sein. Kollektive Identitäten Kaiserswerther Diakonissen 1836-1914 [Because a Deaconess may not be an Everyday Person: Collective Identities of Kaiserwerth Deaconesses 1836-1914]* (Leipzig, Germany: Evangelische Verlagsanstalt, 2006).

Leis-Peters, Annette, *Den kyrkliga diakonins roll inom ramen för två välfärdssystem. En jämförande fallstudie av två diakoniinstitutioner in Sverige och Tyskland* [The Role of Church Diaconal Work within Two Welfare Systems: A Comparative Case Study of Two Diaconal Institutions in Sweden and Germany] (Uppsala, Sweden: Diakonivetenskapliga institutet, 2004).

Leis-Peters, Annette, 'Hidden by civil society and religion? Diaconal institutions as welfare providers in the growing Swedish welfare state', in Pirjo Markkola and Ingela Nauman (eds), *Religion and the Welfare State,* Special Issue of the *Journal of Church and State*, 56:1 (2014).

Loewenthal, Kate Miriam, Andrew K. MacLeod and Marco Cinnirella, 'Are women more religious than men? Gender differences in religious activity among religious groups in the UK', in *Personality and Individual Differences,* 32:1 (2002).

Moller Okin, Susan, 'Mångkulturalism – kvinnor i kläm?' [Multiculturalism – Women in the Squeeze?], in Susan Moller Okin (ed), *Mångkulturalism – kvinnor i kläm? [Multiculturalism – Women in the Squeeze?]* (Göteborg, Sweden: Daidalos, 2002).

Pippa Norris and Ronald Inglehart, *Sacred and Secular: Religion and Politics Worldwide,* 2nd edition (New York: Cambridge University Press, 2011).

Pettersson, Per and Annette Leis-Peters, 'Religion i Sverige: Kontinuitet och förändring' [Religion in Sweden. Continuity and Change], in Mia Lövheim and Magdalena Nordin (eds), *Sociologiska perspektiv på religion i Sverige [Sociological Perspectives on Religion in Sweden]* (Malmö, Sweden: Gleerups, 2015).

Pettersson, Thorleif and Yilmaz Esmer, *Vilka är annorlunda? Om invandrares möte med svensk kultur [Who is different? Om migrants encounter with Swedish culture]* (Norrköping, Sweden: Integrationsverket, 2005).

Roth, Hans Ingvar, *Mångkulturalismens utmaningar [The Challenges of Multiculturalism]* (Lund, Sweden: Studentlitteratur, 2005).

Schmidt, Jutta, *Beruf Schwester: Mutterhausdiakonie im 19. Jahrhundert [Profession Sister. Motherhouse Diakonia in the 19th Century]* (Frankfurt am Main, Germany, and New York: Campus, 1998).

Yanagawa, Keiichi, 'Introductory thesis: Beyond the secularization thesis', in *Journal of Oriental Studies,* 26:1 (1987).

Zackariasson, Maria, 'Being Yourself: Identity and Self-presentation among Youths in Christian Youth Organizations', in *Young,* 22:2 (2014).

Conviviality, Diakonia and Gender

Kari Karsrud Korslien

Introduction

In this chapter I want to examine diaconal work in a parish called Fjell near Drammen in Norway, in a gender perspective.[1] This parish is situated in a multicultural area where believers of different religions live side-by-side. As an important part of the diaconal work, the deacon in one of the local parishes has since 2011 invited women to a gym in the cellar of the church.[2] People from the neighbourhood do gymnastics together; which they do not have the possibility of doing elsewhere; they laugh a lot and they experience a lot of joy when they are together.

The work can be described in different ways. It can be described in terms of fellowship and conviviality. The term 'conviviality' was first used in the contemporary context by the Austrian philosopher and Roman Catholic priest Ivan Illich, who referred to the idea of creative relationships between people, and people and their environment. Conviviality is seen as an art of living, a free give-and-take between people as they create their own reality. It has also been used as a new explanation of multicultural living as it refers to the everyday interactions and practice of living together on equal terms.[3] This approach is connected with the idea of mutual empowerment among people and a better life for marginalised and excluded people and groups.

Similarly the diaconal work connected with the 'Mountain in Movement' can also be described as 'diapraxis' in the sense that its aim is to connect people of different faiths. In 1988, the Danish theologian Lissi Rasmussen proposed the term 'diapraxis' in relation to inter-faith co-operation and co-existence.[4] Diapraxis is action together in solidarity that engages in the promotion of justice, a better quality of life, and the alleviation of human

[1] Fjell is a common name in Norway and means 'mountain'.
[2] The gym is called 'Fjell i bevegelse' and means 'Mountain in Movement'.
[3] Ivan Illich, 'Tools for Conviviality' (London: 2001) in Marion Boyers and Paul Gilroy, *Postcolonial Melancholia* (New York: Colombia University Press, 2005).
[4] Lutheran World Federation, *Diakonia in Context, Transformation, Reconciliation, Empowerment* (Geneva: Lutheran World Federation, 2009), 87.

suffering. [5] This method for diaconal work can also be related to ideas connected with Community Action-Based Learning for Empowerment (CABLE). In 2013 Jouko Porkka and Marja Pentikäinen at the Diaconia University of Applied Sciences edited a report about *Community of the Future* and focused on the Challenges and New Approaches to Community-Based Social Work and Diakonia from the CABLE approach. Originally the aim of the CABLE project, a seven-nation project, was to develop an approach to community-based work and community *diakonia* based on practices that support change and transformation.[6] In my opinion, the method of co-operation and learning from one another in the diaconal work in Fjell may also be characterized as a kind of a local CABLE project.

The theory of gender, with a focus on Martha Nussbaum's theory on capabilities, may be useful in the discussion of methods in *diakonia* and practical diaconal work.[7] The background for Nussbaum's theory is two very simple questions: What are people actually able to do and to be? What real opportunities are available to people? Setting priorities in community work can be a challenge, but the theory of capabilities may give some important perspectives on gender issues in local church development. We will therefore examine why a gym is an important expression of *diakonia*, and in what way the method of conviviality and diapraxis can influence opportunities and help realize women's capabilities.

The Congregation

Fjell congregation is close to Drammen, the fifth largest city in the country and the second largest immigrant city in Norway, after Oslo. 25% of the population are immigrants or born in Norway to immigrant parents. Drammen is divided into eight districts and in one of the districts, Austad / Fjell, almost half the population (44%) are immigrants or born in Norway to immigrant parents. There are nearly 8,000 people living in the district of Austad / Fjell and, unusually for Norway where the Protestant church is the majority church, only 2,000 of the citizens are members of the Church of Norway.[8] Approximately 80% of the pupils in the local school in Fjell have immigrant backgrounds.

---

[5] Lutheran World Federation, *Diakonia in Context, Transformation, Reconciliation, Empowerment*, 88.

[6] Tony Addy, 'New approaches to community-based work, social service, and Diakonia: Challenges from the CABLE approach', in *Diakonia Journal for the Study of Christian Social Practice*, 4:2 (Göttingen, Germany: Vandenhoeck & Ruprecht, 2013), 194-215.

[7] Martha Nussbaum, *Creating Capabilities: The Human Development Approach* (London: Belknap Press of Harvard University Press, 2011).

[8] Ivar Flaten, working as a pastor in Fjell congregation, is the editor of the book *En by på et fjell kan ikke skjules: Fjell kirke 1984-2014 [A town on a mountain cannot be hidden. Mountain church 1984-2014]* (Drammen, Norway: Fjell menighetsråd, 2015), 65.

The church, whose vision is ‘Fjell Church: A meeting place for all’, has in recent years been active in devising a large local project called ‘Fjell 2020’. This project aims to provide the Austad / Fjell district with improvements in terms of both equipment and buildings by the year 2020, but also improvements for the health and welfare of the community. The deacon in the parish, a professional social worker with a master’s in *diakonia*, has been active in this work and, together with others, she created a gym for women in Fjell Church.[9] The initiative was started in partnership between the local church, Drammen Municipality and Buskerud Pakistani Women Association five years ago and, later on, others have contributed to this co-operation. Exercise equipment was purchased and an aerobic trainer engaged.[10] Since then, nearly twenty women have participated every week. The room is not a permanent gym so the rest of the week other activities take place there, but on Mondays and Wednesdays women meet. Friendship, health and well-being are built across cultural and religious boundaries. ‘Mountain in Movement’, as they call it, has in many ways been a concrete expression of the church’s vision: ‘A meeting place for all’.

There are plenty of fitness centres in the Drammen area, but this is exclusively for women. That is important especially for Muslims. The windows have curtains so no-one can look in from the outside. Sometimes you can see children playing while their mothers are in the gym. The gym is not free, but it is not very expensive either, which is good because people’s income in this area has been lower than in the rest of the country and is especially low for women.[11]

In my research I interviewed the deacon. She told me that it was and still is important to recruit good and stable instructors for the training so that the results should be the best possible. The deacon has spent time on ensuring the quality of the training programme. In addition to the deacon and the instructors, volunteers, mainly recruited among the women themselves, are engaged and helpful with unlocking and taking care of registration and facilities. At the gym, women from many countries meet each other. The women who meet have backgrounds from South-East Asia, Africa, Eastern Europe and Norway. Nearly 300 women have attended ‘Mountain in Movement’ since it started.

---

[9] The deacon in Fjell, Signe Myklebust, wrote her master’s thesis in 2010 about integration into plural congregations: ‘Welcome to this holy mess! Kva faktorar er viktige for fleirkulturell integrering i kyrkjelydar i Det Norske Baptistsamfunn og Den Norske kyrkje’ [‘Welcome to this holy mess! What factors are important for multicultural integration in local congregations in the Norwegian Baptist Union and Church of Norway’] (Oslo: Diakonhjemmet University College, 2010).

[10] Ivar Flaten, *En by på et fjell kan ikke skjules*, 74.

[11] Even Høydahl, *Innvandrere og norskfødte med innvandrerforeldre i Drammen* (Statistisk sentralbyrå – Statistics Norway, Oslo-Kongsvinger 2014), 316; Drammen Municipality, *Fjell 2020 – mot en bedre framtid Faktagrunnlag* (Drammen kommune, 2010), 23.

Countries represented in the spring of 2015 were Pakistan, Turkey, Somalia, Cape Verde, Ghana, Thailand, Lithuania and Norway. New people are starting all the time, and in the spring of 2015 no-one had been there longer than a year. The participants have different religions, but most of them are Muslim, and I assume that the facility of the gym for women is an important reason why they take part in this activity. In addition to the gym, the women get acquainted with each other. They receive feedback from each other and get information about local events. Friendship and trust between women is developed through this activity. This is in line with the church's diaconal profile and vision. *Diakonia* has a special responsibility in cases where nobody cares; they want to make an inclusive meeting place for all.[12]

The Deacon's Contribution

I asked the deacon to make a drawing describing 'Mountain in Movement'.

The drawing showed that, to start this activity, more than a room or physical space was needed. The work had to be organized. Co-operation and building trust with a lot of people and groups were fundamental. The realization of this gym required a lot of work with the possibility of learning from each other, planning together and a new kind of co-operation. The drawing showed me the central institutions and groups that were involved. I

---

[12] Church of Norway, *Plan for Diakonia* (Oslo: Church of Norway, 2008), 7.

was impressed because the drawing was such a simple way of showing the complexity of the work. Combined with telling the story about 'Mountain in Movement', the drawing, or what I like to call a map, showed so much more. Co-operation varies a lot and includes people at different levels.

On the map I found a variety of institutions and organizations and people involved in the same project, such as the organization of Fjell 2020, the local mosque, a Somali women's union, the council of the congregation and its diaconal work, the local municipality and physiotherapists, volunteer centres, the tourist association in Drammen, the local Health Living Centre, and physiotherapists at the local hospital, to mention some of those involved.

The deacon works both as a co-ordinator and a facilitator, but before that, she also examines the possibilities for co-operation. It looks like a concrete mapping of the social landscape. Bridge-building is necessary before the work starts, and both inside and outside the church. The drawing helps us recognize what this work has achieved. When we talk about co-operation without the drawing, it is easy to forget this part of the professional work involved. It is, in a way, hidden. This part of the work can of course be done in different ways, but to me it looks as though the deacon works according to a 'snowball-model' where listening and communication are necessary skills. To me it also seems beneficial that the deacon is herself a woman. As part of the discussion about diaconal work with women, we should consider whether men and women are equal as facilitators and co-ordinators.

Working with Relations

As we see, the deacon is a person who works a great deal with relations, as a bridge-builder, networker and trust-builder, but the vision of the congregation also shows us that the congregation wants to be in an active relationship with people in its environment. There is in a way a common will in the local society for change for the better and more participation. People locally take part in a common project to give women a gym and a place to meet each other and to be active citizens.

As a professional deacon you need to work with yourself, relationships, your own biography, your prejudices and your view of what an inclusive fellowship entails. This is not just something that deacons do, but also for many others involved in community work. Professional people need to know how motivation is linked with their formative experiences. As a facilitator and a co-ordinator, it is just as important that the deacon is open to mutual co-operation. In seeking conviviality, this reciprocity is of great importance. *Conviviencia* is a Spanish word and it translates simply as 'conviviality' or 'co-existence'.[13] It has two meanings. The first has to do with living 'left in peace' as Ivan Illich

---

[13] David W. Jardine, *Pedagogy Left in Peace: Cultivating Free Spaces in Teaching and Learning* (London: Continuum, 2012).

explains: 'Peace is that condition under which each culture flourishes in its own incomparable way.'[14] The second meaning indicates something more than the flourishing of each culture or person, and more than co-existing alongside another. In the second meaning, people living together are sharpening, forming and influencing each other.[15] Conviviality refers to the art and practice of living together.[16] But because people may be different and have a variety of interests and goals, we should discuss some principles in enabling organized conviviality.

Principals in Interreligious Work

Community Action-Based Learning for Empowerment or CABLE is an acronym for a seven-nation project, from 2005 to 2008 initiated from the Diaconia University of Applied Science (DIAK) that aimed to develop an approach to community-based work and community *diakonia*, based on practices that support change and transformation. This work includes co-operation and learning together in a safe space to foster self-expression, where stereotypes about 'some', 'a few' and 'many' are avoided. It is necessary to 'go out' and be exposed to the realities of the community you live in, to learn from people living there. The work depends on the fact that trust must be built together if people are to be able to improve nuanced empathetic communication. In this case, the use of 'distancing' and 'simulation' as in role play, theatre or use of cases, may create a safe space for empathy and learning from each other.[17] The method known as 'Exposure' is also mentioned as one of those used in the CABLE project. 'Exposure' is a method of learning that creates an experience of what you see, feel and think about what you experience by going out in known and not so well known areas to be more aware of the specific place and how it influences your understanding and capacity to act under new circumstances. Exposure is done in a systematic way as a part of the CABLE project and expands one's understanding of empathy and action.[18]

I am not sure if the congregation of Fjell has used the method of Exposure systematically, but the team with the pastor, the deacon and their collaborators learn from each other and they also learn from those who use the gym. It is interesting that, after five years, ski groups and swimming groups have been organized, and people become more involved in local work. This is an example

---

[14] David Cayley, *Ivan Illich in Conversation* (Concord, Ontario: House of Anansi Press, 1992), 16-17.
[15] Jardine, *Pedagogy Left in Peace*, 36.
[16] Lutheran World Federation, *Seeking Conviviality, Reforming Community Diakonia in Europe* (Geneva: Lutheran World Federation 2013), 4.
[17] John Keast, *Religious diversity and intercultural education: a reference book for schools* (Council of Europe Publishing, 2007).
[18] Addy, 'New approaches to community-based work, social service, and Diakonia'.

of a flourishing diapraxis and a kind of conviviality that brings people from different religions and cultures together in a new and refreshing way.

The local community acts together to create better conditions of life for their members, and the church has a calling to participate and let others participate. The congregation gathers experience in meaningful processes both for themselves and for others. I assume that if men and women did Exposure together in the neighbourhood of Fjell, they would learn more from each other. Sharing experiences, they might see, judge and act in a new and better way together with people living there. They might talk more concretely about what the main challenges locally are for women's participation. With the participation of the women themselves, the church would learn to act wisely together with people of different religions and cultures. People who are involved are in a way invited to rediscover the place where they live together, with the aim of making it better. Crucial to the flourishing of conviviality are sensitivity to the dignity of each individual, the recognition of human rights as values to be applied beyond religious and cultural diversity, communication between individuals, and the capacity to put oneself in the place of others in order to establish an environment where mutual trust and understanding are fostered. The conviviality approach is both an individual and a common responsibility, and builds on the idea of peace and solidarity.

The Inspiration from Martha Nussbaum

The American philosopher and professor of Law and Ethics, Martha Nussbaum, has, together with the Indian economist and philosopher Amartya Sen, developed a Capability Theory.[19] Nussbaum's central position is that, as a matter of basic justice, each person ought to be afforded a minimum threshold of capabilities. Capabilities represent the freedom a person has to make choices and to act in certain ways: in other words, to achieve a certain 'functioning'. The term 'functioning' includes things like mobility, educating oneself, enjoying recreational activities, and participating in one's political culture. Her list consists of ten different capabilities that are necessary as a prerequisite for a good life. Number one is about life. Nussbaum explains it as being able to live to a normal age – not dying prematurely, or before one's life is so reduced as not to be worth living. Number two is about bodily heath – being able to have good heath, including reproductive health, to be adequately nourished, and to have adequate shelter. Number three is about bodily integrity – being able to move freely from place to place, to be secure against violent assault, including sexual assault and domestic violence, having opportunities for sexual satisfaction, and for a choice in matters of reproduction.

---

[19] Martha Nussbaum, *Women and Human Development: The Capabilities Approach* (Cambridge: CUP, 2000).

The next capabilities concern senses, imagination and thought (fourth), emotions (fifth) and practical reason (sixth). Number seven is about affiliation, which she explains as being able to live in community with others, to recognize and show concern for other human beings, to engage in various forms of social interaction, to be able to imagine the situation of another. Number eight is 'other species' and means to be able to live with concern for and in relation to animals, plants and nature. Number nine is about playfulness. It is about being able to laugh, to play, and to enjoy recreational activities. The last one, number ten, is about control over one's environment, both politically and materially. It is not a list where some parts are more important than others. For a good life you need to *have* all the capabilities, but you don't need to *use* all of them. People should have the relevant freedoms to achieve certain functions, rather than actually *having* to achieve all those functions.

The freedom to act and participate is given in the congregation. It is a concrete action and gives new people a chance to participate. The way 'Mountain in Movement' is facilitated is focused on health, bodily integrity and education. For a deacon who facilitates actions for conviviality, there are always reasons for choices that are made. The question is what are your priorities? Women's health is very important in Drammen as well as anywhere else in the world. Immigrant women from non-western countries more often have obesity and diabetes than Norwegian women, and there are indications that migration to a western country could lead to a less healthy diet. What the deacon does is to offer a space. The gym in the cellar is not only a way of bringing people to church activities, but it is a way of building health and fellowship, and giving birth to a flourishing conviviality and learning together. This is also a way of being church in a pluralistic community. Maybe it is also a step towards a kind of conviviality where people's capabilities flourish just because people are welcomed. This may be a Community Action-Based Learning for Empowerment that the congregation should be a part of and learn from.

Diaconal professionals may also share the opportunities that a house and shelter gives, and also the joy of letting people make progress in their lives, some in the Christian faith and some in the Muslim faith, but together at Fjell. That is also a gift to the congregation – and also a challenge. The example of 'Mountain in Movement' gives no guidance as to whether a man could organize this work. Often a man's role would be different. In this case the deacon is a co-ordinator and a facilitator, but she is also working as a bridge-builder, trust-builder and networker. The key question is how to do that in a good and creative process with empathy and wisdom. Like the vision of Martha Nussbaum, the deacon and the women together make a space where they have a kind of openness to the world, an ability to trust when matters are uncertain or beyond one's control.

Conclusion

The challenges in community work in pluralist areas are complex. Building conviviality takes time, yet such work is valuable and promising. The real challenge however is building bridges between different groups in the local community and in the parish. The second meaning of conviviality indicates something more than each culture or person flourishing. Co-existing alongside one another is not enough. In the art of living together, people are sharpening, forming and influencing each other. Diapraxis and co-operation are necessary. But there should be a better balance between people. We should have in mind the capability approach to create the opportunity for action. This enriches the community. Such work takes time and needs to be understood. Drawings could be helpful to understand the complexity of the work, and sharing it with others could create more ideas of how to build relations in a better way in the future. But such initiatives still depend on trust in one another and in all who are involved.

Bibliography

Addy, Tony, 'New approaches to community-based work, social service, and Diakonia Challenges from the CABLE approach' in *Diakonia Journal for the Study of Christian Social Practice*, 4-2. Göttingen, Germany: Vandenhoeck & Ruprecht, 2013.

Cayley, David, *Ivan Illich in conversation.* Concord, Ontario: House of Anansi Press, 1992.

Church of Norway, *Plan of diakonia.* Oslo: Church of Norway 2008: http://kirken.no/globalassets/kirken.no/om-kirken/samfunnsansvar/diakoni/plan_diakonia2_english.pdf

Drammen Municipality, *Fjell 2020 – mot en bedre framtid Faktagrunnlag.* Drammen kommune, 2010.

Flaten, Ivar, *En by på et fjell kan ikke skjules. Fjell kirke 1984-2014.* Drammen: Fjell menighetsråd, 2015.

Høydahl, Even, *Innvandrere og norskfødte med innvandrerforeldre i Drammen* Rapport 2014/23. Statistisk sentralbyrå – Statistics Norway, Oslo-Kongsvinger 2014.

Illich, Ivan, 'Tools for Conviviality', in Marion Boyers and Paul Gilroy, *Postcolonial Melancholia*. New York: Colombia University Press, 2005.

Jardine, David W., *Pedagogy left in peace: Cultivating Free Spaces in Teaching and Learning.* London: Continuum, 2012.

Lutheran World Federation, *Diakonia in Context, Transformation, Reconciliation, Empowerment*. Geneva: Lutheran World Federation, 2009.

Lutheran World Federation, *Seeking Conviviality, Reforming Community Diakonia in Europe.* Geneva: Lutheran World Federation 2013: https://www.lutheranworld.org/sites/default/files/DMD-Seeking_Conviviality_Diakonia_Europe.pdf

Keast, John, *Religious diversity and intercultural education: a reference book for schools.* Council of Europe Publishing, 2007.

Myklebust, Signe, *Welcome to this holy mess! Kva faktorar er viktige for fleirkulturell integrering i kyrkjelydar i Det Norske Baptistsamfunn og Den Norske kyrkje*. Oslo: Diakonhjemmet University College, 2010.

Nussbaum, Martha, *Women and Human Development: The Capabilities Approach*. Cambridge: CUP, 2000.

Porkka, Jouko and Marja Pentikäinen, *Community of the Future Challenges and New Approaches to Community Based Social Work and Diaconia from the CABLE Approach*. Helsinki: Diaconia University of Applied Science, 2013.

Learning Gender Mainstreaming through Practice: Lessons Learned from Digni's Women's Empowerment and Gender Equality (WEGE) Programme

Heidi Holt Zachariassen

Awareness raising, competence building and learning were the key factors shaping the gender mainstreaming programme, *Women's Empowerment and Gender Equality (WEGE)*. It was initiated and run by Digni, a Norwegian umbrella organization for twenty mission and faith-based organizations (FBOs) which work co-operatively with churches and FBOs in the global South.

As Digni had not previously conducted competence building for its members on gender issues in development assistance, the lack of basic knowledge and awareness on gender equality and women's empowerment was one need that WEGE had to fulfil. At the same time, there was a desire to move beyond gender mainstreaming theory and learn 'how to do gender mainstreaming in practice'. What we learned from the work in practice was shared with all Digni members and served the requirements of both awareness raising and competence building. Here I share very briefly the strategies and conditions that the partners and projects in the WEGE programme experienced to be important in order to do gender mainstreaming in practice and obtain a better life situation for men and women. A book and an article that were written after the WEGE programme was finished will provide the reader with a more in-depth description of the WEGE programme and what we learned about gender mainstreaming in practice through the work undertaken in the projects.[1]

Before sharing what we learned, it is necessary to give a short theoretical and historical introduction to the concept of gender mainstreaming. The term 'gender mainstreaming' refers to the most important mechanism for fulfilling the commitment made to the Beijing Platform for Action in 1995: to achieve 'gender equality and women's empowerment'. There are several definitions of gender mainstreaming, but the one proposed by the UN Economic and Social Council (ECOSOC) has been particularly influential:

[1] Heidi Holt Zachariassen, *Learning gender mainstreaming through practice – Digni's women's empowerment and gender equality programme (WEGE) 2007-2010* (Oslo: Digni, 2012).

> Mainstreaming a gender perspective is the process of assessing the implications for women and men of any planned action, including legislation, policies or programmes, in all areas and at all levels. It is a strategy for making women's as well as men's concerns and experiences an integral dimension of the design, implementation, monitoring and evaluation of policies and programmes in all political, economic and societal spheres so that women and men benefit equally and inequality is not perpetuated. The ultimate goal is to achieve gender equality.[2]

As a strategy, gender mainstreaming contains the hope of transformation, a change in 'how we do development' that includes a gender perspective, with the goal of gender equality and women's empowerment. Gender mainstreaming was put forth as a means, not to look at women's concerns and marginalization as isolated matters, but to raise these issues at all levels, also taking into account the importance of men's involvement in achieving this goal.

With over twenty years of experience working with gender mainstreaming in development aid projects, new insights are formed on 'what it takes' to succeed and in turn to achieve women's empowerment and gender equality. Rao and Kelleher[3] discuss the different areas where change has to take place in order for gender equality to develop. They distinguish between formal and informal areas, and individual and systemic changes. By introducing these areas of change, the authors show a more complex picture of gender mainstreaming. When discussing the importance of religious faith and culture in communities, Wendoh and Wallace further emphasise the complexity in working with gender mainstreaming.[4] Indeed, religion and culture in certain contexts are not always receptive to the current concepts of gender equality championed by NGOs and international agencies, and it is important to be aware of this dimension when introducing the topic. Also, religion and culture are decisive when it comes to defining gender roles in a given context. The norms of religion and culture instruct women and men about what they can and cannot do. The complexities in working with gender mainstreaming require a long-term perspective. Or, as The United Nations Development Fund for Women (UNIFEM) emphasizes, gender mainstreaming is a process rather than a goal.[5]

The overall goal for WEGE was to *increase women's empowerment and gender equality through the work of Digni, its members, and its partners.* In order to get Digni's member organizations, selected partner organizations and

[2] United Nations, *Report of the Economic and Social Council for 1997*, A/52/3, 18th September 1997, 28.

[3] Aruna Rao and David Kelleher, 'Is there life after gender mainstreaming?' in *Gender and Development*, Vol. 13, Issue 2, July 2005.

[4] Senorina Wendoh and Tina Wallace, 'Re-thinking gender mainstreaming in African NGOs and communities', in *Gender and Development*, Vol. 13 Issue 2, July 2005.

[5] J. Sandler, *UNIFEM's Experiences in Mainstreaming for Gender Equality* (New York, UNIFEM, 1997).

their projects on board this process of change, WEGE considered the existence of certain conditions and strategies being in place as decisive in order to achieve this.

Even if the main focus for the WEGE programme was to gather experience at project level from doing gender mainstreaming in practice, it was clear from the start that WEGE had to be embedded at the organizational level in the institutions running the projects. This was important in two ways. First of all, it was important to show all the international partners taking part in WEGE that also Digni and its sister organizations in Norway were putting gender equality high on their agenda. They had to 'put their own house in order', so to speak. From the start, the main focus of the WEGE programme was to gender mainstream development projects abroad. Eventually the need for a more internal focus for the Norwegian partner organizations, including Digni, was identified. For some of the six partner organizations abroad, the gender equality emphasis had already spread from project to organizational level. They had started working on integrating a gender approach at the organizational level, and this was a factor that inspired the Norwegian organizations to concentrate more on themselves. In addition, one of the initial expected results, described in the overall project plan for WEGE, was that Digni, as well as the Norwegian Lutheran Mission (NLM), the Norwegian Mission Society (NMS), and the Mission Alliance, were to develop their own policies for women's empowerment and gender equality during the WEGE programme period. Although some of these organizations had already started their internal gender mainstreaming work, the factors described above increased this focus at home. This was inspiring and motivating for the partner organizations abroad. Digni and two of its member organizations in Norway developed their own gender policies as part of WEGE.

Another decisive factor for achieving any results at all and creating an ownership of WEGE in the organizations, was support from the leaders at every level. By allocating money and promoting gender equality inside and outside the organization, they showed that gender equality was a priority. For instance, throughout the WEGE programme period, the secretary general in Digni took an active part in the programme. He led the WEGE steering committee in Norway and participated in project visits and annual seminars with the partners abroad. This involvement was essential for the status of the programme, and signalled to all Digni member organizations and partners abroad that working for women's empowerment and gender equality should be a prioritized area for all.

The projects included in the programme were situated in very different contexts both in terms of geography (Madagascar, Ethiopia, Bolivia and Ecuador) and type of organization in charge. Some organizations were independent churches, and others faith-based organizations, but they were all engaged in development work. Their theological base was also different. All the projects were quite different in terms of types of activities and stakeholders, but could be categorized in broad terms as community-based projects and organizational development projects. With these variations in geography, organization and project types, some different experiences were encountered when applying a stronger gender focus. One might expect that these experiences would have been heavily tied to their context and therefore not very similar. As WEGE developed, however, we found that, regardless of the differences mentioned above, many of the projects and organizations were faced with common challenges. They also identified similar strategies and conditions that had to be in place in order to achieve gender equality and women's empowerment in their organizations and projects. These were the following:

Make gender a priority.
Involve and commit leaders.
Involve men and women.
Never work alone – create a team.
Understand the context you are working in, and do a gender analysis.
Take the role of religion seriously.
Use a 'bottom-up' approach.
Be flexible and allow room for experimenting.
Spend time on sensitization and competence building.
'Not pressure, but a light push' – gender mainstreaming as a long-term, continual process.
Planning for change makes change possible.

For the purposes of this article, I wish to highlight strategy 7: use a 'bottom-up' approach, as it also encompasses the importance of some of the other strategies.

At its inception, WEGE was 'top down' as it was initiated and planned by Digni in Norway. It had a clear goal of improving women's empowerment and gender equality through the work of Digni, Digni's member organizations and its partners. The means of reaching its goal – competence building and learning from gender mainstreaming in practice – laid the foundation for a 'bottom up' effect from project level to organizational level, although this was not the intention of Digni from the start.

When the projects, like the one in the Combaya community in Bolivia, were given full freedom to identify their own activities for gender mainstreaming, the ones that were initially chosen were mostly women-oriented and met basic needs. In Combaya they also fitted the context well, taking into consideration cultural issues in the area, such as the importance of the local description of gender relation called *chacha warmi*. This concept describes the complementarity between man and woman. Women and men are perceived as a unity and, as such, the relationship between them is perceived as unbreakable. This was decisive for the project's success. The project in Combaya had an effect on individuals in the community where women gained higher self-esteem and men changed their attitude towards the abilities of women. It also created a systemic change in that women entered the political arena and that this organization, Missión Alianza de Noruega en Bolivia (MAN-B), was inspired by good results and started addressing gender issues at the institutional level. It also made plans for mainstreaming gender into all its work. This 'bottom up effect' was also experienced by some of the other partner organizations in the WEGE programme. From the experiences made and the practical lessons learned from the projects in the WEGE programme, it seems that an integrated approach, focusing mainly on improving women's daily life but not challenging their life situation, corresponds well with the complexities in working with gender mainstreaming in different contexts. It also shows us the importance of looking at gender mainstreaming as a process with a long-term perspective.

Through what we learned from the projects in the WEGE programme, we can suggest that starting by working from the 'bottom up', using an integrated approach with activities focused on women that fit the cultural context and take into consideration existing gender relationships, can sometimes be an important starting-point for raising gender equality issues to the institutional level and making them agenda-setting. This, however, calls for flexibility in how we work with gender mainstreaming. We have to let ourselves and others use different and creative approaches in order to reach the goal of women's empowerment and gender equality, and also in relating to those approached that are perceived as 'outdated'. An integrated, comprehensive approach can be powerful when used in the right way. If gender can be placed on the agenda in a certain context by starting at the bottom and using activities that may be perceived as 'old-fashioned', we should reconsider the value of such activities and examine their potential for planning gender mainstreaming agenda-setting also in the future.

As this example illustrates, and the strategies listed above indicate, doing gender mainstreaming in practice taught the participants of the WEGE programme the importance of cultural and religious awareness, flexibility, involvement at both the project and institutional level and, perhaps most importantly, that gender mainstreaming is a long-term and continuous process.

Bibliography

Rao, Aruna, and David Kelleher, 'Is there life after gender mainstreaming?' in *Gender and Development*, Vol. 13, Issue 2, July 2005.

Sandler, J., *UNIFEM's Experiences in Mainstreaming for Gender Equality*. New York, UNIFEM, 1997.

United Nations, *Report of the Economic and Social Council for 1997*, A/52/3, 18th September 1997.

Wendoh, Senorina, and Tina Wallace, 'Re-thinking gender mainstreaming in African NGOs and communities', in *Gender and Development*, Vol. 13, Issue 2, July 2005.

Zachariassen, Heidi Holt, 'From the bottom up: Lessons about gender mainstreaming in the Andes from Digni's WEGE programme', in *Gender and Development*, Vol. 20, Issue 3, November 2012.

Zachariassen, Heidi Holt, *Learning gender mainstreaming through practice – Digni's women's empowerment and gender equality programme (WEGE) 2007-2010*. Oslo: Digni 2012.

'This Is My Beloved Daughter – Listen to Her!' Diaconal Empowerment through Scripture Study among Marginalized Women of the Mekong

Christa von Zychlin

> 'The chutzpah of Zelophehad's daughters in Numbers 27 and Joshua 17 is one of the Hebrew Bible's best kept secrets.'[1]
>
> 'So, the Bible is actually **more** than a book that says what God wants to say; it is also a book that **does** what God wants to do: a book that affects us, that transforms us.' [2]
>
> 'I was a witness of how the Word transforms not only lives but also people's bodies.'[3]

Introduction

In November 2014, I had the privilege of participating with thirty-five women from all four of the Federation of Lutheran Churches in Myanmar gathered for a ground-breaking Women's Biblical Life Conference. Hosted at the historic Bethlehem Lutheran Church in Yangon, the event was co-sponsored by the Mekong Mission Forum (MMF).[4] Some of the women had travelled as far as

---

[1] Margaret C. Hunt, *Dutiful Daughters and the Fathers Who Fail Them: The Application of Feminist Insights and the Retrieval of Resistance Strands of Women's Traditions via a Narrative Analysis of Four Unmarried Daughter Texts in the Hebrew Bible* (PhD thesis, Flinders University, Adelaide, South Australia, 2010), ix.

[2] Diane Jacobson, Mark Allen Powell, Stanley N. Olson, *Opening the Book of Faith: Lutheran Insights for Bible Study* (Minneapolis, MN: Augsburg Fortress Press, 2008), 45.

[3] Elsa Támez, 'The Bible in Mission: Women Facing the Word', in Pauline Hoggarth, Fergus Macdonald, Bill Mitchell and Knud Jørgensen (eds), *Bible in Mission* (Oxford: Regnum, 2013), 224.

[4] The Mekong Mission Forum was formed in 2000 to promote networking and mutual encouragement among LWF-related churches, theological institutions and diaconal outreach programs of Lutheran and Ecumenical partners active in the Mekong River area. See also Hanns F. Hoerschelmann, *Continuing Education Program for Alumni*

seven days' journey in order to reach Yangon. Many of them came from impoverished, far-flung villages, where basic services such as primary education, modern medical care or internet access are still only hoped-for commodities. No more than a few could speak English, nor could all of them understand Burmese, the national language. Instead, translations and conversations were carried on in at least four different dialects, to facilitate sharing within and among the different ethnic groups. But share they did!

Dr Margaret Hunt from the Lutheran Church of Australia (LCA) challenged participants to enter the biblical stories with eyes and ears open to several of the least known, most overlooked women in the Hebrew Scriptures (Old Testament). My co-facilitators and I were deeply affected by the energy and depth of response we witnessed, as women who are living on what many might consider the margins of the modern world interacted with the stories and voices of female characters who might *also* be considered as living on the margins of the *biblical* world.

These were not easy stories: Tamar, Lot's daughters, Ruth, the five Zelophehad sisters; issues raised include rape, incest, widowhood, property rights, and the prophetic calling for women – yes, women! – to function as the voice of God. Dr Hunt encouraged the conference participants to imaginatively identify with one or more of the stories' female protagonists, in order to 'hear a hidden or muted voice which otherwise would not be heard'.[5] For each Biblical passage we asked: *Who? What? Where? When?* And then the big questions: *Why is this story in the Bible? What does God want us to learn from these women's narratives, or from this woman's voice?*

It is widely acknowledged that the three-step methodology of *see-reflect-act* is especially appropriate for diaconal praxis.[6] In the following paragraphs I will use this methodology to explore ways in which marginalized biblical women's voices might elicit and empower *diakonia* in Myanmar, using a modified contextual Bible study approach.[7]

See and Hear – Mekong Women in Context

Diakonia begins with an awareness of context. In particular, this means listening to, '… voices that tend to be neglected… stories of marginalized and excluded people.'[8]

In the Mekong area, women have been marginalized and excluded in a number of ways. A recent graduate of the Lutheran Theological Seminary[9]

(CEPA): An Approach to a Supportive Model of Theological Education in Cambodia (DMin thesis, Lutheran Theological Seminary, Shatin, Hong Kong, 2011).

[5] Hunt, *Dutiful Daughters and the Fathers Who Fail Them*, 75.

[6] LWF, Diakonia in Context, 59.

[7] Gerald O. West, 'Do Two Walk Together? Walking with the Other through Contextual Bible Study'. *Anglican Theological Review* 93.3 (2012), 431-49.

[8] LWF, *Diakonia in Context*, 13.

gives the following description of the place of women in traditional Chin[10] society:

> Women are marginalized and discriminated against… because women's biological [functions] such as menstruation, pregnancy and delivery of babies is regarded as dirty, and women are regarded as inferior to men because of their association with such dirtiness. Women's clothes, especially the sarong (*Hta Mein*) are seen as dirty and untouchable by the men. There are still some practices that women follow because of this, such as keeping their clothes in a private and separate area, and hanging women's laundry out to dry at the back of the house at a lower level, separate from the men's clothes.[11]

Myanmar theologian Dr Khin Swe Oo gives a similar description of traditional and continuing attitudes towards (and even *among*) women in Chin society. Dr Swe Oo argues the consequence of the traditional attitude is that even today, '[The majority] of women accept their low status in all spheres of life and believe in the concept of inferiority to men as natural.'[12]

Displaying a growing awareness of his own context, another recent graduate of the Lutheran Theological Seminary had this to say in a written student reflection a few weeks into his first year of graduate studies:

> I was astonished when we learnt about women's ordination [by meeting a female pastor at LTS]. We… do not have women ordained minister, [nor] women pastor, or women elder until today. We do not elect women even for the Committee of the Church. I see our Church belongs to men. I think it is a burning issue for our Church.[13]

A proverb which reflects the traditional understanding of the respective strength and power of men over women appears to be well known across more than one Mekong country: 'The sun never rises with the hen's crow but only with the cock's.'[14]

---

[9] The Lutheran Theological Seminary in Hong Kong has a special focus on intercultural theological capacity building through Southeast Asian church and seminary leadership development. At any one time, the seminary has thirty or more international students, about twenty of whom come from the Mekong countries.

[10] The Chin State, located in the north-western part of Myanmar, is home to six ethnic minority groups. It is a mountainous, sparsely populated and economically undeveloped state, with little or no economic infrastructure.

[11] Hawi Thawn, *Sex Education in the Church of the Province of Myanmar (Anglican)* (MTh thesis, Lutheran Theological Seminary, Shatin, Hong Kong, 2012).

[12] Khin Swe Oo, *The Role of Women in the Ministry of the Chin Baptist Church in Myanmar* (Yangon: ATEM, 2012).

[13] Male Mekong Student, LTS Scholarship Student Semester Update, 29th September 2013.

[14] Hawi Thawn, *Sex Education in the Church,* chapter 3.

Reflect and Judge – A Modified Contextual Bible Study Tool

Although diaconal literature makes reference to the importance of the connection between the human context and the reading of the Hebrew and Christian scripture,[15] there seems, as yet, little explicit linking of the voices of scripture to the lives of women and men in the Mekong region today. I believe a modified use of a contextual Bible study method, borrowing from the ear-opening Bible studies conducted at the Myanmar Women's Event described above and in the following sections, can provide a foundational tool for making such connections explicit, for the mutual enrichment of the church and its diaconal practice in the world.

Contextual Bible studies may take a number of different forms, as outlined by Gerald O. West in South Africa,[16] and by Suzannah Cornwall with vulnerably-house people in South-West England.[17] I have chosen to experiment with the five-step outline of the Tamar Project,[18] a Bible Study manual specifically created to address the issue of gender-based violence in Kenya. Contextual Bible studies generally employ a similar 5-7 step process for their studies, carefully engineered to promote reflection, critical and creative thinking and sharing, and the generation of action steps among the participants.

Through the dual lens of my role with the MMF and with Mekong students and alumni of the Lutheran Theological Seminary, I will briefly describe the 'God's Beloved Daughters – Listen to Her!' Bible study experiments with which small groups of women related to the MMF are currently engaged. These are as yet only our preliminary findings and experiences.

Step 1 – Choosing a theme

For our 'God's Beloved Daughters' study, we chose the theme of listening expectantly for words of empowerment from women who speak in the Bible. In the context of the Mekong, as described above, women often experience exactly the opposite – women are not listened to – sometimes, sadly, not even by other women. Mekong women are routinely pushed to the sidelines in the home, in church and service organizations, and in the economic sphere.

Step 2 – Finding a biblical text

The Tamar Project suggests, 'Reading familiar texts in unfamiliar ways and reading unfamiliar texts allows the group participants to engage with aspects and parts of the Bible to which they have not previously had access.'[19] The

---

[15] LWF, *Diakonia in Context,* 13.

[16] West, *Do Two Walk Together?*

[17] Susannah Cornwall, 'Contextual Bible Study: Characteristics and Challenges', in Modern Believing (2012):14-22.

[18] Fred Nyabera and Taryn Montgomery (eds), *Tamar Campaign: Contextual Bible Study Manual on Gender-Based Violence* (Nairobi: FECCLAHA, 2007).

[19] Nyabera and Montgomery (eds), *Tamar Campaign,* 9

Mekong women with whom I conferred quickly confirmed my initial hunch – few of the 'daughter texts' seemed familiar (neither, to be honest, were they more than the vaguest of stories for me personally before starting on this journey of diaconal empowerment with my Mekong sisters!). Finding unfamiliar texts relating to our theme was no problem!

Ultimately, for the purpose of these initial one or two-day workshops, we chose the following three texts:

- The Zelophehad sisters (Num. 26:33; 27:1-8) were chosen exactly because they were so unfamiliar to most of us – unconscionably unfamiliar, given that their five individual names are repeated no less than four separate times in the Hebrew Scriptures.
- Tamar, the daughter of David (2 Sam. 13:1-22) was chosen because although she is nearly uniformly portrayed as a mere victim, her prophetic voice rings out loud and clear over the issue of sexual violence perpetrated (in an ironic but unflinchingly truthful situation) on a woman engaged in the very act of *diakonia*. Also, the issue of sexual violence is an especially burning one in the Mekong context, a reality which is routinely ignored out of cultural shame.
- The Syrophœnician woman (Matt. 15:21-28) was chosen because women wanted at least one voice to come from the New Testament, and because this woman seems to be dealing with a situation familiar to many of the ethnic minority women of South-East Asia – she is marginalized not only because of her gender, but also because of her ethnicity.

Step 3 – Questioning and reading

Volunteers take turns to read portions of the text, in English or in their own language, whichever they prefer. During this time, women realize we are already taking more time than usual to literally see and hear different female voices. There is something already empowering about reading an authoritative text in front of a large, attentive group.

For the purposes of our 'God's Beloved Daughter's' study, we begin with an alternative 'in front of the text' approach, in which the women are invited to imaginatively use their senses to see, touch, and especially to hear or *listen* for what they may have experienced if they were standing in front of the scene as it is depicted by the written words. The intention is that this approach 'levels the playing field' between those who are more educated or conversant with biblical stories and those who have had less exposure to an academic setting. Imaginatively 'standing before the scene' is a way of reading the text in an unfamiliar way and in practice it effectively elicits contributions from most of the participants as they quickly contributed impressions such as:

> [Zelophehad sisters] 'I hear the sisters discussed [sic] together and they want their inheritance, because they are also their father's children.'

'We hear those men's voices asking for what do they want, those girls? What are they coming for, to the tent of the meeting place?'

'I hear God laugh and say, of course those sisters are right, man; hey, Moses, you should listen to them!'

[Tamar] 'I hear them bolt the door.'

'I hear the long tear, the tearing sound of her princess's robe.'

'We hear her crying out, not a small cry, but so loud, so all the neighbours can hear her shamefulness.'

[Syrophœnician Woman] 'We hear the word 'dog', and it's not a nice word.'

'We hear her talk right back to Jesus; she trusts him.'

'I hear Jesus listens to her. She gets what she came to him for.'

The women spend some time clarifying exactly what happened in each of the stories, spending time 'on the text' and asking further questions 'behind the text'. Some questions can be answered by other participants; some are questions which may beckon them to more exploration and future biblical studies. Quite naturally they move into the next step of the study.

Step 4 – Articulating and owning

Participants are asked to reflect on the God-given assets and strengths the biblical women possess, and whether they might claim some of these same strengths for themselves or their friends.

[Zelophehad Sisters] Participants cite words such as courage, wisdom, cunning: 'They presented their plight at the appropriate time.' 'They had zeal.' 'They had knowledge of God, willingness to fight for justice.'

Some participants link the Zelophehad sisters to the issue of human rights: 'These sisters are knowledgeable about their rights and the legal way to get it.' 'They are educated. They know the right time, the right place and the right person to approach.'

[Tamar] Participants reflect theologically on whether and how there is any good news (gospel) in the text. One group grappled with whether Tamar's story could be used as a morality tale, to warn girls what not to do, whereas others pointed out that Tamar had done everything 'right' from a moral point of view. This led one woman to say, '... the way she do [speaking up for herself before, during, and even after the rape] is something that is a good example to the other girls... Maybe it was not only Tamar who was, um, treated that way maybe also it was other girls in that society, was done by soldier or by their, maybe father-in-law or something... and then they just keep silent couldn't do nobody do anything for them or find justice for them? [But] the way that that princess do, I think in that

> moment not only Amnon and Absalom's ... household know about that [rape] but maybe people in the whole kingdom will know about that, the princess [tearing her robe and putting ashes on her head] in the public space so many people know and maybe a lot of... girls or boys [are] inspire [sic]and maybe some of them who was silent for a long time have encouragement to speak up... I think it's a good example and something that teaches the young generation to stand up when something bad happens to them.

> [Syrophœnician Woman] Participants were quickly engaged with the question of who the 'outsiders' are in their own context: 'For the church level we think that the drunken people who are addicted to alcohol, they are the outsider because we the regular churchgoer kind of look down on them and they themselves also want to keep aside, 'Don't touch me.' And then the handicapped people and... people who have mental illness, this people are really put in the outside category of society because even those who have that kind of member in a family some people even hide them... in their room... just keep them inside only. So then we don't have any awareness that we should bring them outside and let them connect with nature and common people, yah.

Act – Mekong Women Empowered for Creative Action

The fifth and final step of the contextual Bible study, Step 5 – Developing a Plan of Action, converges neatly with the third part of the three-step methodology of *see-reflect-act*. What specific action plans are developed by Mekong women following such a Bible study?

Step 5 – Developing a plan of action

Here it must be said it is the weakness of having group facilitators who (thus far) are only guests to the Mekong context, and not generally in a position to participate with the follow-up action steps. Nevertheless, key plans for action did and continue to emerge, underscoring the value of the time spent grappling with biblical texts.

First and foremost, every group with whom we've done the study thus far, says, *'Break the silence.'* It seems the act of spending time listening to ancient authoritative texts inspires and empowers women to stand up for their legal rights, against violence, and for marginalized persons in their own contexts.

A second action step is a decision for shared action. As one participant said, '[It is] very important when we come to ask for our rights, like asking the top leaders... when we are alone our voice is very powerless but when we are a lot together, our voice is very powerful.'

A third action step often mentioned is education, especially of women, and here we can listen in on a conversation which took place as Bible study participants were asked to consider a plan of action.

R1: [The] mother favours giving the heritage to their son. Even the women themselves still thinking this, it is very common and familiar to us. Most of the ethnic groups still practise that inheritance goes to sons.

R2: That's why we should educate the women first, to not give the fish head to their son!

Facilitator: What does that mean, about the fish head?

R2: I mean they give the best portion for their sons. I mean if they boil three eggs and two will go to their son and one will go to their daughter. And the reason is: 'My son will one day look after me, you will be given in marriage to the other family.'

R3: But in reality the woman is the one even after getting married, they should realize that.

R2: Actually the woman is the one who looks after them, not the sons.

[Shared laughter]

R1: The education is important for the woman to break the family system. To me personally what I think I can do is sharing this story itself with more people, like students and women in my church.

R 3: Educating women themselves.

R1: Yea, to open up their minds!

The final action step to be mentioned here was greeted by hoots of laughter when it was first brought up by a study participant. But the idea may be an excellent example of a practical and creative diaconal action plan in response to a specific context:

R1: When I think about Tamar, I'm just thinking, is it a suggestion that we have to teach karate to the young generation? (Much laughter)

R2: [Speaking of a young participant, known for her athleticism] If [N.N. –] is in Tamar's place, Amnon would be finished!!

Conclusion

I believe the above voices, observations and conversations of Mekong women give evidence to the tremendous resource Christians have, as we listen to and dialogue with the ancient canonical texts, some of which speak God's word with a woman's voice. Contextual reading of the Bible can be an energizing component of diaconal engagement empowering God's church, female and male, for reflection and prophetic judgement about human situations, and can open creative possibilities for action in the Mekong region, in the light of the God's dawning New Realm.

Bibliography

Cornwall, Susannah, 'Contextual Bible Study: Characteristics and Challenges', in *Modern Believing* (2012).

Dietrich, Stephanie, Knud Jørgensen, Kari Karsrud Korslien, Kjell Nordstokke (eds), *Diakonia as Christian Social Practice: An Introduction.* Oxford: Regnum, 2014.

Hoerschelmann, Hanns F., *Continuing Education Programme for Alumni (CEPA): An Approach to a Supportive Model of Theological Education in Cambodia.* Hong Kong: Lutheran Theological Seminary, 2011. Unpublished dissertation.

Hoggarth, Pauline, Fergus Macdonald, Bill Mitchell and Knud Jørgensen (eds), *Bible in Mission,* Regnum Edinburgh Centenary Series, Vol. 18 (Oxford: Regnum, 2013).

Hunt, Margaret Carolyn, *Dutiful Daughters and the Fathers Who Fail Them: The Application of Feminist Insights and the Retrieval of Resistance Strands of Women's Traditions via a Narrative Analysis of Four Unmarried Daughter Texts in the Hebrew Bible.* Adelaide: Flinders University PhD thesis, 2010 web access: http://theses.flinders.edu.au/public/adt-SFU20101020.113427

Jacobson, Diane L., Stanley Norris Olson and Mark Allen Powell,. *Opening the Book of Faith: Lutheran Insights for Bible Study.* Minneapolis, MN: Augsburg Fortress Press, 2008.

Khin Swe Oo, *The Role of Women in the Ministry of the Chin Baptist Church in Myanmar: Towards Equality of Men and Women in Ministry.* Yangon: ATEM, 2012.

Nordstokke, Kjell, *Liberating Diakonia.* Trondheim: Tapir Akademisk Forlag, 2011.

Lutheran World Federation, *Diakonia in Context: Transformation, Reconciliation and Empowerment.* Geneva: Lutheran World Federation, 2009.

Nyabera, Fred, and Taryn Montgomery (eds), *Tamar Campaign: Contextual Bible Study Manual on Gender-Based Violence.* Nairobi: Fellowship of Christian Councils and Churches in the Great Lakes and the Horn of Africa (FECCLAHA), 2007.

Pitzele, Peter, *Scripture Windows: Towards a Practice of Bibliodrama.* Los Angeles, CA: Alef Design Group, 1998.

Támez, Elsa, 'The Bible in Mission: Women Facing the Word', in Pauline Hoggarth, Fergus Macdonald, Bill Mitchell and Knud Jørgensen (eds), *The Bible in Mission* (Oxford: Regnum, 2013).

Tawng, Seng, 'Why Women Are Missing in Kachin Churches' Leadership.' *In God's Image* 30.2 (2011).

Thawn, Hawi, *Sex Education in the Church of the Province of Myanmar (Anglican)* (MTh thesis, Lutheran Theological Seminary, Shatin, Hong Kong, 2012).

West, Gerald O., 'Do Two Walk Together? Walking with the Other through Contextual Bible Study'. *Anglican Theological Review* 93.3 (2012).

Walking with Hope: Transforming Lives in a Context of Violence through Diaconal Reading and Accompaniment

Hector Fernandez

Challenges of Our Reality

El Salvador is a country of high social vulnerability, which is expressed through its crime rates, unemployment and under-employment, unsatisfied basic needs, migration and low productivity. The end of the armed conflict, through the Peace Accords in 1992, made it possible to establish a space for the social bases to express themselves, although the structural causes that promote injustice continued to be the same – above all, the patters of economic power that exclude the majority of the population.

In 2009, for the first time in the history of the country, the candidate of the left was elected president of the country, creating hope that change would be possible. The networks of injustice, weaving together economic, social and cultural factors, however, resist efforts that envisage real transformation. In our view, poverty is not in the first place an object of study, nor are the poor mere recipients of aid. Through our diaconal approach we opt for a practice that considers impoverished people active subjects, able to build a new story of their lives, to the extent that they become aware of their reality and the root causes of their situation. From this point of departure, they are empowered to organize and co-ordinate with other agencies in order to overcome the limitations that now afflict them and keep them in poverty.

There is another gap, the gender-related one. In El Salvador the literacy rate of a man is seven points above that of a woman. Women do not have the same opportunities as men when it comes to education and getting decent jobs, reflecting a feminization of poverty. Domestic labour, birthgiving and housekeeping are not valued, nor are they distributed among the members of families.

San Salvador, the capital, remains the most violent place in the country. Even before the end of February 2016, 1,772 murders were reported here since the beginning of the year, according to statistics from the National Civil Police. Between 2009 and August 2015, the prison population (adult) increased 48.1%, from 21,032 inmates to 31,148. The number of imprisoned gang members rose from 7,555 to 12,983 in the same period, representing 41.7% of the adult prison population. 70% of the prisoners are young people. A study conducted by the Central American University (UCA) and the Heinrich Boell Foundation concludes that the prisons are overcrowded and insecure, the infrastructure deteriorating, basic services are lacking, and serious insanitary conditions are favouring the spread of diseases.

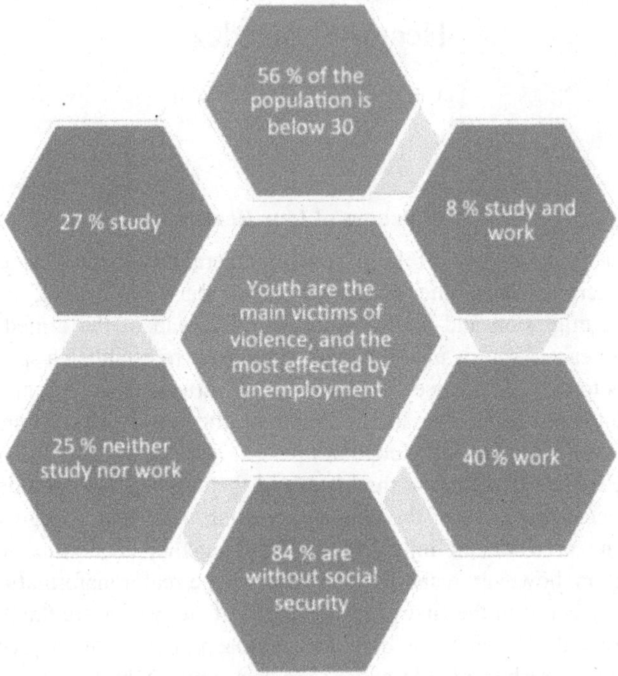

Salvadorian society consists mostly of young people whose reality is quite uncertain, given the few opportunities to study and work. Many of them grow up in a rather turbulent life, in their homes mostly with single parents, or they are children of parents who have migrated abroad. Society often looks upon them with eyes of suspicion, as potential criminals. In fact, too many of them end up joining groups, a kind of 'urban tribes', where they build their own reality, at the margins of society. The group makes them feel free, and to some extent, the same group will protect them.

Among these groups or movements, we find different youth sub-cultures. They break all ties with any authority and with any religious or moral doctrine that seeks to tell them how to live. There is a strong tendency to anarchism; many of these elements came about as a reaction to being marginalized by churches, NGOs, political parties and others. They develop a tremendous ability to survive in the midst of conflicts; they seek refuge in music and in all kinds of addictions. The consequence is that they increase the social risk within which they live.

In general, educational and religious bodies have not been able to respond to this challenge, caused by a reality marked by injustice and marginalization. Instead, they often contribute to uphold this situation, reproducing the pattern of exclusion that is found elsewhere in society.

The Work of IED-E

IED-E (Instituto Ecuménico Diaconal Esteban; English: The Ecumenical Diaconal Institute Stephen) aims at promoting a cultural transformation of young people through an inclusive approach, by developing skills and capacities through relevant training processes that are significant for the dynamics of their daily life.

The following objectives serve as guiding principles for our action:

- Establish ecumenical learning spaces in order to offer theological and socio-political training for students from different faiths, communities and social and political organizations.
- Develop programmes and strategies that foster a new culture with respect for the values of an inclusive democracy, with equal opportunities for women and men.
- Encourage and develop programmes and actions on diaconal reflection and practice, facing the demands of society and the role of Christians in society.
- Contribute to the renewal of incarnated ecclesial, liturgical and pastoral life, in order to strengthen the Christian communities.
- Offer technical and vocational training to young people of different faiths.

We apply the problem posing education, as developed by Paulo Freire in his book on the *Pedagogy of the Oppressed.*[1] This implies a rejection of one-way education, from teacher to student, or 'banking education', as Freire calls it. Instead, communication goes back and forth, eliminating the contrast between teachers and students. The dialogue thus establishes a learning process where both parts educate each other mutually. This method empowers and liberates, it destroys the passivity of the learner, and encourages processes of transformation, in which both oppressor and oppressed find humanizing liberation.

With Whom are We Working?

We aim at two segments of society:

---

[1] Paulo Freire, *Pedagogy of the Oppressed.* 30th Anniversary Edition (London and New York: Bloomsbury, 2000).

- Young women and men with low income who want to be part of spaces in which everyone has a voice, spaces that respect different political and religious beliefs, and that seek to develop models of community-oriented organization. Youth that positively want to transform their lives and their families and influence the positive transformation of Salvadorian society
- Adults, pastors and church leaders who are disposed to participate in processes and inter-generational dialogues, walking together with the youth.

Ecumenical Understanding and Practice

We practise what we understand as Real Ecumenism, seeing it as an intercultural movement that brings together people from different generations and faiths, contributing to the integration of people, creating spaces and strategies. We seek to avoid: a) Prominence of people and confessions, b) These efforts being steered by financial considerations.

We recognize the importance and value of what people say, of the equal participation of women and men, young and old – and not only of active Christians, but of all who are interested in transformation, not only of society, but also of mindsets and attitudes. We avoid references to academic degrees or formal positions; instead we give preference to people's names. We believe this approach is important because it helps to develop freedom of expression, to reaffirm and raise the self-esteem of the participants.

Diakonia

Our thinking and acting is eminently diaconal. We understand *diakonia* as the essential spirit of everyday life that transcends institutionalism; it represents the kind of lifestyle we intend to promote. It is a way of being and acting, something present in ordinary people that makes them act, both inside and outside institutions.

Diakonia contains two important elements of equal importance: 1. Action – organized praxis and other activities (Luke 10:37). 2. Reflection and prayer – contemplation (Ps. 46:10).

We count four 'moments' that may occur separately or in parallel, always being part of a liberating diaconal methodology.

These 'moments' comprise the method that is present in all processes of the institution. They are also developed in an interdisciplinary perspective. We consider it important to provide tools that empower the student to see and judge the economic and ideological powers that cause human suffering. This is how we experience and promote *diakonia*.

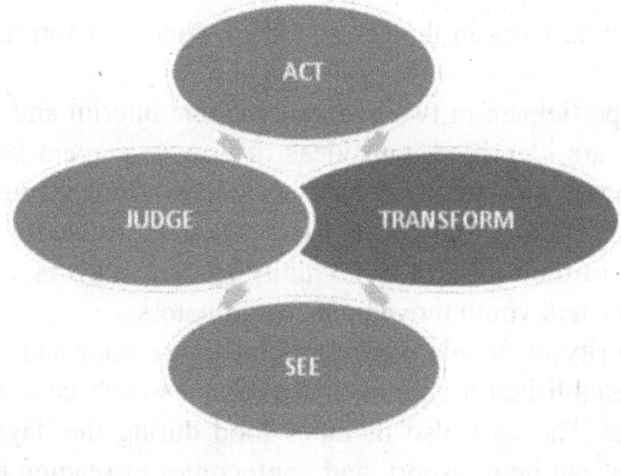

The Institute has developed different ways of putting this into practice:

1. Meeting places called 'Café and Philosophy', 'Café and Diakonia', 'Café and Economy'. We arrange four meetings every month, inviting youth and adults to dialogue, together with experts that share their knowledge.

2. Workshops with youth from 'urban tribes'. The themes have been: Prevention of HIV/AIDS; Deconstruction of masculinity; Communications and personal relationships; Gender; Analysis of reality. We arrange workshops twice a month, organized by the youth themselves. These young people have low incomes, some wash cars at traffic lights, monitor vehicles on public parking, sell water or soft drinks in the streets when there is traffic congestion, and others sell homemade trinkets in the market. Most of them are members of 'urban tribes'; they do painting, graffiti and tattoos. For these young people, the IED-E is an 'open house' in which they find acceptance, and are included, esteemed and appreciated. When we have financial resources available, we organize training courses, teaching them to make soap, shampoo, hand-made jewellery, printing and baking. These young people challenge us, energize us, provide us with hope, and motivate us to improve our methods and diaconal theory.

3. The Diploma Programme in Diakonia. IED-E works together with faith communities, churches and parishes in developing this programme in order to secure its relevance, and that it reflects the reality in which we live. The students follow two modules, for example: Diakonia and Economy, and Political Participation. They meet monthly or bi-weekly, altogether 150 hours, inside or outside the classroom. In addition to studying relevant literature, they also do fieldwork, research and organize diaconal actions. Among the themes are: Diakonia as faith in action; Diakonia and the centrality of human beings in the Bible; Diakonia and citizenship; Diakonia of hope; Diakonia for transformation; Diakonia, action with justice; Diakonia in a globalizing neo-liberal context; Diakonia and the prophets; Diakonia and power; Diaconate, church and society.

Until 2010, we produced annually a book with the main presentations and the conclusions of the participants. These small books still serve as support material for diaconal work in the communities where our former students now are active.

The students participate in two evaluations, one interim and the other final. Here new topics are identified with ideas of how to expand knowledge. This participatory process also includes partner churches and institutions; this has given IED-E high credibility and trust. Overall, students enrol on the recommendation of their pastors, community leaders, mayors, co-ordinators of social movements, and youth movement co-ordinators.

The vast majority of people, who participate, are poor and not able to pay fees. We have established a council that examines each case and proposes a way of financing. The cost also includes food during the days of classroom study, payment of public transport, and photocopies of reading materials. With the support of partners – national and some international – we are able to grant scholarships to those students who are not able to cover these costs.

The Diaconal Method 'Esteban'

Diaconal training presupposes an intimate relationship between theory and practice. It links with a spirituality that embodies ethics for life, friendship, solidarity, and to professionalism and academic insight. Altogether, this forms a multidisciplinary competence that is required for those who serve the poorest sectors of the population.

This method can be described as a pedagogy of welcome, inspired by how Jesus of Nazareth met with people. It expresses hospitality, welcoming without discrimination, value judgements or prejudices.

It envisages continued and holistic accompaniment of persons and their families, and includes visiting their homes, and building relationships of friendship and solidarity. The home of the director of IED-E has from the very beginning been an open house for young people. This adds credibility to our work; it also helps to share painful personal experiences and the complicated impacts of the social, political and economic realities in El Salvador. It fosters resilience and the ability to transform problems or difficulties into opportunities, achievements, progress and happiness.

Transforming Lives

The cases below tell the story of two of the young people who have participated in the workshops. Their names are fictitious.

Ricardo

Ricardo was arrested in 2008 in a *redada*, a police operation that stops and brings in suspicious persons. He was brought to an overcrowded prison, the vast majority of detained being gang members. After five years, he could move outside the prison at daytime, thanks to good behaviour, and got some work at a local school. He then got contact with the IED-E, joined the activity of baking bread, and then started to study *diakonia*. Ricardo was very responsible both in relation to his commitment to the penal institution, and to the school where he was working, and at the same time he developed his skills with the IED-E, becoming part of the team of facilitators. In 2015 Ricardo received his letter of release. Currently he collaborates with the IED-E in various capacities, but mainly in activities with young people. He is also an active member of an evangelical church, engaged in developing a diaconal spirituality.

Marisol

Marisol's mother emigrated to the United States, leaving her six-year-old daughter behind. When she was 15, her father ran away. She then moved to an aunt, who treated her badly, making her self-esteem very low. She started to drink and had difficulties in getting a proper job. Then a friend brought her to the IED-E and to one of the workshops there. She served for a while in the bakery and then decided to enter the diploma course in *diakonia*. Marisol badly wanted to begin university studies; IED-E was able to offer her a small scholarship which made it possible for her to become a radiologist. During this period, she also re-established contact with her father who now had become ill, and she took care of him until he died. With her self-esteem restored, Marisol assumed a leadership position in the local community and in the IED-E, contributing to organizing workshops and café meetings. She is an active citizen, having a home and a good job – in short, a person who has been empowered to manage her own life.

These stories illustrate the methodology of youth work. It starts by establishing relationships, with the main object of being friends and building levels of trust. Religion is not the main, or the primary, driving force: friendship is stronger, with a safe space for exchanging thoughts and experience from one day to the next. Within this space, we sometimes discuss issues related to being human, and ethical values in society and the family. We share important moments in life: birthdays, family celebrations and funerals, both with the young people and those who work in the institution.

Observations and Conclusions

Christian faith and traditions play an important role in everyday life in El Salvador. Unfortunately, a fundamentalist and extremely moralistic Christianity is dominant, causing loss of self-esteem and stigmatization. At the same time, the impact of post-modernism makes young people especially suspicious about the moral authority of church leaders, both Catholic and evangelical. Most of them maintain faith in a superior being, according to Salvadorian spirituality; they expect this 'being' to be friendly and to help them when they encounter difficulties. It is a faith independent of temples or church structures.

Over the last two centuries, Salvadorians have experienced a troubled history with many dramatic events: civil wars, insurrections, riots and coups. It has cost blood, tears and pain. Even with a democratically elected government today, the population experiences a lack of access to social benefits, due to the unjust economic structure. Wealth continues to be concentrated in a very few hands; debts are public, but profits privatized.

On average, a multi-millionaire in El Salvador has an income that is 4,000 times higher than that received by the poorest 20%, according to a recent report published by Oxfam. There are 160 ultra-rich persons in the country; these are people whose net worth is equal to or greater than $30 million. They have accumulated a wealth of $21,000 million, equivalent to 18.8 times the public investment in health, 26.7 times the education budget; it represents 87% of the gross domestic product. In contrast, the legal minimum wage in the country barely covers 66% of what is necessary to reach the average household poverty line, while more than 60% of the population is engaged in the informal labour market.

The present left-wing government often crashes into a wall of impossibilities when it tries to achieve social benefits for the population. The economic structure and its power system do not allow for substantial social advances; progress therefore is still superficial and does not satisfy the basic needs of the population, while poverty remains high and leads, among other things, to high unemployment and migration, in addition to strong levels of frustration, especially among youth.

Within this reality, with its enormous challenges, we practise and reflect on *diakonia*. We continue to be like David versus Goliath – also in the sense that we continue to be signs and spokespersons of hope. Although the scenario seems to be against us, we are confident that truth and justice will one day prevail; therefore we must continue in our diaconal work. And be united in our *diakonia*.

Women En Route to Justice: Migration, Gender and Gender-specific Human Rights

Drea Fröchtling

> 'If you say "migrant", you say: vulnerable.
>
> If you say "women", you say: very vulnerable.
>
> If you say: "women migrating", you say: human rights catastrophe.
>
> If you say "church", you should say: community of faith en route to justice for all.'
>
> Rebecca, 29, Mali

Migration comes in various forms,[1] is induced by various reasons, and leads to a diverse range of experiences. The following contribution will focus on gender-specific human rights violations as a principal impetus for migration.[2] Based on a number of Focus Group Discussions (FGDs) carried out with migrants in Johannesburg and Soweto (South Africa), in Manila (Philippines) and in Amsterdam (Netherlands),[3] the first section will briefly highlight some

[1] Migration is a heavily contested ground – in national and international politics as well as in definitions and in theory formation. Migrants are typified and labelled into free, compelled, voluntary (cf. Annette Treibel, *Migration in modernen Gesellschaften: Soziale Folgen von Einwanderung, Gastarbeit und Flucht* (Weinheim and München, Germany: Juventa, 2011), 164ff.) and forced (cf. Brigitte Hargasser, *Unbegleitete minderjährige Flüchtlinge: Sequentielle Traumatisierungsprozesse und die Aufgaben der Jugendhilfe* (Frankfurt am Main, Germany: Brandes & Apsel, 2014), 19); migrants, and root causes of migration are researched. In this process, more and more researchers are giving up on traditional monolithic ascriptions, categorization and reasoning as well as on long-cherished dichotomies seen between 'migrant-sending' and 'migrant-receiving' countries (e.g. Stephen Castles, Hein de Haas and Mark J. Miller, *The age of migration: international population movements in the modern world* (New York: Palgrave-Macmillan, 2014), 13).

[2] Additional factors affecting a decision to migrate – e.g. poverty or climate-induced migration, though they might affect women more severely than men – will not be considered in this contribution.

[3] In total, there were three FGDs carried out in each of the regional contexts, of 60-90 minutes each. The average number of participants was six, covering men and women. Topical emphases of the FGDs differed, with migration and migration-related

of the areas in which gender and gender-related human rights violations come particularly to the fore in the decision-making stage before migration. The second section will then look at gender-based human rights violations during the migration process. Sections three and four offer a tentative reflection on migration and the need for ecclesial repositioning in diaspora terms, and some suggestions for further reflection and the embedding of diaconal praxis in the intersection of migration, gender-based human rights violations and diaconal engagement.

At the Intersection: Gender and (forced) Migration – Human Rights Violations at the Point of Origin

Gender is at the core of many human rights violations worldwide. Domestic violence, traditional harmful practices such as female genital mutilation or arranged marriages, rape as a weapon of war, polygamous settings, restrictive gender roles and little space for diversified sexual orientation in many countries leave women to be targets of, inter alia, physical, sexualized and psychological violence.

With an increasing awareness of rights, larger numbers of female single parents, changing rural and urban patterns, cultural changes and an official recognition of women's rights in more and more countries, on the one hand, and an increasing global market for traditionally gendered activities such as care-giving and household maintenance, on the other, a constantly increasing number of women leave their places of origin for refuge and survival, dignity, work, educational opportunities, family reunion or marriage purposes.

A feminization of migration[4] has been observed over at least the past two decades, with the 'politics of belonging'[5] playing themselves out at the very

---

experiences being the linking factor in all FGDs. Participants came from various denominational, cultural and professional backgrounds and were selected by a snowballing principle. All but the South African participants cited have migrated due to gender-based violence; the South African participants were involved in outreach programmes towards migrants. All cited participants are female. Names cited in this contribution are the aliases chosen by the participants. The FGDs in South Africa were carried out in July 2013 (Sibongile, 69, South Africa, Ntombi, 61, South Africa, and Naledzani, 65, South Africa) in Johannesburg and Soweto, in the Philippines in June 2014 (Joy, 32, Philippines, Gemma, 31, Democratic Republic of Congo, and Rebecca, 29, Mali), and in the Netherlands in March and December 2015 (Kulumani, 45, Zimbabwe, Faith, 41, Zimbabwe, and Hope, 27, Eritrea).

[4] For the notion and the concept, see e.g. Franz Nuscheler, *Internationale Migration: Flucht und Asyl* (Wiesbaden, Germany: Verlag für Sozialwissenschaften, 2014), 39.

[5] The 'politics of belonging' refer to power-political interplays in which males generally stand a better chance of being considered part of an 'in-group' than females. On a global scale, the chances for male migrants to re-enter an 'in-group' once again after the rupture of migration are decidedly better than those for women who often remain

intersection of migration, integration and gender politics.[6] While, on the one hand, migration has thus regained a much stronger female agency, gender-related human rights violations, on the other, continue to abound on and alongside classical migration routes, as well as off the beaten migratory track. International policies such as e.g. the UNHCR's 'Guidelines on the Protection of Refugee Women'[7] acknowledge gender-related special protection needs. The UNHCR's Dialogues with Refugee Women[8] consider the agency of refugee women, and the 2014 Istanbul Convention[9] acknowledges gender-based violence and persecution in the context of migration and asylum/protection. But women still face what Ntombi (61, South Africa) calls 'the rougher side of migration'.

Women who have experienced migration 'from the underside', often leave a situation in which they, as Naledzani (65, South Africa) observed, 'have lost all that there is to lose anyway: dignity, work, food on the table, your body – because it belongs to your spouse or whoever claims it, and your hope, yes, also your hope that there can be a good life with no pain and with respect for you in your country'.

In similar vein, Kulumani (45, Zimbabwe) describes the push towards an intersection where a decision needs to be made in one way or the other:

> As a woman, you experience so many bad things in your life. Some of them, well, somehow, you get used to them, like poverty, that is. Not because you want to but because you don't have a chance. But for me and all the women I met on the way there was one point where something happened or threatened to happen and you felt like you were thrown at an intersection of roads. You needed to take a decision, here and now.

In the various FGDs in South Africa, the Philippines and the Netherlands, participants highlighted the following areas of gender-related discrimination,

---

excluded e.g. in terms of access to the labour market (beyond the sector for unskilled labour) and of full societal participation.

[6] Here Sauer points, inter alia, to bio-politics coupled with migration politics, to male-dominated and gender-segregated labour markets as well as to gender in breadwinner debates: Birgit Sauer, Politiken der (Nicht-) Zugehörigkeit: Verhandlungen von citizenship und Geschlecht in Diskussionen um das muslimische Kopftuch in Deutschland und Österreich', in Mechthild Bereswill, Peter Rieker and Anna Schnitzer (eds), *Migration und Geschlecht: Theoretische Annäherungen und empirische Befunde* (Weinheim, Germany, and Basel, Switzerland: Beltz-Juventa, 2012), 192-212, 195.

[7] UNHCR. Guidelines on the Protection of Refugee Women (Geneva: UNHCR, 1991).

[8] UNHCR. UNHCR's Dialogues with Refugee Women: Progress Report on Implementation of Recommendations (Geneva: UNHCR, 2013).

[9] Council of Europe: Council of Europe Convention on Preventing and Combating Violence against Women and Domestic Violence (Brussels: Council of Europe, 2014, Treaty No. 210).

violence and cultural harmful practices that for them served as a final impetus amidst an already experienced gendered intersectionality:[10]

a) Arranged marriage: 'In my area, it does not happen often any longer. But my parents they were very traditional, so they had chosen a husband for me when I was born. And when I was fifteen I was supposed to marry that guy – a grumpy person, old, always shouting and so big I felt he once laying on top of me that would be the end of me. I couldn't do it, no, I simply couldn't. [...] My parents, when I told them they got angry and a got a lashing with a belt. Wham! Wham! Wham! When I had no power left to scream they shut me up in an empty hut. My little sister, she helped me to escape.' (Faith, 41, Zimbabwe.)

b) Female genital mutilation: 'When it was time for my girl child to be circumcised... well, I simply couldn't stand it. My circumcision, it was so bad, so bad, with the pain when going to the toilet, my legs tightly bound together for six long weeks, the incredible pain with every period because the opening they left, it was very, very small. And on top, I felt like only half a woman after that. [...] I did not want my daughter to live through the same, I wanted her to be a whole woman, so that one night I simply took her and left.' (Rebecca, 29, Mali.)

c) Education: 'When I was a child I thought that life will be okay if you get a husband who is kind and does not beat you. But, see, when I grew up, I wanted more, I wanted to live out what I had in me. I was much brighter than all my brothers together, but it was them who were allowed to go to school, not me.' (Hope, 27, Eritrea.)

d) Femicide: 'I have heard in other countries it happens much more often. But I had it in my family. After the examination in hospital we knew it would be a girl. My father, he said it would be no good to have another useless person in the family that needs food every day, so he gave me this crushed plant to drink to make the baby go away. [...] My throat, my belly, all was in flames, it was burning and aching so much. The baby girl, it was dead when it came out, dead, dead, dead! [...] When I was expecting a baby again, I ran, because now I wanted my child to live.' (Joy, 32, Philippines.)

e) Gendered violence: 'There is so many things that happen to women everyday here and in so, so many countries. Not in Europe, but here in Africa. There is beating, nobody thinks it's wrong to beat his wife. Or the education that is for boys if a family struggles for money. Or the many things that religion, whatever, Christian or Muslim, what they want you to do or not to do, and that you must be lower than men and so. The bad payment in the job market, if you are lucky enough to get a job that is more than cleaning toilets or being a nurse. And the million other things, looks you get on the streets, rape,

[10] 'Gendered intersectionality' assumes that, amidst inter-sectionalities of discrimination and exclusion such as ethnicity, poverty, age, educational background, abled-bodyness, sexual orientation, etc., gender serves as a factor through which all other areas of (tentative or actual) discrimination are substantially aggravated.

jokes that make you look silly, how newspapers use women, I could go on for ever. But at some stage you have had enough – you don't want it to go on for ever. You want life.' (Rebecca, 29, Mali.)

f) Trafficking: 'In my area people know what happens when a guy comes to you and says he has a nice job for you in Europe, good place to stay, guaranteed holidays, nice pay, bla bla bla. [...] In Eritrea, they take you across to Ethiopia first. And when this guy said he has already talked to my father I knew that I needed to dash for a decent life if I did not want to end in the brothels in Europe or wherever.' (Hope, 27, Eritrea.)

g) Rape (as weapon of war): 'I have seen many, many weapons in my life, way too many. That comes from living in a war area but that also comes from you being a woman. I have had a gun at my head and a machete at my arm. But the worst weapon, it is the penis for me; because a gun kills you fast, but a penis will pierce you and stab you in your body and soul again and again till after years you feel life, it is not worth it any longer. And maybe worse: you also feel that you are not worthy any longer because of that penis that did it to you. The rapes, they were the too much on the already much things against women in our area.' (Gemma, 31, Democratic Republic of Congo.)

h) Gender-based violence in conscript settings: 'In Eritrea we have that National Service. You need to do it, men and women, and you don't know where they put you and for how long. It is bad for all of us Eritreans, but it is doubly bad for the women, because the guys in charge, they would think they own you, you and your body.' (Hope, 27, Eritrea.)

Depending on the context, the list of gender-based human rights violations could be continued. Thus, in many areas, women are disproportionally burdened not only by gender-based violence but also by the fact that (post)-conflict countries show the least likelihood of achieving the UN Sustainable Development Goals and its inherent promise of more gender-equality.

Gendered Violence en Route: Human rights Violations During the Migration Process

Other than men who often migrate across borders or cross continents, women often lack the financial and logistical means to cover larger distances and thus form the majority of the global population of internally displaced people (IDPs) who are (forced into) seeking refuge within the confines of their countries of origin that very often are not able or not willing to protect them from gender-based violence. Little change, despite the various efforts of the UNHCR, has occurred in IDP camps where often neither the security nor empowerment needs of women are considered or met. As Gemma (31, Democratic Republic of Congo) describes it: 'If you look at big politics, for them it does not matter if you are a man or a woman. But it matters for us because we have different needs: we want to be protected from the guys that just come into the tents at night and take us, from the guys robbing us when food is dished out, and we want to learn more about our rights and where we can go to have them.'

In 2015, an estimated average of only 19% of refugees arriving in the EU was female – despite the substantial percentage of women amidst the overall global refugee population. All women participating in the FGDs experienced being en route as women as a 'dangerous, dirty and painful experience that did break you like a firewood gets broken – crack!' (Joy, 32, Philippines) and reiterated that, given a chance and a perspective at home, return would have been a favoured option: 'If I had a chance to go back that day, I think I would. But then, what was waiting for me that was different? So better pick the pieces of your life together and go on' (Faith, 41, Zimbabwe).

Like most male refugees, migrant females also depend on smuggling networks to facilitate their way to what was hoped for as 'countries of equality and peace' (Faith, 41, Zimbabwe). Smuggling-related hardships and human rights violations experienced by the participants in the FGDs included a) abduction and being held captive until a ransom was paid by the family so that the journey could be continued; b) prolonged periods of enforced slave work to pay for a three times increased prize to smugglers; c) forced prostitution and enforced surrogate motherhood; d) continued rapes of both male and female members of the respondent group; e) beatings at border-points if no bribe was paid to the officials who then shared it with the respective smuggler; f) being left alone in the middle of the desert with no food or water; g) threats to inform officials if no slave labour is carried out, and h) enforced nudity of female migrants and parading them around the tents of the smugglers. With the exception of rape as a means of punishment also for male migrants, the above mentioned sexualized forms of gender-based violence were nearly exclusively meted out to migrant women.

Gender thus remains a major reason for migration as well as remaining a high-risk factor during migration and a discrimination factor after settlement in a new context.

Locating Church in Dislocation: Ecclesial Repositioning

Migration, particularly when forced, challenges a sedentary church to reflect about its points of departure as well as about its hermeneutical and physical positioning. In Sibongile's (69, South Africa) words: 'If the church sees millions being pushed away from home because there is no life there, just hurt and death, then that church cannot remain in its big, big stone churches and wait for people to come for the Sunday sermon. Then the church must go in diaspora also, not just remain in Jerusalem.'[11]

---

[11] See also Gemma Tulud Cruz who introduced migration as a locus of theology: Gemma T. Cruz, *An intercultural theology of migration: Pilgrims in the wilderness* (Leiden, Netherlands: Brill, 2010), 121.

Sibongile suggests a diasporic repositioning of the church, a change of location, agency and perspective. Such a repositioning would, in hermeneutical terms, require an inductive, empirical approach that bases doing theology on those on the way from a marginalized, violated and oppressed existence to the regions where survival, dignity and life in justice, equality and peace have a greater likelihood of materializing. Such diaspora repositioning might imply the following:[12]

Liminality

Liminality, coined by van Gennep[13] in his 'Rites of Passage', was reintroduced into anthropological and sociological debates by Turner in the late 1960s.[14] Van Gennep and Turner both apply liminality to describe the threshold or the in-between state occurring in rites of passage between separation, transition and incorporation, the latter associated with a new identity, a new being. Liminality also, to a certain extent, describes the character of theology: liminality is experienced by doing theology in between creation and *eschaton*, the 'already' and the 'not-yet' of the kingdom of God, and in between *missio* and *promissio*. In epistemological terms, knowledge is derived in between biblical faith narratives and human his- and her-stories, and theoretical approaches are assumed in between theological ecclesiologies and sociological, organizational and developmental theories.

Turner sees early Christianity as part of a liminal movement that resulted and results in the formation of ideological *communitas* that interacts differently compared with the mainline social stratification and structure. Liminal diaspora existence thus enables the church to experience as well as critique structures that divide, that outlaw and degrade human beings before, during and after a migration process. It requires an essential interaction with community experiences, on the one hand, and interlocutors from cultural, subaltern, disability and gender studies, on the other.

Anti-structure

Turner defines liminality inter alia in terms of anti-structure. Anti-structure occurs in liminal spaces and is characterized by elements such as transition,

---

[12] A more detailed reflection can be found in Andrea Fröchtling, ''Our Lord was a migrant servant – and who are you?': Suggested signposts on the way towards a subaltern diasporic positioning of Practical Theology and International Diakonia', in Claudia Rammelt, Cornelia Schlarb and Egmont Schlarb (eds), *Begegnungen in Vergangenheit und Gegenwart: Beiträge dialogischer Existenz* (Münster et al: LIT, 2015), 323-33.

[13] Arnold Van Gennep, *Rites of passage* (Paris: 1909; German version *Übergangsriten*. Frankfurt am Main Campus Verlag, 2005).

[14] See Victor Turner, *The forest of symbols: Aspects of Ndembu ritual* (Ithaca and London: Cornell University Press, 1967); Victor Turner, *The ritual process: Structure and anti-structure* (Ithaca and London: Cornell University Press, 1969).

communitas, egalitarianism, a lack of hierarchy, references to religion and experiences of suffering. Structure, as Turner has it, divides people. It allocates them to fixed spaces and positions, and it excludes by established hierarchies and the declaration of in-groups and out-groups. Contrary to structure, anti-structure 'abolishes all divisiveness, all discriminations, binary, social, or graduated'.[15]

Rediscovering anti-structure as a unifying, egalitarian space challenges the current status quo thinking about and living as inclusive communities. It challenges us, from a theoretical and practical point of view, to question the legitimacy of dominant discourses within theology and theologically-based social practices, and calls at the same time for inclusive agency in discourse and practice, here with special reference to women's voices and experiences as particularly 'out-grouped' parts of humankind.

Hybridity and third space

Hybridity as a concept takes centre stage in post-colonial discourses, which understand cultures as inherently hybrid. Hybridity, according to Bhabha, is the 'in-between-space' in which identities are translated as well as negotiated. Bhabha establishes a close connection between hybridity and the third space which he describes as interrogative, enunciative and interruptive. In addition, Bhabha introduces the third space as an ambivalent space that produces meaning and possibilities, and that fosters a counter-hegemonic agency.[16]

Bhabha's third space could thus offer the opportunity to seriously consider intercultural hermeneutics and subaltern agency debates as a constitutive part of the inter-active framework for theology and faith-based social practices. As such, 'third space' could also provide room for a thorough renegotiating of gendered roles and spaces.

Subalternity and strategic essentialism

The term 'subalternity' has been introduced by Antonio Gramsci[17] to denote those (sub-)groups in society which are excluded from access to the dominant, hegemonic sectors and groups of society, their practices and discourses. Subalterns are limited and restricted in access to political participation and decision-making. The notion of subalternity was revitalized during the 1980s by the South Asian Subaltern Studies Group and has become a prominent point

---

[15] Victor Turner, *Dramas, fields and metaphors: Symbolic action in human society* (Ithaca and London: Cornell University Press, 1975), 288.

[16] See e.g. Homi Bhabha, 'Of mimicry and man: The ambivalence of colonial discourse', in Philip Rice and Patricia Waugh (eds), *Modern literary theory: A reader* (London: Hodder Arnold, 1996), 360-67.

[17] See e.g. Antonio Gramsci, *Pre-prison writings* (Cambridge and New York: CUP, 1994).

of reference in post-colonial discourses through Gayatri Chakravorty Spivak's article, 'Can the subaltern speak?' (1988).[18]

Subaltern studies unmask dominant discourses and point to the intersectionality of e.g. the classical triad – race, class and gender – but also in recent years, of religion, sexual orientation and disability. They explore agency from the margins, also in terms of Spivak's strategic essentialism, i.e. by forming alliances of solidarity for change.

Taking diaspora repositioning seriously allows space for an evaluation of notions such as 'agency', 'recipients', 'clients' and 'benefactors', and encourages asset- and community-resource-based approaches. It further challenges us to reconsider the subjects of theology-generating and theology's subversive potential towards change.

A critical framework that engages reflection on liminality, anti-structure and subalternity, and operates within the notion of a third space, could provide the backdrop of a relocation exercise. It could encourage churches to take a more embodied approach that shifts from deductive and dogma-centred positioning of theology in the cathedrals to an inductive, contextually embedded, gendered and embodied diaconal praxis – under way and on the way.

Wayward Diaconal Movements – Gendered Transformation, Reconciliation and Empowerment

Diaconal discourses and practices classically point to the 'margins' as the location of diaconal interaction as well as pointing to the 'centres' of power to be interrogated and challenged, with 'marginalized people' having more and more become interlocutors of theology and diaconal practice during the last decades, and with 'the margins' having emerged as part of the *loci* as well as the location of theology in various regional settings.

As critical theory of and accompanying practice towards transformation, reconciliation, empowerment and justice, *diakonia* is concerned with life-worlds as a point of departure. Taking migration realities seriously requires a rethinking of the impact migration has on e.g. ecclesiology, on approaches to counselling, on the understanding of service and agency, on community-building, on education, on development, on human and gender rights, on advocacy, on 'othering' or 'withering', and on the understanding of resistance.

With migration more and more emerging as a challenge to institutionalized, congregational and individual *diakonia*, in many country contexts *diakonia* has emerged as a hearing aid, magnifying the cries of those moving along between countries of origin and their respective challenges and a preferred scenario. And *diakonia* has emerged as an eye-opener, sharing the insights gained in

[18] Gayatri C. Spivak, 'Can the subaltern speak?' in Cary Nelson and Lawrence Grossberg (eds), *Marxism and the interpretation of culture* (Urbana and Chicago: University of Illinois, 1988), 271-313.

being with migrants, with government officials and policy-makers, pointing to shortcomings and injustices in country- or region-related migration, asylum and protection policies.

Rediscovering the notion of a 'go-between', *diakonia* in many high-migration-affected contexts has surfaced not only as a mediating force but has also developed diaconal spiritualities in terms of resistance: rediscovering a government-critical biblical trajectory and working on a diapraxis that builds on the agency of those marginalized through the intersectionality of a globalized world that had ceased to be a global village. In sequential migration-related traumatization,[19] *diakonia* has transpired as a 'go-between' and interruption, in terms of classical individual counselling as well as in terms of exposing and tackling, by way of advocacy, resistance and lobbying, the forces that lead to traumatization and its corollaries.

Publications such as the 2009 Lutheran World Federation document 'Diakonia in Context'[20] have embedded diaconal discourses and frameworks into concepts such as transformation, reconciliation and empowerment, and have encouraged a *diakonia* that dares to turn the tables. Spelling these essential notions out in terms of the triangle gender-based violence, migration and diaconal engagement, might help to rediscover areas in which current diaconal engagement is – though being an eye-opener to the challenges migrants face in general – still partially blind to gender-specific human rights violations and their impact, as well as to the need for a stronger consideration of gender-based human rights violations in national and international migration-related policy formation.

Acknowledging liminality, anti-structure, and subalternity, *diakonia* might emerge as a third space as unfolded by Sibongile, arguing: 'Justice, in the Bible it is for three groups, isn't it? For widows, orphans and strangers. So yes, we are all citizens of the Kingdom of God, that we are. But *diakonia* needs to be with those who are no longer citizens of a state, because they flee from whatever, like the women flee from all these many things that make your life as a woman unbearable. The church, if they don't listen to the cries of the women, they forget to listen to those God listens to most. And the church, if they forget to be with those with no rights, women first, they forget where God was and is

---

[19] Traumatic experiences include, besides various experiences of violence and threats to life, the following psycho-social and socio-economic losses and challenges: a) leaving friends and family as well as other networks behind, b) often the loss of use of the native language, c) of culture and cultural identity, d) of place and orientation, e) of social status and previous profession; f) with depression and health issues often emerging; Oscar A. Rodriguez, 'A witness to hope: Migration and human solidarity', in Daniel Groody and Gioacchino Campese (eds), *A promised land, a perilous journey: Theological perspectives on migration* (Notre Dame, IN: University of Notre Dame Press, 2008), xi-xvii.

[20] Lutheran World Federation, *Diakonia in Context: Transformation, Reconciliation, Empowerment* (Geneva: Lutheran World Federation, 2009).

most. And the church, if they forget being right there where the millions of migrants are, on the dangerous routes, then they forget where God is: not in the Temple in Jerusalem but right out there, in all the Susas[21] and diasporas of this world where women are suffering the most.'

Engendering *diakonia* would be an essential step along the way – en route to justice, transformation, reconciliation and empowerment.

[21] Reference to the Book of Esther, with Susa being the capital of the Persian Empire; often used in diaspora discourses as a reference to diaspora contexts and its oppressive structures in general.

'Women, use your talents!' Empowerment in the Malagasy Lutheran Church – Madagascar

Zo Ramiandra Rakotoarison

This article will be based mainly on a Diakonia and Christian Social practices' master thesis in 2013 concerning the result of research on church work on the empowerment of women through a development project called 'Use Your Talents' (UYT). The article will try to answer the question about the implication of gender on Christian social practice.

Use Your Talents: A Diaconal Work of the Church

UYT is a national project run by the Malagasy Lutheran Church (MLC) in collaboration with the Norwegian Mission Society (NMS) and funded through Digni,[1] a Norwegian 'umbrella-organization'[2] co-operating with mission and faith-based organizations in Norway and abroad. UYT started in 2008 and is now in its second phase. It was combined into a programme called 'Women Empowerment and Gender Equality' (WEGE) to increase the UYT focus on gender. 'The vision of UYT is: To stimulate and support everybody in the church to use his or her talents to build a better Madagascar.'[3] During the first phase, 2008-2012, UYT principally played the role of facilitator[4] and rural agent, counselling or training peasants in the local community through the church development department structure called FANILO.[5] UYT also provided varied training at a national level on how the church may capitalize on and use the talents of Christians to develop the church and the community. The term 'talents' has no clear definition. It encompasses all areas of human life and activity which the UYT project manager classified into five areas: health, communication, education, rural activities, and other activities. At a grassroots

---

[1] *UYT project application* (2007).

[2] Digni: http//digni.no/en (accessed 13th February 2016).

[3] *UYT project application* (2007).

[4] UYT's main activity is facilitating: linking or relating the local population to organisations or structures which provide development services or materials that can help the population improve their activity and their living.

[5] FANILO is an organizational structure composed of committees with co-ordinators whose role is to ensure that development work is on the agenda of the church and part of its activities.

level, UYT is a church activity implemented with and in the community. Thus, in my opinion, it is considered to be diaconal work.

The project responsible for UYT prefers to present it not as a project but as an approach to development because in responsible opinion, the concept behind 'projects' in Madagascar is strongly embedded in funding from abroad while grassroots development initiatives using UYT depend mostly on faith, local talents, volunteers and group support. Volunteering is the basis of UYT, and its development work rests on local human resources and the network of people and organizations[6] that the grassroots exploit for the purpose of development.

Empowerment in the Context of UYT

According to the UYT narrative report in 2015, the number of women and men volunteering to use their talents in the community, supporting or leading groups that year, is almost the same. A volunteer supports a group when she/he shares and assists the other members of her/his group in improving the techniques of one particular activity they all carry out and hence improve their living. WEGE is a capacity-building programme developed by Digni combined with projects like UYT to increase awareness on gender issues within that project. Two persons from MLC were responsible for the programme and planned the WEGE activities within UYT. The activities were mainly awareness-raising on gender towards the leaders and those involved in the development work initiated by the church. Gender includes the collaboration between women and men in development work. The aims of WEGE are poverty reduction, sustainable development and the improvement of women and children's life.[7] Thus women's empowerment opens access for women to develop. This joins the OECD idea that 'African growth and development agenda can only succeed if the continent is able to draw on all its resources and talents, and if women are able to participate fully in economic, social and political life'.[8]

---

[6] *Use Your Talents – The Congregation as Primary Development Agent* (Senter for Interkulturell Kommunikasjon): www.sik.no/project?96&lang=en (accessed 20th February 2013).

[7] BN/Digni, *Women's Empowerment and Gender Equality (WEGE), BN's overall project plan 2007-2009* (2007).

[8] OECD iLibrary, *'Madagascar' in Atlas of Gender and Development: How Social Norms Affect Gender Equality in non-OECD Countries* (OECD publishing: www.keepeek.com/Digital-Asset-Management/oecd/development/atlas-of-gender-and-development/madagascar_9789264077478-116-en (accessed 12th November 2012)).

Malagasy Women in Society and in the Church

Almost half of the 20 million Malagasy populations are women.[9] The World Bank noted in 2012 that Madagascar is one of the poorest countries in the world[10] while UNDP announced that most of the poor people in the world are women.[11] In the Malagasy Constitution, women and men are given equal access to education, work and land. Ramamonjisoa observes that, in some parts of Madagascar, women ensure the subsistence of their family through farming, crafts and trade.[12] Yet discrimination against women exists[13] and inequalities are determined by the culture of the ethnic group and of the region, which does not allow for any generalization about the situation of women in Madagascar.[14] For instance, in Toliara, many women are illiterate and get married at a very early age.[15]

In the MLC, women form the majority of church members. The women's association is very active and makes the most important local financial contribution, voluntary labour and investment in time to the church. Until now, the MLC has not ordained women; however, 'theologically trained women serve in a variety of ministries at all levels of the church', as stated by the Evangelical Lutheran Church in America.[16]

Methods

Data collection was conducted in Madagascar in January 2013. As gender awareness raising meetings were organized for leaders, a questionnaire was distributed to some national leaders of the church. One-on-one and focus group

---

[9] National Institute of Statistics in Madagascar – INSTAT: www.instat.mg/index.php?option=com_content&view=article&id=33&Itemid=56 (accessed 19th March 2013).

[10] World Bank, *Gross national income per capita 2011, Atlas method and PPP*: http://databank.worldbank.org/databank/download/GNIPC.pdf (accessed 19th March 2013).

[11] UNDP, *MDG report 2012 Assessing progress in Africa toward the MDG*: http://web.undp.org/africa/documents/mdg/2012.pdf, *July 2012* (accessed 19th March 2013).

[12] Suzy Ramamonjisoa, 'Empowerment of Women and Democracy in Madagascar', Setting an Agenda for Change in Africa, in *Review of African Political Economy*, No. 58 (1993).

[13] OECD iLibrary, *'Madagascar' in Atlas of Gender and Development.*

[14] *'Rethinking "la femme malgache": new views on gender in Madagascar'*, Institut de Civilisations-Musée d'Art et d'Archéologie, Taloha 13, Numéro spécial (2000).

[15] Marianne Skjortnes; Heidi Holt Zachariassen, *'Even with higher education you remain a woman': a gender perspective on higher education and social change in the Toliara region of Madagascar*, Gender and Education (Routledge, 2009).

[16] *Madagascar's Young Adults in Global Mission (YAGM)* (ELCA: www.elca.org/Who-We-Are/Our-Three-Expressions/Churchwide-Organization/Global-Mission/Engage-in-Global-Mission/Global-Service/Basics-of-Global-Service/Young-Adults/Madagascar.aspx (accessed 9th March 2013).

interviews of direct and indirect practitioners (church and village meetings) in UYT were held at national, regional and at grassroots level in two regional synods in the south of Madagascar: Ambovombe Androy and South Betioky. The south has ethnic groups that are considered to be 'extremely patriarchal' with a very strong male-dominated system. The research intended to find out if the church through its work is making a difference in that region. The informants were composed of a majority of church members and the rest were inhabitants from two rural villages.

The focal points of the questionnaire and interviews were: the understanding of the terms 'talents' and 'gender', the contribution of UYT in the lives of women in the church and in the community, and challenges women face in using their talents in the church and community. The leaders and the direct practitioners had two additional questions related to the teaching of the church on the role of women and the leaders' role in implementing gender equality. All interviews were video-taped, transcribed and then translated.

Theory of Diakonia and Empowerment

Diakonia is understood as a 'responsible service of the Gospel by deeds and by words performed by Christians in response to the needs of people'.[17] The theory on *diakonia* explains the reason why the church is concerned about promoting women's empowerment. The theory of empowerment will be used to see if women are empowered through the work of UYT.

Diakonia values and dignifies people, and is an instrument of inclusion and participation. Jesus' *diakonia* is the model. It encompasses affirmation and defence of human dignity, and the invitation, inclusion and empowerment of people to participate in Jesus' mission.[18] Diaconal development work makes the difference if it favours working methods that prioritize inclusiveness and processes of empowering people for participation.[19] According to Nordstokke, current diaconal work emphasizes the role and importance of the local congregation.[20] The congregation provides various services for the community and at the same time creates space for individual volunteers.

Empowerment increases the capacity, income and participation of an individual, a group or an organization which are the constituents of development. Increased capacity depends on the level of education,[21] of

---

[17] *Diakonia in context* (Lutheran World Federation quotes The Dictionary of the Ecumenical Movement 2009), 40.

[18] *Diakonia in context*, LWF, 25.

[19] *Diakonia in context*, LWF, 80.

[20] Kjell Nordstokke, *Liberating Diakonia* (2011), 44.

[21] Esther Duflo, *Women's empowerment and economic development* (www.nber.org/papers/w17702 (accessed 3rd April 2013).

personal identity and not at least self-esteem.[22] Participation of women in public discussion, decision-making meetings and political debate are signs of empowerment. Women have access to development when they are part of those who decide. Preparing women for leadership or increasing the number of women for leadership is one way of measuring women's empowerment. Accepting women in leadership means that society, the community or an organization addresses issues such as male-dominated structures and cultures, and promotes working relationships between men and women that are mutually supportive and respectful.[23]

Summary of the Findings

Understanding of terms

Most of the Christians interviewed relate the word 'talents' to God's gifts, their apparent skills and professions. At the same time, people in the villages define talents as their occupation and means of subsistence. Gender equality for church leaders corresponds to women in leadership, while some respondents who are indirect practitioners in UYT associate it with human rights, the superiority of men and the percentage of women in a project. In the villages, the term 'gender equality' is not known or understood.

The contribution of UYT in the lives of women

According to the project manager, UYT is not a special project for women; it is intended to be for all men and women who have talents. From experience, the project manager said that women use their talents more than men even if they are given the same talents. Within the church in general, women are given consideration and Christians accept that they occupy a position of responsibility and leadership, particularly as a treasurer. This attribution is not related to the UYT intervention, but to the common knowledge that women are trustworthy with money. Women in the Ambovombe and Ejeda communities have benefited from church initiatives such as income-generating activities, adult literacy, training in leadership and other things. These activities have improved women's family income, and even their status in the community, helped them to increase their contribution to the church, supported the studies of their children and ameliorated their family's nutrition. In addition, some women have now started to express their opinions in public meetings, and some are elected or appointed to positions of leadership. Using their talents helps women to take responsibility and increase their capacity for action and knowledge.

---

[22] Anthea Sully, Ali Green, *The leading question? Women in leadership in churches and ecumenical organizations* (England, Women's Justice Group, 2011), 12-13.

[23] Sully and Green, *The leading question?, 6.*

Challenges women face in using their talents in the church and community

Women may face three types of challenges: first, personal ones, such as the level of education, self-esteem, and poverty. The second challenges come from the community: attitudes of women and men to change, tradition, a jealous husband, men's protection of position and power, not recognizing women's talents as assets, and women's ordination. The third set of challenges are external, such as unstable weather, market rules, a lack of resources, the question of ownership and decision-making, a lack of follow-up and accompaniment of activities, and opportunities for using their talents.

The church's teaching on the role of women

This teaching was not stated clearly. Answers from some respondents suggested that the practice and the constitution of the church expressed its teaching. Women have an important place within the church as they are the majority and the most active. Men and women are given equal standing before God's call.

The role of church leaders' in implementing gender equality

Some leaders appeared to be engaged in working for and supportive of giving women positions of leadership in the church.

Data Analysis

UYT raises people's dignity

Dignity is shown when the leaders or the UYT workers value the action or characteristics of women, such as honesty and ability in managing money, and when they recognize women's contributions and importance within the church. Two women informants, interviewed individually, stated that the local authority and population showed them respect because of what they were doing in the villages. These two people were supported by the FANILO synod co-ordinator in their work. Respect, in my opinion, reflects the dignified relations these women have with others.[24] Yet not all women are privileged to enjoy the respect of men, especially outside the church when the majority is not Christian. Most of my respondents, leaders as well as church members in Ambovombe Androy and Ejeda, agreed that women both participate actively in church and volunteer for development work initiated by the church. LWF would call their participation 'a visible expression of the dignity of all God's people'.[25]

---

[24] Kjell Nordstokke, *Empowerment in the perspective of ecumenical Diakonia* (Diakonia, Vol. 3, 2012).

[25] *Diakonia in context*, LWF, 31.

However, some active participants in UYT also spoke about challenges they are facing such as their powerlessness to apply what they had learned and a lack of materials. In addition, considering the statements of two male informants, it was observed that unjust structures and unjust ideas are not questioned by the church as the development work the church has initiated does not aim to change the tradition which gives men all authority and power. These two men expressed their compliance with local traditions.

UYT is an instrument of inclusion and participation

Both UYT workers and some of the leaders recognize that success in development work depends on the inclusion of women in all phases of the project. Through the UYT project, participation in development work is open to all Christians who are all given talents, but the manager stated that women are the most diligent in using theirs. The inclusive nature of UYT may be expressed in the response of one of the informants, saying that women are freer to use their talents in church and in opposition of the role and responsibility assigned to women in the local villages; they are also eligible to be members of the church committee. Despite this, women's work in church is limited because the first position of leadership in the church is still held by a man, the pastor. Skjortnes even argues that the church is 'cementing existing gender patterns'.[26] She states that the training for women in the church matches the role attributed to women in society, and does not challenge society's patriarchal structure with the division of labour between women and men. This method of 'cementing existing gender patterns' seems also to be true for UYT. The development work created through UYT, particularly in the south of Madagascar, follows the kind of work attributed only to women, such as basketry, weaving, poultry breeding and green leaf vegetable farming. These activities contribute to the increase of women's income, but the women do not acquire new skills which may enable them to take part in decision-making.

UYT serves the community in a flexible and open way

An example of mutual empowerment is the story of the woman who is leading and encouraging women and men in her village to create and expand income-generating activities for the village's benefit. Empowerment in this case can also be understood as 'power with' [someone] when power comes from the unity and collaboration of individuals to solve a problem.[27] In the same way, Willis thinks empowerment is from within, from individuals and groups, and

---

[26] Marianne Skjortnes, *Religion and Development. A Gender Perspective on the Ambiguous Role of the Churches* (a work in progress, 2012).

[27] Jo Rowlands, *Questioning Empowerment: Working with Women in Honduras.* (Oxfam, 1997), 126.

not from the intervention of a third party like NGOs.[28] In fact, if we apply LWF's idea of empowerment to the UYT project, the talents are Christians' strength; Christians were given talents to share and to enjoy with others. The activities of UYT depend on these talents and the work of the volunteers. So the projects initiated in this way are not governed by the ideas of external sponsors, working methods or funding limitations. According to Musa, the work of the volunteers has increased the local church's ability to generate funds and thus makes its programmes more sustainable.[29] UYT volunteers are also working in co-operation with professional workers of the church, and even people outside the church have the opportunity of working together with other NGOs or professional development organizations, depending on the project's requirements. This openness to other organizations outside the church constitutes an opportunity for UYT, in case the kind of project that the congregation has started is not related to any of the church project(s) in the area. It shows the flexibility and dependence of UYT regarding the choice of partnership.

UYT increases the capacity of women

Empowerment is also about increased capacity to lead, to take responsibility and gain self-confidence. The UYT project has techniques which increase the leading capacity of women, for example, by gathering a small group of women with the same talents and by personal coaching. Occupying the position of leadership for women is an option and can be acquired. However, some women believe that simply being given the opportunity and training for leadership is not enough. For them, leadership actions are not just encouraging words in meetings; they should be accompanied by sharing concrete objectives that improve women's lives. The self-financing of local projects might be one of the weaknesses of UYT in this case, as some of the respondents complained about insufficient funds to sustain income-generating activities which in turn limited UYT actions. LWF states that 'true empowerment' equips an individual or a group of people with the necessary skills for transforming their community.[30] Yet, even if my respondent said that women have knowledge, it seems that they are not transforming their community as far as the male-dominated culture is concerned.

UYT increases the income of women

Women recognize that the various income-generating activities like basketry, embroidery, the breeding of laying hens or growing green leaf vegetables help them with family expenses and with their contribution to the church. In

[28] Katie Willis, '*Theories and Practices of Development*' (Second edition, Routledge Perspectives on Development, 2005), 113.
[29] Danladi Musa, *The Local Church as Primary Development Agent* (2012).
[30] *Diakonia in context*, LWF, 61.

addition, the nutrition of their families has also been improved. To Carr, 'access to and control over resources' like money are part of empowerment.[31] However, the women said that in some cases, the husband did not allow the wife to manage her income, and these activities would have no impact within the family or on the woman's life. Thus an increase of income does not necessarily lead to change in control of resources.

UYT increases the participation of women

Women have a sense of being able to act, to cause things to happen in development projects and activities which were not aimed at 'breaking the tradition', as two women leaders' local associations said. With UYT, the majority of volunteers who use their talents are women and, according to LWF, such a high engagement of women is quite common in diaconal work; this provides an opportunity for women 'both in the church and society.'[32]

Various reflexions

UYT has an advantage when there is a lack of gender equality in both church and society; it is useful to focus on the development of talents in general (not gender-specific) in order to gain the support of the majority of people, even if people have different views on women's empowerment. Working at the grassroots level is one of UYT's strengths, as 'talents' involve personal knowledge and material possessions, and local activities are based on and expanded from these. Working at the grassroots level is one of the diaconal values. UYT is not a donor-driven project, but mutuality-driven – when people are asked if they would like to participate in a certain project independently of the donors' ideology or the planned results. Yet, women's presence in the project's planning does not imply that their role and power change or that they are empowered.

I sometimes felt during my fieldwork that western ideas on development, and perhaps those of the UYT project, do not necessarily correspond with the aspirations of the people I met. I also believe that, as in *diakonia*, reading the context with an interdisciplinary approach[33] is appropriate, even for a local development initiative.

Conclusion

After the field research, it was possible to state that UYT as a diaconal work conveyed human dignity and allowed both Christians as well as community

[31] E. Summerson Carr, *Rethinking Empowerment Theory Using a Feminist Lens: The Importance of Process.* (Sage, 2003: http://aff.sagepub.com/content/18/1/8; accessed 3rd April 2013).
[32] *Diakonia in context,* LWF, 67.
[33] *Diakonia in context,* LWF, 75.

villagers to participate in its activities and support one another. Research shows that the work of the church and UYT in the community changed lives. Some women acquired new knowledge and new status. Others were given the opportunity to improve their own lives and that of others. Their family, church and community all benefited from their involvement in UYT and changed conditions. We also observed that women became more courageous in stepping out of their traditional positions and roles despite challenges. Besides, a number of church leaders inquired tend to promote women's leadership. The transformation of the attitudes of women, church leaders and people in the community would hopefully be a way of opening up more opportunities for women in the future.

This study has also shown that, though women may improve their capacity, have access to resources and be involved in various development activities, power relations in the community may remain unchallenged. This leads to thinking that not all changes in women's life necessarily mean that they become empowered.

Bibliography

BN/Digni, *Women's Empowerment and Gender Equality (WEGE), BN's overall project plan 2007-2009,* 2007.

Digni: http//digni.no/en (accessed 13th February 2016).

Duflo, Esther, *Women's empowerment and economic development*: www.nber.org/papers/w17702 (accessed 3rd April 2013).

Carr, E. Summerson, *Rethinking Empowerment Theory Using a Feminist Lens: The Importance of Process.* Sage, 2003: http://aff.sagepub.com/content/18/1/8 (accessed 3rd April 2013).

Madagascar's Young Adults in Global Mission (YAGM), ELCA: www.elca.org/Who-We-Are/Our-Three-Expressions/Churchwide-Organization/Global-Mission/Engage-in-Global-Mission/Global-Service/Basics-of-Global-Service/Young-Adults/Madagascar.aspx (accessed 9th March 2013).

'*Rethinking "la femme malgache": new views on gender in Madagascar',* Antananarivo: Institut de Civilisations-Musée d'Art et d'Archéologie, Taloha 13, Numéro spécial, 2000.

Musa, Danladi, *The Local Church as Primary Development Agent,* 2012.

National Institute of Statistics in Madagascar – INSTAT: www.instat.mg /index.php?option=com_content&view=article&id=33&Itemid=56 (accessed 19th March 2013.

Nordstokke, Kjell *Empowerment in the perspective of ecumenical Diakonia*, in Diakonia, Vol. 3, 2012.

Nordstokke, Kjell, *Liberating Diakonia,* 2011.

OECD iLibrary, '*Madagascar' in Atlas of Gender and Development: How Social Norms Affect Gender Equality in non-OECD Countries.* OECD publishing: www.keepeek.com/Digital-Asset-Management/oecd/development/atlas-of-gender-and-development/madagascar_9789264077478-116-en (accessed 12th November 2012).

Ramamonjisoa, Suzy, 'Empowerment of Women and Democracy in Madagascar', Setting an Agenda for Change in Africa, in *Review of African Political Economy,*

No. 58, 1993.

Rowlands, Jo, *Questioning Empowerment: Working with Women in Honduras*. Oxfam, 1997.

Use Your Talents – The Congregation as Primary Development Agent, Senter for Interkulturell Kommunikasjon: www.sik.no/project?96&lang=en (accessed 20th February 2013).

Skjortnes, Marianne and Heidi Holt Zachariassen, *'Even with higher education you remain a woman': a gender perspective on higher education and social change in the Toliara region of Madagascar*. Gender and Education, Routledge, 2009.

Skjortnes, Marianne, *Religion and Development. A Gender Perspective on the Ambiguous Role of the Churches*. A work in progress, 2012.

Sully, Anthea and Ali Green, *The leading question? Women in leadership in churches and ecumenical organizations,* England: Women's Justice Group, 2011.

Diakonia in context, The Lutheran World Federation, 2009.

UNDP, *MDG report 2012 Assessing progress in Africa toward the MDG*: http://web.undp.org/africa/documents/mdg/2012.pdf, *July 2012* (accessed 19th March 2013).

Use Your Talents project application. 2007.

Willis, Katie, '*Theories and Practices of Development*'. Second edition, Routledge Perspectives on Development, 2005.

World Bank, *Gross national income per capita 2011, Atlas method and PPP*: http://databank.worldbank.org/databank/download/GNIPC.pdf (accessed 19th March 2013).

The Africanisation of Diakonia: Care in Community with *Femmes Pour Christ* in Cameroon

Terese Bue Kessel

I have been touched by some women I met during field research in Cameroon, in the heart of Africa. In the midst of a church, they practise a system of communal living built on the value of care in community.[1] I have not experienced anything like this in my Norwegian church context. Reciprocal care is part of their local tradition and refers to a close relationship between young and old in an intimate community of belonging – of care in community.[2] Through the women's active involvement in the movement *Femmes Pour Christ* (FPC), or Women for Christ, in Eglise Evangélique Luthérienne au Cameroun (EELC) they care for the individual through the community.[3] As a Christian community, they demonstrate acts of compassion to relieve suffering.[4] They are africanising *diakonia*.

The women's movement is organised in local groups in EELC congregations across the nation. The symbol of the movement consists of a cross, an open Bible and praying hands. This reflects the identity and practice of an everyday *diakonia*. This identity is rooted in the Christian faith, and the practice is carried out publicly without embarrassment in local neighbourhoods and health centres. The women visit, not individually but as a group, those who are sick and those who mourn. They comfort them, pray for them and provide practical help.

In what follows, I will reflect on how Christian women are transforming local traditions of care into becoming the church's everyday *diakonia*, and what I mean by the africanisation of pastoral care as diaconal practice. The term 'pastoral care' refers to practices of care and compassion carried out by

---

[1] Peter Lechion Kimilike, 'Integrating the African perspective', in Øyvind M. Eide et al (eds), *Restoring Life in Christ: Dialogues of Care in Christian Communities: An African Perspective* (Erlanger Verlag für Mission und Ökumene, 2008), 30.

[2] John Lansley, 'Reciprocity', in *Modern Churchman,* 32:3 (1990), 41-47.

[3] EELC has, since 1975, been an independent church. It grew out of American and Norwegian Protestant missions. Kåre Lode, *Appelés à la liberté: Histoire de l'Eglise Evangélique Luthérienne du Cameroun* (Amstelveen, Netherlands: IMPROCEP éditions, 1990).

[4] Kjell Nordstokke, *Liberating Diakonia* (Trondheim, Norway: Tapir akademisk forlag, 2011).

members of a Christian community to relieve suffering.[5] I also ask if the africanisation of pastoral care from a gender perspective includes dimensions of a dilemma for women who bear heavy responsibilities at home. Does diaconal duty, which creates spaces of inclusion and initiates healing processes, also disturb the rhythm of women's daily chores? I start the discussion with a brief introduction to the context with reference to my research on the FPC movement.

The Research Context and a Diakonia from Below

Femmes pour Christ was established in 1975 in the context of the young church, Eglise Evangélique Luthérienne du Cameroon (EELC),[6] to address rural and semi-rural women. The aim was to enable women in a patriarchal culture to be active participants in life at home, in church and in society. Forty years later, FPC is still a dynamic movement with more than 25,000 members who are involved in various diaconal practices in the congregations of the EELC.[7]

In 2010 and 2011, I did field research in Ngaoundéré and interviewed seventeen women actively involved in the movement.[8] I participated in group meetings in church and in private homes and observed their practices. I interacted informally with FPC members in addition to my informants, and with pastors and lay people in the church. All informants were semi-rural women who identified themselves as farmers, *débrouillard* or *bayam-sellam*. *Bayam-sellam* is a Pidgin English word composed of the words 'to buy' and 'to sell'. It points to the activity of buying goods in order to sell them at some profit – a 'small-business, day-to-day market woman'.[9] A *débrouillard* refers to people with an unpredictable life situation who in various ways improvise strategies for survival.[10] The term 'semi-rural' refers to people who live in urban contexts but make their living as farmers or market women similar to the conditions of rural areas. All informants were responsible for large households, and many were married to husbands with no regular income. Citations of the

---

5 Øyvind M. Eide, 'Introduction', in Eide, *Restoring Life in Christ*, 3.

6 The church has since changed its name by altering the particle 'du' to 'au', cf. the introductory section.

7 Terese Bue Kessel, 'Between God's Sharing Power and Men's Controlling Power: A Quest for Diaconal Empowerment and Transformation in Femmes Pour Christ in Cameroon' (PhD thesis, Stavanger, Norway: Misjonshøgskolen, 2014).

8 For the selection of informants and research ethics, see Bue Kessel, 'God's Sharing Power', 30-33.

9 Juliana Makuchi, *Your Madness, not Mine: Stories of Cameroon* (Ohio City, OH: Center for International Studies, 1999), 27.

10 Trond Waage, '"Chez nous on se débrouille": Om håndtering av uforutsigbarhet: Fortellinger fra syv ungdomsmiljøer i den polyetniske byen Ngaoundéré i Nord Kamerun' (Tromsø, Norway: Cand.polit. University of Tromsø, 2002).

interviewees are my translations from French and for ethical reasons are referred to with fictitious names.[11]

The EELC has understood *diakonia* primarily as a practice carried out by trained health staff in diaconal institutions, in hospitals and health centres built by American and Norwegian Protestant missions in the 1950s and 1960s.[12] The diaconal heritage brought from the West mirrors a *diakonia* from above, a *diakonia for* others performed by trained, salaried and professionals.[13] It is a service performed by active agents to passive recipients. Institutional *diakonia* developed due to the modern diaconal movement in Europe in the nineteenth century.[14] It started in Germany and spread to the Nordic countries and America before finding its way to Africa with the help of western missions.

Contrary to a *diakonia for* others as compassion carried out in institutions, FPC women practise a *diakonia from* below. It is a *diakonia* between equals and *with* others.[15] In my thesis, I provide a detailed description and analysis of these practices.[16] The system of reciprocity in the FPC community persists because the women share the same values and have similar needs. One day they act as care-givers, the next day the roles change. They are neither trained nor paid for their efforts. Reciprocity is instead a pattern of social relationships based on some kind of exchange between those who belong to a given community. This requires an obligation and duty to repay favours within the relationship.[17] The idea of reciprocity is rooted in local traditions and a worldview based on collectivism and aimed at caring for the individual, an essential task in a society with no public welfare.

Semi-urban women who have traditionally acted within two spheres – the home and the field/market – were, with the entry of Christianity to the region in 1925, provided a new sphere in which to act, namely, the church. The church has been a source of knowledge that has initiated processes of self-consciousness, empowerment and transformation. As a result of Christian

---

[11] There are more than 250 ethnic languages in Cameroon, and therefore French was therefore used in the interview setting. Since French is not the mother tongue of any of the informants, their way of speaking is coloured by ethnic languages. In order to respect their integrity, I have sought to combine their oral French competence with some corresponding English without providing a correct Standard English translation.

[12] Lode, *Histoire de l'Eglise*, 36-49.

[13] Bue Kessel, 'God's Sharing Power', 41-44.

[14] Øyvind Foss, *Kirkens diakoni i bibelteologisk, historisk og etisk belysning: En studie i den kristne kirkes socialhistorie med baggrund i urkristendommens forståelse af kærlighedens gerninger* (Aarhus, Denmark: Aarhus Universitetsforlag, 1992), 95-108.

[15] Lutheran World Federation, *Diakonia in Context: Transformation, Reconciliation, Empowerment: An LWF Contribution to the Understanding and Practice of Diakonia* (Geneva: LWF, 2009).

[16] Bue Kessel, 'God's Sharing Power', 137-55.

[17] Lansley, 'Reciprocity', 41-47.

teaching, women view themselves in a new way. Church affiliation has given them a new identity in Christ as dignified and equal to men, before God. These same women have brought their local traditions of care to the church from which they have developed an African pastoral care in the Christian community to relieve pain.

'When One of our Members is Sick, it Means that We Are All Sick.'[18]

The pillars of the FPC movement are teaching and sensitisation and an everyday diaconal practice. A characteristic of their activities is weekly meetings in church and private homes. A liturgical framework makes the meetings predictable week after week with singing, prayers, and a session of mutual discussion on biblical and social issues taken from an annual manual.[19] However, the group meeting is not only an opportunity for cognitive and spiritual development. It is from this community of sharing life and belief that pastoral care arises.

When they meet, they notice if and why a member is absent. In case of sickness and death, 'we choose two or three women and the leader, and we go and do the prayer'.[20] The meeting is a chance to plan their outreach:

> When one of our members is sick, it means that we are all sick. We have to visit her. We have to take care of her needs. And when a woman is grieving… we have to be there. We have to embrace her. We have to comfort her. We have to remember her in our prayers and give her some help. But here, we don't have money. We defend ourselves with our small business. We collect 100 francs [1.15 Euros] to help our sisters[21] who are sick or who are in need because of illness and grief.[22]

There is no distinction between the individual and the community. They belong to one another in an intimate relationship. When one person suffers, the community responds by reaching out in support. Money collected is used to help the sick who have no medical insurance to pay for treatment. The visits respond to a need for comfort and care in a context of frequent disease and death: 'There are many diseases, many diseases, malaria, diarrhœa, many diseases.'[23] In addition, the pandemic of HIV/AIDS has made life worse. The FPC women's approach echoes an African collectivistic worldview and community lifestyle and the biblical model of a Christian fellowship as

[18] Jabilin, 20th February 2010.
[19] Bue Kessel, 'God's Sharing Power', 107-35.
[20] Jabilin, 20th February 2010.
[21] They refer to one another in family terms that reflect both the biblical term of 'sister in Christ', and the wider African family beyond blood ties.
[22] Jabilin, 20th February 2010.
[23] Sapin, 21st September 2011.

described in Romans 12. This stands in contrast to a individualistic western lifestyle. While listing what happens during a visit, Jabilin describes the everyday condition of struggle common to all of them. The context yearns for a mutual diaconal practice.

A characteristic of the visit is giving ear to the sick: '… and you have to sit down with her and understand her needs and pray with her.'[24] Sensitive listening, prayers and songs, affirm belonging to the fellowship even when they are sick. My material confirms that the communal lifestyle within the church context initiates healing processes:

> When people come like that, you are happy. The illness goes away. And when they leave, the illness starts again. When you start thinking again, the illness comes back. And when they come to you, to pray with you, and talk with you, it is very good. […] I talk about everything, the disease, or this or that, what bothers me in my home. I say everything. And then, we finish. And then, we pray.[25]

Sasemi and other informants tell about an experience of a healing process when surrounded by the sisters. They create a space of inclusion where pain is relieved. Without theoretical training in pastoral care, the FPC women have a natural competence in caring through 'learning by doing' in their traditional corporate communities of reciprocity. In church, they continue to shape this competence to include both cultural and theological values.

The Africanisation of Diakonia from Below

Africanisation refers to a renewed interest in Africa and its way of life. It is about affirming the resources of African culture and identity.[26] In recent decades, African theologians have been developing a contextual theology that derives from the African continent, reflects an African worldview and is concerned with the challenges of peoples' everyday life in dialogue with the Bible.[27] African Theology is theological reflection and expression by African Christians. Women theologians engage in this task as well, as seen in the Circle of Concerned African Women Theologians (the Circle) initiated in Ghana in 1989.[28] African theology opposes a dominant academic western theology, brought to the continent by missionaries, which has often been distant from the

---

[24] Jabilin, 20th February 2010.

[25] Sasemi, 5th February 2010.

[26] Kimilike, 'Integrating the African Perspective', 28-37.

[27] Kwame Bediako, *Christianity in Africa: The Renewal of a Non-Western Religion* (Edinburgh: Edinburgh University, 1995); John Parratt, *Reinventing Christianity: African Theology Today* (Grand Rapids, MI: Eerdmans, 1995); Lamin Sanneh, *Disciples of All Nations: Pillars of World Christianity* (Oxford: OUP, 2008).

[28] Oduyoye, *Beads and Strands: Reflections of an African Woman on Christianity in Africa* (Maryknoll,
NY.: Orbis Books, 2004).

concerns of peoples' everyday life. The term 'africanisation' is a conscious quest of nothing more or less than the right to be an African and embrace the African heritage. It asks if pastoral care and counselling can 'be both sensitive to African cultural values and genuinely theological'.[29]

Neither American nor Norwegian missionaries to Cameroon taught local women to visit one another when sick. The women already did so before getting involved with the church. When they heard stories of Jesus, a missionary in the 1980s recalls them saying: 'We didn't know that Jesus also visited the sick'.[30] Care practices as demonstrated in FPC did not originate from western theology. Its origin is indigenous and reflects Kimilike's point of view that 'African insights of care suggest that tradition has something which is not immediately apparent when using westernized lenses'.[31] FPC has promoted African culture when they have built their movement on a pillar of care. Simultaneously, the way they plan and practise the visits reflect three core values of ecumenical *diakonia*. First, it is rooted in the belief of the church. Second, it responds to the social context that challenges the church. Third, it is planned rather than spontaneous action.[32] Pastoral care as diaconal practices in FPC has an ecclesiological identity that, when combined with African values and expressions of care, demonstrates an africanisation of Christian practice. To semi-rural women, pastoral care in FPC substitutes the system of social security they lost when they moved from the village to the city. Contextual needs challenge church practices to be sensitive to both African cultural values and diaconal understanding.

This does not mean that traditional values are, by definition, consistent with theological values. According to informants, traditional care practices include caring primarily for those of the same ethnic affiliation. A nation with more than 250 ethnic groups experiences ethnic challenges. FPC acknowledges this fact and encourages caring practices that overrule ethnic barriers. It teaches the biblical standard that 'there is neither Jew nor Greek, slave nor free, male nor female, for you are all one in Christ Jesus' (Gal. 3:28). FPC reshapes traditional care expressions. It affirms genuine African values that correspond to biblical models of ecclesiology while trying to oppose practices of exclusion.

Missionaries to Africa have for the most part taught pastoral care and counselling from a classical perspective. [33] Pastoral counselling refers to a specialised form of pastoral care that takes place within a relationship between a trained counsellor and the person in need. A classical model emphasises that humankind is sinful and in need of salvation. The task is to help the person repent and get into a right relationship with God with less focus on the person's

---

[29] Kimilike, 'Integrating the African Perspective', 24.
[30] Bue Kessel, 'God's Sharing Power', 150.
[31] Kimilike, 'Integrating the African Perspective', 36.
[32] Nordstokke, *Diakonia in Context,* 40-43, 47-49.
[33] Eide, 'Introduction', 17-21.

other burdens. African voices challenge the individualistic perspective seen in both the classical and the clinical model that separate the counsellor and the confidant from the community of the church. [34] According to the African perspective, pastoral care and counselling must reflect how people organise their lives. It must acknowledge cultural consciousness, the African worldview, and build on knowledge of African care practices.[35] It cannot be confined, as in the West, to a relationship between the counsellor and the confidant because that is not how Africans live their lives: '... caring is far more than the work of a single individual or a professional practitioner.'[36] Therefore, there is a need for a communal and contextual care practice in the churches of Africa. As far as I can see, this is what the FPC women are demonstrating: a contextual pastoral care rooted in community that is different from the western classical and clinical approach.

Dimensions of Dilemma in Gender-Imbalanced Care Practices

The FPC has from its beginning addressed rural and semi-rural people who are farmers, *débrouillard* and *bayam-sellam.* These women have, as already mentioned, traditionally acted within two spheres, at home as mothers/wives, and as farmers/businesswomen at the local market. When the church was established, the women got a new sphere in which they could live and belong. They gained access to new knowledge and a new identity of gender equality through Christian teaching. This contrasted the identity of inferiority they had had in patriarchal society.

The FPC upholds local traditions of care that represents an advantage for those who have moved from the community life of the village to the city. However, to be an African woman at home and in church requires two sets of duties and obligations which may become a dilemma:

> As for me, I have chosen the road of the church. I do not have time to look for money every day. I am busy with all the group meetings. I do not have time to sell at the market until 6 pm for the sake of money. Since our meeting is on Thursday at 3 pm. Well, from 3 pm till 5.30 pm. Then it finishes. Well, in our group we are many. There are many women. Well, there will be cases of mourning, as I have told you, cases of illness, and all those who didn't come to the meeting. I as responsible will have to go and search for them to visit and pray with them in their home or at the hospital. You see, I don't have time. [...] Yes, yes. I don't have much time to engage in small business. Because there are times when I will

[34] According to the clinical model, pastoral counselling needs to engage not only with biblical doctrine but also with psychology. Charles V. Gerkin, *The Living Human Document: Re-Visioning Pastoral Counseling in a Hermeneutical Mode* (Nashville, TN: Abingdon Press, 1984).

[35] See Tanzanian scholarship on the issue in Eide, 'Introduction', 19-21.

[36] Kimilike, 'Integrating the African Perspective', 35.

> go and visit. […] And they live far, far, away in another neighbourhood. […] … and you have to sit down with her and understand her needs and pray with her. That also takes time.[37]

An FPC woman who tries to combine the duties of the family with the duties of the church often experiences a conflict of interest and priorities. To manage a consistent business in parallel with the FPC engagement is difficult because both activities take place at the same time. Several informants confirmed that this clash was a dilemma. I heard about many women who had been involved in the movement but had withdrawn due to the incompatible obligations of home and church.

African women theologians claim that African culture is a two-edged sword. It is both a creed of community and solidarity, and it is an arena of genders preventing one another's development. Cultural values are used to justify differences and harm women.[38] According to the patriarchal context of this discussion, women belong to men. They experience limitation of freedom.[39]

Market business is a woman's affair, for the sake of the family. It is unlikely that a husband, even without job and with time to spare, will step in and keep the business going so the wife can take care of her responsibilities in the FPC. Even if her engagement in the FPC may one day benefit the family in times of crises, any sharing of family duties for this purpose is not common.

During the 1990s, the Circle had a major focus on researching the oral stories and rituals that shape women's roles and implement norms in the relationship between men and women.[40] Gender as a social construction defines gender roles.[41] The everyday language of FPC women reflects how the responsibilities of home are women's duties, and how this prevents participation in FPC. Care practices as diaconal practices 'from below' are sustainable only when a system of reciprocity functions. Therefore, it seems that the africanisation of diaconal care has a weak joint. By being mainly a female task, women unable to participate because of gender roles at home, may be set apart because 'care practices *with* others in church' depend on mutual efforts.

There are profound difficulties related to the liberation of culture in Africa. To be critical of culture can threaten the security of the community because culture is 'the very veins through which the solidarity of communities is

---

[37] Jabilin, 20th February 2010.

[38] Musimbi Kanyoro, *Introducing Feminist Cultural Hermeneutics: An African Perspective* (Cleveland, OH: Pilgrim Press, 2002), 64.

[39] Bue Kessel, 'God's Sharing Power', 61-80.

[40] Rosemary Edet, 'Christianity and African Women's Ritual', in Mercy Amba Oduyoye and Musimbi R.A. Kanyoro (eds), *The Will to Arise: Women, Tradition, and the Church in Africa* (Maryknoll, NY: Orbis Books, 1992), 25-39.

[41] Oduyoye, *Beads and Strands: Reflections of an African Woman,* 78-89.

nurtured'.[42] However, according to the Circle, African women can only experience transformation of living conditions if men agree to a radical examination of gender in relationships. Men and women together must develop an engendered communal theology where gender issues are incorporated.[43] Related to the FPC, this means that only when Christian husbands are included in a discussion of cultural and theological expressions of care, will the Africanisation of diaconal practices become sustainable. The current practices seem to inhibit liberating processes and the inclusion of all.

Concluding Comments

Women in the movement *Femmes Pour Christ* are africanising pastoral care and acts of compassion to relieve suffering in their local environments. Through caring in community, they are shaping contextual care practices in the crossing of cultural and theological values. On the one hand, they demonstrate practices that are clearly community-based. On the other hand, they demonstrate practices different from academic western theology which has often been distant from the concerns of people's everyday life. The FPC women's care practices did not originate in western theology. Their origin is rather indigenous and affirms African theological perspectives, such as Kimilike's point of view that 'the African insights of care suggest that tradition has something which is not immediately apparent when using the Westernized lenses'.[44]

However, the africanisation of pastoral care and counselling, as seen in the distinctive contextual identity of a mutual *diakonia* from below, has a weak joint because care practices at home and in church are gender-imbalanced. This assumption needs closer attention in the ongoing discussion on pastoral care in Africa in order for gender mainstreaming to take place. Otherwise, the benefits of inclusion in diaconal practices may become a dilemma for those who act as care-givers in a community with overwhelming needs.

Bibliography

Bediako, Kwame, *Christianity in Africa: The Renewal of a Non-Western Religion.* Edinburgh: Edinburgh University Press, 1995.

Bue Kessel, Terese, *Between God's Sharing Power and Men's Controlling Power: A Quest for Diaconal Empowerment and Transformation in Femmes Pour Christ in*

---

[42] Kanyoro, *Feminist Cultural Hermeneutics*. 14.

[43] Musimbi Kanyoro, 'Engendered Communal Theology: African Women's Contribution to Theology in the
21st Century', in Nyambura J. Njoroge and Musa W. Dube Shomanah (eds), *Talitha Cum!: Theologies of African Women* (Pietermaritzburg, South Africa: Cluster Publications, 2001), 158-80.

[44] Kimilike, 'Integrating the African Perspective', 36.

Cameroon. PhD thesis. Stavanger, Norway, Misjonshøgskolen, 2014.

Edet, Rosemary N., 'Christianity and African Women's Rituals', in Mercy Amba Oduyoye and Musimbi R.A. Kanyoro (eds), *The Will to Arise: Women Tradition, and the Church in Africa*. Maryknoll, NY: Orbis Books, 1992.

Eide, Øyvind M., 'Introduction', in Øyvind M. Eide et al (eds), *Restoring Life in Christ: Dialogues of Care in Christin Communities: An African Perspective*. Erlanger Verlag für Mission und Ökumene, 2008.

Foss, Øyvind, *Kirkens diakoni i bibelteologisk, historisk og etisk belysning: En studie i den kristne kirkes socialhistorie med baggrund i urkristendommens forståelse af kærlighedens gerninger*. Aarhus: Aarhus Universitetsforlag, 1992.

Gerkin, Charles V., *The Living Human Document: Re-Visioning Pastoral Counseling in a Hermeneutical Mode*. Nashville, TN: Abingdon Press, 1984.

Kanyoro, Musimbi, R.A., 'Engendered Communal Theology: African Women's Contribution to Theology in the 21st Century', in Nyambura J. Njoroge and Musa W. Dube Shomanah (eds), *Talitha Cum!: Theologies of African Women*. Pietermaritzburg, South Africa: Cluster Publications, 2001.

Kanyoro, Musimbi R.A., *Introducing Feminist Cultural Hermeneutics: An African Perspective*. Cleveland, OH: Pilgrim Press, 2002.

Kimilike, Peter Lechion, 'Integrating the African perspective', in Øyvind M. Eide et al (eds), *Restoring Life in Christ: Dialogues of Care in Christian Communities: An African Perspective*. Erlanger Verlag für Mission und Ökumene, 2008

Lansley, John, 'Reciprocity', in *Modern Churchman*, 32:3 (1990).

Lode, Kåre, *Appelés à la liberté: Histoire de l'Eglise Evangélique Luthérienne du Cameroun*.

Amstelveen, Netherlands: IMPROCEP éditions, 1990.

Lutheran World Federation, *Diakonia in Context: Transformation, Reconciliation, Empowerment: An LWF Contribution to the Understanding and Practice of Diakonia*. Geneva: LWF, 2009.

Makuchi, Juliana, *Your Madness, not Mine: Stories of Cameroon*. Ohio City, OH: Centre for International Studies, 1999.

Nordstokke, Kjell, *Liberating Diakonia*. Trondheim, Norway: Tapir akademisk forlag, 2011.

N'Sangou, Arouna, 'La contribution des buy'em sell'em au développement', in Jean Claude Barbier (ed), *Femmes du Cameroun: Mères pacifiques, femmes rebelles*. Bondy: Orstom, 1985.

Oduyoye, Mercy Amba, *Beads and Strands: Reflections of an African Woman on Christianity in Africa*. Maryknoll, NY: Orbis Books, 2004.

Parratt, John, *Reinventing Christianity: African Theology Today*. Grand Rapids, MI: Eerdmans, 1995.

Sanneh, Lamin, *Disciples of All Nations: Pillars of World Christianity*. Oxford: OUP, 2008.

Waage, Trond, '"Chez nous on se débrouille": om håndtering av uforutsigbarhet: Fortellinger

fra syv ungdomsmiljøer i den polyetniske byen Ngaoundéré i Nord Kamerun'. Tromsø, Norway: Cand.polit. University of Tromsø, 2002.

Gender Analysis and Development Work: A Case Study from Ethiopia

Marit Breen

Introduction

The goal of all development work is human well-being, and human resources are crucial to the achievement of such a goal.[1] What follows such logic, then, is that the whole process of development interventions – design, plans, implementation, monitoring, and evaluation – should be conducted with this goal in mind. If so, the identification and meaning of *human well-being* in a given context becomes important, and people must be put at the centre of all development intervention. Before entering a specific context with a certain intervention, it is necessary to carefully investigate *who the people are, how they experience their realities and perceive well-being, and what influences this*. It is also important to understand the connections between these findings. The concept of *empowerment* is central in many development initiatives. Here I will use the concept in accordance with Naila Kabeer's[2] definition: 'Women's empowerment is about the process by which those who have been denied the ability to make strategic life choices acquire such an ability.'[3] I will add the following to this definition: 'In order to find the paths to help themselves in their own development.' When working with empowerment as a means to improve well-being, which in the case of women's empowerment links with achieving gender equality, it is crucial to understand the universe of complex social relationships in which development interventions take place. Interventions always enter into a universe where power balances are shaken and unpredictable outcomes may occur. It is therefore necessary to gain a deep understanding of the context and how the different practitioners and institutions in the field interact. Gender relations are one of the most important social relations in society; hence understanding the differences between women and men's lives and experiences is crucial. A *gender analysis* is a kind of socio-

---

[1] Naila Kabeer, *Reversed Realities: Gender Hierarchies in Development Thought* (London and New York: Verso, 1994).

[2] Naila Kabeer, 'Resources, Agency, Achievements: Reflections on the Measurement of Women's Empowerment', in *Development and Change,* 30, 1999.

[3] Kabeer, 'Resources, Agency, Achievements', 435.

economic analysis, which provides us with the necessary tools to investigate these social relations and how its different practitioners interact, by recognising the differences and inequalities that might otherwise be taken for granted in a particular society.

By drawing on my three years' experience with the Ethiopian Evangelical Church Mekane Yesus' (EECMY) Western Ethiopia Women Empowerment Programme (WEWEP), I will demonstrate the importance and usefulness of applying the gender analytical framework of Kabeer, the *Social Relations Framework* (SRF).[4] Her framework highlights the importance of understanding relationships and institutions, how they interact, and how they are connected with the context in which development interventions operate. Through an institutional analysis provided by this framework, important factors to consider in the continuous programme implementation of WEWEP are revealed. Thus, this paper provides a practical example of how a gender analysis is useful for evaluating an existing programme in order to improve the way we engage with gender in development work – and women's empowerment in particular.

The paper is organised in three main sections: 1) A presentation of Kabeer's SRF and the institutional analysis within her framework, 2) A presentation of EECMY and WEWEP, and 3) An institutional analysis of WEWEP through the application of the SRF. Some central concepts are presented separately in the following.

Central Concepts

Well-being is a complex concept without clear definition in development literature. Here, I will use Robert Chamber's understanding of the concept, as perceptions of 'self-esteem, security, happiness, stress, vulnerability, power, exclusion, and material concerns'.[5] This means that human well-being depends on one's personal perception of it and this will differ from context to context. Such an understanding has implications for development work.

A ***gender analysis*** identifies the types of gender differences and inequalities that might otherwise be taken for granted in a particular society, by asking: *Who does what? Who has what? Who decides? How? Who gains? Who loses?*[6] Such an analysis, however, is only a means to a larger end, namely that of –

[4] The principles of the Social Relations Framework is found in Kabeer's book, *Reversed Realities,* but is mentioned in particular in chapter 10, 264-305.

[5] Ian Scoones, 'Sustainable Rural Livelihoods: A Framework for Analysis', in *IDS Working Paper* 72 (Sussex, UK: IDS, 1998), 6.

[6] Candida March, Ines Smyth and Maitrayee Mukhopadhyay, *A Guide to Gender Analysis Frameworks* (Oxford, Oxfam Publishing, 1999), 18.

> devising and implementing policies and programmes which do not exclude or harm women, which take their needs and perspective into account, and which may help redress some of the existing gender imbalances.[7]

Gender analysis frameworks[8] are practical tools designed to help users integrate a gender analysis. Using a framework may help raise questions, analyse information, and develop strategies to increase women and men's participation in projects so that both can benefit from them. A framework is always designed to fit a particular context at a time, by which its methods and steps will also be influenced. Therefore, a certain framework must be chosen carefully and not be perceived as a 'quick fix' to gender equality: 'No set of methods are in themselves sensitive to differences and inequalities between men and women; each method is only as good as its practitioner.'[9] The *Social Relations Framework* (SRF) designed by Naila Kabeer in the early 1990s, is one such framework.[10]

The Social Relations Framework[11]

The SRF takes a socialist feminist approach, focusing especially on the *social relations of gender* and the role of *institutions* in shaping gender relations. SRF investigates the relations between the different practitioners involved in the field, the power relations at work, and the wider context in order to identify constraints to gender equality and women's *strategic needs.*[12] The framework locates the institution of *the family or kinship* within the network of social relations connecting them also to three other key institutions: *the community, the market, and the state*. According to Kabeer, *institutions* are:

[7] March, Smyth and Mukhopadhyay, *A Guide to Gender Analysis Frameworks*, 12.

[8] This paragraph is informed by March, Smyth and Mukhopadhyay, *A Guide to Gender Analysis Frameworks*, 22-28.

[9] Naila Kabeer, 'Targeting Women or Transforming Institutions? Policy Lessons from NGO antipoverty efforts', in *Development in Practice*, 5 (2), 1995, 108-16, 112.

[10] Further readings on other types of frameworks can be found in March, Smyth and Mukhopadhyay, *A Guide to Gender Analysis Frameworks,* 32-100.

[11] The presentation of the SRF is based on Kabeer, *Reversed Realities,* 264-305 in particular, and March, Smyth and Mukhopadhyay, *A Guide to Gender Analysis Frameworks,* 102-19.

[12] Women's *strategic needs* relate to important life decisions and involve power and control. In order to change women's strategic needs, the existing relationship of unequal power between men and women would have to change. These relate to the gender division of labour, power, control, legal rights, etc. (March, Smyth and Mukhopadhyay, *A Guide to Gender Analysis Frameworks,* 20.)

> frameworks of rules for achieving certain social or economic goals. Institutions ensure production, reinforcement, reproduction of social relations, and thereby create and perpetuate social differences and social inequality.[13]

Organisations are then the specific structural forms that institutions take – or how they are manifested. This means that for the institution of family, a household can be the organisational form; for the community it can be an NGO or a church; for the market it can be a company; and for the state it can be a ministry department or government school. The aim of the SRF is:

> to be a method of analysing existing gender inequalities in the distribution of resources, responsibilities and power, and for designing policies and programmes which enable women to be agents of their own development.[14]

Already here we see how the SRF relates well to the concept of empowerment, and that of well-being as a goal for development; the target group appears as agents of their own development, and their needs and perspectives are at the centre.

The SRF is a comprehensive framework when applied as a whole. In this paper, I will focus only on the part of *institutional analysis.*[15] We have seen that there are four key institutions in the SRF: the family, the community, the market and the state. In our case and, as we will see, the EECMY and WEWEP take the organisational forms of the institution of *the community.* By applying the institutional analysis from Kabeer's framework on these organisations, the important role of gender analysis in development is revealed and demonstrated.

Gender analysis and assumptions about institutions

According to Kabeer, the SRF challenges general assumptions about institutions – that they are ideologically *neutral* and *separate entities.* Following such assumptions, development interventions are perceived to have the same effect on all people, regardless of gender, class, age or other social categories. A change in one of the institutions is not then believed to affect the others also. This is, however, often not the case in the field. Social practitioners, governing norms, rules, cultures and traditions constitute institutions and shape them. These are never neutral bodies operating in a vacuum, but they produce, reinforce and reproduce social difference and inequalities. Institutions also interact in relationship with one another as part of – and conditioned by – a certain context. They are not static entities, but vary from each context in which they operate and can therefore change.

---

[13] March, Smyth and Mukhopadhyay, *A Guide to Gender Analysis Frameworks*, 104.
[14] March, Smyth and Mukhopadhyay, *A Guide to Gender Analysis Frameworks*, 102.
[15] For a full understanding of the framework and its underlying principles, see Kabeer, *Reversed Realities*. For a more practical explanation of its application, as a whole, see March, Smyth and Mukhopadhyay, *A Guide to Gender Analysis Frameworks*.

Social relationships within institutions

Following Kabeer, there are five dimensions of social relationships within institutions: *rules, resources, people, activities, and power*. These are important to investigate in order to reach underneath the surface of official appearance. Organisations often show great commitment to gender on paper or through official documents, but the reality of their values and assumptions may tell a different story. It is the latter which may reveal constraining or enabling factors to the work. When evaluating inequalities in development interventions, it is exactly this institutional analysis provided by the SRF that is helpful, and even more so when dealing with gender inequality.

This also sums up why it is important to undertake gender analysis in development work; if human well-being is an ultimate goal of development work, this must apply equally to both men and women. Without understanding the social relations of gender and how they operate in a particular society, and what may cause barriers to – or enable equality of – well-being cannot be achieved. In order to conceptualise well-being and promote it in a culturally sensitive way, one must have a listening ear to the people themselves, and know the realities and experiences of both men and women. The gender analysis provides us with tools to identify and establish such knowledge.

The Western Ethiopia Women's Empowerment Programme and the Ethiopian Evangelical Church Mekane Yesus

WEWEP is funded by the Norwegian Agency for Development Co-operation (NORAD), through Digni and the Norwegian Mission Society (NMS). The owners and implementers of the programme are the seven synods of the EECMY in the western part of Ethiopia – also the area where NMS has been present and partnering with the church since 1969. EECMY is a national church with twenty-five autonomous synods across the country.[16] The synods function with their own administrative offices, presidents, boards and departments. WEWEP consists of seven of these synods, formed into seven separate projects and one Co-ordination Office. Through the signing of a *Joint Agreement*, these synods established co-operation in 2012 to implement the programme.

Some of the WEWEP activities overlap with and are integrated into the work of the Department of Women's Ministry (DWM) in the church. The purpose of placing WEWEP within this structure is to make it sustainable and create ownership of a work that is often associated with 'foreign money' and not considered a priority. This also contributes to empowering the DWM and the overall church's work on gender and women empowerment.

The mandate of the programme's work is based on the following general problem statement:

---

[16] EECMY, Annual Report 2015 (Department for Mission and Theology, 2015), 76.

> The women of Ethiopia have a low position in society and little influence over their own lives. They have limited access to resources and many of them are victims of various harmful traditional practices that threaten their health and their well-being, and are against national laws. The majority is illiterate and do not know their own rights.[17]

The overall programme goal of WEWEP 2015-2017 is stated in the Programme Document for the same period: *To increase women's empowerment and gender equality in the synods and their target areas.*[18] The processes needed for such achievement are understood as long-term and connected with the overall work of the EECMY. It also links with the policy environment and attitudes on gender issues within the local community and the Ethiopian state. The programme's three focus areas and their areas of activities are summarised in Table 1 below:

Focus areas	Areas of activities
1. Institutionalise the women's empowerment process – and mainstream gender throughout the synods	1.1 Empower the DWM 1.2. Establish a functional monitoring and evaluation system
2. Enhance participation in socio-economic life for target girls and women	2.1. Increase educational opportunities 2.2. Increase income-generating opportunities
3. Increase gender sensitive – and responsive church – and community members	3.1. Mobilise resources and communities 3.2. Standardise training material and resources 3.3. Increase social empowerment

Table 1

The main strategies applied to achieve these objectives can be summed up by the concepts of *ownership* and *sustainability*. The strategies are visible in activities that are focused on two levels: at the *structural* level and at the *grassroots* level. The *structural* level is represented by the seven synods that in Kabeer's SRF make up WEWEP as an *organisation* of the institution of the *community*. It has its own structure, strategies, employees and attached norms, values and attitudes. The synods also reflect EECMY as the national organisation. The *grassroots* level refers to the beneficiaries who are mainly in the target congregations.

I will now turn to the analysis of the institution most relevant to WEWEP in this regard, namely *the community* – being the programme itself (the seven synods) and the EECMY. Due to the limitations of this paper and the comprehensive task of applying the SRF as a whole, the roles of the other three

[17] WEWEP, Programme Document 2012-2014, 2.
[18] WEWEP, Programme Document 2015-2017, 18.

key institutions – the state, the family and the market – will not be dealt with here. The institutional analysis of the SRF is summarised in the table below, which provides a helpful guide for analysis.

Example of Concept Three in the Social Relations Framework: Institutional Analysis *Institutions are key to producing and maintaining social inequalities*		
Key institutions	**Example of organisational forms of institutions**	**Dimensions of social relationships within institutions**
Family/Kinship	Households and lineage groups	• Rules • Resources • People • Activities • Power
Community	NGOs and community organisations: *EECMY* and *WEWEP*.	
Market	Companies, labour unions	
State	Ministry departments, schools	

Table 2

Institutional Analysis of WEWEP and EECMY: Getting One's Own House in Order

To undertake an institutional analysis means asking the questions of *Who does what? Who gains what?* and *Who loses?* (which men and women). This will help establish an idea of the social relations and inequalities at play within the organisation – and the gender inequalities in particular. Moreover, it will identify factors that are either constraining or enabling the programme implementation, thus forming a basis for evaluating to what extent the programme promotes gender equality and women's empowerment.

The importance of focusing on *the community* as one of the five institutions in SRF is in line with the idea that, as development practitioners, we need to get our own house in order.[19] Concerns about gender inequality cannot be raised if the organisation – in our case, WEWEP and EECMY as programme owners and implementers – is doing nothing about the matter in 'its own house'. We will now go through the five dimensions of social relationships within institutions: *rules, resources, people, activities and power*, in relation to WEWEP and EECMY.

[19] Penelope J. Plowman, 'Organisational change from two perspectives', in *Development in Practice*, 10 (2), May 2000, 190.

The far-reaching implications of rules

The rules of an organisation are both official and unofficial. They go together with norms, values, attitudes, traditions, customs and laws, and constitute how things are done in the organisation. Compared with other churches in Africa, EECMY is quite progressive in the area of women's empowerment and gender. To ordination of female pastors and several women-friendly resolutions are evidence of this. However, it is also known that many of these resolutions have not been implemented, and that practical steps are slow. The Programme Document from WEWEP's previous phase states the following about the situation of gender justice within EECMY: 'The situation has been bottlenecked by a lack of organizational commitment and capacity, political will, technical capacity, organizational culture, budget and accountability'.[20] The Baseline Survey from the same phase supports this impression, stating the following about the situation in the six synods at the time:

> The study showed that there were no policies, strategies and guidelines, and monitoring and evaluation systems in the entire synods with regard to gender and women ministry… Almost all of the synods have been conducting the women's ministry work in an unorganized and ad hoc basis.[21]

Several sources[22] attribute a low status in society to Ethiopian girls and women, and the country is reported to have one of the highest rates of gender-based violence in the world.[23] The low status of Ethiopian girls has an impact on their lives from an early age, and relates to a range of human rights violations and what is categorised as 'Harmful Traditional Practices and Beliefs' (HTPBs): the right to make decisions about their own bodies, access to suitable health care, to choose when and whom to marry, when to have sex and negotiate condom use, and opportunities in education and employment. Ethiopian girls are likely to marry at a young age, experience sexual abuse and violence in the form of rape, abduction, Female Genital Mutilation (FGM) and widow inheritance.

The socially constructed notions of what constitute female and male in Ethiopian society underpin this description.[24] Since the church members are

---

[20] WEWEP Programme Document 2012-2014, 12.

[21] WEWEP Baseline Report 2013, 17.

[22] Country progress report on the HIV response, 2014 (Federal Democratic Republic of Ethiopia 31st March 2014): www.unaids.org/sites/default/files/country/documents/ETH_narrative_report_2014.pdf (accessed 8th February 2016), National Adolescent and Youth Reproductive Health Strategy 2006-2015 (Federal Democratic Republic of Ethiopia, Ministry of Health): http://countryoffice.unfpa.org/filemanager/files/ethiopia/ayrh_strategy.pdf (accessed 8th February 2016).

[23] Country progress report on the HIV response, 2014.

[24] When referring to *Ethiopian* or *Ethiopian culture* or *tradition* in this paper, it is mainly in the context of West Ethiopia, which means the Oromo culture since the majority of the work is implemented in the Oromo region. Some of the WEWEP

part of Ethiopian culture and society, the gender relations from these notions will also be found within the church organisation and influence: 'how things get done' there. How different rules are reflected and played out in the organisational life, and in WEWEP, is likely to be influenced by the same notions, so that a perception of women's low status can even be perceived as natural. This can help to explain why progress has proved to be slow, but it also shows why commitment to enhance the efforts in order to bring change is urgent. WEWEP is trying to push for change and hold the church accountable to her commitments, and signs of improvement are showing.

WEWEP is designed to meet some of these challenges through the activities within the first programme component – *to institutionalise the women's empowerment process – and mainstream gender throughout the synod structure* (see Table 1). The target group here is mainly the synod leadership. Main activities are gender training and workshops where synod leaders are actively involved. Since the leadership in the church is heavily male-dominated, the majority of the participants have been men, and most of the departments in each of the synods have been represented during this training and the workshops. Especially encouraging has been the commitment and presence of the top leaders – the church presidents; this has sent a powerful message to the other departments to participate actively. One of the workshops has resulted in the formation of a Gender Guideline, which was based on joint work from the synods where main challenges and solutions for the work on gender and women's empowerment were identified and suggested. These processes will, however, always be threatened and influenced by the social gender relations that dominate Ethiopian society. The church is no exception, and must at all times keep her eyes wide open in order to be aware of these threats and manifestations in her organisation's rules, norms, values and commitments – both the official and the unofficial ones.

Resource allocation in EECMY

The same 'lack of organisational commitment' described above has implications for the allocation of resources among church departments.

In 2010, the EECMY national office decided that all synods should have the same structure with an independent DWM that should report directly to the Executive Board in their respective synod. A successful establishment of these departments in the twenty-seven synods of EECMY requires commitment and resources. In 2015, many of the DWM still lacked a budget, power and even a leader. In the synods where WEWEP operates, the establishment and strengthening of these departments have been an important undertaking of the programme. To allocate the budgets entitled to them, however, is still a work in

activities are also implemented in the Beninshangul-Gumuz region or among women of other minorities, which differ culturally. Where referred to in general, the traditional features overlap.

progress. It has been difficult to identify the amount of budget allocated to the DWM within the synods. This may be a confirmation of the long-term process of the nature of this work, but most importantly it also shows how the allocation of resources in an organisation corresponds to the institutional rules and norms described above. It makes it imperative to keep empowering the DWMs so that they themselves can demand the resources they are entitled to. As a donor, it may be tempting to support these departments financially, but this would undermine the commitment to empowerment. The concept of empowerment is based on giving capacity to the beneficiaries – the organisational leaders and the organisation itself – to take charge of their own development. It means to guide and support the departments in the direction that enables them to claim their own rights and entitlements – in this case, their budgets.

Who are the people involved?

All the WEWEP staff, except the driver and accountant, are women: six project managers, one programme leader, one social co-ordinator, and one gender advisor – most of them young women. All these positions require qualifications within one of the following fields: social work, social science and/or gender and development. Management and administrative skills are additional preferences. Women are encouraged to apply, and in fact very few men have ever applied and none have been professionally qualified.

Theologians dominate the synod staff, and most of these are men. The synod leadership has sometimes communicated its discontent regarding the WEWEP positions not being open to people with theological education. The nature of the WEWEP activities, however, requires other qualifications. There is a desire that the profession and specific sets of qualifications, skills and knowledge from the WEWEP staff, can complement the theology-dominated environment in the church. With their profession and understanding of the social dynamics of both organisations and gender relations, the WEWEP staff have much to contribute to the work of the church – especially the diaconal service. Given the value, authority and respect ascribed to theologians, it has been important for WEWEP to keep its position within the church structure and promote these qualities as valuable and necessary for the church organisation.

To challenge the current hierarchies of positions is not easy. These hierarchies reflect the social categories of age, gender, profession, degree of education and also ethnic group, all of which hold different degrees of power and control. Once challenged or threatened, these hierarchical categories reveal complex social relations. This has occurred in situations of recruitment, in the expansion of activities, in cases of complaints, and when decisions by someone higher in the hierarchy may be questioned. It is when these encounters occur that one realises the importance of joint efforts and partnership in the work on gender and women's empowerment. Trust and respect are key components to such co-operation. If conducted successfully, I assert, power relations within the social relationships will be shaken, so it is important to be able to rely on a supportive network.

Activities

WEWEP is designed to carry out its activities in order to achieve its programme goal. The way these activities are conducted will generate routine patterns of practice that reconstitute the organisation through such practice, and will either work to support or constrain the achievement of its goal.[25] Awareness and constant evaluation of how WEWEP's activities are carried out is therefore necessary. The question of *What is done?* in the programme must be accompanied by *Who does what?*, *Who gets what?* and *Who claims what?*

Young educated women mainly carry out WEWEP's activities. These may be biased in their encounters with beneficiaries of older women or women from ethnic minority groups. In fact, the programme in its design may be biased in how it views and expects the beneficiaries to respond to the different activities. The activity of the women's *Self Help Groups* (SHG) may illustrate some of these challenges.

According to Ethiopian tradition, men, as household heads, are expected to be in charge of the household finances. Most women learn little about how to manage finances, savings and business. This activity is therefore designed on the assumption that Ethiopian women are not economically empowered; hence, empowering them in this area will contribute towards their well-being. The SHG members themselves, however, emphasise other features of this activities when prompted:

> 'We save 5 ETB (about $0.05 US) each time we meet. Before, we didn't believe that we could do anything by ourselves, but now I know that I can help myself,' says Holiti. Zawude tells how she was about to leave her physically disabled husband before she joined the SHG: 'My sisters advised me to stay with my husband. Now they support me through the challenges I face in my home.' Another woman continues: 'We work together and are very happy for the fellowship provided through the Self Help group.' One of them says that the group gives them the opportunity to come out of their homes and meet as sisters: 'Before I was home all the time, but now I have an activity of my own that I can go to and be part of.'[26]

These quotes reveal another perception of well-being or 'development' than that of the programme. Increased income, financial growth and economic empowerment – these are all part of development, and thus the ideas and perceptions of the programme designers have led to an emphasis of these activities. The women themselves, however, appreciate another side of these

---

[25] Kabeer, *Reversed Realities*.

[26] These quotes were collected during a project visit to the WEWEP Self-Help Group in the Handu congregation in the Birbir Dila Synod of West Ethiopia in 2014.

activities, which have led to increased self-confidence, opportunities to get out of their homes and organise themselves, fellowship with other sisters, being part of something of their own and supporting each other's life challenges. Economic empowerment remained a minimal part of their stories, which also implies another perception of well-being and that of 'development'.

As development practitioners, we are always biased in our approaches, and we bring our assumptions into the work. Our assumptions are either expressed through the design of our activities or the ways in which we conduct them. Unless we are aware of the environment and the social relationships in which we implement our work, we cannot successfully contribute to people's well-being. The women in the SHGs brought valuable insights when their true motivation for attending the activities was revealed. Unless WEWEP keeps the needs of fellowship and meeting places for these women at the centre of this activity, no-one will turn up and 'be economically empowered'. The design of the activity itself may even be subject to evaluation.

Power

Social individuals who embody relations of authority and control make up institutions. We saw how the social categories of profession, position, age and gender influence the relationship between the WEWEP staff and the people in church leadership. Ethiopian culture attributes authority and power to people high up in the social hierarchy based on these categories. It is a challenge to negotiate and manoeuvre in this landscape. Change is often a result of slow processes where power relations and authorities have been challenged step-by-step over a longer period of time. The risks of backlash from those in power – those who are challenged – require patience. This is also the reason why focusing on social gender relations – as opposed to only women or only men – is crucial, but also demanding. It implies that when changes take place in the roles of women, the positions of men will naturally be threatened unless they are involved in the processes of change.

During the life-span of WEWEP, visible changes or shifts in power in the positions of authority have been observed. One relates to the decision by the EECMY from 2010 when the national office decided that all synods should establish their own independent DWM. Becoming an independent department had implications for opportunities to apply for funds, to have a seat at the table with the leadership (the synods' Management Committee (MC)), to enhance the decision-making authority by moving it under the Executive Board and thus closer to the power centre of the synods, to have some degree of autonomy and entitlement to a share of the budget allocated equally to the different departments. Another piece of evidence of a potential shift in power is the mandate given by the synod presidents to the DWM Directors to be the only members of the WEWEP MC. Since the programme started, this responsibility was shared with the Executive Secretaries of the synods. From 2015, the presidents simply expressed that it was now time for their DWMs to stand on their own feet and take full responsibility of what it means to be an independent department within the church. This structural change within WEWEP and the constitution of its MC is considered a milestone in the work. But any structural change in favour of gender equality, in administration or in legislation, is never worth more than its enforcement. This takes us back to the people in the organisation, and their willingness and commitment to carry out the work in a gender-sensitive manner. This is always influenced by the constructed social relationships in the context.

Conclusion

Through the application of Kabeer's institutional analysis in the SRF to WEWEP and EECMY, this paper has demonstrated the importance of gender analysis in development work. We have seen how gender relations, as one of the most important social relations in society, are at play within organisations. Due to their nature of being social constructs, they will either perpetuate or challenge existing inequalities. Unless we unpack these relations in our organisations through analysis and evaluations, we may carry out our work in a gender-blind manner. Interventions that were designed to challenge gender inequalities may thus end up perpetuating and reproducing them.

WEWEP and EECMY as organisations in the community must be aware of who they are in relation to their context. They can never be neutral, because unequal social relations within them interact with and reflect the norms and values of the wider community as well. In analyzing the rules, resources, people, activities and power within WEWEP and EECMY, important insights were revealed. The governing official and unofficial rules within the organisation affect the resource allocation; the people have different positions in the social hierarchy that affect the work and how they carry out their activities in different ways, and, finally, power relations within the different social categories such as gender, age, profession and ethnicity govern these relationships. Here we can see how a gender analysis also enables us to take other social relations into account – and not only that of gender.

In the case of the women SHG members, we have seen how a gender analysis can help draw our attention to the target group and their contexts, and in fact put the beneficiaries at the centre of our work. If we are not aware of their perceptions of well-being, their life realities, needs and assets, any development intervention may fail to contribute to their well-being. More importantly, the gender analysis has revealed how gender relations in their context influence their lives and the extent to which they are empowered or disempowered. Empowerment, however, is a process, which looks different to different people and contexts, so careful investigation and knowledge is required before entering the field and planning an intervention. A gender analysis is helpful also in this regard.

Human resources are crucial to the achievement of human well-being as a development goal; a development intervention and its tools and methods can never be better than its development practitioner. This means that each and every one of us in the field of development must be aware of our gendered identities and how these interact with others and the context. Since gender relations are social constructs, they can also change. This is the crucial point for work in gender and development: it is what fuels and inspires any process of change, and which gives relevance and credibility to gender analysis as a powerful tool to promote gender equality and increase women's empowerment. It also emphasises the important role of gender analysis in the achievement of the goal of all development work: human well-being.

Bibliography

Federal Democratic Republic of Ethiopia, Country progress report on the HIV response, 31st March 2014: www.unaids.org/sites/default/files/country/documents/ETH_narrative_report_2014.pdf (accessed 8th February 2016).

Federal Democratic Republic of Ethiopia, Ministry of Health, National Adolescent and youth reproductive health strategy, 2006-2015: http://countryoffice.unfpa.org/filemanager/files/ethiopia/ayrh_strategy.pdf (accessed 8th February 2016).

Kabeer, Naila, *Reversed Realities, Gender Hierarchies in Development Thought.* London and New York: Verso, 1994.

Kabeer, Naila, 'Targeting Women or Transforming Institutions? Policy Lessons from NGO antipoverty efforts', in *Development in Practice*, 5 (2), 1995.

Kabeer, Naila, 'Resources, Agency, Achievements: Reflections on the Measurement of Women's Empowerment', in *Development and Change,* 30, 1999.

March, Candida, Ines Smyth, Maitrayee Mukhopadhyay, *A Guide to Gender Analysis Frameworks*. Oxford, Oxfam Publishing, 1999.

Momsen, Janet H. *Gender and Development*. New York, Routledge, 2004.

Plowman, Penelope, 'Organisational change from two perspectives', in *Development in Practice*, 10 (2), May 2000.

WEWEP Baseline Report, 2013.

WEWEP Programme Document 2012-2014.

WEWEP Programme Document 2015-2017.

Scoones, Ian, 'Sustainable Rural Livelihoods: A Framework for Analysis', in *IDS Working Paper* 72. IDS, Sussex, UK, 1998.

Part 3

Reflections and Key Issues in Diakonia and Gender

Gender Perspectives on Power

Isabel Apawo Phiri and Chammah J. Kaunda

Introduction

The chapter engages with the notion of power in *diakonia* within the World Council of Church (hereafter, WCC) and the ecumenical movement from a gendered perspective. From the outset, it is important to emphasise the fact that power dynamics permeates every dimension of human relationships and life. It has been rightly argued at a WCC Faith and Order consultation that human ability to control, oppress and exploit others, or to enable, empower and emancipate them, is essentially determined by the possession and use of power.[1] Imbalance of power is a situation in which power travels along a one-way street. This tension can also be found in diaconal work that seeks to emancipate the marginalised but which has always been implicated in structures of control and domination.[2] *Diakonia* is entrenched with power that, if used in life-giving ways, has the potential to allow the margins to gain greater control over their lives. Yet the diaconal capacity that can produce this liberation is too often entangled within a web of a power struggle and has exerted control and domination over women and youth, and in the discrimination and exclusion of others based on their sexual orientation, the very groups it aspires to emancipate. Thus, the 'means' can then become an instrumental tyranny that threatens to destroy the 'end' being sought.'[3]

This chapter engages the concept of power in *diakonia* from a gendered perspective through the lens of African feminist post-colonial theory. Musa Dube is one of the prominent African scholars who have engaged this theory. According to Musa:

---

[1] WCC, 'Interrogating and Redefining Power – A Theological Consultation' (Faith and Order, Crêt Bérard, Puidoux, Switzerland, 10th-13th December, 2003): https://www.oikoumene.org/en/resources/documents/commissions/faith-and-order/x-other-documents-from-conferences-and-meetings/theological-reflection-on-peace/interrogating-and-redefining-power-a-theological-consultation (accessed 23rd Dec 2015).

[2] Martin Robra, 'Theological and Biblical Reflection on Diakonia: A Survey of Discussion within the World Council of Churches', in *The Ecumenical Review,* 46, No. 3 (1994), 276-86.

[3] WCC, 'Interrogating and Redefining Power.'

> The struggle for liberation of post-colonial feminist readers is located within the framework of resisting global and natural structures of oppression – be they politically, economically, socially or culturally based. Since gender oppression pervades all sectors of life, post-colonial feminist readers add gender analysis to the struggle of Two-Thirds World communities of resistance to ensure that national and international efforts of establishing justice do not sideline gender justice. Post-colonial feminists thus ask how various forms of national oppression affect women and men, how international forms of oppression affect men and women, how gender oppression functions with other forms of oppression such as class, race, ethnicity, age and sexual orientation. They also propose various ways of reading that will chart social justice and that take on gender justice in national and international relationships.[4]

While Dube's post-colonial discourse focuses on biblical interpretation and exegesis, and what she terms as other 'world' texts in communities of faith within Botswana, this chapter will deal with the engagement of the WCC and its member churches, focusing on two issues: a) The roles of women, and b) How sexual minorities are defining power dynamics in determining partnerships for *diakonia*. Furthermore, our analysis of this topic is influenced by our social location – as an African woman theologian from the Presbyterian tradition, and as an African male theologian from the Pentecostal tradition. Both of us have deep connections with the WCC, which has shaped our ecumenical grounding in the pursuit of gender justice.

Following Dube's guiding theoretical thinking which she uses in her post-colonial feminist strategy of reading the Bible, this chapter investigates the expressions of powers of imperialism and patriarchy in the work of *diakonia*. It examines how the issues of homosexuality and sexual and reproductive health have highlighted the power dynamics between churches in the global North and the global South. It also identifies power relations that promote the dignity of all humanity within church partnerships. We conclude by arguing that the pilgrimage of justice and peace offers a safe space for dialogue and action on contested issues, and still works towards using power in a culturally sensitive way for gender justice.

How We Have Come to the Conversation

African feminist scholars have argued for experience as the foundation and valid starting-point for any liberating theology.[5] These experiences are believed

---

[4] Musa W. Dube, 'Rahab Says Hello to Judith: A Decolonizing Feminist Reading', in R.S. Sugirtharajah (ed), *The Postcolonial Biblical Reader*, 142-58 (Malden, MA: Blackwell, 2006), 142.

[5] For a detailed discussion on the significance of experience for feminist theological thinking, see Isabel A. Phiri and Sarojini Nadar, 'African Women's Theologies', in Diane B Stinton (ed), *African Theology on the Way: Current Conversations*, 90-100 (London: SPCK, 2010), 91-93.

to be contextually based, but even within the same context, these experiences take different turns due to various factors such as culture, religion and status. Thus, feminist thought emphasises the need to consider specifics and the location of experience. Given the significance of this argument, it is important to specify our own locality of experiences, especially as related to ecclesiastical location.

Isabel Apawo Phiri is a woman theologian from the conservative Presbyterian tradition in Malawi. Coming from a country where more than half the population do not have formal education, she cherishes the privilege of having come from a family that valued education, especially of female children. Having worked in secular institutions in the academic world while being closely connected with institutions of the church, she has come to experience the complexity of power dynamics when a female lay person who identifies with a feminist framework is significantly contributing to the education of the male clergy. Working for the World Council of Churches has been an opportunity to bring local activism informed by prophetic theology to an international platform of power.

Chammah J. Kaunda is a male theologian from a Pentecostal tradition in Zambia. He grew up in a context of struggle against extreme poverty and social hardship. He saw his six sisters and a brother drop out of school. As he went further in pursuing education, he came to realise that poverty is the darkness that robs people of the ability to forge their own destiny. He resolved at all costs to acquire an education so that he could immerse himself in understanding, analysing and seeking to bring the light of socio-economic development to those who live in the darkness of poverty. His present involvement with the WCC has been largely as a result of the conviction that if Jesus is the 'Light of the world', then every human being has the right to live in the light through fair access to resources to help make life liveable. His theological thinking is grounded in this passion and a vision for a just, healed and whole society.

Both these authors have deep connections with the WCC and experiences of struggle, which have shaped their ecumenical grounding in the pursuit of gender justice. They are convinced that understanding the complexities of power is essential for achieving a greater degree of gender justice. For this to be achieved, *diakonia* must be grounded in the post-colonial experiences of the marginalised groups.

Musa W. Dube's Post-Colonial Feminist Theory

The second entry point into the conversation on power dynamics in *diakonia* is through the post-colonial feminist theory. Musa Dube's initial reflections on post-colonial feminist theory are found in *Postcolonial Feminist Interpretation of the Bible*.[6] This theoretical lens helped her to note that, at the root of exploitation and oppression in the world today, is established global power dynamics which have direct and indirect implications on the way Christian ministry is done on the continent. Dube's position within the African cultural heritage enabled her to use post-colonial thinking to critique material legacies of colonialism maintained through imperialist and patriarchal structuring of global power relations. She stresses that 'post-colonial is not a discourse of historical accusations, but a committed search and struggle for decolonization and liberation of the oppressed'.[7] Post-colonial theory helps us to understand that the dialectic between the powerful and the powerless cannot be overlooked in diaconal social analysis. Dube's post-colonial thinking sought to overcome the dichotomy between theory and praxis. Her post-colonial discourse is a tapestry of reflection and practice which brings radical diaconal work to the forefront in the struggle against sexism, heterosexism, and HIV/AIDS.[8]

Dube's writings on gender justice (including justice for sexual minorities), HIV/AIDS are aimed not only at a scholarly audience, but also at church and faith readers. In *Africa Praying*, which she edited, Dube observes that HIV has brought *diakonia* schemes and methods to the cul-de-sac threshold, and that the only tangible option was to find another way. She emphasises:

> In the HIV/AIDS era, the discrimination of homosexuals means they are often deprived services that pertain to prevention and provision of quality care. This discrimination means that some homosexuals are forced to hide their identity, to marry wives, and then to live with double sexual life, a secret one and a publicly accepted one.[9]

In the light of this view, Dube calls the church to repent as its lack of love has caused the deaths of millions, hampered HIV prevention and exposed women and homosexuals to HIV infection. She is arguing for a gender-sensitive mission undergirded by justice and humane approaches in the light of the struggle for gender justice, and against discrimination of sexual minorities

---

[6] Musa W. Dube, *Postcolonial Feminist Interpretation of the Bible* (St Louis MO: Chalice Press, 2000).

[7] Musa W. Dube, 'Toward a Postcolonial Feminist Interpretation of the Bible', in *Semeia,* 78 (1997), 11-26, 14.

[8] More examples of Dube's post-colonial praxis thinking can be found in Musa W. Dube, 'Social Location and Storytelling Method of Teaching in HIV/AIDS Contexts', in Musa W. Musa (ed), *HIV/AIDS and the Curriculum: Methods of Integrating HIV/AIDS in Theological Programmes*, 43-58 (Geneva: WCC, 2003); Musa W. Dube (ed), *Other Ways of Reading: African Women and the Bible* (Atlanta, GA: Society of Biblical Literature and Geneva: WCC Publications, 2001); Musa W. Dube, 'Fighting and Crying With God: Who Cares for Children and Women in the HIV/AIDS Era?', in *Journal of Theology for Southern Africa,* 114 (2002), 31-42.

[9] Musa W. Dube (ed), *Africa Praying: A Handbook on HIV/AIDS Sensitive Sermon Guidelines and Liturgy* (Geneva: WCC, 2003), 210.

which urgently needs to be tackled, especially in the context of the HIV struggle. Dube notes that Jesus' mission was targeted at those who were marginalised in society, those in need of care and compassion; he identified himself with the less privileged. She believes that engaging in *diakonia* 'for decolonisation is... imperative for those who are committed to the struggle for liberation'.[10] In post-colonial *diakonia,* 'practice must be dedicated to an ethical task of promoting decolonization, fostering diversity, and imagining liberating ways of interdependence'.[11]

Dube describes globalisation as a direct descendant of colonization. She argues that, while 'distribution of goods and services'[12] is not negative in itself but remains a one-way traffic which makes globalisation an 'anti-social and anti-life force', worsening 'poverty, escalating mobility, the trafficking of women and girls and sex workers'.[13] In another article, 'Looking back and forward', she writes:

> If we understand post-colonialism as a study of international relations; of how ideology of domination, collaboration and resistance are expounded and enacted between nations, globalization finds its place very well in this framework. If we understand post-colonialism as underlining the fact that relationships of domination and subordination, created in modern imperialism, did not end when geographical independence was won, then globalization is a 'mutation', a new form of an old problem.[14]

Dube's verdict on colonial mission is simply 'guilty' – guilty for promoting the globalization of the world based on unequal global power relations. In the light of this view, she then articulates a people-centred mission approach that resists globalising forces – especially because they affect the global South negatively. She suggests 'villagisation' as an alternative to globalisation. She argues that villagisation functions with a concept of power that is multi-directional, based on the promotion of ethics of community care, an economic system from below which strives to empower all its members and encourage reverence for life.[15] Villagisation must not be understood in the sense of the 'grouping of population into centralised planned settlements', as was proposed

---

[10] Musa Dube, 'Villagizing, Globalizing, and Biblical Studies', in Justin S. Ukpong et al, *Reading the Bible in the Global Village: Cape Town*, 49-63 (Atlanta, SBL, 2002), 60.

[11] Musa W. Dube, 'Reading for Decolonization (John 4.1-42)', in *Semeia,* 75 (1996), 37-59. 57.

[12] Musa W. Dube, 'Praying the Lord's Prayer in a Global Economic Era', in *The Ecumenical Review,* 49, No. 4 (1997), 439-50, 441.

[13] Musa W. Dube, 'Theological challenges: Proclaiming the Fullness of Life in the HIV/AIDS and Global Economic Era', in *International Review of Mission, 91*, no. 363 (2002), 535-49, 536.

[14] Musa W Dube, 'Looking Back and Forward: Postcolonialism, Globalization, God and Gender', in *Scriptura* 92 (2006), 178-93, 183.

[15] Dube, 'Villagizing', 62.

in Tanzania and Ethiopia,[16] but in the sense of reclaiming the values and norms that undergirded African philosophy and wisdom within village life.

To articulate mission within villagisation is to empower ordinary women and sexual minorities to articulate their own sexualities and sexual reproductive health in an oppositional stance against imperialism and patriarchal structuring of society and the forces of international injustice. It is about embracing diversity and global justice within the context of villagizing, in which all share mutual respect for each other and seek to know each other by name, face, locality and consent to mutual concerns for each other.[17] Thus, Dube's post-colonial feminist thinking is grounded in experiences from the margins as valid and authentic sources for articulating *diakonia* in the era of globalisation.[18] *Diakonia* from the margins 'promotes marginal voices, by taking up the rainbow colours of the world rather than the continued 'whitening' of the global village.'[19] Understanding *diakonia* within post-colonial feminism means that *diakonia* is a search for how power can be used to promote gender justice, healing from sexism and the heterosexism syndrome, and realising social wholeness. It seeks to decolonize *diakonia*, its practitioners and institutions from which it is articulated so that *diakonia* can become a practice of liberation and a tool for promoting liberating interdependence.

The Concept of Power in Selected Documents

The WCC's *diakonia* seeks to develop a culture for promoting peace and justice in the world. For this reason, the recovery of proactive social commitment to post-colonial *diakonia* is a critical element in overcoming gender injustice and advancing economic justice. The WCC continues to work for climate change, the promotion of life-giving masculinity, overcoming gender-based violence and creating safe spaces, and spaces of grace in human sexuality. Within this approach, we intend to discuss through the lens of post-colonial feminist discourse how the WCC's Diakonia has been engaging with the notion of power

Together Towards Life

WCC's ecumenical mission affirmation by the Commission on World Mission and Evangelism (CWME), *Together Towards Life* (TTL), deals with the

---

[16] Survival International 1988, cited in Christy Cannon Lorgen, 'The Experience of Villagisation: Lessons from Ethiopia, Mozambique, and Tanzania Oxfam-GB': http://mokoro.co.uk/wp-content/uploads/villagisation_ experiences_eth_moz_tanz.pdf (accessed 9th February 2015).

[17] Dube, 'Villagizing', 53ff.

[18] Chammah J. Kaunda and Roderick R. Hewitt, '"Together towards Life": Reconceptualising *Missio*-Formation in the Changing Landscape of World Christianity', in *Pharos Journal of Theology*, Vol. 96 (2015), 1-16, 11.

[19] Dube, 'Villagizing', 59.

changing landscape of world Christianity that has been taking place over the past three decades. The TTL statement is about the search for authentic life. It calls for discerning feasible and adequate mission approaches within the framework of human rights. It also demands a search for justice to facilitate and enable the margins realise fullness of life. TTL calls for mission from the margins with an understanding of the complexities of power dynamics which were overlooked in the past, resulting in domination of the people that the missions sought to empower. The document challenges therefore that –

> The cross calls for repentance in the light of the misuse of power and use of the wrong kind of power in mission and in the church… The Spirit empowers the powerless and challenges the powerful to empty themselves of their privileges for the sake of the disempowered.[20]

The document further argues that:

> Mission from the margins recognizes that being in the centre means having access to systems that lead to one's rights, freedom and individuality being affirmed and respected; living on the margins means exclusion from justice and dignity.[21]
>
> The aim of mission is not simply to move people from the margins to the centres of power but to confront those who remain in the centre by keeping people on the margins. Instead, churches are called to *transform* power structures.[22]

The key phrase in the statement above is 'transform power structures'. TTL argues for overcoming power abuse through a two-way process of engaging with power with a clear dialogue with those on the margins from where mission emerges. The document calls for social analysis to help identify and understand how everyday choices, or the lack of them, have functioned as sources of abuse, and to seek for ways to 'promote human rights, gender justice, climate justice, unity and peace'.[23] While TTL mentions gender justice and includes women among those who are on the margins, it does not go far enough to explain how women have contributed to the transformation of the church and society.

Theological Perspectives on Diakonia in the 21st Century

The concern in relation to power and how to ensure that *diakonia* does not become a project of domination for the marginalised is central to the WCC

---

[20] Jooseop Keum (ed), *Together towards Life: Mission and Evangelism in Changing Landscapes* (Geneva: WCC, 2013), 14.
[21] Keum, *Together towards Life,* 15.
[22] Keum, *Together towards Life,* 16 (italics as found).
[23] Keum, *Together towards Life,* 28.

document on 'Theological Perspectives on Diakonia in the 21st Century'.[24] The document argues that, 'In Christ, the Church is called to hold forth the power of service over the power of domination, so that life, in all its fullness, may be possible for all. Therefore, the Church presents itself not only as a sign of the coming reign of God but also of the way leading to it, Christ's way.'[25] Similarly to TTL, the statement calls for a paradigm shift from '*diakonia* to the margins' to '*diakonia* of the marginalised'. The focus is the distinctive contribution of the people from the margins. The document further argues that, 'Jesus announces his *diakonia* as one that liberates the oppressed, opens the eyes that are blind, and heals the sick (Luke 4:16-17).'[26] In so doing, Jesus identified and located himself with the marginalized in his context. This means that Jesus' *diakonia* rejected abusive power (Luke 4:1-12), refused to give in to the prevailing logic of power (Mark 10.45), and defied oppressive religious traditions (Luke 11:37-54). The centrality of power in *diakonia* resulted in the call for rights-based *diakonia*, 'from the perspective that the struggle for justice and peace are core issues in any diaconal activity, and that it will be successful only when the poor and vulnerable themselves are empowered to claim their rights and have an active role in the shaping of society.'[27] Yet the most serious setback of the document, like TTL, is that the marginalised remained unnamed, and therefore women and sexual minorities remain voiceless.

Empowering Diakonia

Carlos Ham's doctoral thesis argues that significant work has been done in the area of empowerment and *diakonia* within the WCC and the ecumenical movement in general. He proposes a new model which he calls 'empowering *diakonia*'.[28] 'This model,' Ham argues, 'synthesizes, combines and binds both concepts together, namely, a new method, using the steps and tools that are described in the thesis. Arguments are made that this model can become an effective way for diaconal engagement today, since it is being built on a concept and practice of *diakonia* that are both empowered and empowering.'[29]

[24] WCC, 'Theological Perspectives on Diakonia in the 21st Century' (The Conference jointly organized by the Justice and Diakonia, Just and Inclusive Communities, and Mission and Evangelism programmes of the World Council of Churches in Colombo, Sri Lanka, 26th June 2012): https://www.oikoumene.org/en/resources/documents/wcc-programmes/unity-mission-evangelism-and-spirituality/just-and-inclusive-communities/theological-perspectives-on-diakonia-in-21st-century (accessed 23rd December 2015).

[25] WCC, 'Theological Perspectives'.

[26] WCC, 'Theological Perspectives'.

[27] Kjell Nordstokke, 'Ecumenical Diakonia: Responding to the Signs of the Times', in *The Ecumenical Review*, 66, Issue 3 (2014), 265-73, 265.

[28] Carlos E. Ham, *Empowering Diakonia: A Model for Service and Transformation in the Ecumenical Movement and Local Congregations* (doctorial dissertation, Amsterdam: Free University (VU) of Amsterdam, April 2015), 8.

[29] Ham, *Empowering Diakonia*, 275.

He employed the theoretical thinking of Don S. Browning's, *A Fundamental Practical Theology*, in which Browning emphasises '"five dimensions of practical reasons", as foundational elements that conform his understanding of practical theology'.[30] Ham summarises them as visionary, normative, needs-oriented, contextual and transformative. He argues that these 'dimensions are an essential tool not only to interrelate both the theory and practice, but also as a helpful diagnosis instrument for analysis, description and interpretation'.[31] Ham concludes that the 'empowering *diakonia*' model seeks to identify the complexities of power dynamics and empowers the churches to aspire to promote the integration of creation, human rights, gender justice and economic justice. Ham is aware of the power dynamics which *diakonia* must always seek to navigate. He defines empowering *diakonia* as 'the driving force' to lead churches towards 'self-fulfilment as social actors, denouncing power over people' and function, sharing power with people on the margins.[32] Ham's new pragmatic and operational method for *diakonia* does not adequately demonstrate how it can function in the context of the search for gender justice, sexuality and sexual reproductive rights. For example, his use of the theory of Browning to build empowering *diakonia* communities does not take into account the reality that churches have used the scriptures to discriminate against people living with HIV, sexual minorities in accessing treatment, and pregnant girls in accessing sexual reproductive health services in hospitals and clinics owned by churches.

Diaconal Community through a Pilgrimage of Justice and Peace

The Pilgrimage of Justice and Peace is an initiative of WCC member churches which emerged from WCC's Tenth Assembly in Busan, South Korea, in 2013. Thus, it is important to note that, in relation to diaconal work, the Pilgrimage is engaging the notion of power. Isabel Apawo Phiri and Kim Dongsung 'reflect on how the WCC envisions a response to some aspects of *diakonia* in its programmatic work within the framework of the pilgrimage of justice and peace, where the Christian value of dignity for all is upheld'.[33] They argue that theology of life undergirds this pilgrimage. They see theology of life as a theology 'in service to life and in opposition to the life-denying, death-dealing theologies, ideologies, and practices of youth unemployment, unpaid and underpaid employment for women, and social exclusion and marginalization'.[34] For Phiri and Kim, 'at the centre of the pilgrimage of justice and peace, human dignity, health, reconciliation, healing and transformation are essential aspects

---

[30] Ham, *Empowering Diakonia*, 275.
[31] Ham, *Empowering Diakonia*, 275.
[32] Ham, *Empowering Diakonia*, 278.
[33] Isabel A. Phiri and Kim Dongsung, 'Called to Be a Diaconal Community through a Pilgrimage of Justice and Peace', in *The Ecumenical Review*, 66, Issue 3 (2014), 252-64, 252.
[34] Phiri and Dongsung, 'Called to Be a Diaconal Community', 263.

for life in its fullness'.[35] Yet, as in all the WCC documents mentioned above, gender justice, sexuality and reproductive health are not explicitly emphasised as key dimensions for understanding *diakonia*.

Thus, all four theological documents analysed above have in common a blind spot on gender analysis. They work with the assumption that the *route de pèlerinage* is level and non-discriminatory for men, women, children and sexual minorities in the way power is used to transform their relationships. They seem to take an essentialist approach to the concept of the marginalised and, in doing so, marginalise specific experiences of various marginalised groups.

Our argument is that gender bias plays a role in stigmatisation and discrimination of at-risk populations or people on the margins (e.g. sexual minorities, adolescent girls, sex workers, married women) when it comes to access to diaconal services owned by churches.

Conditional International, Ecumenical and Local Relations in Diakonia

The ecumenical movement is now being faced with new challenges in terms of power relations and human sexuality. The unity of the churches is threatened when it comes to issues of gender and sexual orientation. Conservative churches who normally disagree with each other unite to oppose United Nations (UN) women's documents when it comes to gender, sexual minorities and sexual reproductive health. The Vatican works together with Pentecostal and Evangelical churches in North and South America, Africa and Asia, and with Orthodox churches to oppose gender justice for women and girls. Unfortunately, these fights are now linked with governmental and church aid as the aid is usually given by the haves to have-nots. A few examples will suffice. The cases of Nigeria, Uganda and Malawi saw the circular and ecumenical funding agencies withdrawing aid to those countries on the basis of protesting against the criminalisation of same-sex relationships.

Towards Gender Justice on Power in Diakonia

If operating within the framework of the pilgrimage of justice and peace, and if it also uses the lens of post-colonial theory, how do we bring reconciliation and healing over ethical issues that divide the churches in their understanding of gender perspectives on power in *diakonia*?

First, we call for the egalitarian inclusivity of the Jesus community. The church is Jesus' inclusive, relational, dynamic, interdependent community envisioned to function as an alternative model of God's dealing with the world. In this context, *diakonia* is not the end but the means of catalysing the radical inclusivity and egalitarian essence of the Jesus community. The empowering and life-

[35] Phiri and Dongsung, 'Called to Be a Diaconal Community', 263.

affirming inclusiveness of the Jesus community has no identity apart from its inclusion of the marginalised. Jesus' messianic identity was embedded in his inclusiveness of tax collectors and sinners, lepers, women, children, prostitutes – and many others. Indeed, it cannot qualify to be the pilgrimage of justice and peace in the name of Jesus if its *diakonia* functions within a paradigm of exclusion.

Second, we need a recognition of the marginalised as agents of change as a new location from which to view and transform gender struggles in the world. The pilgrimage of justice and peace in post-colonial thinking can only be meaningful and transformative from below 'at the margins because transformation never genuinely happens at the centre but at the margins, where the reality of people seeking fullness of life "that becomes a new creative core"'.[36] This also means that women and sexual minorities have the power to name their realities, and that those seeking to be in solidarity with them acknowledge such experiences.

Third, we also call for reaffirming that the starting-point for *diakonia* in a post-colonial time is not a doctrine but the experiences of women and sexual minorities. The struggle is not whether marginal experiences can be sources of theological construction – for most theologians have long recognised them as 'valid and authentic sources'[37] – but how to accurately and authentically represent these voices. Therefore, *diakonia* in the pilgrimage of justice and peace calls the churches to learn to be quick to listen and to do so in love with grace.

Fourth, we call for the creation of safe spaces and spaces of grace for dialogue. *Diakonia* in the pilgrimage of justice and peace calls for an open and honest dialogical encounter where those engaged in the process can feel and perceive genuine forgiveness, diversity, equality and acceptance. The main obstacles to dialogue in most cases are not only spoken words during interaction, but also the way the dialogue takes place and how words are spoken, along with non-verbal gestures, past experiences and entrenched attitudes and beliefs. Therefore, in the pilgrimage of justice and peace, creating safe spaces and spaces of grace for dialogue requires setting ground rules acceptable to all engaged in dialogue. It also means becoming empathetic and vulnerable listeners. The church has been talking too much and listening very little. Perhaps it is time to listen as Jesus did.

Fifth, we call for critical and authentic solidarity. Throughout Church history, the Bible has been used negatively to promote oppression and the discrimination of women and sexual minorities. In a context that has become sensitive to justice for all, the Bible must be interpreted within the paradigm of the hermeneutics of life. This is a justice for all hermeneutics in which the scriptures are used as an instrument for promoting life. In the context of the

---

[36] Kaunda and Hewitt, 'Together towards Life', 11.
[37] Kaunda and Hewitt, 'Together towards Life', 11.

pilgrimage of justice and peace, life is an overarching frame for reading and interpreting the scriptures. The scriptures are read and interpreted, not as an end in themselves, but as a means for promoting life in its fullness for all people, including women, girls and sexual minorities. Therefore, we call for unconditional love to undergird *diakonia* in the context of the pilgrimage of justice and peace. Kaunda argues elsewhere that 'the church was created by God to be God's social instrument for manifesting his unconditional love, unconditional acceptance and unconditional appreciation of the world as his [sic] good creation'.[38] The church cannot claim to be Jesus' community if its love for other human beings is based on conditions. The love of Jesus is unconditional – which means that, in its profoundest sense, it knows nothing about any conditions.

Conclusion

From the above analysis, we conclude that engaging power in *diakonia* work within the pilgrimage of justice and peace is undergirded by three imperatives. First, there is a need to expose the negative impact of a one-way *diakonia* on women and sexual minorities. This calls for searching for life-giving ways of the use of power in *diakonia* as central to the pilgrimage of justice and peace. Second, there is also a need to unveil historical injustice towards women and sexual minorities which have been used as an ecclesiastical strategy for oppression, exploitation and exclusion. Third, this means that there is a need to support emerging non-western approaches to contemporary *diakonia* work. In this sense, the post-colonial theory can help extend the work of feminist critique to issues of power in *diakonia*. In this way, *diakonia* becomes a post-colonial spirituality of struggle for transformation of social relations of power so that power can be shared with women and sexual minorities.

[38] Chammah J. Kaunda, 'Betrayed by Cultural Heritage: Liminality, Ambiguous Sexuality and Ndembu Cultural Change – An African Ecclesia-Ethic of Openness', in *Alternation Special Edition,* No. 14 (2015), 22-44, 38.

Mainstreaming Gender Leadership in Diakonia

Knud Jørgensen

> Around the globe, more women than men are practising Christians. Measured by regular church attendance, pilgrimages, prayers at home, fund-raising, and teaching children about the faith, Christianity is a women's religion. The ratio of female to male Christians is approximately two to one. Within Catholicism, sisters outnumber brothers and priests by more than fifty percent. Yet because the priests, preachers, theologians, public leaders, and famous missionary entrepreneurs are typically male, the crucial roles of women in mission remain buried in the unwritten stories of human relationships. In the late nineteenth and twentieth centuries, in both Catholicism and Protestantism, the majority of missionaries were women. However, until recently, overview histories of mission have scarcely analyzed women's roles or acknowledged that women typically make up the majority of active believers.[1]

I guess I am a typical western man who has had to learn gender thinking the hard way – from my wife, my children, my colleagues, my reading, and from living in different cultural contexts (Scandinavia, Africa, America and Asia). My Scandinavian background and experience of 'complementarity' between men and women were, however, not automatic but attained through a process of gender learning and new legislation in church and society. Deep-down, my inclination, as a member of the fallen race, was domination.

In a manner of speaking, the following describes my itinerary en route to a more mature and more biblical understanding of gender. I shall start off with some definitions and assumptions and then continue with perspectives on gender and leadership in a broader scope, before I turn to leadership in Scripture, church and *diakonia*. I shall finally enumerate some approaches to mainstreaming gender.

My desire is that women should be *empowered*. This implies a shift of power. It means deconstructing mindsets that give exclusive power to men, and putting environments and policies in place that secure equality in participation and leadership. This is the purpose of mainstreaming gender leadership and the aim of this chapter.

---

[1] Dana L. Robert, *Christian Mission: How Christianity Became a World Religion* (Chichester, UK: Wiley-Blackwell, 2009), 118.

Definitions and Basic Assumptions

Gender refers to socially constructed differences in attributes and opportunities associated with being female or male, and to the social interactions and relationships between women and men. Gender determines what is expected, allowed and valued in a woman or a man in a given context. In most societies, there are differences and inequalities between women and men in roles and responsibilities, in activities, and in access to and control over resources, as well as in decision-making opportunities.[2]

Gender equality means equal opportunities, rights and responsibilities for women and men, girls and boys. Equality does not mean that women and men are the same but that women's and men's opportunities, rights and responsibilities do not depend on whether they are born female or male. It implies that the interests, needs and priorities of both women and men are taken into consideration. While gender equality is about being equally valued by society, *gender equity* is the process of being fair to men and women. This will often include measures to compensate for the historical and social disadvantages that prevent women and men from operating on a level playing field.[3]

This means that gender is the way we organize our lives as males and females, our relationships, our roles and responsibilities. Most of us have been socialized into believing that the different roles and status accorded to men and women in society are determined by biology, i.e. sex, and that these are natural, constant and unchangeable. These roles are shaped and maintained by structures like family, community, society, ethnicity and race. They are sustained and perpetuated through forms of culture, language, education, media and diverse faith beliefs. But such a view does not explain the inequalities that exist between women and men. Inequality between women and men is created by historical, social, religious and cultural constructs. They should, therefore, be questioned, challenged and changed.

Gender analysis is part of this process: it is a tool to understand the disparities between women and men's realities in any context. Gender analysis may bring to light previously hidden or obscure anomalies like differing social realities, socialization processes, role expectations, economic circumstances, and access to and power over resources. Some perspectives or criteria are particularly important in a diaconal context: *the understanding and use of power, the role and methods of empowerment, leadership as transformation, and ideologies of patriarchy*. Patriarchy is a belief system according to which men are held to be superior and responsible for those under their care or control. Religious interpretations, cultural practices and institutionalized

---

[2] UN report, 'The World's Women 2005: Progress in Statistics', Introduction, 1.

[3] Heidi Holt Zachariassen, *Learning gender mainstreaming through practice: Digni's Women's Empowerment and Gender Equality programme (WEGE)* (Oslo: *Digni*, 2012), 50.

structures have played a key role in creating and perpetuating the patriarchal ideology in social behaviour and socio-economic structures. Christian theology and mission have again and again contributed to this thinking.[4] Sometimes this thinking appears so natural that women themselves perpetuate the system.

Gender analysis is also a helpful tool for collecting information on roles, including leadership roles: men and women perform different roles. As a result, they possess different experiences, knowledge, talents and needs. Some of these roles are imported and imposed; some grow out of the local context and culture. These roles may provide access to leadership for both sexes, but they may also prevent women from sharing leadership in *diakonia* – in church and society.

Mainstreaming gender is also part of this process. It is the process of addressing gender from the beginning to the end of any planned action. It is a strategy for making women's as well as men's concerns and experiences an integral dimension of the design and implementation, monitoring and evaluation of policies and programmes in all political, economic and societal spheres so that women can benefit equally and inequality is not perpetuated. We mainstream gender concerns to achieve gender equality and improve the relevance of development agendas. [5] Gender mainstreaming is essential to overcome sectoral approaches that splinter topics and issues. The linkages are also essential just as it is essential that each gender contributes to our thinking on *diakonia.* In an example from the Lutheran World Federation (LWF) on gender analysis of *diakonia*, such analysis led the participants to understand the following:

- Offering and receiving such services are intended for both men and women, but service should be distinguished from the *servitude* that is often required of women. Service is a free offer women extend willingly, while servitude is a subjugation imposed on them by others.
- If *diakonia* is promoted over the existing development paradigms, one needs to look into whether gender as an analytical tool would be integral in *diakonia* as it has been for development.
- Most importantly, it should be insisted that, in diaconal deliberations, women are not once again relegated to being the traditional, humble service providers with less options for being initiators and leaders, with less or no remuneration, with fewer opportunities for leadership, nor to be relegated once again to traditional feminized areas of service.[6]

---

[4] Lutheran World Federation, 'It will not be so among you!' (Mark 10:43): A Faith Reflection
on Gender and Power (Geneva: Lutheran World Federation, 2009), 14.

[5] Zachariassen, *Learning gender mainstreaming through practice*, 92; Lutheran World Federation, 'It will not be so among you!', 48.

[6] Lutheran World Federation, 'It will not be so among you!', 49.

It should be added that some consider gender mainstreaming a 'soft approach'.[7] They fear that a gender approach may eventually lead to women's concerns becoming invisible rather than being transformed. Or that gender mainstreaming may be an attempt to integrate women's work to cut costs and reduce staff. These critics have a point. Gender jargon and gender mainstreaming can become a smokescreen that hides a continued inequality.

Dimension of Leadership

Many years ago, Geert Hofstede[8] developed some dimensions of leadership. One of the dimensions is Masculine-Feminine: Hofstede is here using the stereotyped western difference between the sexes to describe a cultural difference. Within the feminine worldview, care and concern receive priority, the roles of the sexes are not so strict, there is equality between the sexes, quality of life and mutual dependence are important, you work to live, people take care of the losers, and small is beautiful.

In masculine cultures, the sex roles are fixed in such a way that men dominate and women serve; independence, ambition and masculinity are important; you live to work. All Nordic countries fall in the feminine camp, while the USA and most countries in Latin America are masculine.

It is essential to be aware of this dimension of leadership when we cross cultural borders. At the same time, we must be critical of attempts to polarize gender as the church has so often done. Such attempts are mostly based on stereotyping: masculinity has to do with being strong, taking the initiative, being goal-oriented, taking chances, and being an arbitrator; while femininity stands for beauty, mercy, understanding, a preoccupation with detail, and being relational. Such simplified views are not supported by Scripture, but created by culture – and by men. Many churches have been described as 'patriarchal' – and some still are – in their organisation and understanding of gender. This is based on a belief in inequality between the genders and therefore a right for men to be leaders over women. We do not share this view. But neither do we share the views of a radical feminism when it tends to claim that the man's sexuality is inherently violent.

Women and Leadership

The study of leadership requires an interdisciplinary perspective. As we discuss gender and leadership in *diakonia*, this is particularly important since *diakonia* spans both religious and secular arenas and institutions. Probably the majority of leaders in *diakonia*, at least in the West, carry out their leadership in the

---

[7] Lutheran World Federation, 'It will not be so among you!', 21.

[8] Geert Hofstede, 'Motivation, Leadership and Organisation: Do American Theories Apply Abroad?', in *Organisational Dynamics,* Summer 1980.

public sphere. General models and theories of leadership therefore apply, perhaps even more so than 'biblical' models.[9] Let us therefore listen to some insights from general leadership theory on gender.

In the West and South-East Asia, increasing numbers of women are moving into leadership positions, and we find a growing number of women in academia. This has fuelled an interest in studying and discussing female leadership: are there differences between women and men in terms of leadership style and leadership effectiveness?[10] Some have argued that gender has little or no bearing on leadership style or effectiveness. Others have found that women lead in a more democratic or participatory manner. Research on transformational leadership[11] seems to indicate that, with regard to inspirational motivation, stimulation and consideration, women's styles tended to be more transformational than men's.

An essential finding in various studies is that men and women are equally effective leaders, but there are gender differences such that women and men are more effective in leadership roles that were congruent with their gender. Thus, women are less effective in military positions, but more effective in education and social service organisations. And women are more effective than men in middle management positions where interpersonal skills are highly valued.

In many societies, women are as educated as men and make up half the labour force. A growing number obtain leadership positions, but not at the top level within business, church and politics. Some authors talk about a 'glass ceiling', i.e. an invisible barrier preventing women from ascending into elite leadership positions. Some ethnic minority groups share the same experience. There is therefore a need for promoting a diverse group of women into leadership roles to help make social institutions, business, government and church more representative. We also believe that there is a connection between gender diversity and organisational performance: an organisation, an institution or a church performs better with a gender balance.

---

[9] This does not imply that secular and biblical models of leadership need contradict one another. Actually, good leadership is good leadership, irrespective of the arena. See also Knud Jørgensen, *Equipping for Service: Christian Leadership in Church and Society* (Oxford: Regnum, 2012), 23ff.

[10] See Peter G. Northouse, *Leadership: Theory and Practice* (Los Angeles, London, New Delhi, Singapore, Washington: Sage Publications, 2010, 302-03.

[11] Transformational leadership includes the key components of situational leadership, but takes them a step further by looking at leadership as a process that changes and transforms people. It is concerned with emotions, values, ethics, standards and long-term goals. It includes assessing followers' motives, satisfying their needs, and treating them as full human beings. Transformational leadership moves followers to accomplish more than what is usually expected of them. It is a process that often incorporates charismatic and visionary leadership (see Northouse, *Leadership: Theory and Practice,* 171ff).

The Leadership Labyrinth

Crystal L. Hoyt describes the barriers and hindrances as a 'leadership labyrinth' with three components:[12] human capital, including education, experience, development opportunities, and work-home conflict; gender differences, including style and effectiveness, commitment and motivation, and self-promotion; prejudice, including gender stereotypes, biased perceptions, vulnerability, and cross-pressures. Women may often suffer because of motherhood. They may have to give up work for family reasons. They may be forced to work fewer hours than women without children. The same family situation does not seem to affect men. They continue working as they did before. These domestic expectations are an added burden on women on the way to leadership. Generally, many women struggle with the work-home conflicts much more than men do. This may also lead to women having fewer opportunities for self-development and receiving further education.

Women are no less effective at leadership, but they do seem to be less likely to self-promote and negotiate than men. One reason could be that the social costs of being demanding are higher for women than for men.

As regards prejudice, we should be particularly on guard for stereotyping and preconceptions of women's roles and abilities. Here lies a major contributing factor to a leadership gap in church and society. These stereotypes may look 'nice' (women show a concern for others – sensitivity, warmth, helpfulness), but are dangerous when misused as arguments about who should be in which leadership positions. Gender stereotypes are pervasive and highly resistant to change.

Unfortunately, most of this research on gender in leadership has taken place in western contexts. Research from the global South seems to be sparse. We may therefore not generalize too quickly across cultures. Yet even cross-culturally, understanding the obstacles of the labyrinth and developing tactics to confront them, will make for a more sound gender balance in leadership.

Taking Gender Seriously

The concept of gender can become jargon among church leaders and in diaconal circles. The term may be included to be politically correct or to secure approval for our projects and endeavours, among grassroots non-governmental organizations (NGOs), or church-run projects. The projects may be designed by men in leadership who still consider women as 'vulnerable groups' or 'beneficiaries'. This tendency does not open the door to empowering women or transforming men. Neither should 'gender' become an 'add-on' component, only allotting certain specific or restricted roles for women: running training

[12] Crystal L. Hoyt, 'Women and Leadership', in Northouse, *Leadership. Theory and Practice*, 301-33.

workshops in sewing, soap-making and kitchen gardening for women.[13] Sometimes, or even often, people think they are talking about gender but actually are only discussing women's needs and issues. This might deter men who want to be counted in, who expect their needs to be expressed and their issues included in discussion on gender. Gender is larger than women's issues; therefore having men on board as partners and advocates of gender is a step towards equality and fairness. Gender should not be used as a 'halfway house' for women and men to reduce gender discrimination and injustice or as a tool to maintain gender differences, and work around problem areas for amicable and workable solutions. There must be room for addressing the concerns of men, including their fear of losing their place in a patriarchal setting. At the same time, churches must avoid a sort of tokenism, by allowing just a few women to sit at the round table or by ordaining just a few women.

> Allowing prescribed roles and social expectations to govern male and female behaviour limits men's understanding of the issues and inhibits them from active involvement. Men should therefore welcome gender analysis as a tool that enables them to focus more on male behaviour and attitudes and how these can change for the better. It is indeed possible for men to change. Taking more responsibility in ensuring that we respect and protect women's rights is possible for men.[14]

Gender and Ministry[15]

Both women and men are called to ministry. Ministry is service (*diakonia*), and every Christian, male and female, young and old, is called to follow in the footsteps of him who came to serve. Some may object, as Elisabeth Fiorenza did, who criticises the 'servant ecclesiology' of the 1970s and 1980s. This theology may allow for more 'ministries', particularly for women, but it does not seriously challenge the church's structures of patriarchal hierarchy and the 'class' division between ordained and non-ordained ministries. It easily becomes 'theological double-speak' since the theology of service has different implications for men and women, ordained and non-ordained, powerful and powerless. The servant rhetoric has not resulted in any change of actual power relations or privileges. 'Service' may become 'servility' or simply a token acceptance of existing hierarchies. Fiorenza is equally critical of feminist attempts to redefine *diakonia* and retrieve a sound theology of service. These attempts do not, in her opinion, obfuscate 'the fact that the patriarchal church

---

[13] Lutheran World Federation, 'It will not be so among you!', 23-24.

[14] Jonah Gokova, 'Men for Women', in *Connections* (Netherlands: Vrouwenberaad Ontwikkelingssamenwerking, March 1999), 13-14. Quoted from Lutheran World Federation, 'It will not be so among you!', 24.

[15] See, in regard to this section, Knud Jørgensen, *Equipping for Service*, 113-20.

continues to exercise its ministry as "power over". It remains structured into a hierarchy of power dualisms: ordained/non-ordained, clergy/laity, religious/secular, church/world'.[16] In her opinion, *diakonia* should rather be used as a critical category challenging those who have actual power and privilege. The basis for such a use she finds in Mark 10:42-44 where Jesus challenges those in position and power to become equal with those who are powerless. Here is an 'equality from below'. I think it is helpful and essential to pay attention to Fiorenza's warnings of a widespread misuse and misinterpretation of *diakonia*. We need such feminist hermeneutical readings of key concepts in Scripture. Servant ecclesiology must not be allowed to motivate women to acquiesce in any second class status. Having said that, one wonders how Fiorenza would look at John Collins' reinterpretation of *diakonos* as a 'messenger' and 'go-between'.[17]

Let me reiterate: both women and men are called to ministry. All would agree to this, but some/many would want to deliberate on what forms women's ministry should take, whether any limits should be placed on it, and whether women should be ordained.

The Roman Catholic and Eastern Orthodox Churches have no women priests; they are still firmly against this development. Most other churches, and particularly Protestant churches, have women pastors or priests, including the Anglican, Reformed and Lutheran Churches. There are, however, within all churches some who oppose having women in ordained positions. Part of their argument is that all the apostles and the presbyters of New Testament times were men. In addition, we have the specific instructions that women must be 'silent in the churches' and 'not teach or have authority over a man' (1 Cor. 14:34; 1 Tim. 2:12).

In my view, a strong biblical case can be made for active female leadership in the church, including a teaching ministry. In the Old Testament there were prophetesses called and sent by God – Huldah, Miriam, Deborah (Deborah was also judging the people). In the New Testament it was to women that Jesus first revealed himself after the resurrection. The Acts and the epistles contain many

---

[16] Elisabeth Schüssler Fiorenza, '"Waiting at Table": A Critical Feminist Theological Reflection on Diakonia', in Norbert Greinacher and Norbert Mette (eds), *Diakonia: Church for Others* (Edinburgh: T. & T. Clark, 1988), 90, 84-94.

[17] The Australian scholar John N. Collins has an alternative understanding of *diakonia*. Rather than charitable or humble service, it describes a task or a mission for a person as an envoy and spokesperson. The deacon is a 'go-between' entrusted with an important message, a mediator on behalf of someone in authority and with a vital task. This reinterpretation of the biblical meaning of *diakonia* opens up new perspectives when we develop a theology of *diakonia*. *Diakonia*'s biblical background presents it as 'bold action that announces good news for the poor'. Secondly, *diakonia* cannot be limited to professional work; it belongs to the mandate given by the triune God to the church as an integral part of its mission. John N. Collins, *Diakonia: Re-interpreting the Ancient Sources* (New York/Oxford: OUP, 1990).

references to women speakers and women workers – women with the gift of prophecy, Priscilla as a leader, together with her husband Aquila, many of Paul's fellow workers (e.g. Euodia and Syntyche in Philippi and the eight women mentioned in Romans 16). If God could call women into these roles, why should the church today not appoint women to similar responsibilities?

We may add the evidence of Pentecost: God poured out his Spirit on 'all flesh', including 'sons and daughters', and his 'servants, both men and women'. If the gift of the Spirit was bestowed on all believers of both sexes, so were the spiritual gifts. The charismata have never been restricted to men. Christ gives gifts, including teaching gifts, to women, and issues a call to develop and exercise them in his service.

To use 1 Corinthians 14:34-35 and 1 Timothy 2:11-15 as a prohibition of all talking by women in church does not square with Paul's references to prophetesses and to how he allows everyone to contribute a hymn, a word of instruction, a revelation, a tongue or an interpretation (1 Cor. 14:15-19). One may, however, argue that Scripture teaches male headship in terms of the man caring for and being responsible for his wife. As her 'head', he gives himself up for her in love, just as Christ died for his body, the church. So the husband's concern is to liberate her, to create the conditions within which she may grow into the fullness of her femininity. If this is what Scripture teaches (which I doubt), then I would interpret the texts in 1 Corinthians 14 and 1 Timothy 2 to be cultural applications of this for a particular situation and time.

Following this line of argument, one may then claim that God calls women to leadership and to teaching, provided that, in so doing, they are not usurping authority over men. The biblical model for leadership seems to be one of plural pastoral oversight. Members of the pastoral team may in this way capitalize the sum total of their gifts. Within such a pastoral team there should be women, but the team leader should be a man. Such an arrangement, the argument goes, would be an appropriate expression in our time and age of male headship. I can sympathise with this way of arguing, but I am far from convinced.

What then of ordination? One's understanding of ordination will depend on one's understanding of the 'ministerium', the office. If we are talking about priests in a Catholic sense (as the person in charge of a sacrificial meal – *sacerdos*), ordination makes sense. My view of the office is pastoral, an office that can be more fluid, modest and varied, offering different kinds and degrees of ministry. In such a broad view of ministry, ordination would imply a public recognition of God-given gifts, together with the public authorisation to exercise these gifts in a team. Such an understanding would definitely include the ordination of women.

God endows women with gifts and calls them to exercise them for the common good. The church must therefore recognise God's gifts and calling, make appropriate spheres of service available to women, and ordain and commission women to exercise their God-given ministry.

My reading of the New Testament's view on gender takes Galatians 3:26-28 as the hermeneutical key: 'For you are all sons of God through faith in Christ Jesus. As many of you as were baptized into Christ have clothed yourselves with Christ. There is no longer Jew or Greek, there is no longer slave or free, there is no longer male or female, for all of you are one in Christ Jesus' (Gal. 3:26-28). Women and men are together in mission and *diakonia*. In principle, participation in everything that happened in the congregation and community was open to both. Gender differences played no role in the experience of God's Spirit. The early church treated women and men equally, from planning worship to leadership tasks in the community. Indeed, women's leadership in the primitive church was exceptional, not only by the standards of Judaism and the Greco-Roman world, but also by those of the later Christian church. The theological basis for this is found in Galatians 3:26-28. The change came with the Pastoral Epistles and the transition from house churches to gatherings in public buildings or basilicas. When Christianity moved out of private homes, worship life and organizational structures had to adapt to the patterns in culture and society. And eventually the Constantinian church structures removed women from leadership.[18] Today, with the breakdown of the Constantinian church model, the way is open for re-imagining the gender leadership of the early church. An interesting example of such re-imagining may be found within neo-Pentecostal churches in East Africa. Here women have not only ritual power but authority to lead due to the democratization of charisma in Pentecostalism. The mission of God demands the full mobilization of all sectors. So neo-Pentecostalism has created openings for women to make an impact in *diakonia*, in mission and in society.[19]

Female Deacons

The New Testament talks in several places (1 Tim. 3:11; Rom. 16:1-3) about women in leadership roles. Phoebe is described as a deacon and as one who has been a good friend to many people. What we cannot read out of Scripture is whether Paul talks about deacon in a general sense or about Phoebe as a deacon consecrated for a specific service. Neither do we know in which ways she has been a good friend and how she may have helped people in need, but the verses do make it clear that she held some sort of leadership position and had been

[18] Christine Lienemann-Perrin, 'Biblical Perspectives on Women's Impact in Mission', in Christine Lienemann-Perrin, Atola Longkumer and Afrie Songco Joye (eds), *Putting Names with Faces: Women's Impact in Mission History* (Nashville, TN: Abingdon Press, 2012), 23-44.

[19] Philomena Njeri Mwaura and Damaris Parsitau Seleina, 'Gendered Charisma: Women in Mission in the Neo-Pentecostal Churches and Charismatic Movements in Kenya', in Lienemann-Perrin, Longkumer and Songco Joye (eds), *Putting Names with Faces*, 123-46.

entrusted with authority.[20] There is on the whole evidence to show that women played important roles in the early church. This would also seem to be a natural consequence of Jesus' attitude to women and his practice of inviting them into his service and ministry (*diakonia*).

1 Timothy 5 paints a picture of the widows having tasks of caring in the congregation, in terms of hospitality, washing the feet of Christians, helping those in need and 'devoting herself (themselves) to doing good'. Whether these widows were deacons we do not know, neither do we know how they related to the deacons. The same applies to mention of deaconesses in the fourth century. One of their tasks was to guide the female candidates for baptism through the process of baptism, while the deacons performed the same task for the male candidates.

We find other early indications also in non-Christians sources that women in many places were entrusted with important leadership tasks. When this later changed (after Christianity became the religion of the state), the reason was probably the development of a more hierarchical structure and adjustments to local cultures.

Women and Diakonia

We may safely say that women have always played a key role in diaconal work.[21] It is quite common that more women than men are engaged both as volunteers and as employees. Deaconesses played a central role in the diaconal movement in Germany in the 1830s. This also had to do with the fact that there were few other job opportunities for women at that time. In that way, the movement significantly contributed to providing opportunities for women, both in church and society.

At that time, women were, and in some cases still are, normally excluded from leadership positions in society and in the churches. Even the Motherhouse of the deaconesses would have a man, most often a pastor, as its leader. Today, women may be in leadership, but decision-making and budgeting are done by men. In addition, in most parts of the world men are better paid than women, even if they are holding the same job.

Also today, we may run into the assumption that *diakonia* is, first and foremost, a task for women, and that *diakonia* is 'female' work. Does this reveal a misunderstanding that *diakonia* is of secondary importance in the life of the church? Such 'feminization' of *diakonia* is not in line with its theological basis since *diakonia* belongs to the whole body of Christ in which both men and women are called to participate.

---

[20] For this section, see Stephanie Dietrich, Kari Korsrud Korslien and Kjell Nordstokke, *Diakonen – kall og person* (Oslo: Tapir akademisk forlag, 2011), 57.

[21] See in regard to this section, Lutheran World Federation, *Diakonia in Context: Transformation, Reconciliation and Empowerment* (Geneva: LWF, 2009), 66ff.

Approaches to Mainstreaming Gender

We need a gender approach in diaconal work. This includes both practical and strategic dimensions. Gender roles in diaconal work should be related to an analysis of roles and functions: should these roles and functions just reflect what is practised in the concrete context, or could they present an alternative for equal participation by women and men? A new approach should be rooted in what *diakonia* is all about and a diaconal commitment to inclusiveness and a participatory society.

A working document from the Lutheran World Federation, 'It will not be so among you! A faith reflection on Gender and Power' from 2009[22] suggests four approaches towards mainstreaming gender leadership:

1. **A practical approach** that continues to educate, empower and enable women, since they are still by far the most disadvantaged group. This approach provides them with basic needs to become informed practitioners working towards transformation for themselves, their families, churches and communities. This approach may include the provision of scholarships and education, skills training, and opportunities that are women-specific. Such initiatives will build self-esteem and develop a collaborative style of leadership.

2. **A conceptual approach** whereby gender becomes the analytical tool to understand and address the disparities between women and men. This would include a gathering of gender-disaggregated data, dialoguing with women and men, and ensuring that gender is included in the agenda through the provision of adequate space, time, and a platform for discussion. Those who are not in power would be given adequate space to voice their opinions, and those in power to listen and learn.

3. **A strategic approach** where proactive policies on gender are formulated, and organizational structures are designed, to ensure that gender commitments are applied, systematically accounted for, and consciously monitored. This creates an enabling context that informs, affects and updates how the organization plans, articulates and executes its work. Some churches and organisations have, for example, a policy of a 50% participation of women and men.

4. **A systemic approach** makes gender an integral organizational culture that moves beyond individual intent or specified projects and programmes. It becomes an ethos of the organization that builds on the gender interventions made and the learning experienced. It promotes a cycle of action, reflection and events. Such an organizational culture will then enable the organization to have gender as an institutional discipline and an undisputed profile.

What happens when women and men are treated equally and given the same leadership roles in *diakonia*? The church arena is still lagging behind when it

[22] Lutheran World Federation, 'It will not be so among you!', 47-49.

comes to gender and leadership. I believe that *diakonia,* by giving priority to equality and by seriously mainstreaming gender leadership, will set an example that will challenge the church at the local and the national level. Furthermore, the leadership models chosen by *diakonia* will mirror values inherent in a broad understanding of *diakonia* (go-between, mediator, advocacy) and will bring to light the assets of *diakonia*[23] (including ethos, relationships, trust, moral authority), and in that way contribute new thinking towards both secular and Christian leadership.

Conclusion

'The history of Christian mission must focus on women, for the majority of Christians in the world are women,' says Dana L. Robert.[24] A focus on gender can therefore not escape a primary focus on women. As a man, I should not be 'gender-blind' and thus fail to recognize that gender is an influencing factor in mission, *diakonia*, projects, programmes and policy.

Women and men are made in the image of God, with equal stewardship, and they are baptized into equal communion and empowered by the Holy Spirit to be equally responsible for the whole of God's creation. We should therefore reflect on how women and men can jointly take their share in diaconal work. Are their capacities and roles similar or different?

Could it be that engagement in diaconal work will change the roles of men and women, in both church and society? Or is the opposite experienced, i.e. that churches delay processes in society to recognize and promote the roles of women? Are our churches blinder to gender than the society in which they work and live?

Women should be empowered. This implies a shift of power. It means deconstructing mindsets that give exclusive power to men, and putting environments and policies in place that secure equality in participation and leadership.

---

[23] See Kjell Nordstokke, 'Mapping Out and Mobilising Diaconal Assets', in Stephanie Dietrich, Knud Jørgensen, Kari Karsrud Korslien and Kjell Nordstokke (eds), *Diakonia as Christian Social Practice: An Introduction* (Oxford: Regnum, 2014), 214-25.

[24] Robert, *Christian Mission: How Christianity Became a World Religion*, 141.

Global Development:
Why a Religious and Gender Perspective Matters

Marianne Skjortnes

Introduction

Increasing awareness among faith-based communities, especially within the Christian tradition, indicates that all work which aims at creating positive processes of change needs to include a gender perspective. A community will always be marked by the fact that conditions are different for women and men, and that there are different perceptions of what women's and men's roles in society are, based on social and cultural constructions and understandings of what is 'natural'.

A Christian faith and perspective on life are experienced by many as a good starting-point for mobilizing and stimulating a broader perspective on a worthy life. The Christian church has shown that, through its activity, it can stimulate more people to create better living conditions and life situations for themselves and their families as well as to contribute to giving greater capacity and ability to reach this goal. A Christian ideology that emphasizes the worth of human beings can also bolster perceptions of a more humane and meaningful life, where women and men gain access to opportunities and rights that are given, as religious faith and practice are manifested. In working for dignified lives, people's worldview, their culture and religion[1] are important resources.[2]

Religion has until recently largely been ignored in development studies, politics and practice. In the modern world, there has for many years been a tendency to devalue the role of religion in the public sphere and religion's significance for individuals. One of the reasons for this has been an assumption in the secular world that religion disappears as societies are modernized. This 'secularization theory' argues that modernization leads to a weakening of

---

[1] When I refer to religion or religious bodies, my focus in this chapter will mainly be Christian religious entities.

[2] Berma Klein Goldewijk and Bas de Gaay Fortman, *Where needs meet rights: Economic, social and cultural rights in a new perspective,* Vol. 88 (Geneva: WCC Publications, 1999).

religion both in society and in individuals' faith and practice.[3] However, social development towards the end of the twentieth century has led many to question the sociological secularization hypothesis, partly because religious affiliation and activity seem to be more relevant than was previously assumed. Even though the sociologist Peter L. Berger has been among those who have argued for the secularization theory, he has in more recent years suggested that we live – not in a secularized world – but in a world that today is more religious than it has ever been.[4]

Over past years, several practitioners have challenged secularization theories and debated the role of religion in social development. The World Bank has in several contexts taken up the question of religion's positive potential for development.[5] Several books, such as *God Is Back: How the Global Revival of Faith Is Changing the World*,[6] and *Religion in development: Rewriting the secular script*[7] have made important contributions that emphasize the place of religion in the social arena.

The tendency within secular modernity to overlook religion as a factor declined after the attack on the World Trade Center and the Pentagon on September 11th, 2001. After this event, it was clear that religion could be used to justify extreme, violent actions, and that religion could be used as an identity marker, and therefore could play a significant role in conflict creation, but also in conflict resolution. This has led to increased interest in the role of religion in society. Attention has been paid to religion's destructive role, but there has also been growing insight into religion's positive and constructive role in the development, peace and reconciliation work that is carried out by faith-based communities.[8]

---

[3] Steve Bruce, *God is dead: Secularization in the West* (Oxford: Blackwell, 2002), and Charles Taylor, *A Secular Age* (London: Harvard University Press, 2007).

[4] Peter L. Berger, *The desecularization of the world: Resurgent religion and world politics* (Washington, DC: Ethics and Public Policy Center, 1999).

[5] Gerard Clarke, 'Agents of transformation? Donors, faith-based organisations and international development', in *Third World Quarterly,* 28, No. 1, 2007, 835-48; Katherine Marshall and Marisa Van Saanen, *Development and faith: Where mind, heart, and soul work together* (Washington, DC: World Bank, 2007).

[6] John Micklethwait and Adrian Wooldridge, *God Is Back: How the Global Revival of Faith Is Changing the World* (New York: Penguin, 2009).

[7] Severine Deneulin and Masooda Bano, *Religion in development: Rewriting the secular script* (London: Zed Books, 2009).

[8] Leah Selinger, 'The forgotten factor: The uneasy relationship between religion and development', in *Social Compass,* 51, 2004, 523-43; Oslosenteret for fred og menneskerettigheter. *Religion og utvikling. En rapport for prosjektet Religion og utvikling 2011-2012* (Oslo: Oslosenteret for fred og menneskerettigheter og Utenriksdepartementet).

In this chapter I will use examples of development work, also termed diaconal work,[9] carried out by the Lutheran Church in Madagascar.[10] How does commitment to Christian faith have implications for women's and men's daily life in Madagascar? In a situation marked by economic crises and social transformation, how does commitment to Christianity influence gender structures?

Theoretical Views of the Topic: Religion and Global Development

It has been a challenge for anthropologists to translate religious phenomena in a non-ethnocentric and comparatively useful way. This is because religious concepts have a particular meaning in the anthropologist's own society and professional terminology, and do not correspond with concepts used by those who are being studied.[11] Ever since anthropologists began to study beliefs in traditional societies, there has been a disagreement as to what religion is. From an anthropological perspective, the aim is to analyse and translate the life-world of a group into a common professional language and not necessarily to find out whether others' views 'are right or wrong'.[12]

Many researchers have participated in a professional conversation on what religion is, and in an anthropological context Clifford Geertz has been influential.[13] His starting-point is that the study of religion should be about how religion is created from within a society, and how it provides meaning and direction to people's existence. An insider perspective points to what believers themselves understand to be part of a religious universe, and how their religion is lived. According to Geertz, religion is a way of making the world meaningful. Instead of studying religion's 'social functions' or the social

---

[9] The concept of *diakonia* is used in the sense of faith-based, Christian development work related to improving people's living conditions. According to the Lutheran World Federation (LWF), *diakonia* is central to what it means to be a church, and the work reaches out to all persons who are created in God's image. While *diakonia* begins as unconditional service to a neighbour in need, the LWF document argues that it inevitably leads to social change that restores, reforms and transforms (Lutheran World Federation 2003, 6).

[10] The empirical research related to the development work of the Lutheran Church took place in the beginning of 2010 and spring 2012. In addition to this research, since 1979 I have returned regularly to Madagascar for studies and fieldwork. My research themes have been gender and development, and social, cultural and religious processes of change in different parts of Malagasy society, primarily related to the Bara group in the southern part of Madagascar, and to the Merina group in the highlands.

[11] A discussion on the concept of religion is elaborated further in my book, *Restoring Dignity in Rural and Urban Madagascar* (Peter Lang, 2014).

[12] Thomas Hylland Eriksen, *Small Places, Large Issues: An introduction to social and cultural anthropology* (London: Pluto Press, 2010) (3, revised edition), 222.

[13] Clifford Geertz, 'Religion as a cultural system', in Clifford Geertz (ed), *The interpretation of cultures: Selected essays* (New York: Basic Books, 1973), 87-126.

reasons for religion, we ought to study religion in itself, he argues, and the point of such studies must be to understand how life in the world appears to be meaningful for the believer. According to Geertz, it is not sufficient to explain the role of religion in social and cultural processes, but by focusing on the system of meanings, we can explain the role of religion as one of the factors that motivate change.[14]

However, when we attempt to define what a religion is in terms of substantive cross-cultural attributes in order to distinguish religion from other social phenomena, we reinforce particular western views of what religion should be, Emma Tomalin explains.[15] As anthropologist Talal Asad argues, 'there cannot be a universal definition of religion, not only because its constituent elements and relationships are historically specific, but because that definition is itself the historical product of discursive processes'.[16] Talal Asad's argument that there cannot be one universally valid definition of religion is generally acknowledged among scholars of religion today. According to Asad, religion is in many ways a Christian and Western concept, and carries with it Christianity as a model of what religion is.[17] The concept carries baggage, including the history of its interpretation and perception of values, which cannot automatically be made valid in other parts of the world. Asad argues that the concept of religion must be understood and interpreted in the cultural context in which it is used, without assuming a western experiential background as a precondition.

On one hand, as Tomalin emphasises, there is a need to approach the topic of religion in ways that are reflexive and do not just replicate modernist ideas about what religion should be, including the view that it is likely to disappear.[18] On the other hand, 'world religions'[19] tend to demand exclusivity, and while conversion is normally a possibility, people are not permitted to 'belong' to more than one religion at a time.[20] However, the existence of 'religious hybridity' in many parts of the world – for instance, in mainland Africa and large parts of Madagascar where Christianity has become an integrated part of the life of millions of people – the boundaries between different religious

---

[14] Geertz, 'Religion as a cultural system', 87-126.

[15] Emma Tomalin, 'Introduction', in Emma Tomalin (ed), *The Routledge Handbook of Religions and Global Development* (New York: Routledge, 2015), 8.

[16] Talal Asad, *Genealogies of religion: Discipline and reasons of power in Christianity and Islam* (London: Johns Hopkins University Press, 1993), 29.

[17] Asad, *Genealogies of religion.*

[18] Tomalin, 'Introduction', 9.

[19] The world's principal religions and spiritual traditions have often been classified into major groups, even though scholars since the 1960s have questioned the idea of the existence of discrete 'world religions' that are differentiated from one other according to the beliefs they promote (Tomalin, 2015: 7-9).

[20] Emma Tomalin, 'Introduction', 9.

traditions are less clear-cut.[21] In a context where Christianity may be perceived as part of Malagasy culture, it is not necessarily meaningful to speak of a divide between a world religion as Christianity and local cultural traditions.

Gender and Development

Gender is a complex and dynamic set of ideas, actions and feelings about what it means to be a woman or a man in a specific place, culture and time.[22] My theoretical perspective is based on the assumption that femininities and masculinities are historical, social and cultural constructions.[23] As Simone de Beauvoir put it: 'One is not born a woman; one becomes one.'[24] When gender involves cultural constructions, we cannot assume what gender means in different cultures and contexts; rather, we have to empirically study what it means. This is also the case when it comes to gender in the context of religions.

The area of gender and development has become more political in recent years.[25] A clear expression of this is the World Bank *World Development Report* for 2012, where the World Bank recognizes gender equality as a development aim in its own right.[26] The report argues that 'empowerment' of the individual is not sufficient in order to achieve gender equality, but points out the need for changed social structures. The report marks a first step in rethinking – 'from equal rights for women as economically efficient' to 'strengthening gender equality as a process of social and political change'.[27]

Religion and Gender in Madagascar

Large parts of the population in the Merina group think of themselves as Christian and participate as members in a Christian church. For many Merina, elements from the ancestral religion they were committed to before Christianity are nevertheless to a large extent present in their life and worldview, in parallel

[21] A. Hastings, 'Christianity in Africa', in U. King (ed), *Turning points in religious studies: Essays in honour of Geoffrey Parrinder* (Edinburgh: T. & T. Clark, 1990); Eva Keller, *The road to clarity: Seventh-Day Adventism in Madagascar* (New York: Palgrave Macmillan, 2005); Emma Tomalin, 'Introduction'.

[22] Naila Kabeer, *Reversed realities: Gender hierarchies in development thought* (London: Verso, 2003).

[23] Judith Butler, 'Performative acts and gender constitution', in Katie Conboy, Nadia Medina and Sarah Stanbury (eds), *Writing on the body: Female embodiment and feminist theory* (New York: Columbia University Press, 1997).

[24] Simone de Beauvoir, *The Second Sex* (New York: Bantham, 1952), 249.

[25] Andrea Elisabeth Harrison Cornwall and Ann Whitehead (eds), *Feminism in development: contradictions, contestations and challenges* (London: Zed Books, 2007).

[26] World Bank, *World Development Report 2012* (New York: World Bank, 2012).

[27] DIE (Deutsches Institut für Entwicklungspolitik), 'Gender equality and development: Conceptual turning point – but no change in practice?' in *World Development Report 2012* (Briefing Paper 2).

with their Christian identity. This is also true for the Bara group in the southern part of Madagascar, where a far smaller percentage of the population is Christian. In order to understand religion's social significance for Merina and Bara women and men, it is necessary to explore the believers' use of religion. It is not sufficient to view religion as an abstract system of ideas.[28]

In a Malagasy ancestral context, religion encompasses a person's life from birth to death, and also includes the soul's continued existence after death. Religion is all-encompassing and is a natural part of existence. It encompasses gods, the deceased ancestors, holy animals and mountains, and plays a decisive role both in everyday life and on special occasions, in both illness and health. The presence of the ancestors in people's lives is of the utmost importance all over Madagascar, and is, in one way or another, described in a range of studies of Malagasy society.[29]

Christianity has played an important role in Madagascar for almost two centuries, having been taken there by missionaries and incorporated with local traditions and beliefs. The significance of Christianity in Madagascar is unquestionable when looking at its spread and the central role it has played in political and social life.[30] Of the total population of 22 million in Madagascar, 57% are official members of a Christian church, Protestant or Catholic, while 40% adhere to traditional beliefs and 2% are Muslims.[31] In addition, there is a proliferation of smaller churches, mostly evangelical or Pentecostal.[32]

---

[28] Religions in Madagascar are further elaborated in my book, *Restoring Dignity in Rural and Urban Madagascar* (Peter Lang, 2014), 39-60.

[29] Maurice Bloch, *Placing the dead: Tombs, ancestral villages, and kinship organization in Madagascar* (London: Seminar Press, 1971); William Richard Huntington, *Religion and social organization of the Bara people of Madagascar* (Ann Arbor, MI: University Microfilms, 1974); Marianne Skjortnes, *Kvinner og utvikling: Kvinners rolle i Fifamanor-prosjektet på Madagaskar [Women and development: The role of women in the Fifamanor-project in Madagascar]* (Stavanger, Norway: Rogalandsforskning, 1990); Rita Astuti, 'Kindreds and descent groups: New perspectives from Madagascar', in J. Carsten (ed), *Cultures of relatedness: New approaches to the study of kinship* (Cambridge: CUP, 2000); Sandra Evers, *Constructing history, culture and inequality: The Betsileo in the extreme southern highlands of Madagascar* (Leiden, Netherlands: Brill, 2002); Michael Lambek, *The weight of the past: Living with history in Mahajanga, Madagascar* (New York: Palgrave Macmillan, 2002); Eva Keller, *The road to clarity: Seventh-Day Adventism in Madagascar* (New York: Palgrave Macmillan, 2005); David Graeber, *Lost people: Magic and the legacy of slavery in Madagascar* (Bloomington, IN: Indiana University Press, 2007).

[30] B. Hübsch (ed), *Madagascar et le christianisme* (Paris: Karthala, ACCT; Antananarivo: Editions Ambozontany, 1993); L. Jacquier Dubourdieu, 'De la guérison des corps à la guérison de la nation: Reveil et mouvements évangéliques à l'assaut de l'espace publishede', in *Politique Africaine*, No. 86, 2002), 70-85.

[31] The Catholic church has five million members (25%), the Lutheran church 3.4 million (16.4%), the United Church 2.8 million (13.5 %), and the High Church Anglican 400,000 (1.9%).

[32] World Christian Database, 2010: http://worldchristiandatabase.org/wcd/esweb.

In Malagasy religious traditions, it is accepted that women can be religious leaders.[33] In pre-colonial Madagascar, women held important positions in the local community as queens and as religious leaders. Through the Malagasy monarchy's encounter with European ways of understanding and thinking, and also in order to please European guests – both state representatives and visitors from mission organizations – women lost their power and the roles that they initially had so that the monarchy could hold on to its power.[34] Through the revival movement in the Protestant church, women regained their leadership roles, even though the historical churches[35] in Madagascar were often restrictive about appointing women to religious leadership.[36]

Across Madagascar, religion and culture have influenced social relations and gender in profound ways, which in turn has had significance for women's and men's opportunities for development.

Religious conversion to Christianity has played a role in transforming gender role patterns. However, Christian churches[37] can be seen to block as well as to support equality between men and women.[38]

Narratives from Madagascar

People's encounter with the church changes them – some more, others less – the leader of the Lutheran Church, Rakoto Endor Modeste says. He claims that the reason for this is simple. Through development work, people encounter a church and individuals whom they are neither related to, nor owe anything, yet who offer them goods and welfare. People will ask what drives these people to do good, and what makes them seek out strangers whom they do not know in order to offer their services? Such encounters make people question what the reason might be for someone to provide development work. They will assume

asp?WCI=Results&Query=183&PageSize=250&cntxt=1 (accessed 4th April 2013); Todd M. Johnson and Kenneth R. Ross, *Atlas of Global Christianity: 1910-2010* (Edinburgh: Edinburgh University Press, 2009).

[33] Marianne Skjortnes, *Kvinner og utvikling. Kvinners rolle i Fifamanor-prosjektet på Madagaskar [Women and development: The role of women in the Fifamanor project in Madagascar]* (Stavanger, Norway: Rogalandsforskning, 1990).

[34] Cynthia Holder Rich, *The Fifohazana: Madagascar's indigenous Christian movement* (Amherst, NY: Cambria Press, 2008).

[35] The four historical churches in Madagascar are FJKM (the United Church), FLM (the Lutheran Church), EEM (High Church Anglican), and EKAR (the Catholic Church).

[36] Of the historical churches, only FJKM allows women to become pastors.

[37] When I refer to Christian churches, my focus in this chapter will be the Malagasy Lutheran Church.

[38] Marianne Skjortnes, *Restoring Dignity in Rural and Urban Madagascar: On How Religion Creates New Life-stories* (New York: Peter Lang, 2014a); Monica Lindberg Falk, 'Religion and gender in developing South-East Asia', in Emma Tomalin (ed), *The Routledge Handbook of Religions and Global Development* (New York: Routledge, 2015), 268.

that there must be reasons other than purely material ones; that there must be spiritual forces behind such actions. This, Modeste argues, means that the encounter with the church's development work changes people.

How does commitment to Christian faith have implications for women and men in Madagascar? I will present two stories to describe how vulnerable human beings have succeeded in improving their quality of life. Rabary and Voahangy have met the diaconal work of the Malagasy Lutheran Church, resulting in a better life for themselves and their families.

Rabary

During the years that I have conducted fieldwork among the Bara, I have been struck by how those who were previously self-reliant, independent and proud agro-pastoralists without much desire for contact with the surrounding world, today find themselves in a situation where they realize that they are dependent on the world around them, and thus wish to change their worsening living conditions. Old solutions no longer work – new challenges demand new solutions. This is what Rabary expresses when he talks about how all his cattle were stolen. It happened at night, when everyone was sleeping. Strangers with stronger weapons than Rabary's family snuck into the village, stole the cattle and disappeared. Rabary got several of the men in the village to go with him to find the stolen cattle, without success.[39]

Rabary, who was fifty years old, grew up in Ankasy in the Ihorombe region. He is married to Soa, one of his relatives from the same village. The marriage was arranged by their parents. Rabary and Soa have had nine children altogether, five girls and four boys, but two of the children died when they were little. Neither he nor his wife can read or write, since the nearest school was still far away when they grew up. But after the village built a school in 2000, in collaboration with the Malagasy Lutheran Church, their children of school age have attended school. Rabary thinks it is necessary to go to school today. It is not easy to get by in life without being able to read or write. Even when the cattle need to be registered with the local government, those who cannot write have to pay people to draw up lists of the animals, and this writing skill is expensive. Even though he himself no longer has animals, he hopes that his children will in due course be able to acquire cattle, so that they can experience the security and satisfaction that comes with owning a cattle herd. After their own herd was stolen, Rabary and Soa have to borrow animals from

[39] For agro-pastoralists such as the Bara, cattle have traditionally been their most important capital and livelihood. Since the 1980s and 1990s, there has been a sharp increase in organized cattle theft, not least from groups who live in bordering areas and who have modern weapons. Several families in the village where Rabary lived have had all their cattle stolen. Others have had to sell their animals one by one when family members have become ill or when the family has been hit in other ways by hard times. The lack of available cattle has created a cultural identity crisis, and many, especially the men, are asking how one can manage life without a herd of cattle.

their relatives when they need to work the fields and prepare them for rice planting.

In 2005, a church was built in the village, and in the same way as with the school, the village population worked to construct the church building. Rabary and Soa decided a few years ago that they and their children would become Christians. 'The whole family is Christian. All my children have been baptized,' says Rabary. It started when Rabary became seriously ill. He went to the traditional healer to receive advice on how to get well. First he visited the healer who lived in the neighbouring village, and later he travelled all the way to the town of Ihosy, a day's journey north-west, to get help at the hospital, but did not get well from the medicines he was given there either. Rabary spent a lot of resources on this, without seeing any improvement in his health. It was only when he was prayed for in church that he became well. This made up his mind – he and his family decided to join the Lutheran Church in Ankasy.

For Rabary it is safe to be part of the church. When the children fall ill, he and Soa bring them to church to be prayed for so that the shepherds can drive out the evil spirits from the sick person, or take them to the village's new health clinic so that the midwife can give them medicine. 'The good thing about being a Christian is that you get healed. It gives good health – there is nothing shady about that.' Rabary is pleased with his new life as a member of the church.

Voahangy

Voahangy works in Antsirabe in the Merina region as a street seller. She invited me to visit her pizza bakery and we sat together and tasted her pizzas as she shared her story. 'Now, I am not poor any more. That is the most important. I can manage well today; I am independent and not dependent on anyone. Before I didn't sleep well – I thought of all the problems, the worries. Now I sleep well at night. Now life is good.' Voahangy is a 34-year old single mother, with responsibility for a four-year old daughter. The man she married fell ill and died four years ago.

Voahangy is the seventh in a family of nine. Her family was never well off, and when she was four her parents divorced and life became even more demanding for the children. The children lived with their mother, and the family managed to prioritize sending the children to school. Voahangy finished junior high school, but never passed her final exam. She tried various small jobs, without succeeding in them. A few years later, Voahangy got married. When her husband died, Voahangy was left with nothing, and had to find a new job. She began to take in washing for people, but that did not make income for herself and her daughter. Voahangy was in despair and did not know what to do.

She heard about the Diaconal Centre through the Lutheran Church she belonged to, and she thought she fulfilled the criteria: unemployed, young, and a single mother with some education. She was accepted and began the compulsory course in general education: how to present oneself when seeking work, how to manage time and money, how to receive customers, how to bring up children, and all about hygiene and nutrition. But what sort of work should she go for to bring in an income? Voahangy was given a place on a three-month baking course, and she decided to start her own pizza shop. The Centre gave her help with the expenses for building the oven and buying the necessary kitchen equipment for setting up her own pizza and bakery business. Voahangy gets up at three or four in the morning to make the dough for the day's pizzas and pies. By ten she is ready to sell the newly-baked wares and positions herself outside the city's public swimming pool to sell the small round pizzas and pies. 'There is demand for my new pizzas and everything is sold,' she tells me proudly. Voahangy sells sixty pizzas and pies every day, and on Saturdays and Sundays and during the school holidays she can sell up to a hundred.

Voahangy has long working hours and is not home before four or five in the afternoon. By then she has usually sold her pizzas and pies and has prepared the purchase of ingredients for tomorrow's baking. 'I have succeeded with my small business,' she says. Voahangy has learnt to manage for herself, and she has learnt at the Diaconal Centre how to take care of her daughter. She has also learnt the importance of prioritizing education for her children. 'My goal is that my daughter will have a good education and succeed' For Voahangy, the support she has received through the Centre and congregation has given her hope and faith in the future. As far as Voahangy is concerned, the good life is one that is put into the hands of Jesus every day, she says.

Religion, Gender and Global Development: Concluding Remarks

Through the diaconal work of the Lutheran Church in Madagascar, opportunities for women and men have increased. The two stories I have told are examples of the extremely vulnerable life conditions that many women and men in the country face. The stories also tell us something about how these individuals live in a religious universe, in which religion plays a decisive role in life, not just at a surface level, but as part of the daily existence that people live in and relate to.

The Lutheran Church plays an important role and inspires people who experience crises in their own life or the life of the family. Through prayer and Christian fellowship, women and men are healed from illness that they were not able to find any other cure for.

The story about Rabary and others who have chosen to become Christian are examples of people who have been in difficult life situations, and who have seen the Christian religion as a solution to their new life challenges, both in the form of healing from illness and as an aid in finding spiritual and material rootedness at a time when cattle disappear and co-existence breaks down. For these people, the church can provide a new way of understanding reality and new alternatives for action in situations that are experienced as challenging and critical. The Christian religion becomes a basis for handling their life in new ways, and because of Christianity they see themselves as people with human dignity.

The Lutheran Church in Merina region has been active in social work with people who fall through the cracks in the city of Antsirabe. Migration from the countryside to Antsirabe has created a number of challenges for the city with regards to receiving and integrating newcomers by providing housing, work, schooling and welfare services. The Diaconal Centre plays an important role in reaching unemployed youth in difficulty, and especially single mothers, in order to provide them with the opportunity of finding paid employment or setting up their own business through income-generating activity.

These youth see themselves as Christians, and through the training at the Diaconal Centre, their Christian identity is confirmed. This gives them support and motivation to believe in themselves, and to take hold of their everyday lives, not only in terms of setting goals for their lives, but also in terms of a broader spiritual, psychological and general formation which they receive at the Centre.

It is often argued that women in Madagascar enjoy a higher status than in mainland African countries. The bilateral kinship system is believed to have influenced the relative autonomy that women in Madagascar have enjoyed.[40] Women in this society are likely to control money and engage in economic activity, and to inherit on nearly the same terms as men. Access to education and the enrolment rate at primary school level is almost the same for boys as for girls. Like other low-income countries, Madagascar has very few students in higher education, but the gender ratio is less skewed than in many other countries. However, this does not necessarily imply gender equality in all parts of society. The realms of religion and politics are areas of male dominance, not least in the ways most historical churches are restrictive in relation to women in religious leadership positions. Religion shapes gender order in ways that both stand out as a hindrance to change and as agents of change. Greater gender equality is not an automatic result of commitment to Christian faith.

However, religion has the capacity to create hope, give meaning and transform society, especially in times of difficulty.[41] When the Lutheran Church in Madagascar offers its Christian faith, this is borne out of a desire to relate meaning and Christian values to the experiences and life situations that women and men find themselves in. For individuals and families who

---

[40] Maurice Bloch, *Placing the dead: Tombs, ancestral villages, and kinship organization in Madagascar* (London: Seminar Press, 1971); Marianne Skjortnes, *Kvinner og utvikling. Kvinners rolle i Fifamanor-prosjektet på Madagaskar [Women and development: The role of women in the Fifamanor-project in Madagascar]* (Stavanger, Norway: Rogalandsforskning, 1990); Eva Keller, *The road to clarity: Seventh-Day Adventism in Madagascar* (New York: Palgrave Macmillan, 2005).

[41] Monica Lindberg Falk, 'Religion and gender in developing South-East Asia', in Emma Tomalin (ed), *The Routledge Handbook of Religions and Global Development* (New York: Routledge, 2015), 275.

encounter the church's message and diaconal actions, the spiritual dimension that the Lutheran Church represents is experienced as a significant part of the good life that is created, a life that provides security, peace, protection against the devil and evil spirits, a changed heart, and freedom from fear.

The Lutheran Church, in common with other Christian Malagasy churches, is a religious agency with strong roots in local Malagasy society in large parts of the country. The church is therefore an effective diaconal force with a high level of legitimacy and credibility among large parts of the population. In a country characterized by a state of emergency and economic and social deprivation, the church has a solid starting-point for being there when people need it most. Christian faith and Christian values reflect a religiosity and spirituality that comes to expression as collective practice in a community of faith, in rites, prayer, blessings, Bible reading, trust and credibility. In these religious fellowship acts, there is an assumption that the church wishes the best for people.

Bibliography

Asad, Talal, *Genealogies of religion: Discipline and reasons of power in Christianity and Islam*. London: Johns Hopkins University Press, 1993.

Astuti, Rita, 'Kindreds and descent groups: New perspectives from Madagascar', in J. Carsten (ed), *Cultures of relatedness: New approaches to the study of kinship*. Cambridge: CUP, 2000.

Beauvoir, Simone de, *The Second Sex*. New York: Bantham, 1952.

Berger, Peter L., *The desecularization of the world: Resurgent religion and world politics*. Washington, DC: Ethics and Public Policy Centre, 1999.

Bloch, Maurice, *Placing the dead: tombs, ancestral villages, and kinship organization in Madagascar*. London: Seminar Press, 1971.

Bruce, Steve, *God is dead: Secularization in the West*. Oxford: Blackwell, 2002.

Butler, Judith, 'Performative acts and gender constitution', in Katie Conboy, Nadia Medina and Sarah Stanbury (eds), *Writing on the body: Female embodiment and feminist theory*. New York: Columbia University Press, 1997.

Clarke, Gerard, 'Agents of transformation? Donors, faith-based organisations and international development', in *Third World Quarterly* 28, No. 1, 2007.

Cornwall, Andrea, Elisabeth Harrison and Ann Whitehead (eds), *Feminism in development: contradictions, contestations and challenges*. London: Zed Books, 2007.

Deneulin, Severine, and Masooda Bano, *Religion in development: Rewriting the secular script*. London: Zed Books, 2009.

DIE (Deutsches Institut für Entwicklungspolitik), 'Gender equality and development: Conceptual turning point – but no change in practice?' in *World Development Report 2012* (Briefing Paper 2).

Eriksen, Thomas Hylland, *Small Places, Large Issues: An introduction to social and cultural anthropology*. London: Pluto Press, 2010. 3, revised edition.

Evers, Sandra, *Constructing history, culture and inequality: The Betsileo in the extreme southern highlands of Madagascar*. Leiden, Netherlands: Brill, 2002.

Falk, Monica Lindberg, 'Religion and gender in developing South-East Asia', in Emma Tomalin (ed), *The Routledge Handbook of Religions and Global Development*. New

York: Routledge, 2015.

Geertz, Clifford, 'Religion as a cultural system', in Clifford Geertz (ed), *The interpretation of cultures: Selected essays*. New York: Basic Books, 1973.

Graeber, David, *Lost people: Magic and the legacy of slavery in Madagascar*. Bloomington, IN: Indiana University, 2007.

Hastings, A., 'Christianity in Africa', in U. King (ed), *Turning points in religious studies: Essays in honour of Geoffrey Parrinder*. Edinburgh: T. & T. Clark, 1990.

Huntington, William Richard, *Religion and social organization of the Bara people of Madagascar*. Ann Arbor, MI: University Microfilms, 1974.

Hübsch, B. (ed), *Madagascar et le christianisme*. Paris: Karthala, ACCT; Antananarivo: Editions Ambozontany, 1993.

Jacquier Dubourdieu, L., 'De la guérison des corps à la guérison de la nation. Reveil et mouvements évangéliques à l'assaut de l'espace published', in *Politique Africaine,* No. 86, 2002.

Johnson, Todd M., and Kenneth R. Ross, *Atlas of global Christianity: 1910-2010*. Edinburgh: Edinburgh University Press, 2009.

Kabeer, Naila, *Reversed realities: Gender hierarchies in development thought.* London: Verso, 2003.

Keller, Eva, *The road to clarity: Seventh-Day Adventism in Madagascar*. New York: Palgrave Macmillan, 2005.

Klein Goldewijk, Berma, and Bastian de Gaay Fortman, *Where needs meet rights: Economic, social and cultural rights in a new perspective,* Vol. 88. Geneva: WCC Publications, 1999.

Lambek, Michael, *The weight of the past: Living with history in Mahajanga, Madagascar*. New York: Palgrave Macmillan, 2002.

Marshall, Katherine, and Marisa Van Saanen, *Development and faith: Where mind, heart, and soul work together*. Washington, DC: World Bank, 2007.

Micklethwait, John, and Adrian Wooldridge, *God Is Back: How the Global Revival of Faith is Changing the World*. New York: Penguin, 2009.

Oslosenteret for fred og menneskerettigheter. *Religion og utvikling. En rapport for prosjektet Religion og utvikling 2011-2012*. Oslo: Oslosenteret for fred og menneskerettigheter og Utenriksdepartementet.

Rich, Cynthia Holder, *The Fifohazana: Madagascar's indigenous Christian movement*. Amherst, NY: Cambria Press, 2008.

Selinger, Leah, 'The forgotten factor: The uneasy relationship between religion and development', in *Social Compass,* 51, 2004.

Skjortnes, Marianne, *Kvinner og utvikling: Kvinners rolle i Fifamanor-prosjektet på Madagaskar [Women and development: The role of women in the Fifamanor-project in Madagascar].* Stavanger, Norway: Rogalandsforskning, 1990.

Skjortnes, Marianne, *Restoring Dignity in Rural and Urban Madagascar: On How Religion Creates New Life-stories.* New York: Peter Lang, 2014.

Skjortnes, Marianne, 'A gender perspective on the ambiguous role of the churches', in Tomas Sundnes Drønen (ed), *Religion and development: Nordic perspectives on involvement in Africa*. New York: Peter Lang, 2014.

Taylor, Charles, *A Secular Age*. London: Harvard University Press, 2007.

Tomalin, Emma, 'Introduction', in Emma Tomalin (ed), *The Routledge Handbook of Religions and Global Development*. New York: Routledge, 2015.

World Bank, *World Development Report 2012.* New York: World Bank, 2012.

World Christian Database, 2010: http://worldchristiandatabase.org/wcd/esweb.asp?WCI=Results&Query=183&PageSize=250&cntxt=1

Human Rights and Diakonia in a Gender Perspective

Hans Morten Haugen

Are human rights with their strong emphasis on non-discrimination between men and women seen as a useful tool by diaconal practitioners – and are they actually used by such practitioners and churches alike? Or, alternatively, are there other approaches that improve women's standing and participation in communities with traditional views on social and family roles of women?

These questions, while being rather broad, are nevertheless at the core of debates about religion, gender and human rights. These questions can also be approached in another way: 'Whose power is enhanced when religious organisations and leaders are to be agents of change and development?'[1] Put differently, do religious leaders promote the *status quo*?

In the history of the Christian church and the global mission movement, the exercise of traditional authority has frequently impeded women's empowerment.[2] While educating girls has been a central priority for churches and missionary organisations alike, the type of specialized education they have been offered has emphasized their roles as housewives.

An adequate level of education is nevertheless of crucial importance for families and for society overall. Investing in women's education in order to enhance equality has been shown to reduce child malnutrition in South Asia by 13%, and in sub-Saharan Africa by 3%.[3] Another study finds that gender

---

[1] Aud Tønnessen, 'Trosbaserte organisasjoner, utvikling og kjønn – utfordringer og muligheter', in Asle F. Jøssang and Arne Olav Øyhus (eds), *Religionens rolle i bistand og utvikling* (Kristiansand, Norway: Portal Akademisk 2012), 98-110, 98 (author's translation).

[2] Miriam Adeney, 'Do Missions Raise or Lower the Status of Women? Conflicting Reports from Africa', in Dana Robert (ed), *Gospel Bearers, Gender Barriers: Missionary Women in the Twentieth Century* (Maryknoll, NY: Orbis Books, 2002), 211-21, noting at 215: 'Christian missionaries [were] not equipped to see African women's strong role in traditional society.'

[3] Lisa C. Smith, Usha Ramakrishnan, Aida Ndiaye, Lawrence Haddad and Reynaldo Martorell, *The Importance of Women's Status for Child Nutrition in Developing Countries, IFPRI Research Report 131* (Washington DC: International Food Policy Research Institute, 2003).

disparities in education contribute to between 0.4 and 0.9% less annual growth in gross national income per capita.[4]

This chapter first outlines alternative theories and approaches to women's concerns and needs. Then the essence of a human rights theory is explained. Finally, there is a discussion of a human rights approach as applied by church-based agencies.

The overall research question that this chapter seeks to answer is: *What are the strengths and weaknesses of a human rights approach, taking into account other theories of the roles and positions of women, and what are the main obstacles to a broad and effective application of a human rights approach among diaconal practitioners?*

Assessing Five Theories

Acknowledging that it is not possible to give a full account of the theories, the core elements of theories are presented, emphasizing their concerns with injustices against and exclusion of women: the social constructionism tradition, as outlined by Parsons,[5] Gilligan's theory on care ethics,[6] Sidanius' and Pratto's social dominance theory,[7] Crenshaw's theory on intersectionality,[8] and Nancy Fraser's justice theory.[9] They are presented so that those traditions that have the most negative approach towards human rights are presented first. Each theory or tradition is presented and then assessed.

Parsons presents social constructionism as an anti-thesis to the liberal tradition, in which human rights are embedded.[10] While the liberal tradition

---

[4] Klasen, Stephan, 'Low schooling for girls, slower growth for all? Cross-country evidence on the effect of gender inequality in education on economic development', in *World Bank Economic Review* 16:3 (2002), 345-73.

[5] Susan Parsons, *Feminism and Christian Ethics* (Cambridge, UK, and New York: Cambridge, 1996).

[6] Carol Gilligan, *In a Different Voice: Psychological Theory and Women's Development* (Cambridge, MA: Harvard University Press 1992). See also Nel Noddings, *Caring, a feminine approach to ethics and moral education* (Berkeley, CA: University of California Press, 1984); Joan C. Tronto, *Moral Boundaries, A Political Argument for an Ethics of Care* (New York: Routledge, 1993); Joan C. Tronto, *Caring Democracy. Markets, Inequalities, Justice* (New York: New York University Press, 2013); Virginia Held, *The Ethics of Care: Personal, Political and Global* (Oxford: OUP, 2006).

[7] Jim Sidanius and Felicia Pratto, *Social Dominance: An Intergroup Theory of Social Hierarchy and Oppression* (Cambridge: CUP, 1999).

[8] Kimberle Creenshaw, 'Demarginalizing the Intersection of Race and Sex: A Black Feminist Critique of Anti-discrimination Doctrine, Feminist Politics and Anti-racist Politics', *University of Chicago Legal Forum,* 1989: 139-67.

[9] Nancy Fraser, *Social Justice in the Age of Identity Politics: Redistribution, Recognition, and Participation. The Tanner lectures on human values, delivered at Stanford University April 30-May 2, 1996.*

[10] Parsons presents a third approach: naturalism, saying that all gender differences are due to natural differences.

emphasizes human freedom, autonomy and dignity, the social constructivism tradition specifies that all moral values and social orders are culturally created, shaped primarily by the influence of the powerful. Hence, according to social constructionism, there are only context-specific and no universal norms. Applied to gender, social constructionism emphasizes that there is no essential, universally distinct, character that is masculine or feminine, as social relationships are shaped by culture.

In the context of oppression and injustice against women, social constructivism can be criticized, due to its emphasis on the contemporary norms operating within a given society. These norms are subject to change, but cultural and social change can take time. In the meantime, to advocate mental, cultural and structural changes in accordance with universal norms is difficult, given that the prevailing norms accept that women are of a lower rank than men. Hence, women living in less inclusive social contexts will risk being abandoned to their fate, which is contrary to an inclusive humanism.[11]

Care ethics is more inclusive. Acknowledging that women and men have different approaches to ethical issues, Gilligan highlights the ethics of justice as central to men, and the ethics of care as central to women. While care ethics is concerned with disconnection, abandonment and indifference, justice ethics is concerned with oppression and inequality. The implications of Gilligan's approach is that women are attentive to the realm of practice and close relationships, embedded in the ethics of proximity, while men are attentive to the public and political sphere, relating to more abstract principles of retribution and distribution.

The criticism against Gilligan is that she presents stereotyped images of women and men.[12] Moreover, structural issues like power asymmetries, impediments on participation, direct oppression and inadequate protection are not adequately addressed.[13] The data upon which Gilligan's book is based are primarily American: women's choices regarding whether to take abortion or not, which obviously mobilizes ethics of proximity (Buber, Levinas, Løgstrup) and relationality. Women in other parts of the world face much grimmer and more severe prospects for their lives. Values of co-operation, interdependence and collective responsibility, being central to care ethics, do, however, find strong resonance in most cultures.

Turning to social dominance theory, the essence is that inequalities are maintained through institutional and individual discrimination, as well as power asymmetries maintained by dominant social groups over non-dominant

---

[11] Kate Soper, *Humanism and Anti-Humanism* (London: Hutchinson, 1996).

[12] Sarah Banks, *Ethics: Accountability and the Social Professions* (Chichester, UK: Wiley-Blackwell, 2004).

[13] Olena Hankivsky, 'Rethinking Care Ethics: On the Promise and Potential of an Intersectional Analysis', in *American Political Science Review,* 108:2 (2014), 252-64, 258, specifying power relations in care ethics.

social groups. The term 'social dominance orientation' (SDO) is applied, being defined as 'the degree to which individuals desire and support group-based hierarchy and the domination of 'inferior' groups by 'superior' ones.[14] Such attitudes can be measured by surveys and are embedded in so-called 'legitimizing myths'. These group distinctions are difficult to alter, and include gender, age and what is termed 'arbitrary group-based hierarchies', such as ethnicity and caste.

The criticism of the social dominance theory is that it is self-fulfilling.[15] In essence, presupposing that social hierarchies exist, this will make researchers search for and confirm such hierarchies. These hierarchies and hegemonic relationships are then presented as constituting something 'inevitable'.[16] According to Romm, while describing and analyzing dominant attitudes and perceptions, researchers should engage in reconstructing dominant perceptions. Acknowledging that social structures produce patterns of discrimination is valuable, however.

Intersectionality theory, with its strong emphasis on patterns of discrimination, has grown to become probably the most dominant gender theory. Its essence is to identify how different systems of oppression intersect and affect women, most notably oppression based on gender and race, but also poverty, caste, disability and other forms of stigmatization. By studying the interactions between the various forms of oppression, this results in what is termed 'synergistic effects'.[17] By this analysis, a basis might be built for creating alliances between agencies who have worked against various forms of oppression.

The argument against intersectionality is that it is affirming a US-led research agenda, due primarily to the central role that 'race' plays in the theory. Hence, there are several forms of social organisation and patterns of oppression that are not adequately encompassed by intersectionality theories. Moreover, from leftist circles, intersectionality has been perceived as a version of identity politics that ignores class struggle.

Identity politics is part of Fraser's theory of justice. Embedded in critical theory, Fraser warns against a politics of recognition, seeking to promote identity that makes a politics of distribution more difficult. To ensure that both recognition and distribution are promoted, this requires adequate

---

[14] Sidanius and Pratto, *Social Dominance*, 48.

[15] Norma R.A. Romm, 'Revisiting Social Dominance Theory: Invoking a more retroductively-oriented approach to systemic theorising', in *Systemic Practice and Action Research,* 26:2 (2013), 111-29; see also Norma R.A. Romm, *New Racism: Revisiting Researcher Accountabilities* (Heidelberg, Germany, and New York: Springer, 2010).

[16] Romm, 'Revisiting Social Dominance Theory', 123.

[17] Hankivsky, 'Rethinking Care Ethics', 257.

representation, or what Fraser terms 'participatory parity', which is crucial in order to combat both 'over-feminization' and 'under-feminization'.[18]

The criticism against Fraser's theory of justice is that it 'oversimplifies the literature on distributive justice',[19] as distributive justice scholars from a liberal tradition have addressed not only inequality, but also ethnicity, culture and gender. Amartya Sen's capability approach is found to meet the requirements of a social justice theory as specified by Fraser.[20]

Sen's capability approach is essentially about how the context influences one's abilities to function and live a fulfilling life with dignity,[21] and the capabilities approach has been developed further, being applied specifically to women.[22] Being poor, differently abled (disabled), a sexual minority or LGBT (lesbian, gay, bisexual, transpersons), or a woman, will make one more vulnerable in some contexts than in others. One's vulnerability obviously depends on psycho-social and religio-cultural conditions, but also on public education and public institutions.

This emphasis on public policies brings us to the core of human rights theory.

Human Rights Theory

The theories, approaches and traditions outlined above do address cultural, social and psycho-social relations, but do not address the role of probably the most important enabler and facilitator – or impeder and destroyer – of human well-being and a life in safety: the state. Addressing the negative side of political measures by states, the greatest famines in peacetime, like Ukraine in the early 1930s, Bengal in the early 1940s, China in the early 1960s, Ethiopia in the early 1980s, and North Korea in the early 1990s, can all be ascribed to catastrophic policies – and limited political freedoms. Hunger is still a reality for 795 million persons, which is an avoidable human catastrophe, as more than enough food is produced. Sustainable development goals (SDGs) 1 and 2 are ending poverty and hunger by 2030.[23]

---

18 Fraser, *Social Justice*, 58.

19 Ingrid Robeyns, 'Is Nancy Fraser's Critique of Theories of Distributive Justice Justified?', in *Constellations,* 10:4 (2003), 538-53, 543.

20 Robeyns, 'Is Fraser's Critique Justified?', 551.

21 Sen's capability approach, saying that two seemingly equal persons' different contexts imply different capabilities to achieve their functioning, is outlined in Amartya Sen, *Poverty and Famines: An Essay on Entitlements and Deprivation* (Oxford: OUP, 1982).

22 Martha Nussbaum, *Women and Human Development: The Capabilities Approach* (Cambridge: CUP, 2000), 78-85, listing ten various capabilities under three main headings: basic, internal and combined, the latter relating to external conditions, a list that Sen does not approve of; see Amartya Sen, 'Human Rights and Capabilities', in *Journal of Human Development*, 6:2 (2005), 151-66, 158.

23 For all SDGs with targets, see https://sustainabledevelopment.un.org/?menu=1300

Human rights are to be enjoyed by all human beings simply by belonging to the human family. The end of the Second World War represented a breakthrough in that states willingly took upon themselves international law obligations by negotiating, adopting and later ratifying human rights treaties. Hence, how a state treats its own inhabitants – not only its citizens[24] – gradually became part of international law. By ratifying these treaties, states also agree to be monitored by supervisory bodies and in some cases subject to court rulings.

Human rights are recognized by the international community of states in two ways: first, by emerging through the natural law tradition, and being acknowledged through state practice and legal opinion (*opinio juris*) as forming part of international customary law. Prohibitions of piracy or torture are two examples. Second, by being recognized by states through negotiating, adopting and ratifying human rights treaties. Human rights do not exist because states have made treaties, but treaties specify the content of the human rights and their corresponding duties. Currently there are nine United Nations human rights treaties and nine protocols, with the Convention on the Elimination of All Forms of Discrimination against Women (CEDAW) having 189 ratifications.[25] In addition there are regional systems.

Most relevant is the 2003 Protocol to the African Charter on Human and Peoples' Rights on the Rights of Women in Africa, which is ratified by 36 states, and which an additional fifteen states have signed, but not ratified. Women's rights to property and inheritance is strongly recognized.[26] The European and American human rights systems are advanced. Two Asian regions have adopted human rights instruments, the 2004 Arab Charter on Human Rights, and a 2012 ASEAN (Association of South East Asian Nations) Human Rights Declaration. Both are criticized by the United Nations High Commissioner for Human Rights.[27]

---

[24] The state can restrict the enjoyment of political rights to citizens, and developing countries can – in accordance with Article 2.3 of the 1966 International Covenant on Economic, Social and Cultural Rights (ICESCR) – limit the enjoyment of economic rights to citizens ('nationals').

[25] CEDAW is the human rights treaty with the highest number of reservations, with more than 60 still in force; on all reservations and objections to these reservations: www.un.org/womenwatch/daw/cedaw/reservations.htm. The 1999 Optional Protocol that institutes an individual complaints procedure is ratified by 106 states.

[26] No less than six provisions regulate land and property: Articles 6(j), 7(d), 15(a), 19(c), 21.1 and 21.2.

[27] The Arab Charter, ratified by thirteen states, is, for instance, criticized due to its wording on women's rights: http://iheu.org/arab-charter-human-rights-incompatible-international-standards-louise-arbour; the ASEAN Declaration is criticized for its attempt to balance individual rights and individual duties: www.un.org/apps/news/story.asp?NewsID=43536#.UPgVKGckSOI, with further links that specify the criticism.

Expanding human rights to more rights-holders and more rights is often controversial. It is wrong to suppose, however, that extending human rights enjoyment to collectives, and not only to individuals, is a recent phenomenon. The rights of the family, members of minorities and (indigenous) peoples had already been recognized in the 1966 International Covenant on Civil and Political Rights (ICCPR), in Articles 23, 27 and 1, respectively. Hence, it is wrong, as alleged by Susan Parsons, that human rights promote only a liberal individualism.[28]

Another criticism is that human rights promote only rights,[29] and not duties. This can be challenged simply by referring to the last preambular paragraph of the 1948 Universal Declaration of Human Rights (UDHR), which reads: 'Every individual and every organ of society… shall… promote respect for these rights and freedoms…' Individuals, non-governmental organisations (NGOs), corporations and other powerful agencies have moral duties. There are processes to move from mere 'responsibility' towards 'accountability' for NGOs and corporations.[30] Accountability implies that conduct is assessed in relation to externally set norms, with the possibility of sanctions in cases of non-compliance with these norms. It is only states that have the international law duties, often termed 'obligations'.

Emphasizing the nature of obligations is a means of making the enjoyment of human rights more effective, and obligations are generally specified as implying respect (not interfering), protecting (prevent other's interference, also in the domestic sphere) and fulfilling (facilitate and, if required, provide).[31] These obligations apply to all human rights, but with different emphases. For instance, most would agree that the state should not play an important role in handing out food, as this might distort the local markets and producer incentives, but that the state has a much more active role to play in the realm of education and health.[32]

---

[28] Parsons, *Feminism and Christian Ethics*, 53.

[29] Rights can be understood claims (legitimate demands on duty-holder) or liberties (non-interference), as well as powers or immunities: see Wesley N. Hohfeld, *Fundamental Legal Concepts as Applied in Judicial Reasoning* (New Haven, CT: Yale University Press, 1919); see also http://plato.stanford.edu/entries/rights/#2.1; also Robin Bradley Kar, 'The Psychological Foundations for Human Rights', in Dinah Shelton (ed), *The Oxford Handbook of International Human Rights Law* (Oxford, OUP, 2013), 104-43, 110.

[30] For NGOs, see CHS Alliance, *Core Humanitarian Standard on Quality and Accountability* (2014). CHS encompasses the previous Humanitarian Accountability Partnership (HAP).

[31] On international obligations, see Hans Morten Haugen, 'Diakonia as rights-based practice', in Stephanie Dietrich et al (eds), *Diaconia as Christian Social Practice: An Introduction* (Regnum, Oxford, 2014), 123-38.

[32] SDG 3-6 encompass health and education: https://sustainabledevelopment.un.org/?menu=1300

A final criticism is that human rights have a limited approach and is too little concerned with power and income asymmetries. It is correct that there are relatively few provisions in human rights treaties that call for a general overhaul of societal structure – with Article 28 of the UDHR being an exception. Human rights realization depends, however, on a proper analysis of the prevailing legal, institutional and cultural structures, seeking to challenge the impediments for inclusion of women and other inadequately represented groups.

Adequate human rights intervention requires a good societal analysis and broad involvement, as the state cannot alone ensure a full realization of human rights. The state, however, has to facilitate 'every individual and every organ of society' in promoting respect for human rights. We meet more restrictions for NGOs, for instance, in countries like Vietnam,[33] Ethiopia,[34] and the Russian Federation.[35] In vulnerable states and states with security challenges, attention to security measures tends to reduce human rights awareness.

Human rights principles (dignity, non-discrimination, the rule of law, transparency, accountability, participation and empowerment)[36] set minimum standards for adequate conduct in any decision-making process. Of these, the most decisive principle is that of non-discrimination. As seen above, when reviewing the social dominance theory and the intersectionality theory, the structures of oppression can be deeply embedded in prevailing norms and societal institutions. Non-discrimination does not imply that one cannot treat persons differently. Favourable treatment might be needed to ensure substantive equality.

Moreover, empowerment for individuals, families and communities is understood as the end-result of a good decision-making process where human rights principles have been adequately observed. Such decision-making processes will promote justice for the most vulnerable and marginalized, in accordance with Fraser's justice theory.

Among the human rights principles, the rule of law has been seen as highly problematic, as it 'institutionalizes the power of men… and… power in its male form…'[37] While it is true that laws tend to be formulated, administered

---

[33] Decree 12 of 2012 on the Registration and Management of the Operations of Foreign Non-Governmental Organizations in Vietnam, particularly Section 4.1.

[34] Ethiopian Proclamation 621 of 2009 on Charities and Societies, particularly Section 14.

[35] The full title of the 2012 law is: 'On Amendments to Legislative Acts of the Russian Federation regarding the Regulation of the Activities of Non-profit Organisations Performing the Functions of a Foreign Agent.'

[36] These seven principles are frequently applied by the UN Food and Agriculture Organization: see FAO, *A right to food-based approach to enhance the contribution of non-wood forest products to food security and nutrition. Background Paper 3 for the International Conference on Forests for Food Security and Nutrition* (2013), 3.

[37] Held, The Ethics of Care, 66.

and enforced primarily by men, the main purpose of the rule of law is to prevent power abuse, unpredictability and injustice.

In summary, it is possible to counter the objections against human rights for promoting individualism, selfishness and an unjustified 'claim mentality'. Individuals' conduct, as well as the conduct of 'organs of society', is important for the realization of human rights. Care ethics' unease with 'principles' can also be addressed by emphasizing that principles are about responsible conduct towards others. The objection against human rights by social constructivism is also open to challenge, as altered linguistics and altered perceptions are not the only ways that will bring about change. States shall, in accordance with CEDAW Article 5, take appropriate measures to modify prejudices and any idea of inferiority.

Why Diaconal Agencies Apply a Human Rights Based Approach – and Why Not?

Among diaconal agencies working with international development, the rights-based approach is increasingly applied. The ACT Alliance EU (formerly Aprodev) outlines the relationship between a rights-based and a faith-based approach. The ACT Alliance EU confirms human rights principles, with a focus on structural and root causes, equality and non-discrimination, accountability, empowerment, participation, community and the inter-relatedness of human beings.[38] These will guide community development, education and health programmes.

Moreover, the ACT Alliance EU clarifies that states' capacities will be enhanced by the efforts of church-related and faith-based agencies, so that states are better able to fulfil their legal human rights obligations.[39] Faith-based agencies engage in human rights work as a part of overall justice work as required by Christian ethics, because justice promotion requires that 'structural determinants of oppression and discrimination are overcome'.[40] Such efforts will be of crucial importance in building broad-based coalitions for making demands and holding the state accountable. A vibrant faith community that engages with civil society will also provide important training in democratic decision-making. Various churches and church traditions have different approaches towards political authorities, and Orthodox thinking of *symphonia* or harmony between church and state is one notable example.

When examining the rights-based practice of twenty Norwegian Christian organisations receiving public development, it was found that there was hardly any principled hesitation in promoting a human rights approach. There was an

[38] ACT Alliance EU, *Rights-based development from a faith-based perspective* (2008), 12-13.

[39] ACT Alliance EU, *Rights-based development*, 11.

[40] ACT Alliance EU, *Rights-based development*, 8.

inadequate implementation of a rights-based approach in planning and implementation of programmes, however, and too many programmes were not sufficiently specific on gender equality.[41] Churches that have a theology saying that women are not to hold senior positions in the church can nevertheless promote the standing of women in society.

It is reasonable to state that those European diaconal organisations working in the realm of international development are more open to human rights terminology as compared with European diaconal organisations that work primarily in a domestic context.[42] This might be explained by the fact that the back donors in the realm of international development frequently refer to human rights.[43] Is this also reflected in an increased openness towards human rights in churches in the states where such programmes are implemented?

As an example, the Ethiopian Evangelical Church Mekane Yesus (EECMY) is chosen. The Ethiopian 2009 Proclamation, referred to above, applies to its Development and Social Services Commission (DASSC), not to the EECMY. The EECMY has Objectives, Guidelines and Prospects for diaconal ministry.[44] An Objective states: 'Empower congregations [to]… be critical towards injustice, violence, oppression, inequality, gender abuse, poverty and pandemic diseases…' The Prospects advocate 'transformational diakonia… to confront injustice'.

While there is no explicit reference to the term 'human rights', engaging in work in line with EECMY's three strategy documents will obviously promote human rights. The Objectives, Guidelines and Prospects also identify the EECMY itself as a duty-bearer.

Church-based and diaconal agencies frequently apply terms like 'dignity' and 'accountability', which have a direct relationship to human rights. These terms do not create tensions in co-operation with conservative churches. Two characteristics of conservative churches are that they neither ordain women nor

---

[41] Elsa Døhlie, Shamim Meer and Hans Morten Haugen, *Faith and rights – a participatory global learning evaluation with Digni members and partner organizations,* Diakonhjemmet University College Report 2015/4.

[42] The term applied in the Lutheran World Federation (LWF) and Interdiac, *Seeking Conviviality: Re-forming Community Diakonia in Europe* (Geneva: LWF, 2013) is 'human dignity', because the term 'human rights' would create more disagreements than 'human dignity', according to a member of the so-called Solidarity Group.

[43] Norad and Norwegian Ministry of Foreign Affairs, *Assessment of Sustainability Elements / Key Risk Factor. Practical Guide* (Oslo: Norad/MFA, 2010), having one section on Gender Equality and Women's Empowerment, and one section on Human Rights and Equality. See also the UN Development Group, *The Human Rights-Based Approach: Statement of Common Understanding* (2004). For a criticism of the World Bank's human rights record, being a specialized agency, and obliged to promote human rights in accordance with Article 59 of the UN Charter, see UN, *Report of the Special Rapporteur on extreme poverty and human rights, A/70/274* (2015).

[44] The documents were available on EECMY's former web page. Summary versions are available via the author.

accept legalisation of relationships between LGBT persons, because they believe that both of these, according to the Bible, are wrong.

The divides over LGBT persons between mainstream churches is currently deep, and human rights are applied by those promoting same-sex marriage. Therefore, to illustrate the dilemmas in the context of international development work that diaconal agencies face, and the role of human rights in this dilemma – same-sex marriage – the role of Lutheran churches is chosen, acknowledging that the divide within the global Anglican Church is wider.

The Lutheran World Federation (LWF) has a long process of facilitating dialogue among member churches. In 2007, the LWF Council adopted Guidelines for Processes and Dialogue, in order to guide discussions among member churches on issues relating to family and sexuality.[45] Nevertheless, dialogue among three of the main LWF members did not prevent EECMY's formal disassociation from two of the world's largest Lutheran churches in 2013 – the Church of Sweden (CoS) and the Evangelical Lutheran Church in America – as a protest against these churches approving a liturgy for same-sex marriage.[46]

If entering into same-sex marriage is presented as a human right, this appeals to large segments of the Americas and western Europe, but not in Africa or the Middle East.[47] When the Church of Sweden approved a liturgy for same-sex marriage in 2009, a background report stated that this decision would strengthen human rights.[48] The European Court of Human Rights states that the right to marry does not imply that states need to legislate for same-sex marriage.[49]

---

[45] For the report containing the Guidelines, see LWF Task Force, *The Lutheran World Federation: Marriage, Family and Human Sexuality. Proposed Guidelines and Processes for Respectful Dialogue* (Geneva: LWF, 2007); for other LWF resources, see https://www.lutheranworld.org/family-marriage-and-sexuality

[46] EECMY, *EECMY Terminates her Partnership Relations with ELCA and CoS* (2013).

[47] Pew Research Center, *Morality Interactive Topline Results* (2014), 5, measuring approval of homosexuality.

[48] Church of Sweden, *Kyrkostyrelsens skrivelse 2009:6 Vigsel och äktenskap* (2009), 60. Note that Norwegian Church Aid (NCA) says in its multi-year strategy that 'harmful religious and cultural traditions fuel intolerance and discrimination, especially for women, girls, and sexual minorities'; NCA, *Global Strategy: Faith in Action* (2015), 11; on sexual minorities, see also 20.

[49] European Court of Human Rights, Grand Chamber, Hämäläinen v. Finland, case 37359/09 (2014), finding (14-3) that Article 12 of the European Convention on Human Rights and Fundamental Freedoms does not encompass an 'obligation… to grant access to marriage to same-sex couples' (para 96). In the European Court of Human Rights, Oliari and others v. Italy, cases 18766/11 and 36030/11 (2015), Article 8 on the right to family life was found to be violated, as marriages entered into in Spain were not given legal recognition in Italy. This does not imply recognition of same-sex *marriages*, but recognition of same-sex *unions*; see paras. 37, 139, 185.

Based on this clarification, it might be wiser for churches and diaconal agencies to find a common platform on the obvious, and not adopt too confrontational an approach. Churches should stand up against harassment and unjustified discrimination of LGBT persons.[50] Arguing that same-sex marriage is to be promoted because it is a human right might, however, risk alienating large segments of the Christian population in many countries of the global South from giving general approval of human rights. Similar arguments apply to abortion.[51]

As there are so many important struggles that still have to be engaged in to improve the lives of women around the world, we need common rather than divisive platforms. This does not imply that challenging other churches over exclusionary practices should never be done. Challenging must be based on trust, as good friends should criticise each other's conduct.

Summary

While the theories presented initially are, to various degrees, able to explain patterns and structures of oppression, exclusion and injustice, it is human rights theory that brings in the agency that is able to do most, both to prevent and to foster inclusion and justice. Many of these changes are incremental, and while not addressed in this chapter, appropriate public institutions will influence human perceptions and conduct. The human rights approach has an unfulfilled potential, and there are several commonalities between a religious and a secular approach to human rights – for instance, dignity and accountability.

As concerns the essential human rights principle of non-discrimination, it is important to stress that a church should not be seen as hypocritical if it engages in combating harassment against anyone, but still believes that it is correct to treat persons differently due to their reading of the Bible. Working with conservative churches will still raise dilemmas.

Bibliography

ACT Alliance EU, Rights-based development from a faith-based perspective, 2008: www.aprodev.eu/files/Development_policy/Dev-RBA/Rights-Position-Paper_E-2008.pdf

Adeney, Miriam, 'Do Missions Raise or Lower the Status of Women? Conflicting Reports from Africa', in Dana Robert (ed), *Gospel Bearers, Gender Barriers: Missionary Women in the Twentieth Century*. Maryknoll, NY: Orbis Books, 2002.

---

[50] LWF Task Force, The Lutheran World Federation: Marriage, 16, bullet point 5: 'Encourage churches to advocate for the dignity and the rights of those who risk being criminalized because of their sexual orientation.'

[51] General Secretary of Norwegian Church Aid, Anne Marie Helland, argues for access to safe abortion, to save women's lives.

CHS Alliance, *Core Humanitarian Standard on Quality and Accountability*, 2014: http://chsalliance.org

Church of Sweden, *Kyrkostyrelsens skrivelse 2009:6 Vigsel och äktenskap [Consecration and marriage]*, 2009: www.svenskakyrkan.se/default.aspx?id=675426

Creenshaw, Kimberlé, 'Demarginalizing the Intersection of Race and Sex: A Black Feminist Critique of Antidiscrimination Doctrine, Feminist Politics and Antiracist Politics', *University of Chicago Legal Forum*, 1989.

Døhlie, Elsa, Shamim Meer and Hans Morten Haugen, *Faith and rights – a participatory global learning evaluation with Digni members and partner organizations, Diakonhjemmet University College Report 2015/4*: http://brage.bibsys.no/xmlui/handle/11250/285636

EECMY, EECMY terminates her Partnership Relations with ELCA and CoS, 2013: www.eecmy.org/?page=!news&article=141

European Court of Human Rights, Grand Chamber, *Hämäläinen v. Finland, case 37359/09*, 16th July 2014.

European Court of Human Rights, *Oliari and others v. Italy, cases 18766/11 and 36030/11*, 21st July 2015.

FAO, *A right to food based approach to enhance the contribution of non-wood forest products to food security and nutrition. Background paper 3 for the International Conference on Forests for Food Security and Nutrition* 2013: www.fao.org/forestry/82456/en/

Fraser, Nancy, *Social Justice in the Age of Identity Politics: Redistribution, Recognition, and Participation. The Tanner lectures on human values, delivered at Stanford University April 30–May 2, 1996*: http://tannerlectures.utah.edu/_documents/a-to-z/f/Fraser98.pdf

Gilligan, Carol, *In a Different Voice. Psychological Theory and Women's Development*. Cambridge, MA: Harvard University Press, 1992.

Haugen, Hans Morten, 'Diakonia as rights-based practice', in Stephanie Dietrich et al (eds), *Diakonia as Christian Social Practice: An Introduction*, Regnum, Oxford, 2014.

Hankivsky, Olena, 'Rethinking Care Ethics: On the Promise and Potential of an Intersectional Analysis', in *American Political Science Review*, 108:2 (2014).

Held, Virginia, *The Ethics of Care. Personal, Political and Global*. Oxford: OUP, 2006.

Hohfeld, Wesley N., *Fundamental Legal Concepts as Applied in Judicial Reasoning*. New Haven, CT: Yale University Press, 1919.

Kar, Robin Bradley, 'The Psychological Foundations for Human Rights', in Dinah Shelton (ed), *The Oxford Handbook of International Human Rights Law*. Oxford, OUP, 2013.

Klasen, Stephan, 'Low schooling for girls, slower growth for all? Cross-country evidence on the effect of gender inequality in education on economic development', in *World Bank* Economic Review, 16:3 (2002).

LWF Task Force, *The Lutheran World Federation: Marriage, Family and Human Sexuality. Proposed Guidelines and Processes for Respectful Dialogue*. Geneva: LWF, 2007.

LWF and Interdiac, *Seeking Conviviality: Re-forming Community Diakonia in Europe*. Geneva: LWF, 2013.

NCA, *Global Strategy. Faith in Action*, 2015: www.kirkensnodhjelp.no/globalassets/strategiske-dokumenter-og-foringer/globalstrategy-2015.pdf

Noddings, Nel, *Caring, a feminine approach to ethics and moral education*. Berkeley, CA: University of California Press, 1984.

Norad and Norwegian Ministry of Foreign Affairs, *Assessment of Sustainability Elements / Key Risk Factor. Practical Guide*. Oslo: Norad/MFA, 2010.

Nussbaum, Martha, *Women and Human Development: The Capabilities Approach*. Cambridge: CUP, 2000.

Parsons, Susan, *Feminism and Christian Ethics*. Cambridge and New York: Cambridge 1996.

Pew Research Center, *Morality Interactive Topline Results*, 2014: www.pewglobal.org/files/2014/03/Morality-Topline-FINAL.pdf

Robeyns, Ingrid, 'Is Nancy Fraser's Critique of Theories of Distributive Justice Justified?', in *Constellations*, 10:4 (2003).

Romm, Norma R.A., 'Revisiting Social Dominance Theory: Invoking a more retroductively-oriented approach to systemic theorising', in *Systemic Practice and Action Research*, 26:2 (2013).

Romm, Norma R.A.,, *New Racism: Revisiting Researcher Accountabilities*. Heidelberg, Germany, and New York: Springer, 2010.

Sen, Amartya, 'Human Rights and Capabilities', in *Journal of Human Development*, 6:2 (2005).

Sen, Amartya, *Poverty and Famines: An Essay on Entitlements and Deprivation*. Oxford: OUP, 1982.

Sidanius, Jim, and Felicia Pratto, *Social Dominance: An Intergroup Theory of Social Hierarchy and Oppression*. Cambridge: CUP, 1999.

Smith, Lisa C., Usha Ramakrishnan, Aida Ndiaye, Lawrence Haddad and Reynaldo Martorell, *The Importance of Women's Status for Child Nutrition in Developing Countries, IFPRI Research Report 131*. Washington DC: International Food Policy Research Institute, 2003.

Tronto, Joan C., *Caring Democracy. Markets, Inequalities, Justice*. New York: New York University Press, 2013.

Tronto, Joan C., *Moral Boundaries, A Political Argument for an Ethics of Care*. New York: Routledge, 1993.

Tønnessen, Aud, 'Trosbaserte organisasjoner, utvikling og kjønn – utfordringer og muligheter', in Asle F. Jøssang and Arne Olav Øyhus (eds), *Religionens rolle i bistand og utvikling*. Kristiansand, N: Portal Akademisk 2012.

UN, *Report of the Special Rapporteur on extreme poverty and human rights, A/70/274*, 2015.

UN Development Group, *The Human Rights Based Approach. Statement of Common Understanding*, 2004: www.unicef.org/sowc04/files/AnnexB.pdf

Dialogical Spaces of Gender in Pastoral Care and Counselling

Anne Austad

The Story of Sarah[1]

Every semester, my class of international students in the Pastoral Care and Counselling course writes an assignment. The assignment is a case description, followed by a transcribed dialogue and a reflection. One of my students presented the following case, which I have received permission to reproduce:

> I was confronted by Sarah, who had a family problem and needed help. Sarah was a young lady of 15. She was a brilliant student who wished to become a doctor. Sarah came from a poor family background with six siblings: two brothers and three sisters. She was the eldest among her siblings. Sarah's parents were farmers who cultivate on a small scale to make a living. I was able to get to know much about Sarah and her tenacious goal in life to become a doctor during my first visit to the community. Though her family was living hand-to-mouth, she was determined to achieve her ambition.
>
> Sarah had a serious problem in her family that was affecting her academic performance. She was introduced to a man who was three times her age as her husband-to-be. This meant she had to end her education to be able to join her husband if the marriage went through. As it was common for most girls in the community to be given for early marriage, it would not be strange that my client should be given away to be married at that age. The practice is common in the community because most of the people are illiterate and do not value education. My client's parents wanted to offer her in marriage to the husband to free the family from their economic hardship. Sarah was planning to commit suicide if she had to sacrifice her education for the marriage.

[1] Sarah is a fictitious name created for this presentation.

Framing Gender Positions in Pastoral Care and Counselling[2]

In the case presented above, many readers will probably find the gender perspective most striking: as a young woman, Sarah is told to quit her academic career to marry a man who is three times her age. However, readers may detect other themes in the narrative as well, such as poverty, cultural norms, family relations, personal ambition and vulnerability. In fact, one can find a multitude of 'voices'[3] in Sarah's story. The case is not unique in that sense.

When approaching Sarah, as well as other people in Pastoral Care and Counselling, there are different ways to address these various voices. The following article rests on the idea that exploring the counsellees' voices, including how they relate to one another, may create opportunities for change. Accordingly, the objective of the text is to contribute to a framework for such an exploration. Further, through the theoretical framework, the aim is to determine how gender can be addressed in Pastoral Care and Counselling as connected with other themes in the life story of the counsellee.

One way to frame theoretically complex intermingling stories and themes on gender could be to apply the *intersectionality theory*.[4] As implemented in recent and commonly used publications in pastoral care, the intersectionality theory has been included as a theoretical framework, particularly in intercultural and feminist pastoral care.[5] The intersectionality theory comes from the black feminist theory and it states that a person's gender position is best understood as intersecting with other roles or positions. Thus, a woman's gender status cannot be separated from her class, sex or racial status.[6] Instead, the intersectionality theory holds that 'gender, class and race work together in creating an overarching structure of domination, creating different outcomes for individuals and for groups positioned at the point at which a particular race meets a particular gender and a particular class status'.[7] When integrated into

---

[2] The concepts 'pastoral care' and 'pastoral counselling' are often used in tandem to include two aspects of the pastoral ministry. Pastoral care refers to the 'supportive and crisis care offered by ordained and lay leaders', whereas pastoral counselling is an 'extension of pastoral care which is undertaken by specially trained counselors attending not only to emergent needs but also to underlying causes of emotional or psychological distress and how a client's religious/spiritual life relates to this distress' (C. Doehring, *The Practice of Pastoral Care: A postmodern approach* (Louisville, KY: Westminster John Knox Press, 2015), 190). In the following article, I take a broad perspective, and I refer to both pastoral care and counselling. Accordingly, I will use the combined term.

[3] The term 'voices' will be described and defined later in the article.

[4] P.H. Collins, *Black Feminist Thought* (Oxford: Taylor & Francis, 1990).

[5] See, for instance, E.Y. Lartey, *In Living Color: An Intercultural Approach to Pastoral Care and Counseling,* second edition (London: Jessica Kingsley, 2003); and Doehring, *The Practice of Pastoral Care*.

[6] Collins, *Black Feminist Thought.*

[7] H.J.M. Hermans and A. Hermans-Konopka, *Dialogical Self Theory: Positioning and Counter Positioning in a Globalizing Society* (New York: Cambridge University Press, 2010), 75.

the practice of pastoral care, one can say the intersectionality theory helps care-givers and care-seekers explore how multiple systems generate privileges and disadvantages.[8]

In this way, the intersectionality theory could be a possible take on the presented case, and more generally, on pastoral care from a gender perspective. Yet, I have opted for another theoretical framework, that is, the *dialogical self theory* (DST).[9] The DST has some similarities with the intersectionality theory, as it also looks at the intersections between different positions and agrees that identity can be subjected to the relations of social domination.[10] However, the DST is interested not only in processes on the interface of 'social positions', such as gender, class and race, but also in 'personal positions'. The DST explicitly holds that personal positions and social positions (roles) are interconnected elements of the self. Related to the presented case, the DST certainly focuses on gender, class, race and poverty, but the theory also provides conceptual frameworks for addressing Sarah's voices of ambition, brilliancy, vulnerability and tenacity, positions that can be categorized at a more personal level. Further, a DST approach would look at the interconnections of social and personal positions. The gender perspective in Sarah's story would thus not be elicited by adding gender to the analysis, but by placing gender within a network of other themes, positions and voices – both on a socio-cultural level and on a personal level.

The DST is developed within the discipline of psychology and is increasingly applied as a theoretical understanding and conceptual tool in secular counselling and psychotherapy. However, few publications have applied the theory to Pastoral Care and Counselling.[11] In the following, I will aim at making that connection. The DST can, according to my view, be a fruitful conceptual framework in pastoral care and, more specifically, in looking at a gender perspective. That is because the DST combines the different aspects of personal, social and cultural positions; in that way, it matches the Counselling situation with an individual, yet socially and culturally embedded, person. Another reason for bringing the DST into the field of Pastoral Care and Counselling is the theory's focus on dialogue – a concept

---

[8] Doehring, *The Practice of Pastoral Care*, 189.

[9] The DST was launched in the early 1990s by Hubert Hermans (now professor emeritus at Radboud University in the Netherlands) and has been developed since then. It is widely used in different psychological disciplines, but also in wider domains, as well as in counselling and psychotherapy. Hermans and Hermans-Konopka, *Dialogical Self Theory*, 19-20.

[10] Hermans and Hermans-Konopka, *Dialogical Self Theory*, 75.

[11] However, Hetty Zock presents DST and the role of religious voices in the theory, and states that the theory is relevant for both clinical and pastoral professionals. H. Zock, 'The existential self in a culture of multiplicity: Hubert Hermans' theory of the dialogical self'. In J. Wentzel van Huyssteen and E.P. Wiebe (eds), *In search of self: Interdisciplinary perspectives on personhood* (Grand Rapids, MI: Eerdmans, 2011).

that is helpful in encountering people in a globalized society and, in particular, in approaching gender issues.

The Dialogical Self Theory in Pastoral Care and Counselling

As the article focuses on Pastoral Care and Counselling, I will, in addition to the DST literature, draw on some literature on Pastoral Care and Counselling. The process of moving between the pastoral care and DST theories will be hermeneutical, with the aim of moving towards a more thorough understanding. Combining the DST and Pastoral Care and Counselling theories certainly produces some tensions. For instance, there is a difference in the use of an immanent and transcendent language between the two disciplines.[12] The primary aim of this article is, however, not to create a dialogue between a 'religious' pastoral care and a 'secular' psychology, but to use the DST as an analytical take on stories and dialogues in Pastoral Care and Counselling. The DST will work as a means of concretizing themes and concerns in pastoral care, and pastoral care literature will be used to concretize the context of the practice. The hermeneutic interplay between the two disciplines rests on the assumption that theology and psychology ensure a mutual broadening of both fields of study.[13] Using psychological theories and insights in pastoral care may help pastoral care-givers 'to avoid a kind of "transcendentalist spirituality" alienated from concrete, historical life conditions',[14] and to provide a better understanding of human personhood and behaviour. I should emphasise, though, that the DST is only one take among many possible on Pastoral Care and Counselling from a gender perspective. I do not propose a new paradigm, but one way of addressing gender issues in pastoral care in a concrete way.

Pastoral Care as a Diaconal Practice

I consider pastoral care an integrated part of *diakonia*. As part of diaconal practice, pastoral care has the possibility of going deep into individual suffering

---

[12] The DST as a psychological theory describes the voice of god (with lower case 'g') in the self as an 'imaginal voice', whereas pastoral care would speak of God as a transcendent reality, presupposing the existence of God.

[13] A. Austad, '"Don't tell me this is only taking place in my head.' Dialogues between theology and psychology on anomalous experiences', in *Tidsskrift for praktisk teologi,* 2 (2015); R. Satler-Rosa, 'The Emergence of Cultural Difference and Pastoral Care. Conflicts and Opportunities of Encounter and Healing', in D. Louw and U. Elsdörfer (eds), *Encounter in Pastoral Care and Spiritual Healing: Towards an Integrative and Intercultural Approach* (Zürich Switzerland: Verlag Münster, 2012).

[14] Ronaldo Sathler-Rosa, 'The Emergence of Cultural Difference and Pastoral Care: Conflicts and Opportunities of Encounter and Healing', in D. Louw and U. Elsdörfer (eds), *Encounter in Pastoral Care and Spiritual Healing: Towards an Integrative and Intercultural Approach* (Zürich, Switzerland: Verlag Münster, 2012),.131.

and listening to the emotional conflicts and feelings of oppression. At the same time, pastoral care-givers are agents confronting abusive and oppressive power structures.[15] That can be done through listening and dialogical conversation, as well as through addressing structural injustice.

In my view, the following approach to pastoral care[16] falls into a diaconal tradition: pastoral care can be seen as 'a co-creative process of intermingling stories that takes into account the interacting multilayered stories of people embedded in overlapping familial, communal, and social systems'.[17] Doehring's approach underscores further that 'the link between the personal and the political is in the DNA of care-giving'.[18] This understanding relates to what has been called the *contextual paradigm* in Pastoral Care and Counselling.[19] The contextual paradigm holds that the individual is a relational being and is always part of a larger network of communal and social life. Pastoral care-givers in this tradition interpret people's lives as interwoven in their contexts and, further, give room to the prophetic dimension of speaking up against social injustice.

Linking the DST with Pastoral Care and Counselling – as I do in this article – will correspond with contextual understanding, as the DST values the intersection of personal, social and political voices. The socio-cultural approach of DST further refutes one of the critiques that has been put forward on Pastoral Care and Counselling, namely that, using psychological theories makes pastoral counselling too individualistic, which means that people's suffering and deprivation due to social structures and cultural norms are not accounted for. Feminist and liberation theology has seen voices speaking against this psychological individualism in pastoral care.[20] However as mentioned, this critique does not hold for the DST, as DST opens the scope of psychology to cultural voices and structural social positions.

---

[15] L.G. Engedal, 'Theological foundation of pastoral care and counseling', in Ø. Eide, L.G. Engedal, L.P. Kimilike and E. Ndossi (eds), *Restoring Life in Christ. Dialogues of Care in Christian Communities: An African Perspective* (Germany: Erlanger Verlag für Mission und Ökumene, 2008).

[16] In the following citation, Doehring refers to intercultural pastoral and spiritual care.

[17] Doehring, *The Practice of Pastoral Care*, 188

[18] L.K. Graham, 2013, 471-72 in Doehring, *The Practice of Pastoral Care*, xxi.

[19] The contextual paradigm is described as different from the classical paradigm and clinical pastoral paradigm. The classical paradigm emphasizes pastoral care as preaching the word of God for the individual. The clinical pastoral paradigm is influenced by a liberal Protestant tradition, and it values an inductive approach and psychological resources in relating to the counselling process, while the contextual paradigm draws on liberation theology, hermeneutics, feminist theology and communitarian ethics. For a further description, see J. Patton, *Pastoral Care in Context: An introduction to pastoral care* (Louisville, KY: Westminster John Knox Press, 1993).

[20] Doehring, *The Practice of Pastoral Care*, xix

The Dialogical Self Theory as an Interpretive Framework

Now I will turn to a short presentation of the DST. To get a better understanding of the relevance of the theory, I will illustrate some of the concepts and ideas with elements from the case about Sarah.

DST brings together two basic concepts: *self and dialogue*. In contrast to a view where self and dialogue are seen as being differently positioned on the internal-external axis,[21] DST combines the two concepts so that dialogue also takes place within the self. DST holds that the self is not only something 'within the skin', and dialogue is not only something between two or more people. In DST, the notions of self and dialogue are put together in the concept of an extended self. [22] Thus, there is no sharp separation between the internal life of the self and the outside world. Figure 1[23] shows one of the core issues in the DST, namely that the border between 'inner' and 'outer' is porous in what Hermans (the founder of DST) calls the extended self. In terms of the DST, the self does not have an existence separate from society, but is part of society. The self becomes a 'society of mind', inhabited by people, groups or traditions, such as a mother, a teacher, a religious figure or a congregation.[24]

Related to the idea of a society of mind are two core concepts in the DST: 'I-positions' and 'voices'. The concept of the I-position refers to how the self can take different positions depending on particular social contexts. Further, the DST holds that human cognition and emotions, as well as social functioning, are based on the dialogical relationships between different I-positions. I-positions may have a more social character (e.g. I as a woman and I as poor), or a more personal character (e.g. I as ambitious and I as vulnerable), but the personal I-positions are always part of and intertwined with the social and cultural positions, and the social positions are voiced through individual positions.[25] I-positions may be situated in the 'internal' domain (e.g. I as ambitious, tenacious, and vulnerable) or in the 'external' domain, which is the other in the self (e.g. I as my mother) (see Figure 1). The DST emphasizes

---

[21] The self is, at least in western traditions, seen as a reflexive concept that deals with what takes place within the person, while dialogue is taking place externally, that is, between person and other (Hermans and Gieser, 2012: 2).

[22] H.J.M. Hermans and T. Gieser, 'Introductory chapter: history, main tenets and core concepts of dialogical self theory', in H.J.M. Hermans and T. Gieser (eds), *Handbook of Dialogical Self Theory* (Cambridge: CUP, 2012), 1-22.

[23] The figure is from H. Hermans, *Between dreaming and recognition seeking: The emergence of Dialogical self theory* (Maryland: University Press, 2012), 38. The particular I-positions are written in by me.

[24] H.J.M. Hermans and H.J.G. Kempen, *The Dialogical Self: Meaning as Movement* (San Diego, CA: Academic Press, 1993).

[25] H. Zock, 'Religious voices in the dialogical self: Towards a conceptual-analytical framework on the basis of Hubert Hermans' dialogical self theory', in M. Buitelaar and H. Zock (eds), *Religious Voices in Self-Narratives* (Berlin: Walter de Gruyter, 2013), 11-36.

further the importance of recognizing not only actual others, but also 'imaginal' others. Thus, an imaginal position can also be part of the self. Imaginal positions may draw on cultural traditions, such as religion.[26] Within the conceptual framework of the DST, it is possible to think of the soul, the spirit, or God as an I-position existing in imaginal space.[27] Thus, the line is not only porous between the inner and outer, or self and society; it is also porous between what in the DST is called the 'actual' and the 'imaginal'.[28]

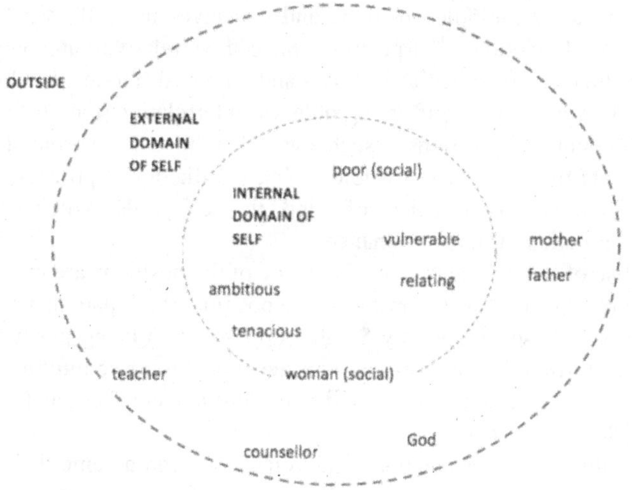

Figure 1

The I-positions have their different 'voices'. The voices tell different stories from different perspectives. All voices are 'colored by the ideas, values, emotions, expectations and behavioral patterns of the various social and cultural and also religious groups one is part of'.[29]

---

[26] Hermans and Kempen, *The Dialogical Self: Meaning as Movement*, 70.

[27] Rowans, 'The use of I-positions in psychotherapy', in Hubert J.M. Hermans and T. Gieser (eds), *Handbook of Dialogical Self Theory* (Cambridge: CUP, 2012), 244.

[28] The DST assumes the existence of an imaginal space, side-by-side and interwoven with physical space. A multiplicity of I-positions located in the imaginal space connects with physical appearance in different ways. It may or may not be congruent with the actual perspective of the actual other (which can be checked by entering into a conversation with the other). It may be largely the product of imagination, and it can even be completely imaginary (H.J.M. Hermans, H.J.G. Kempen and R. van Loon, 'The Dialogical Self. Beyond Individualism and Rationalism', in *American Psychologist*, 47:1 (1992), 23-33.)

[29] Zock, 'Religious voices in the dialogical self, 17.

Related to the case of Sarah, we can assume that her 'society of mind' consists of her mother, her father, her teacher (who appears later in the conversation), gender positions, poverty positions, and more. In addition, the voice of God appears later in the conversation through a prayer initiated by the counsellor. Some positions are situated in the internal domain and some in the external. The different positions are all part of Sarah's self and each speaks with a voice.

Hermans articulates that the I moves in space and time, and it is positioning, repositioning and counter-positioning. He emphasizes the plural, polyphonic self, constituted by multiple positions and conceives the self as a 'dynamic multiplicity of I-positions'.[30] I-positions have their relative autonomy in the self, have their own specific history, and show different developmental pathways. However, the self is capable of interrelating the different and relatively autonomous positions in such a way that they can be brought together as components of an organized whole.[31] Yet, the dialogical processes are not always harmonious. As a society of mind, the self is also voicing tensions, conflicts, contradictions and dominance.

In the case of Sarah, one can see that some of the positions are in a dynamic interplay with one another. For instance, the position of her parents wanting her to marry is counter-positioned by Sarah's opposition to being positioned as a submissive, married girl, as well as with her thoughts of committing suicide. Sarah's story shows how the self includes tensions and conflicts, and how some voices can dominate others.

Relating this to gender positions and voices, one can assume there are two conflicting gender positions in the self of Sarah. The first is the '*traditional gender orientation*', which is voiced by the idea of getting married to secure a living. This position is intersected with a poverty position, and both can be considered social positions. The poverty and traditional gender positions are voiced through Sarah's parents, who have external personal positions in the self of Sarah. The other gender position is the '*equal opportunity orientation*', based on the idea of the importance of women in academic studies. This position is voiced through Sarah's teacher and in Sarah's own personal positions of tenacity and ambition. In the dialogue with the counsellor, Sarah expresses how these two voices are in conflict. Because they – in different ways – are both important to her in their consequences, they provoke strong emotional reactions. Sarah states, 'I cannot stand it losing my education to early marriage and cannot also face family rejection.' Facing the dilemma of either losing her education or losing her parents, Sarah cannot see how the two positions are able to dialogue with each another. In this dilemma, Sarah puts forward the solution of suicide.

---

[30] Hermans and Gieser, 'Introductory chapter: history, main tenets and core concepts of dialogical self theory', 2.

[31] Hermans and Kempen, *The Dialogical Self: Meaning as Movement*, 92-93.

How may the pastoral counsellor approach this situation of conflicting gender voices? How can pastoral care address gender perspectives in such a way that it opens spaces for liberating change?

Spaces of Dialogue, Spaces of Change

In the introduction, I mentioned dialogue as a core concept and approach in Pastoral Care and Counselling. Dialogue is a way of exploring different dynamics in the intermingling stories of the counsellee. In the following, I will look more closely at what it means in the light of the understanding of dialogue in the DST.

The concept dialogue in the DST is used to describe two or more related utterances.[32] However, it is also used in a more qualified sense, where dialogues are conceptually differentiated from monologues. Related to the latter understanding, the DST holds that dialogue and monologue can be regarded at an analytical level on a continuum.[33] At one end is the monological exchange, where the participants try to dominate or win the discussion. At the other end, one finds dialogue, where the participants listen carefully to others' viewpoints and are willing to learn from each other.[34] Between these poles are different mixtures of dialogical and monological elements. Dialogue is thus unequal to any communication or movement between positions. Hermans states that, in dialogue, there is 'an exchange between different positions in such a way that the original positions of the participants are changed and developed on the basis of the preceding phases of the interchange'.[35] He adds that, 'more than conversation, discussion and debate, dialogue has innovative potentials'.[36]

In pastoral care, dialogue means that the counsellor listens to the counsellee and vice versa, and both parties respond, based on what is said. In other words, they do change or move from their initial ideas and positions. However, dialogue as a mutual exchange does not mean that the asymmetry in terms of professional and ethical responsibility on the side of the counsellor is taken away. Neither does it imply that the counsellee's story becomes out of focus at the expense of a mutual conversation. Dialogue does not mean that the counsellor's life stories are examined in the pastoral care setting, but that the counsellor's internal positions may change due to responses from the counsellee, and vice versa. In contrast to traditions of pastoral care, which

[32] Hermans, Kempen and van Loon, 'The Dialogical Self. Beyond Individualism and Rationalism', 27.

[33] By this, Hermans states that dialogue is not always there. Dialogue is not equal to any exchange. (Hermans and Gieser, 'Introductory chapter: history, main tenets and core concepts of dialogical self theory.')

[34] Hermans and Gieser, 'Introductory chapter: history, main tenets and core concepts of dialogical self theory.'

[35] Hermans and Hermans-Konopka, *Dialogical Self Theory*, 80.

[36] Hermans and Hermans-Konopka, *Dialogical Self Theory*, 80.

involve deductively preaching to the counsellee, as well as to approaches that value authority, dialogical approaches have the potential to obstruct patriarchal relations of power domination.

Having said that, a monologue from the counsellor can – in certain situations – be appropriate. In encountering Sarah's desperate cry, in which suicide is an imminent danger, or in other crises or emergencies, the counsellor might have to give instructions to make the counsellee safe. Monological responses in crisis contexts can be a means of immediate help. However, in a counselling relationship in which the emergency is less acute, the dialogical approach is a fruitful way of letting the different voices learn from each other and of listening to the small voices that might have been silenced by other voices.

In counselling, one may, according to DST, speak of *three spaces of dialogue*. The first is the spoken dialogue between the counsellor and the counsellee, as I have previously discussed. The two other spaces are the inner dialogues of the counsellor and counsellee, respectively. The counsellor's inner dialogues may contain ponderings on how to respond to the utterances from the counsellee. The ponderings may be dialogues with collective voices such as theologies and gender theories, as well as personal voices of lived religion, emotions that arise as a reaction to the story of the counsellor, and dialogues with God. The inner dialogue may start before the session, anticipate how the session will unfold, continue through the session, and stay after. Likewise, the counsellees have inner dialogues more or less related to the counselling situation. The three spaces of dialogue are not totally separated; they influence each other mutually. It is the professional task of the counsellor to be aware of his or her inner voices, as well as how they affect the conversation. It is also the responsibility of the counsellor to be sensitive to how his or her inner dialogues are intertwined with the social position of being a pastoral counsellor, as well as how the combination of personal voices and social position may communicate power in more or less subtle ways.

Back to the story of Sarah, the counsellor explores how the different gendered voices are connected with other voices in Sarah's self. The following picture emerges: 'the traditional gender voice' is closely intersected with poverty and cultural norms in the local community, but also with Sarah's vulnerability and her relation to and love for her parents. The 'equal opportunity voice', on the other hand, is connected to her brilliance, ambition, autonomy and passion for becoming a doctor. In the language of the DST, the two gender positions create two '*coalitions*'.[37] The two coalitions are in conflict and Sara cannot choose one of them over the other. In order to solve the conflict, the counsellor introduces a possible movement. He asks whether the poverty voice could just as well find a place in the other coalition, together

[37] Hermans and Hermans-Konopka, *Dialogical Self Theory*, 9.

with education: in other words, if education could be understood as a way out of poverty. Sarah agrees to that.

Following the idea of moving the poverty position, the counsellor introduces a *fourth space of dialogue*, that is, to include Sarah's important external voices in the conversations. This inclusion relates to the idea that change is not uni-directional, from people's inner worlds towards relationships, families, communities and beyond, but rather 'intermingling effects of change that move back and forth across relational webs'.[38] In the case of Sarah, the counsellor then invites Sarah's parents to dialogue about the future of their daughter. This is not an easy task as Sarah's parents have made up their minds based on their cultural norms and their poverty. However, the counsellor is able to move some steps by being aware of the contextual meaning of the parent's voices. By being sensitive to the parents' perceived position, learning from their perspectives, and understanding their relationship with the collective voices of gender in the community, the counsellor creates dialogical spaces of possible change, although there are immediate economic obstacles to the plans for education.

The story of Sarah thus illustrates how different positions are linked with each other, as well as how the gender voice cannot be seen separately but as intertwined with other voices in the self. When it comes to change, it becomes clear how intersecting structural positions of marginalization, gender and poverty make change difficult. Accordingly, the call for Pastoral Care and Counselling is to voice the intersecting gender perspective at all levels – the personal, the local and the global.

Summary

In this article, I have shown how gender positions and gender voices intersect with other positions and voices. By using the DST as a conceptual framework, various positions and coalitions may be identified. From this perspective, gender is not essentialized, but explored from different positions attached to different voices – both personal and socio-cultural. When addressing gender issues in pastoral care, the DST may contribute with analytical concepts to the exploration. It may further concretize a dialogical approach, which may buffer against patriarchal power structures and open spaces of liberating change.

Bibliography

Austad, Anne, ''Don't tell me this is only taking place in my head.' Dialogues between theology and psychology on anomalous experiences', in *Tidsskrift for praktisk teologi,* 2 (2015).

Collins, Patricia Hill, *Black Feminist Thought.* Oxford: Taylor & Francis, 1990.

[38] Doehring, *The Practice of Pastoral Care*, xix.

Doehring, Carrie, *The Practice of Pastoral Care: A postmodern approach*. Louisville: Westminster John Knox Press, 2015.

Engedal, Leif Gunnar, 'Theological foundation of pastoral care and counseling', in O. Eide, L.G. Engedal, L.P. Kimilike and E. Ndossi (eds), *Restoring Life in Christ: Dialogues of Care in Christian Communities: An African Perspective*. Erlanger Verlag für Mission und Ökumene, 2008.

Hermans, Hubert J.M., *Between dreaming and recognition seeking: The emergence of Dialogical self theory*. Maryland: University Press, 2012.

Hermans, Hubert J.M., 'The dialogical self. Between exchange and power', in Hubert J.M. Hermans and G. Dimaggio (eds), *The Dialogical Self in Psychotherapy*. New York: Brunner Routledge, 2004.

Hermans, Hubert J.M. and T. Gieser, 'Introductory chapter: history, main tenets and core concepts of dialogical self theory', in Hubert J.M. Hermans and T. Gieser (eds), *Handbook of Dialogical Self Theory*. Cambridge: Cambridge University Press, 2012.

Hermans, Hubert J.M. and A. Hermans-Konopka, *Dialogical Self Theory. Positioning and Counter Positioning in a Globalizing Society*. New York: Cambridge University Press, 2010.

Hermans, Hubert J.M. and H.J.G. Kempen, *The Dialogical Self. Meaning as Movement*. San Diego, CA: Academic Press, 1993.

Hermans, Hubert J.M., H.J.G. Kempen and R. van Loon, 'The Dialogical Self. Beyond Individualism and Rationalism', in *American Psychologist* 47:1 (1992).

Lartey, Emmanuel Yartekwei, *In Living Color: An Intercultural Approach to Pastoral Care and Counseling*. Second Edition. London: Jessica Kingsley, 2003.

Patton, John, *Pastoral Care in Context: An introduction to pastoral care*. Louisville, KY: Westminster John Knox Press, 1993.

Rowan, J., 'The use of I-positions in psychotherapy', in Hubert J. M. Hermans and T. Gieser (eds), *Handbook of Dialogical Self Theory*. Cambridge: CUP, 2012.

Satler-Rosa, Ronaldo, 'The Emergence of Cultural Difference and Pastoral Care. Conflicts and Opportunities of Encounter and Healing', in D. Louw and U. Elsdörfer (eds), *Encounter in Pastoral Care and Spiritual Healing: Towards an Integrative and Intercultural Approach*. Zürich, Switzerland: Verlag Münster, 2012.

Snorton, T.E., 'Gender issues in pastoral care', in S.B. Roberts (ed). *Professional Spiritual and Pastoral Care: A Practical Clergy and Chaplain's Handbook*. Woodstock: Skylight Paths, 2011.

Zock, H., 'The existential self in a culture of multiplicity: Hubert Hermans' theory of the dialogical self', in J. Wentzel van Huyssteen and E.P. Wiebe (eds), *In search of self. Interdisciplinary perspectives on personhood*. Grand Rapids, MI: Eerdmans, 2011.

Zock, H., 'Religious voices in the dialogical self: Towards a conceptual-analytical framework on the basis of Hubet Hermans' dialogical self theory', in M. Buitelaar and H. Zock (eds), *Religious Voices in Self-Narratives*. Berlin: Walter de Gruyter, 2013.

Sexual Misconduct in Church: A Gender Perspective

Tormod Kleiven

Introduction

Sexual abuse in churches has been an issue for several decades. The enormous degree of attention to the sexual abuse of boys in the Catholic Church has been one of the main reasons for this.[1]

'Is Nothing Sacred?' was published in 1989,[2] and is a classic study in this field. Marie M. Fortune[3] recounts a story about her encounters with women and denominational leaders where the pastor of a congregation was accused of sexual misconduct during pastoral counselling.

My own initiation into this field was like almost everyone else's; in 1995, I had to listen to a story. Some men told their stories, and after a while we understood a scary reality: about twenty men had been abused as children and youths by the spiritual leader of a Christian fellowship. I myself was a member of the same fellowship, and I was the director of the Health and Social Department of this community. Together with the pastor of the local church and the director of the community, I was responsible for taking action. Consequently, a twenty-year story of abusive behaviour by a spiritual leader was brought to an end.

Since 1995, I have been engaged in exposing and preventing sexual misconduct in churches. This has been the focus of my practice and research, along with developing competence in responding to sexual abuse in church contexts. I have not taken a specifically gender approach. Nevertheless, the gender perspective is so closely connected with this field that it is impossible not to let it be a focal point.

---

[1] Merle W. Longwood, 'Introduction' in Marie M. Fortune and W. Merle Longwood (eds), *Sexual abuse in the Catholic Church: Trusting the Clergy?* (Binghampton, NY: Haworth Pastoral Press, 2003), 1-7.

[2] Marie Fortune, *Is Nothing Sacred? The story of a pastor, the women he sexually abused, and the congregation he nearly destroyed* (Cleveland, OH: United Church Press, 1999).

[3] The Lutheran pastor Marie M. Fortune is one of the pioneers working in this field. In 1977, she founded the Center for Prevention of Sexual and Domestic Violence, now named the Faith Trust Institute (www.faithtrustinstitute.org) in Seattle. The Institute edited the *Journal of Religion & Abuse* from 1999 to 2009.

Sexual abuse has existed since the fall of man. I believe it has also been an issue in churches for all time. Nevertheless, among the leaders of the global church, there has been an awareness of such abusive attitudes and behaviour among trusted people in churches only since the 1980s. Denominational policies concerning sexual misconduct in churches indicate how increasing this has come to be understood as a serious problem.[4]

The Lutheran Church of Norway and the Free Churches in Norway have been at the forefront in the Nordic countries and western Europe in developing such policies.[5] One important reason was research by the theologian Eva Lundgren published from 1985.[6] She accused Christian men in high positions of misusing power in relation to their wives and girlfriends by mixing a patriarchal approach with sexuality. This devalued women, making them tools for satisfying men's needs. Her research was based on interviews with women. Later, Lundgren also interviewed the men involved. This research provoked a public debate, which raised awareness of the topic, and encouraged women to tell their stories. Church leaders had to acknowledge that the church was not a safe zone. Sexual abuse by clergy, deacons, other trusted people and church leaders was a reality. The stories were eye-openers. These stories had not been told earlier for a number of reasons: one of the main reasons was that the power misused by such abusers engendered a false self-understanding in its victims, making those abused feel responsible, guilty and ashamed.[7]

Sexual abuse is about power and sexualisation. The stories so far tell us that it is mainly men who are the abusers. The statistics seem to indicate that

---

[4] Examples of similar policies in different continents illustrate this. In America: *Denominational Policies on Clergy / Congregant Sexual Contact: www.adults abusedbyclergy.org/denominational_policies.html; Sexual Misconduct Policy and its Procedures – Presbyterian Church, USA (2013): https://www.pcusa.org/resource/ presbyterian-church-us-sexual-misconduct-policy-an; Resources for the Prevention of Sexual Misconduct in Orthodox Church: https://oca.org/about/sexual-misconduct.* In Africa: *Policy on Clergy Sexual Misconduct in the Doctrine and Discipline of the African Methodist Episcopal Church (2000).* In Australia: *Policy for Dealing with Complaints of Sexual Misconduct made against a Member or Adherent of The Uniting Church of Australia (2001): www.clergyabuseaustralia.org/Policy2001Sexual MisconductUCA.pdf.* In Europe: *'Guidelines for the Handling of Sexual Misconduct' for four Norwegian Mission Organizations: www.nlm.no/en/nlm-the-world-for-christ-norwegian-lutheran-mission/ressurser/dokumenter/instrukser-og-retningslinjer/guidelines-for-the-handling-of-sexual-misconduct2*

[5] Policies were adopted in the Church of Norway in 1995, and the largest Free Churches had adopted policies before 2000.

[6] Eva Lundgren, *I Herrens vold. Dokumentasjon av vold mot kvinner i kristne miljøer.* (Oslo: Cappelen Forlag, 1985).

[7] Flora A. Keshgegian, 'Power to Wound, Power to Mend: Toward a Non-Abusing Theology', in *Journal of Religion and Abuse* (Binghampton, NY: Haworth Pastoral Press, 1999), 39-41.

between 80% and 90% of all sexual abuse is perpetrated by men.[8] In the church, it is committed by trusted men in leadership positions, those who preach the gospel and salvation in the name of Jesus Christ. Their theology is often conservative and founded on classic Christian views, and they may be active in mission organizations working to spread the word of God in their neighbourhoods and abroad. It is mainly children, youth and women who are abused.[9] The gender perspective is also apparent if we examine the history of how this situation has been revealed: women's movements and feminist organizations have been at the forefront. They have very often struggled with a stubborn and blind Christian leadership that mainly consists of men. Most feminist theology has a power analytic approach, in regard both to the interpretation of biblical material and to the historical and current situation of the church. The influence of a patriarchal culture in family and church/religious systems is used to understand and uncover repression and abusive interactions.[10]

We often say: 'We can't believe it before we see it.' The story of sexual abuse in the church is the reverse: 'You can't see it before you believe it.'

Method and Topic

My topic is sexual misconduct from a gender perspective. My approach is diaconal. Helping others to 'autonomy and interdependence' by empowering 'not by power *over*, but power *to*, *with* and *within*' are the core terms used to describe a diaconal approach in this context.[11] This approach requires an understanding of sexual misconduct from the position and perspective of the vulnerable. It is crucial to empower abused people by creating opportunities to remove the invalid sense of responsibility and guilt that has been created.

The chapter is intended to provide answers to the following question:

---

[8] David Finkelhor, 'The international epidemiology of child sexual abuse', in *Child Abuse & Neglect, 18,* 409-17; Norwegian Competence Center on Violence and Traumatic Stress: www.nkvts.no/tema/Sider/BarnogUnge_Definisjonerogomfang-seksuelleovergrep.aspx

[9] Gary Richard Schoener, 'Historical Overview', in John C. Gonsiorek (ed), *Breach of Trust: Sexual Exploitation by Health Care Professionals and Clergy* (London: Sage Publications, 1995), 3-17.

[10] Keshgegian, 'Power to Wound, Power to Mend', 37-65; Janet L. Jacobs, 'Charisma, Male Entitlement, and the Abuse of Power', in Anson Shupe, William A. Stacey, and Susan A. Darnell (eds), *Clergy Misconduct in Modern America* (New York and London: New York University Press, 2000), 113-30.

[11] Stephanie Dietrich, 'Reflections on Core Aspects of Diaconal Theory', in Stephanie Dietrich et al (eds), *Diakonia as Christian Social Practice: An Introduction* (Oxford: Regnum, 2014), 14-15.

How can we understand the mechanism of sexual misconduct[12] *in church from a gender and power perspective?*

This question is massive, and it is necessary to refine it. A core question is: what is a gender perspective on the topic 'sexual abuse in church'? The question can be answered in different ways. In this chapter, I have chosen to discuss the ways in which the gender perspective is relevant to understanding sexual abuse, not only when this perspective is included, but also in approaches where it is absent. My premise is that we have to see sexual abuse through the lenses of the abused (a diaconal perspective) to understand the problem truly as a church. This entails the need to use a theoretical power framework to make the mechanism of abuse visible. The gender perspective is anchored mainly in a cultural and relational understanding. My position is that gender is not an explanation of evil or good, right or wrong. A gender perspective is more about a critically conscious approach to every way of evaluating human beings that uses stereotypes about gender to categorize individuals and groups into degrading positions. Evil (which sexual abuse represents) can never be interpreted as and limited to gender phenomena. Evil from a Christian point of view is a consequence of sin and the fall of man.

To understand sexual abuse, we must start by briefly describing the content of sexuality in a power-analytical framework. As mentioned above, the gender perspective promoted by feminist movements, and research is central to understanding the reasons why this issue has at last become a visible reality for the leadership of churches. Nevertheless, different approaches have offered different ways of understanding sexual abuse, the abuser and the abused. I discuss these approaches from a gender perspective together with theological, traditional and cultural factors in the church context. This is done in the context of a definition of sexual misconduct based on the use of power.

Sexuality, Gender and Power in a Church Context

What is the relationship between sexual misconduct and sexuality? My view is that sexual abuse is not about sex, but about misuse of power – and misuse of sexuality itself.[13] The challenge is that both sexuality and power as verbalized issues are, in many ways, far from the consciousness of Christian fellowships and of the church. Derek Farrell claims that the content of sexuality has never been an issue in church. He writes:

---

[12] The term 'sexual misconduct' is used because it is usually the headline term used for denominational policies. It is not meant to devalue the seriousness of sexual abuse, and may be understood as a headline for all kinds of misuse of sexuality as a power tool to objectify and devaluate another.

[13] James Newton Poling, *The Abuse of Power: A Theological Problem* (Nashville, TN: Abingdon Press, 1991), 25; Marie Fortune, *Sexual Violence: The Sin Revisited* (Cleveland, OH: Pilgrim Press, 2005), 38-46.

> In 2,000 years, no Christian church has developed an adequate theology of sexuality, or developed an over-arching, comprehensive, and integrative understanding of the nature and place of sexuality within the scheme of salvation and theological systems. Religious pronouncements on sex are ordinarily moralistic and marked by rhetorical, polemical, and highly charged emotional overtones designed to compensate for the essential lack of substantive foundation.[14]

We may talk about *the silent church* not talking about the content of sexuality at all. However, this church may also be described as *the limit-conscious church*; it focuses unilaterally on the framework of decent and moral acceptable sexual behaviour.[15] The consequence of this is *the adoptive church*, adopting the mainstream understanding of sexuality. This reveals the lack of discussion in the church about sexuality using theology and the Christian view of humanity as a framework. Michel Foucault describes civilization in the western part of the world as having a 'science of sexuality' approach. The focus is on right and wrong, on legal or criminal behaviour, or on a diagnostic medical approach to different kinds of unacceptable sexual behaviour. This is unlike the ancient Greek and Eastern practices of what he calls 'the art of erotica':

> Our civilisation possesses no *ars erotica*. In return, it is undoubtedly the only civilisation to practise a *scientia sexualis*, or rather the only civilization to have developed over the centuries procedures for telling the truth of knowledge-power strictly opposed to the art of initiations and the masterful secret.[16]

The essence of sex seen from a Christian and humanistic point of view is an act based on a symmetrical power balance where both parties have a freedom to choose intimacy, or not. This seems obvious, but it is not. The approach to sex in our culture seems to focus primarily on individual experience, and not on its basically relational character. The other person is an object for one's own sexual satisfaction. The sex industry has at all times given women a kind of instrumental role, requiring them to fake common pleasure as a part of the agreement. This perverted version has a link with the ethics of the church by

[14] Derek Farrell, 'A Historical Viewpoint of Sexual Abuse Perpetrated by Clergy and Religious', in *Journal of Religion and Abuse,* Vol. 6, No. 2 (Binghampton, NY: Haworth Pastoral Press, 2004), 64.

[15] Michel Foucault, *The Care of Self. The History of Sexuality: Volume 3* (London: Penguin Books. 1990), 165. Foucault has discussed the understanding of sexuality in the Greek culture around the centuries before and after Christ. He correlates this in some ways with the history of the Christian Church.

[16] Michel Foucault, *The Will to Knowledge. The History of Sexuality: Volume 1* (London: Penguin Books, 1998), 58.

silencing sex as an issue and adopting a focus on the individual at the expense of the relational interplay in freedom and equality.[17]

A power-analytical approach is necessary both to describe the content of sex and of sexual abuse. Regarding power, Michel Foucault offers a relevant theoretical framework for focusing on its relational dimension. He characterizes power as 'omnipresence', claiming that 'power is everywhere; not because it embraces everything, but because it comes from everywhere'.[18] No power-free interaction exists. Power is impossible to characterize or categorize. 'Power is exercised rather than possessed,' says Foucault.[19] This way of understanding the power issue focuses on the relational interaction, on both the personal and the institutional level. This shows that the primary question is not *who* exercises power, but *how* we do so.

Foucault's aim in developing his analysis of power was a wish to challenge 'every abuse of power, whoever the author, whoever the victim' because he believed that this kind of confrontation created freedom.[20] Johannes van der Ven concretizes this understanding when he describes 'the dissymmetry of violence', which may be understood in terms of the distinction between 'power to do' and 'power over'.[21] This approach makes the link between the exercise of power and the position of power in relationships visible. Power is an exercise, but in a power-asymmetric relationship the responsibility for exercising influence over another's life is always that of the person in a position of 'power over'. This shows the need of being in a power-symmetric relationship when sex is on the schedule. This is also the reason for claiming that sexual abuse and sex are disparate. James Poling expresses this as follows:

> Erotic power, or sexual power, is the holistic expression of communion and freedom between persons in ways that are appropriate to their relationships. Sexual violence is both a violation of the *telos* of sexuality and an abuse of power.[22]

Another way of describing the same sentiment is that sex is a fusion, but sexual abuse is an occupation. If sexual abuse has to do with power misuse, we

---

[17] Derek Farrell, 'A Historical Viewpoint of Sexual Abuse Perpetrated by Clergy and Religious', in *Journal of Religion and Abuse,* Vol. 6 No. 2 (Binghampton, NY: Haworth Pastoral Press, 2004).

[18] Foucault, *The Will to Knowledge*, 93.

[19] Quoting Foucault in Flyvbjerg, *Real Social Science,* 117; see Foucault, *Discipline and Punish* (New York: Vintage Books, 1979), 26.

[20] Bent Flyvbjerg, *Making Social Science Matter: Why Social Inquiry Fails and How It Can Succeed Again* (Cambridge: CUP, 2001), 100.

[21] Johannes A. van der Ven, 'An empirical or a normative approach to practical-theological research? A false dilemma', in Johannes van der Ven and Michael Scherer-Rath (eds), *Normativity and Empirical Research in Theology* (Brill, Netherlands: Empirical Studies in Theology, Vol. 10, 2004), 162.

[22] Poling, *The Abuse of Power*, 25.

must analyze both the risk zones and the blind zones in church in relation to a view of gender. The need for transparency in relationships that actualize vulnerability is obvious. The feminist movement and feminist theology in church have been crucial in uncovering sexual misconduct based on trust given both from above and from the perspective of the vulnerable. Nonetheless, it is dangerous to isolate this as a gender issue. It is more an issue of good and evil. Yet the gender perspective illuminates some presuppositions for creating (and preventing) arenas for abusive behaviour.

What is Sexual Misconduct?

A definition and a story

A starting-point is to introduce a definition:

> 'Sexual misconduct' means that the person with more power in an asymmetric relationship uses sexualisation of the relationship in such a way that the other person's boundaries of intimacy are violated.[23]

Sexual misconduct occurs when a person in power misuses the sexualisation of a relationship as a means to cross the intimacy boundaries of another. The other should have the power to define when she or he experiences this crossing of boundaries. Yet a complex issue is that an offender has the power to use a position of trust to impose an understanding of mutuality and agreement on the violated person.

A gender perspective is close to this definition, although it is not explicitly expressed. The gender perspective is in many ways about relational power.[24] The question concerns how gender and related factors influence the understanding of role and position in a relationship. The biblical understanding of gender (especially in the Old Testament) is historically and traditionally based on a patriarchal gender view. James N. Poling claims that 'the consequences of the patriarchal system are that women's labour is sexualized and women's subordination is eroticized'.[25] A story from the Old Testament illustrates how this might apply to the context of sexual abuse (2 Samuel 13). Amnon, a son of David, 'fell in love with Tamar'. She was his half-sister. He pretended to be ill, and he deceived his father so that Tamar might help him. He used this opportunity to rape her. When she told her brother Absalom, who took care of her, he said, 'He is your brother. Don't take this thing to heart,' but from that day Absalom hated Amnon. 'When King David heard all this, he was furious.' However, he did nothing to take care of his daughter, nor did he

---

[23] Kleiven, *Intimitetsgrenser og tillitsmakt,* 487.
[24] Keshgegian, 'Power to Wound, Power to Mend'.
[25] James Newton Poling, 'God, Sex and Power', in *Theology & Sexuality, January 2005, Vol. 11,* 261.

punish Amnon. Absalom took revenge two years later by killing Amnon. He did it because the half-brother of Absalom had offended the honour of the family. The man in focus was the abuser. The aim was not to take care of the abused daughter, but either to do nothing (David) or to take revenge (Absalom). The story emphasises that women in general were not sufficiently important as humans to be subjects. Caroline Blyth describes another biblical narrative from a gender perspective (Genesis 34) in the same way: 'The character of Jacob appears to conceptualize Dinah's rape, not as a serious assault upon his daughter's physical and sexual integrity, but rather as an event that had serious political repercussions for *him*.'[26]

This reminds us of well-known stories in our church when children, youths and women have been abused by clergy or other trusted leaders. The main person has often been the abuser. The reputation of the church is in focus. The abused are made invisible.[27]

Different approaches to sexual misconduct

Different approaches represent different perspectives. I will describe some approaches to sexual abuse, and discuss these from a gender and power perspective.

Sexual abuse may be understood (1) as an issue of sexuality, (2) as being about pathology or personality abnormalities in the abuser, or (3) as an injustice that requires remedial justice. These frameworks for understanding are well known in church and in society.[28] These perspectives are also recognizable in denominational policy documents about sexual misconduct.

Understanding sexual abuse as *sexuality* has been discussed above. Fortune reflects on sexuality and sexual violence by pointing out what she calls 'erroneous beliefs'. One of these is that 'the widely accepted "romantic love ideal" requires a dominant-subordinate relationship between two people'.[29] She states that male sexuality 'as defined by the dominant culture' includes a need to objectify, a desire to use another person, and an ability to rationalize the experience as a mutual desire.[30] It is an illustration of sexuality defined as a kind of quasi-relationship based on the dominant person's right to define the content as a mutual agreement. This understanding makes it almost impossible

---

[26] Caroline Blyth, *The Narrative of Rape in Genesis 34: Interpreting Dinah's Silence.* (Oxford: OUP, 2010), 119.

[27] Fortune, *Is Nothing Sacred?* tells a story about making the abused invisible. My own book is entitled *Når den utsatte blir usynlig [When the deferred become invisible]*, and it emphasizes the same aspect: Tormod Kleiven, *Når den utsatte blir usynlig: Om seksuelle overgrep i kristne miljøer* (Oslo: Luther, 2003).

[28] Philip Jenkins, *Pedophiles and Priests: Anatomy of a Contemporary Crisis* (Oxford: OUP, 1996); Fortune, *Sexual Violence*; Anson Shupe, *In the Name of All that's Holy: A Theory of Clergy Malfeasance* (Westport, CT: Praeger Publishers, 1995), 16-23.

[29] Fortune, *Sexual Violence: The Sin Revisited,* 15.

[30] Fortune, *Sexual Violence: The Sin Revisited,* 20.

to differentiate between sex and sexual abuse. Abuse and rape are then 'just sex that got out of hand'.[31] The power to define is usually held by the person in power, and the offended party will experience responsibility, guilt and shame – and be silent. In a church context, this approach also has to be interpreted as an adoption of a current understanding of sexuality. This is depicted in the sex and trafficking industry in a perverted manner, but it also influences the science of sexology.

A *pathological approach* lets the 'otherness' of the abuser be the core point. He or she is different from me, and the problem can be diagnosed. Abusing children is, for example, named *paedophilia* as a description of sexual preference. Nevertheless, more recent empirical research claims that 'many men who abuse children do not have deviant sexual preferences, and many men who do have such preferences never abuse children'.[32] The diagnostic system may be helpful in providing pathological descriptions for deviations. However, it may also be used to provide a framework for apologetic explanations. Diagnosis provides a kind of excuse for behaviour, and it is difficult to allege responsibility. 'It potentially compromises both the nature of abuse as an act of power and the need for the perpetrators to be held accountable,' writes Flora Keshgegian.[33] The consequence of this search for valid reasons for abusive behaviour will also be to place the abused outside the visible zone. A provocative question is: will pathological explanations primarily help the church and society to excuse, not only the abuser, but also themselves for not preventing the abuse? Eva Lundgren claims an alternative cultural and procedural gender approach, naming it 'the process of Normalization of Violence' (in Swedish: 'Våldets Normaliseringsprocess'). She calls this process a 'Constitution of Gender' (in Swedish: 'Könskonstitueringsprocess') where man creates masculinity.[34] I discuss some feminist frameworks for understanding later, but here I simply emphasize the need to understand abuse as a social construction based on normalizing abusive behaviour. It may very well be linked with the understanding of male sexuality presented by Fortune above, and together they emphasize gender as a core aspect of normalizing abuse. It is tempting to let gender (biological or cultural) define the evil of the sexuality of men. In my view, this is a misuse of both sexuality and the understanding of gender.

The aim of creating justice is the third approach mentioned. Keshgegian claims that this understanding holds the abuser responsible It results in a performance where the wrong can be made right through some decisions. This understanding is the basis for revenge, as we saw in the biblical story. In our

[31] Fortune, *Sexual Violence: The Sin Revisited*, 38.

[32] Marie Keenan, *Child Sexual Abuse and the Catholic Church: Gender, Power, and Organizational Culture.* (Oxford: OUP, 2012), 93.

[33] Keshgegian, 'Power to Wound, Power to Mend', 55-56.

[34] Eva Lundgren, *Våldets normaliseringsprocess* (Stockholm: ROKS, 2004)

society today, it is closely related to a legal framework that emphasizes judicial interpretations of the law rather than sexual abuse as a relational matter. Common to the stories in the Old Testament and to a juridical approach is that the abuser is the only subject. The abused is in many ways out of mind as the owner of her or his story, because the focus is on what the law says about responsibility and punishment.

Understanding sexual misconduct from the perspective of gender and power

Marie Keenan uses theories from feminist scholars and from the study of masculinities. 'The feminist approach to understanding child sexual abuse is to emphasize power and control, the role of patriarchy, and the gendered context in which the problem comes to be,' she says, and stresses (as does Eva Lundgren) the context of normality.[35]

The history of the feminist movement is helpful in understanding why sexual abuse has been exposed as a common challenge in society and in church. Keenan describes this as three waves. The first wave 'placed the issues of women and sexuality, gender and sexual violence on the public agenda'. The second wave focused on men in general as presumptive abusers and claimed that male socialization facilitated this attitude. 'Women were essentialized as good; men were essentialized as bad; and children were essentialized as innocent and good.' Third-wave feminism rejects some of these perspectives and universal explanations. It challenges 'the notion of gender and power as being fixed and stable'.[36] However, the source of the problem of sexual abuse is still placed on the social construction of masculinity.

The study of masculinities attempted to address some of the issues raised by the feminist theories. The theory suggests that 'hegemonic masculinity is not a fixed character type', but relates more to 'a given pattern of gender relations'.[37] J.W. Messerschmidt argues that 'a consideration of competing masculinities provides a better explanation' of the cultural normalization of abusive behaviour.[38] It seems that scholars approaching the issue from both feminist and masculine perspectives have substantial common ground. A social and cultural construction of gender is important as an analytical tool to interpret what sexual misconduct is about. This is also important in a church context because of our strong patriarchal tradition, and therefore the need to create 'competing masculinities'. But it is also relevant because of the positions of spiritual power of church leaders. They speak in the name of God, encountering the vulnerable because of age (and gender), spiritual needs and the use of Christian (pastoral) care and counselling ministries. I believe it is also crucial to understand the complexity of power and not merely the stereotypical power

35 Keenan, *Child Sexual Abuse and the Catholic Church,* 115.
36 Keenan, *Child Sexual Abuse and the Catholic Church,* 116-17.
37 Keenan, *Child Sexual Abuse and the Catholic Church,* 120.
38 Keenan, *Child Sexual Abuse and the Catholic Church,* 121.

of domination and coercion.[39] It opens up the landscape by emphasizing the dynamics between people.

Sexual Misconduct in the Church Context: Summary and Concluding Remarks

How can we understand the mechanism of sexual misconduct in church from a gender and power perspective?

Sexual abuse must be understood from a gender perspective if it is to be truly understood. Nevertheless, as mentioned above, gender stereotypes can be misused to categorize individuals and groups into degrading positions. Therefore, it is crucial to use a power-analytical approach to visualize ways in which gender perspectives may be a key to interpreting the misuse of power in this context.

From my point of view, the most appropriate term to use in understanding sexual abuse is *misuse of power*. From this position, it is possible to understand sexuality and gender as tools to legitimate, normalize and legalize the abuse. I have emphasised the power-analytical approach understood as primarily the exercise of power and not the possession of it, based on Foucault's theoretical analysis. Thus, it is also necessary and essential to understand both the exercise and possession of power in a dynamic interplay if we want to understand sexual abuse from a diaconal approach – a perspective from below.

The patriarchal history and tradition of the church challenges the possibility of *preventing sexual misconduct in church.* A dominant male culture has to be identified not just among individuals but also, and no less importantly, at the organizational level. The challenge is that the power to define is from above. Being in positions of power also creates blind zones by defining the misuse of power as something else. Gender is about identification. Women may traditionally prefer to identify themselves with women and children. Therefore, the extent of the blind zones among the church leadership will increase because of the lack of females in positions of power.

A characteristic of eviln is that it creates confusion, and the evildoer may also be a part of this confusion. Nevertheless, we are not only responsible for what we understand to be evil, but also for what we do. Therefore, the crucial point is to develop a culture in relationships and organizations that increases transparency, especially in the risk zones connected with vulnerability. Transparency has to be created by giving the vulnerable the opportunity to speak. This is why today we know that sexual misconduct occurs in church. Trusted people have to be watched, and we should be made to accept being watched, especially in our interactions with vulnerable individuals and groups. This is about living in the light (John 8:12).

---

[39] Keenan, *Child Sexual Abuse and the Catholic Church,* 123.

The definition of sexual abuse emphasises the fact that abuse presupposes an asymmetric relationship. The position of having 'power over' provides opportunities for exercising power to do good or evil. Sexuality is misused as a tool to legalize and implement an understanding that defines an interaction as a sexual relationship. It creates an illusion of power symmetry and volunteerism. Gender may then be misused as a tool to define and facilitate roles as a confusing mix between subordination and repression. Subordination is a difficult term in our culture, but it can be used to represent the opposite of abuse and repression. Jesus modelled subordination by washing the disciples' feet (and, in this cultural context, acting as a slave), but he did it from a position of power. Moreover, he said afterwards that this was a model for his disciples (John 13:1-11). Subordination can never be healthy if the subordinated have no power to choose not to be subordinated. A diaconal attitude and behaviour from a position of power is to be submissive to the other by serving him or her in a way that empowers and creates freedom.

A gender perspective very often focuses on gender as such. In the culture we meet in the Bible and in church tradition, the male has been the dominant gender. In language and roles, masculinity has in many ways dominated the positions of shepherds and leaders. A dominant group will always be tempted to misuse power, and define it as something else. Opportunities for the misuse of power have to do with power possession. Power possession has to do with position, status and role. In this context, I believe it may be appropriate to focus on the interplay between power and powerlessness, and to create opportunities for 'competing masculinities' (and perhaps also 'competing femininities'). There is a strong link between power and powerlessness. The link is obvious in relational interplay, but is not so obvious in what we might call individual interplay. Sexual abuse is about the misuse of power, but the perpetrator very often attributes the background and reasons for abusive behaviour to being powerless (i.e. because of heavy pressure from work, difficulties in their marriage, or loneliness). This may of course be an excuse, but it can also be helpful in understanding how to prevent sexual abuse. As parents, we know very well that we are in a position of power, yet we can also experience powerlessness in this role. The choice is to admit it, or to escape from this experience by transferring our helplessness to the child by accusing him or her. Sexual abuse can be interpreted in the same way. Jesus' way of modelling equivalence between men and women, and between children and adults, in his attitude and behaviour is radical and different. Even more radical in our cultural context may be his way of modelling subordination from a position of power. One approach to prevent sexual abuse may be to provide an opportunity for the experience of being powerless from a position and role of power. This is not about uncovering the power asymmetry in the relationship. It is more about legalizing the experience of powerlessness and using the differences in gender to discover a language, an attitude and a behaviour that reveal and prioritize this issue. This may provide the opportunity for a process of moving from being alone in ourselves to accepting the need for interdependence, independent of gender and positions.

A gender approach is crucial to understanding sexual abuse, both generally and in church contexts, not least because sexuality and power issues are so firmly intertwined with the gender perspective. However, a gender approach may also be used to legalize sexual abuse. Therefore, differentiating between being equitable and being equal is very important when discussing sexual abuse. Using the possession and positions of power to coerce others into roles and behaviour is not connected primarily with gender, but with the misuse of the power-asymmetric relationship. Gender may perhaps give eviln different faces, but eviln is not a gender question. It is about humans misusing their power.

Bibliography

Blyth, Caroline, *The Narrative of Rape in Genesis 34. Interpreting Dinah's Silence.* Oxford: OUP, 2010.

Farrell, Derek, 'A Historical Viewpoint of Sexual Abuse Perpetrated by Clergy and Religious', in *Journal of Religion and Abuse,* Vol. 6, No. 2. Binghampton, NY: Haworth Pastoral Press, 2004.

David Finkelhor, 'The international epidemiology of child sexual abuse', in *Child Abuse & Neglect, 18.*

Dietrich, Stephanie, 'Reflections on Core Aspects of Diaconal Theory', in Stephanie Dietrich, Knud Jørgensen, Kari Karsrud Korslien and Kjell Nordstokke (eds), *Diakonia as Christian Social Practice: An Introduction.* Oxford: Regnum, 2014.

Fortune, Marie, *Is Nothing Sacred? The story of a pastor, the women he sexually abused, and the congregation he nearly destroyed.* Cleveland, OH: United Church Press, 1999.

Fortune, Marie, *Sexual Violence: The Sin Revisited.* Cleveland, OH: Pilgrim Press, 2005.

Foucault, Michel, *The Care of Self. The History of Sexuality: Volume 3.* London: Penguin Books, 1990.

Foucault, Michel, *The Will to Knowledge. The History of Sexuality: Volume 1.* London: Penguin Books, 1998.

Flyvbjerg, Bengt, Todd Landman and Sanford Schram (eds), *Real Social Science: Applied Phronesis.* Cambridge: CUP, 2012.

Flyvbjerg, Bent, *Making Social Science Matter: Why Social Inquiry Fails and How It Can Succeed Again.* Cambridge: CUP, 2001.

Jacobs, Janet L., 'Charisma, Male Entitlement, and the Abuse of Power, in Anson Shupe, William A Stacey and Susan A. Darnell (eds), *Clergy Misconduct in Modern America.* New York and London: New York University Press, 2000.

Jenkins, Philip, *Pedophiles and Priests: Anatomy of a Contemporary Crisis.* Oxford: OUP, 1996).

Keenan, Marie, *Child Sexual Abuse in the Catholic Church: Gender, Power, and Organizational Culture.* Oxford: OUP, 2012.

Keshgegian, Flora A., 'Power to Wound, Power to Mend: Toward a Non-Abusing Theology', in *Journal of Religion and Abuse.* Binghampton, NY: Haworth Pastoral Press, 1999.

Kleiven, Tormod, *Når den utsatte blir usynlig: Om seksuelle overgrep i kristne miljøer [When the Abused Becomes Invisible: About sexual abuse in Christian communities].* Oslo: Luther, 2003.

Kleiven, Tormod, *Intimitetsgrenser og Tillitsmakt. Kirkesamfunns forståelse av og handlingsstrategier i møte med anklager om seksuelle krenkelser sett i lys av et diakonifaglig perspektiv [Intimacy Boundaries and Power of Trust. Understanding and policies of denominations encountering accusations of sexual misconduct elucidated from a diaconal perspective].* Oslo: Diakonova, 2010.

Kleiven, Tormod, 'Power to Serve OR Serving the Power', in *Theology & Life. Annual Theological Journal, No. 36, 2013.* Hong Kong: Lutheran Theological Seminary, 2013.

Longwood, W. Merle, 'Introduction', in Marie M. Fortune and W. Merle Longwood (eds), *Sexual Abuse in the Catholic Church: Trusting the Clergy?* Binghampton, NY: Haworth Pastoral Press, 2003.

Lundgren, Eva, *I Herrens vold. Dokumentasjon av vold mot kvinner i kristne miljøer [In the violence of the Lord. Documentation of violence against women in Christian communities].* Oslo: Cappelen Forlag, 1985.

Lundgren, Eva, *Våldets normaliseringsprocess [The Process of Normalization of Violence].* Stockholm: ROKS, 2004.

Poling, James Newton, 'God, Sex and Power', in *Theology & Sexuality,* January 2005, Vol. 11.

Poling, James Newton, *The Abuse of Power: A Theological Problem.* Nashville, TN: Abingdon Press, 1991.

Schoener, Gary Richard, 'Historical Overview', in John C. Gonsiorek, *Breach of Trust: Sexual Exploitation by Health Care Professionals and Clergy.* London: Sage Publications, 1995.

Shupe, Anson, *In the Name of All That's Holy: A Theory of Clergy Malfeasance.* Westport, CT: Praeger Publishers, 1995.

Shupe, Anson (ed), *Wolves within the Fold: Religious Leadership and Abuses of Power.* New Brunswick: Rutgers University Press, 1997.

Van der Ven, Johannes A., 'An empirical or a normative approach to practical-theological research? A false dilemma', in Johannes van der Ven and Michael Scherer-Rath (eds), *Normativity and Empirical Research in Theology.* Leiden, Netherlands: Brill – Empirical Studies in Theology, Vol. 10, 2004.

Index

Editors and Contributors

Editors

Stephanie Dietrich, b. 1966. Associate professor at Diakonhjemmet University College, now VID Specialized University, Diakonhjemmet, Oslo. Studied theology in Neuendettelsau and Erlangen, Germany, and in Oslo. Dr Theol from Menighets Fakultetet (MF) Norwegian School of Theology in 1998 with 'Das schweigende Gebet: Zur fundamentaltheologischen Grundlage des Gebets in ökumenischem Blickwinckel' (Silent prayer: On the theological basis for understanding prayer in an ecumenical context). Teacher and PhD scholar at MF 1991-1998. 1998-2007 senior advisor on ecumenical theology with Church of Norway Council on Ecumenical and International Relations. Since 1997, associate professor at Diakonhjemmet University College. For many years involved in national and international bi- and multilateral ecumenical dialogues, especially on understanding and practice of *diakonia* in an ecumenical context and the deacon's ministry. Member of presidency of CPCE (Community of Protestant Churches in Europe) 2006-2012, and since 2012 convener of the Church of Norway Theological Committee. Has edited several books (in Norwegian) and published numerous articles on *diakonia* and ecumenical theology.

Knud Jørgensen, b. 1942. MTh from University of Copenhagen, PhD in Missiology, Fuller Theological Seminary. Journalist and theologian, served with Radio Voice of the Gospel, Addis Ababa, Ethiopia, the Lutheran World Federation, Geneva, the International Mass Media Institute, Kristiansand, the Go out Centre, Hurdal, Norway, Norwegian Church Aid, the Mekane Yesus Seminary, Addis Ababa, and the mission foundation Areopagos. Dean of Tao Fong Shan, Hong Kong, until 2010. Adjunct professor at the MF Norwegian School of Theology. Published several books and articles on journalism, communication, leadership and mission, including 'Equipping for Service: Leadership in Church and Society' (Regnum 2012). One of the editors of the Regnum Edinburgh 2010 Series.

Kari Karsrud Korslien, Assistant professor at Diakonhjemmet University College, now VID Specialized University, Diakonhjemmet, Oslo, Norway, since 2016. Professional social worker, deacon and lecturer for several years. Can San from University of Oslo, 2003. Contributed to various textbooks in Norwegian about recognition as a central part of *diakonia* (2009), methodical reflections of *diakonia* (2011), and the deacon as pilgrim and leader (2012). Working with education in the field of *diakonia*, contributed to establishing a Master's in Diakonia (2004), and developing different subjects for a Master's degree in Diakonia and Christian social practice (2010). Since 2014, participated in the project Youth at the Margins (YOMA). Specialised in *diakonia* as science, practical *diakonia*, voluntary work, and the deacon's liturgical work.

Kjell Nordstokke, b. 1946. Professor emeritus at Diakonhjemmet University College, now VID Specialized University, Diakonhjemmet, Oslo; studied theology in Stavanger and Oslo. Dr Theol from University of Oslo, 1990, with 'Council and Context in Leonardo Boff's Ecclesiology: The Rebirth of the Church among the Poor'. Lived ten years in Brazil, first as pastor with Evangelical Church of Lutheran Confession in Brazil (1974-1981) and later as professor of theology at Escola Superior de Teologia in São Leopoldo (1994-1996). Since 1990, at Diakonhjemmet in Oslo, mainly responsible for training for the diaconal ministry in Church of Norway and developing the science of *diakonia* as an academic discipline. CEO of Diakonhjemmet Foundation 1998-2005, Director of the Department for Mission and Development at Lutheran World Federation, Geneva, 2005-2009, responsible for LWF's Diakonia Programme resulting in publication of 'Diakonia in Context', 2009. Since 2009, lecturer in Science of Diakonia. Published books and articles on *diakonia*, including 'The Diaconate: Ministry of Prophecy and Transformation', in *The Ministry of the Deacon*, ANDREP 2 (Nordic Ecumenical Council, 2000), 'Diakonia in Context: Transformation, Reconciliation and Empowerment', in *Mission as Ministry of Reconciliation* (Regnum, 2013), and *Liberating Diakonia* (Tapir, 2011).

Contributors

Anne Austad, Associate professor in Pastoral Care at VID Specialized University, Diakonhjemmet, Oslo, since 2006, MTh from MF Norwegian School of Theology, minor degrees in Psychology, University of Oslo and University of Manchester, PhD in Psychology of Religion, MF Norwegian School of Theology. Student Chaplain at MF (1997-1998) and Diakonhjemmet University College (1997-2005). Publications in psychology of religion and pastoral care.

Marit Breen, since 2012, gender advisor to Western Ethiopia Women Empowerment Programme in Ethiopia, Norwegian Mission Society; MA in Gender Analysis in International Development, University of East Anglia, UK; MA in Global Studies, VID Specialised University School of Mission and Theology (MHS), Stavanger, Norway; Assistant professor in science of religion and science of culture at MHS; Deputy leader at a department for asylum seekers in Sandnes, Norway, Hero Norway AS; various consultancies for the teaching and production of information materials for HIV/AIDS, general North/South issues, youth work, mission and life skills. She has published an article in the Regnum Edinburgh Centenary Series.

Father (Abouna) Alexi Chehadeh, an Orthodox priest, serves as Director of the Department of Ecumenical Relations and Development (DERD) of the Greek Orthodox Patriarchate of Antiochia and All the East (GOPA), co-ordinating the development and relief work of DERD in Syria. PhD from University of Münster, Germany, on 'Islam, Staat und Gewalt. Hassan al-Turabis islamistisch-politisches Denken' (Islam, State and Violence. The Islamist-Political Thoughts of Hassan al-Turabi). MA in Islamic Studies from the University of Hamburg. Lectured on a variety of topics at University of Balamand, Lebanon, and Institute of Mission, Ecumenism and Religious Studies and the Asia-Africa Institute, University of Hamburg; also participated in many international consultations on peace, the ethics of peace, the war in Syria, and Christian-Islamic conversations. 1993-2013, served as priest of the Antioch-Orthodox Archdiocese of Europe; 2000-2007, vicar of the Metropolitan and, since 2007, 'Exarchos of Antioch-Orthodox Archdiocese of Germany'. At the end of 2013, His Beatitude Patriarch John X asked Father Alexi to move to the Middle East to assist him in the main residency in Syria and Lebanon. A member of the Lutheran-Orthodox Joint Commission and Chief Editor of the Patriarchal Magazine 'AL-NASHRA'.

Hector Fernandez, El Salvador. Director of Instituto Ecuménico Diaconal Esteban (Esteban Ecumenical Diaconal Institute), San Salvador. Lived as political refugee in Mexico 1980-1992. Graduated in theology at Comunidad Teológica de México (CTM) in 1991, ordained minister of the Salvadorian Lutheran Church in exile. Postgraduate studies in Brazil (Instituto de Pós-Graduação e Pesquisa at Escola Superior de Teologia), São Leopoldo, 1995-1997. Director of Lutheran University in El Salvador (Universidad Luterana Salvadoreña – ULS) 1998-2005. Since 1998, organized programmes of capacity building in *diakonia* at informal and formal levels, now integrated in activities of the Instituto Ecuménico Diaconal Esteban. Has published study material on *diakonia*.

Drea Fröchtling, currently at University of Applied Sciences for Intercultural Theology in Hermannsburg, Germany, as Professor for Practical Theology in intercultural perspective and for International Diakonia. She is a Lutheran pastor and previously worked in South Africa, inter alia for the South African Council of Churches and for HIV/AIDS programmes of the Evangelical Lutheran Church in Southern Africa. Research interest includes questions of migration and justice, gender and *diakonia* from an intercultural, justice-based perspective.

Hans Morten Haugen, professor in International Diakonia at VID Specialized University, Diakonhjemmet, Oslo, MA (Cand Polit) in political science, 1995; PhD (Dr Jur), 2006. Senior Executive Officer on International Affairs and Human Rights in Church of Norway (CoN) 1996-2002, Representative in Jerusalem for Norwegian Church Aid, 2005-2006. Through CoN, a member of World Council of Churches' Ecumenical Team at two UN conferences: Geneva

2000 and Financing for Development, 2002. Chair of the Norwegian Crossroads movement, 2006-2009; Chair of Oslo Diocese (CoN) Environment, Consumption and Justice Group, 2004-2016. His two English books are (short version): *The Rights to Food and the TRIPS Agreement* (2007) and *Technology and Human Rights* (2012). Has written extensively on law and justice issues, focusing on trade, conflicts over land and resources, and immigration.

Chammah J Kaunda, PhD, is Postdoctoral Research Fellow in Christlike Spirituality/ Christian Spirituality of University of South Africa, Pretoria. Particular interest in how African religio-cultural heritage can inform African Christianity, politics, theological education, African Pentecostal theology, missiology and ecumenical theology. Most recent published article (with B.J. Pokol) is 'Re-Inculturating Suum-Ngi Creation Worldview within Church of Christ in Nations in Nigeria: An African Feminist Missiological Perspective', in *Pharos Journal of Theology*, 97: 1-13 (2016).

Terese Bue Kessel, associate professor in Practical Theology at VID Specialized University, Campus Misjonshøgskolen (MHS), Stavanger, since 2015; Cand Theol at MHS. Dr Theol in Practical Theology/International Diakonia, MHS. missionary and pastor in Osaka, Japan, with the Kinki Evangelical Lutheran Church in partnership with the Norwegian Missionary Society, 1993-2006. Research fellow, MHS, 2009-2013. Chaplain, Tasta Sykehjem, Stavanger, 2013-2015.

Tormod Kleiven, Director of Research, Diakonova University College since 2011; Social Worker and Deacon; Master's in Health Studies, Diakonia Specialization, University of Oslo, Faculty of Theology; PhD in Practical Theology/Diakonia, MF Norwegian School of Theology. Director of the Department for Health and Social Work in Rømskog municipality, 1986-1998, Head of Studies in Diakonia and Christian Counselling in Diakonova University College, 1999-2011. Several publications on *diakonia* and pastoral counselling.

Kristian Larsen, Master's in Diaconia, Diploma Programme in Administration, and Nursing degree from Diakonhjemmet University College, Oslo. Further education in multi-disciplinary rehabilitation from Oslo University College. Since 2006, Senior Advisor at Digni – the umbrella organization for the long-term development work for twenty Norwegian mission organizations and churches. Missionary for Mission Alliance in Bolivia, 1983-1998, several years as Director of the Diaconia and Development work. Manager of a Health Rehabilitation Centre, 1999-2006.

Elieshi Ayo Mungure, Bachelor of Theology from Tumaini Makumira University, STM (Hons) from Wartburg Theological Seminary, and PhD in Pastoral Care and Counselling, Luther Theological Seminary, Minneapolis, USA. An ordained theologian of the Evangelical Lutheran Church in Tanzania, served in the parish, lecturer at Tumaini Makumira University. Currently, area secretary for Africa in the Lutheran World Federation in Geneva.

Annette Leis-Peters, PhD in theology. Associate Professor in Sociology of Religion at University of Uppsala and head of the Department for Diakonia and Leadership at VID Specialized University, Oslo, Norway. Research focuses on role of religion and religious organisations in welfare and civil society. Currently involved in the research programme 'Impact of Religion – Challenges for Society, Law and Democracy' and the research project 'Youth at the Margins: a comparative study of the contribution of faith-based organisations to social cohesion in South Africa and Nordic Europe'.

Atola Longkumer, b. 1971, a Baptist from Nagaland, north-east India. She teaches Religions and Missions at South Asian Institute of Advanced Christian Studies (SAIACS), Bangalore. Longkumer is one of the editors of volume on *Mission and Power* (Regnum, 2016). Also serves as member of BWA Commission on Interfaith Relations, and as Asian representative in the International Association of Mission Studies.

Elaine Neuenfeldt, Secretary for Women in Church and Society – Department for Theology and Public Witness, Lutheran World Federation. An ordained pastor from the Evangelical Church of the Lutheran Confession in Brazil (IECLB). 2005-2008, professor of feminist theology at the Faculdades EST (Escola Superior de Teologia) in São Leopoldo, Brazil. Master's degree (2001) and doctorate in theology (2004) at Instituto Ecumênico de Pós-Graduação (Ecumenical Institute of Graduate Studies) in São Leopoldo. 1995-1998, worked in missionary partnership with the Lutheran Church in El Salvador, specifically with the Lutheran University. Active participation in the popular reading of the Bible movement, organized in the CEBI – Centro de Estudos Biblicos – Biblical studies centre, where she served in the co-ordination board for several years.

Isabel Apawo Phiri, PhD, University of Cape Town, South Africa, is Associate General Secretary for Public Witness and Diakonia of the World Council of Churches and honorary professor in the School of Religion, Philosophy and Classics at the University of KwaZulu-Natal, South Africa. A Presbyterian lay person from Malawi, was Dean and Professor of African Theology and Feminist Theology, School of Religion, Philosophy and Classics at the University of KwaZulu-Natal, South Africa. Former General Co-ordinator of the Circle of Concerned African Women Theologians, and former co-Editor of the Journal of Gender and Religion in Africa. Most recent published article (with Maxwell Agabu Phiri) is 'HIV and AIDS, Gender Violence and Masculinities: A Case of South Africa', in *Journal of Human Ecology*, 53(1), (2016).

Zo Ramiandra Rakotoarison, Programme Leader of Empower FLM, Malagasy Lutheran Church, Madagascar since 2014; Assistant for the Malagasy Lutheran Church Head Office 2013-2014; Master's in Diakonia and Christian Social Practice, Diakonhjemmet, Oslo, 2013; Secretary for the Malagasy Lutheran Church Head Office 2005-2011; Communication assistant for 'Programme de Professionalisation de l'Agriculture', Antananarivo, 2000-2001; Bachelor in Geography, University of Antananarivo, 1999.

Marianne Skjortnes, Professor in Social Anthropology at VID Specialized University, Campus School of Mission and Theology, Stavanger since 2004; Mag art in Social Anthropology, University of Oslo, 1985. Served in Norwegian Mission Society working with Malagasy Lutheran Church as a teacher, 1978-1982. Research fellow in Research Council of Norway, 1986-1989, International Research, Institute of Stavanger, 1990-1997, Centre for Intercultural Communication, Stavanger, 1997-2004. Extensive experience with development issues in several African countries, particularly Madagascar, where she has lived and worked with research and consultancy in development issues for several years. Several publications on culture, social change, gender, religion and development.

Heidi Holt Zachariassen, Master of Arts in Sociology, University of Boston, USA. Senior adviser for Committee for Gender Balance and Diversity in Research (Kif) at Norwegian Association of Higher Education Institutions since 2014; Visiting scholar at Centre for Gender Research, University of Oslo (2013); Senior adviser at Digni 2006-2014; Researcher/ consultant at Centre for Intercultural Communication (SIK) at the School of Mission and Theology 2001-2006. Books and articles on gender mainstreaming and gender equality.

Christa von Zychlin, ordained pastor of the Evangelical Lutheran Church in America (1985); lecturer at Baboua Seminary in Central African Republic (1991-1995); since 2011 Assistant Co-ordinator of the Mekong Mission Forum (MMF); Co-ordinator of International Student Affairs at the Lutheran Theological Seminary, Hong Kong. Co-editor of MMF publications. Workshop leader and author of dozens of popular articles in the area of women, spirituality and the Bible. Currently working on a D Min research project in biblical empowerment for *diakonia*.